THE HISTORY OF
AVIATION

THE HISTORY OF
AVIATION

AIRLINERS • MILITARY AIRCRAFT • PIONEERS • LANDMARKS • RECORD BREAKERS

BARNES & NOBLE

NEW YORK

© 2007 Amber Books Ltd

This 2007 edition published by Barnes & Noble, Inc. by arrangement with
Amber Books Ltd.

Editorial and design by
Amber Books Ltd

Project Editor: James Bennett
Picture Research: Terry Forshaw, Kate Green
Design: Tony Cohen

ISBN-13: 978-0-7607-8892-9
ISBN-10: 0-7607-8892-8

Printed and bound in Singapore

1 3 5 7 9 10 8 6 4 2

Contents

Introduction

Of all the major technological advances made by mankind over the centuries, arguably the most important has been aviation. Commercial aviation has shrunk the globe to an extent that would have seemed incredible only a century ago, while the military aircraft has become the instrument that dictates the outcome of battles.

This book presents an authoritative chronology of civil and military aviation, blending facts, figures, personalities and achievements in a single-volume work of reference. Tracing the major developments in aviation from its origins in ancient China to the supersonic jets of today, this book celebrates some of the most significant and momentous events in the history of flight.

Aviation has always been a pioneering world, from the day when François Pilâtre de Rozier became the first man to be carried aloft in a Montgolfier balloon, through the momentous achievement of the Wright Brothers at Kitty Hawk, to today's suer-efficient airliners and stealth bombers. It has produced the means to deliver awesome weapons of mass destruction capable of wiping humanity from the planet, and the tools that have enabled mankind to take his first faltering steps to the stars. Which path the human race will take, only time will tell.

The Lockheed Constellation, with its graceful dolphin-shaped fuselage and distinctive triple tail, was the first pressurized airliner to see widespread use.

A fanciful depiction of an early attempt to fly, showing an oriental king with birds attached to a kind of gondola.

8

The Dream of Flight

No one will ever know exactly when humankind first took to the skies. The legends of ancient times are littered with tales of flying beings and flying machines, and over the years pseudo-science had cited these as 'evidence' that lost civilizations knew the secret of flight. A Babylonian set of laws called the Halkatha reportedly contains a passage that reads: 'To operate a flying machine is a great privilege. Knowledge of flying is most ancient, a gift of the gods of old for saving lives.' Another fragmentary Babylonian script, the Epic of Etana, which dates back to between 3000 and 2400 B.C.E., appears to describe a flight high over the Middle East by a shepherd, who was carried aloft by an eagle whose life he had saved. A similar tale, dating from 1500 B.C.E., involves a Persian king named Kai Kawus.

Some of the richest and most descriptive accounts of ancient flying machines occur in Hindu sacred literature, particularly in the Samaranga Sutradhara, a collection of texts compiled in the eleventh century, but possibly based on material of much greater antiquity. The ancient craft were called Vimanas, and were allegedly fitted with an engine that derived its power from some form of energy latent in mercury.

Intriguing though such tales may be, the true recorded history of flight only begins to emerge in the meticulous records of the Chinese emperors, who are known to have experimented with flying machines of various types, notably man-carrying kites. Their purpose was warlike. In 206 B.C.E. the Chinese general Han Hsin used a kite to calculate the distance between his forces and the palace of Wei Yang Kong, situated in the town he was besieging, and in 549 C.E. the defenders of the town of King Thai, besieged by enemy forces, used kites to send out calls for help to nearby villages, using a form of signalling not unlike semaphore. Chinese man-lifting kites were described by the Venetian explorer Marco Polo in the fourteenth century, and he introduced the concept to Western Europe, where it became a novelty.

Other adventurous souls, however, not content to be shackled to earth, tried to emulate the birds. They made wings, strapped them to their bodies and leaped dramatically from high places, to be killed in equally dramatic fashion when the wings failed to keep them aloft.

Early Theory of Flight

Despite the early dramatic failures, there were those who approached the problems of achieving manned flight in a much more scientific manner. Foremost among them, in the thirteenth century, was an English scholar and Franciscan friar called

9

The thirteenth-century English friar Roger Bacon concluded that a flying machine that was lighter than air would be humankind's passport to flight.

Roger Bacon, who produced a scientific manuscript entitled *Opus Magus* (Great Work), in which, among other topics, he envisaged the construction of flying machines. Bacon had always been fascinated by the possibility that one day men would fly, but at first he dropped into the pitfall of believing that, in order to fly, man had to emulate the flight of a bird as closely as possible, which meant beating the air with artificial wings.

Bacon's knowledge of languages enabled him to study non-ecclesiastical records containing accounts of earlier attempts at manned flight, and he gradually came to realize that the real reason behind the repeated failures lay in the inability of man's puny muscles to sustain the weight of his body in true birdlike flight, prompting him to write, '… a flying machine can be constructed so that a man sits in the midst of the machine revolving some engine by which artificial wings are made to beat the air like a flying bird'. The concept of the powerplant was born.

It was at this point that Bacon's originality led him into a new channel of thought. If the attempts at manned flight so far had failed because of weight, then the solution was obviously to build some kind of apparatus light enough not only to lift a person clear of the ground, but also to sustain him in the air. He

A model of an airship proposed by Francesco de Lana, a seventeenth-century Jesuit priest who was a native of Brescia in Italy. De Lana envisaged copper globes from which air had been removed carrying his airship aloft.

discussed how this might be achieved in his two major scientific works, envisaging a gigantic globe of extremely thin metal that would be filled with 'the thin air of the upper atmosphere, or with liquid fire, thus rising high into the heavens'. Although it was beyond even Bacon's scientific genius or vivid imagination to elaborate, his writing does give us the first recorded instance of serious thought on the lighter-than-air principle.

It was to be nearly four centuries before there was a return to the embryo idea of a man-carrying balloon. This time, the scientist involved was a Jesuit priest named Francesco de Lana. Born in Brescia, Italy, in 1637, de Lana took an active interest in natural sciences, and gave considerable thought to the application of the latest scientific discoveries. After studying the experiments of scientists Blaise Pascal and Evangelista Torricelli, who found that the density of the atmosphere could be measured and that it decreased with altitude, and the discovery by Otto von Guericke that a vacuum could be artificially created, de Lana worked out a design for a flying ship that was to be carried into the air by four large globes of thin copper, from which all the air had been exhausted.

Although the principle was sound enough, de Lana's design could not possibly have worked in practice for the simple reason that his copper globes would have been instantly crushed by atmospheric pressure. By the middle of the eighteenth century, however, scientists were beginning to make the discoveries which, ultimately, would enable men to turn the dream of de Lana and others into reality.

In 1766, the British scientist Henry Cavendish, a Fellow of the Royal Society, discovered a gaseous agent which he called 'inflammable air', later to be named hydrogen by Antoine-Laurent Lavoisier in 1790. Meanwhile, in 1774,

Antoine-Laurent Lavoisier named hydrogen in 1790, but it was Henry Cavendish who had first discovered the gaseous agent in 1766. During the nineteenth century, hydrogen would be used in balloon flights.

the Birmingham chemist and physician Dr Joseph Priestley was to continue his research into his new discovery of 'dephlogisticated air', or oxygen, as Lavoisier was subsequently to call it, and published his findings in a work entitled *Experiments and Observations on Different Kinds of Air*.

The Montgolfier Brothers and Their Dream of Flight
Priestley's book aroused considerable interest among Europe's scientists, but it fired the imagination

The first demonstration of a Montgolfier balloon at Annonay, France, on 5 June 1783. The success of the flight persuaded the Montgolfier brothers to demonstrate their creation at the Court of Versailles.

of one man in particular: 36-year-old Joseph Montgolfier, who obtained a copy when the French translation appeared in 1776. Joseph Montgolfier had more than a passing interest in the possibilities of flight, and his younger brother Étienne was, if not quite so enthusiastic, at least an interested observer. Later, Étienne was to become as passionately interested in the subject as was his brother, but it was Joseph who was

encouraged to carry out his own experiments after reading the work of Priestley and other scientists.

Joseph's first tentative experiments involved the use of hydrogen, which he produced himself. He made a small paper balloon – a natural choice of material and one available in abundance, thanks to the Montgolfier family trade of paper-making – and filled it with the gas, expecting it to rise into the air. But the experiment was a failure, and so was a subsequent one using a silken balloon; the reason was simply that the hydrogen passed easily through both silk and paper.

Joseph consequently abandoned the use of hydrogen, and he began to experiment with hot air as a means of producing the necessary lift. His thoughts on lighter-than-air flight were finally translated into practical form in November 1782, when he built and tested his first model balloon at Avignon in the south of France, where he was living at the time. He held the silken envelope over a fire until it filled with hot air, then let it go. It rose to the ceiling and hung there for half a minute, until the air inside it cooled and the balloon came spiralling down.

Joseph, joined now by his brother Étienne, went on to build three test balloons, each larger than the one before. The third, with a diameter of 10.6m (35ft), flew on 25 April 1783 and reached an altitude of about 244m (800ft), before descending to land a mile from its starting point.

The next balloon to be built was far larger than anything the Montgolfiers had attempted previously, with a capacity of 622.6 cubic metres (22,000 cubic feet) and a total weight of 226kg (500lb). The envelope, which was made of cloth and lined with paper, had a circumference of 33.5m (110ft) and was reinforced by a spider's-web network of strings, the bottom ends of which were attached to a square wooden frame surrounding the aperture. It was demonstrated before a huge crowd at Annonay on 5 June 1783, ascending to 1830m (6000ft) and drifting for a mile and a half (2.5km) on the breeze before coming down to earth.

The First Aeronauts

Following their success at Annonay, the Montgolfiers decided to take a huge risk and demonstrate their next balloon at the Court of Versailles, before King Louis XVI and his queen, Marie Antoinette. They overcame a series of setbacks and, on 19 September 1783, suspended their latest creation over a platform at Versailles, concealing it from view by curtains draped from scaffolding. As an added precaution, soldiers of the Royal Guard were posted around the platform to act as a deterrent to anyone who might inflict damage on the balloon, maliciously or otherwise.

After dining at a banquet held in their honour, the Montgolfier brothers set about inflating the balloon, watched by Louis and his queen. Within an hour, the balloon was fully inflated and billowing

This rather imaginative painting depicts the Montgolfier balloon carrying Pilâtre de Rozier (seen waving his hat from the basket) soaring over the River Seine.

above its platform. In a wicker cage attached to its neck sat three bewildered passengers: a sheep, a cockerel and a duck. Originally, the Montgolfiers had wanted the flight to be made by a human being, but King Louis did not share the brothers' confidence and absolutely forbade the idea, believing the venture to be fraught with extreme peril. And so it was that the honour of becoming the first aeronauts in history fell to three dumb animals.

Heralded by four cannon shots, the mooring ropes were cast off and the balloon rose into the air, climbing to about 500m (1700ft) before drifting away on the breeze. Eight minutes later and 3km (2 miles) away, it came to earth in the forest of Vaucresson. It proved a disappointingly short flight, for the Montgolfiers had worked out that the flight would last for at least 20 minutes and that the balloon would reach a height of 3660m (12,000ft). Later, they found some small holes in the fabric, which they held responsible for the premature descent.

Some of the spectators had followed the flight of the balloon on horseback, racing to be the first at the scene of its landfall. Those who had expected to see the mangled remains of the three animal passengers were disappointed. The wicker cage had broken open as the balloon

came down through the trees, and the sheep was standing nearby, giving its undivided attention to a patch of grass. The duck was waddling around, apparently unconcerned. Only the cockerel had suffered in any way, having sustained a slight injury to one of its wings.

Man Takes to the Skies

A matter of days after the Versailles demonstration, the Montgolfiers announced a project to build an even bigger balloon, designed to carry two men. The king remained sceptical, but eventually gave his consent, and, on 15 October 1783, a Montgolfier balloon made a tethered ascent with a volunteer on board. His name was Jean-François Pilâtre de Rozier, a 29-year-old chemistry and physics teacher who had witnessed the earlier Montgolfier demonstrations. De Rozier made four ascents, each one higher than the previous one; on the third, the ballast was removed and a passenger, Girond de Villette, climbed into the gallery in its place. With the two men on board, the balloon rose to a height of 100m (324ft), descending to the platform after nine minutes. De Villette then got out and his place was taken by the Marquis d'Arlandes, a wealthy and influential nobleman who had been instrumental in persuading Louis to change his mind over the passenger-carrying issue.

An attempt to make a free flight had been scheduled for 20 November, but it was frustrated by wind and rain. The weather improved considerably by the following morning, and preparations for the flight went ahead. The Montgolfiers asked de Rozier to make one more captive ascent to check the balloon's lifting power, and the envelope was duly inflated. Suddenly, an unexpected gust of wind caught the balloon and plucked it off the launching platform that had been erected in the gardens of the Château la Muette, in the Bois de Boulogne. The balloon was hauled down with difficulty, but not before several holes had been torn in the envelope.

The Montgolfiers were now faced with the prospect of having to call off the attempt; however, they had an unexpected stroke of good fortune when a number of seamstresses came forward from the assembled crowd and offered to repair the damage.
Within two hours, the Montgolfiers were able to inflate

The French aeronaut Jean-François Pilâtre de Rozier and of his assistant Romain Pierre-Angel were both killed when their balloon caught fire and plunged to earth during an attempt to cross the English Channel on 15 June 1785.

Inflating a hydrogen balloon. Hydrogen's flammable nature meant that it was a dangerous agent to use, but it was the only one available until helium was produced.

the balloon again, and, at 1.50 p.m., de Rozier and the Marquis d'Arlandes climbed into the gallery. Four minutes later de Rozier gave the signal to cast off, and the balloon rose steadily into the air accompanied by a great cheer from the spectators. An even bigger cheer went up when, at a height of about 91m (300ft), the two aeronauts waved their hats in salute just before the gentle northwesterly breeze caught the balloon and took it towards the Seine.

Twenty-five minutes later, de Rozier and his passenger came safely to earth on the Butte aux Cailles, near where the Place d'Italie now stands, some 8km (5 miles) from La Muette. The whole flight had been made at relatively low altitude – less than 305m (1000ft) – and it had not been uneventful; several times, the two men had been forced to apply wet sponges to glowing holes in the fabric of the envelope caused by flying sparks. The margin between success and disaster had been narrow, but, for the first time, man had cut the thread that bound him to the earth. The conquest of the air had begun in earnest.

Meanwhile, another Frenchman, Jacques Alexandre César Charles, had been experimenting with hydrogen-filled balloons. He demonstrated a prototype of his work on 27 August 1783, the unmanned balloon ascending from the

Jacques Alexandre César Charles pioneered the use of hydrogen-filled balloons. On one of his early ascents, he became the first man to see the sun set twice in one day.

Champ de Mars, Paris, and reaching an altitude of 915m (3000ft). It drifted in and out of cloud on a flight that ended 45 minutes and 24km (15 miles) away, not far from the village of Gonesse. By the time Charles and his assistants reached the scene, however, all that remained of the balloon was a mass of shredded fabric, scattered over a field – the work of local peasants who, in their superstitious fear and ignorance, had attacked the writhing envelope with scythes and pitchforks.

15

Charles raised the necessary funds to build a man-carrying hydrogen balloon; its basic design, with only minor changes, would be used by hydrogen balloons for a century to come. Spherical in shape and with a diameter of just over 8.2m (27ft), it was made from tapered sections of silk treated with a special rubber solution devised by Ainé and Cadet Robert, who were Charles's close collaborators. It had an open neck, allowing gas to escape on expansion – so avoiding the hazard of the balloon bursting as a result of the decrease in pressure at altitude – and more gas could be released through a spring-loaded valve at the top of the balloon, operated by a cord that hung down through the interior of the envelope. A somewhat ornate car, resembling a boat, was suspended below the balloon's neck.

The maiden voyage of the balloon took place on 1 December 1783, with Charles and Ainé Robert on board. It ascended from the Tuileries Gardens in Paris and, borne on a southwest breeze, drifted across the French countryside for 43.5km (27 miles), before alighting at Nesle, after having been airborne for two hours. The balloon was held fast by peasants and a group of townspeople from Nesle, and the two aeronauts settled down to write a short account of the flight while the details were still fresh in their minds and to await the arrival of anyone who had been pursuing the balloon's flight from the Tuileries.

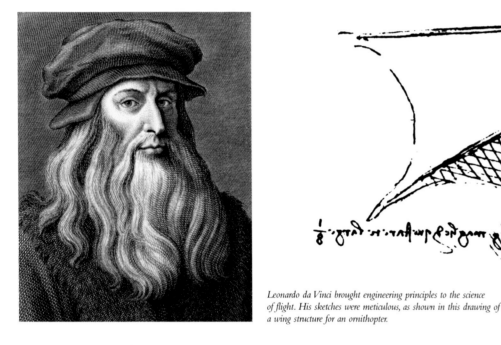

Leonardo da Vinci brought engineering principles to the science of flight. His sketches were meticulous, as shown in this drawing of a wing structure for an ornithopter.

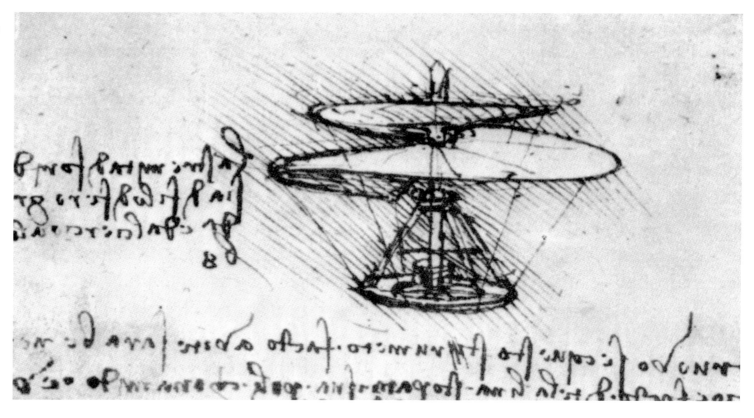

Leonardo da Vinci's sketch of a helical screw showed a firm grasp of the principles that would later result in the helicopter. Da Vinci annotated his sketches in a curious backhand script.

Three riders came galloping up just as the sun was setting and embraced the aeronauts enthusiastically. Charles, who was filled with the exhilaration of success, immediately insisted on making another short flight, alone this time. Climbing back into the balloon's car, he signalled to his volunteer ground crew to let go. The balloon shot up in the dusk, and a few moments later a great cry went up from the spectators as the last rays of the dying sun caught it and turned it into a glowing bubble of light far above their heads.

Golden Sunlight

The balloon climbed rapidly to a height of nearly 3050m (10,000ft). The cold was intense, but Charles hardly noticed it. He was alone in golden sunlight, while down below men passed unnoticed in the shadows of approaching night. As the light faded over the horizon, a new wonder filled the aeronaut as he realized that he had become the first man to see the sun set twice in one day. Suddenly, an excruciating pain in his right ear – the result of his rapid climb to nearly 3km (2 miles) above the earth – interrupted his daydream. He pulled the valve-release line and the balloon began a descent that brought it to rest, half an hour after the start of the second dramatic flight, in a ploughed field three miles from Nesle.

Whether Jacques Charles was overwhelmed by the sheer wonder of his experience, or whether his solo balloon flight frightened him deeply, we shall never know. We only know that he never flew again, even though the Robert brothers, Aîné and Cadet, were to make several more ascents.

While some pioneers of flight turned to the use of balloons filled with hot air or hydrogen to cut themselves loose from the earth, others would not rest until they could emulate the flight of birds, or come as close to it as possible.

Roger Bacon was one; another was Leonardo da Vinci, who appears to have been preoccupied with the problems of human flight for a decade of his life, between 1495 and 1505. Like Bacon, Leonardo's ideas were far ahead of his time; unlike Bacon, he brought a considerable knowledge of engineering to the task in hand. He was the first to expound the true principles of flight; he knew that both water and air were fluids, and that the behaviour of a solid body moving through both media must be essentially the same.

In 1505, da Vinci wrote a remarkably detailed treatise on the flight of birds, a work of genius written in a secret backhand script. At a time when the Church had an unpleasant way of dealing with what it considered to be heretical attitudes, Leonardo went to great pains to conceal what he was doing in the way of scientific research. The result was that much of his scientific work was lost to the world for nearly 400 years after his death; had it been otherwise, later pioneers of flight might have been spared a great deal of heartbreak and tragedy.

Da Vinci knew, for example, that a bird with outstretched wings could not fall vertically through the air, but had to glide down at an angle. He also knew that birds made use of their wings and tails as air-brakes to check their descent, and that they also took advantage of rising currents of air to gain height. He even understood the importance

One of George Cayley's designs was a convertiplane, a helicopter cum aeroplane, seen here in model form. It was a century before the concept reached fruition.

of sufficient height in enabling a flying bird that suddenly loses its equilibrium to recover safely. In all, da Vinci's writings on the subject of flight amounted to about 35,000 words.

Model Gliders

While it was Leonardo da Vinci who laid the foundation, in his writings, of the principles of flight, it was an Englishman who, 300 years later, was the first to define the principles of mechanical flight – the relationship between weight, lift, drag and thrust. His name was Sir George Cayley. He lived at Brompton Hall near Scarborough, in Yorkshire, and without doubt was one of the most talented and versatile pioneers in the history of aviation.

In 1804, after experimenting with various model glider designs, Cayley built what is considered to be the first rigid aircraft in history, a glider about 1.5km (5ft) long, with a fixed wing set at an angle of six degrees and a cruciform tailplane attached to the fuselage by universal joints. Five years later he built a larger glider, which was flown successfully in ballast, and sometimes for a few yards with a man or boy clinging to it. No record of this machine's configuration exists, and there are no drawings of it, but Cayley himself left this tantalizing account in 1810:

'Last year I made a machine, having a surface of 300 square feet [28 square metres], which was accidentally broken before there was an opportunity of trying the effect of the propelling apparatus; but its steerage and steadiness were perfectly proved, and it would sail obliquely downward in any direction, according to the set of the rudder. Even in this state, when any person ran forwards in it, with his full speed, taking advantage of a gentle breeze in front, it would bear upwards so strongly as scarcely to allow him to touch the ground; and would frequently lift him up, and convey him several yards together.'

Cayley never lost his interest in aviation; he went off at various tangents

George Cayley's enormous contribution to aviation was later acknowledged by the Wright brothers. He was the true father of heavier-than-air flight.

over the next 30 years, experimenting with ornithopter and dirigible balloon designs and also inventing stabilizing fins for artillery projectiles. Then, in 1843, after having built several more models, and producing an ingenious design for a convertiplane (a sort of helicopter), he built a triplane glider in 1849, first of all carrying out trials with ballast, then with the 10-year-old son of one of his servants. The manned flights of the so-called 'Boy Carrier' are likely to have been hops of only a few yards.

In 1853 Cayley completed his Glider No. 3, which was almost certainly a triplane similar to the previous one, and sometime after June of the same year this aircraft made a famous brief flight with Cayley's coachman on board. Although the coachman has been referred to by the name of John Appleby, the fact remains that his true identity remains a mystery to this day. The glider, with its terrified occupant, is said to have flown about 500m (1500ft) across a small valley behind Brompton Hall, before crashing to the ground. There is no doubt at all that this flight took place. It may fairly be described as the first manned (but not piloted) glider flight in history. Incidentally, the coachman (or, according to one account, the butler) is said to have broken a leg in the crash and resigned on the spot. Many years later, Cayley's granddaughter Dora Thompson recalled the incident:

'I remember in later times hearing of a large machine being started on the high side of the valley behind Brompton Hall where he lived, and the coachman being sent up in it, and he flew across the little valley, about 500 yards [500m] at most, and came down with a smash. What the motive power was I don't know, but I think the coachman was the moving element, and the result was his capsize and the rush of watchers across to his rescue. He struggled up and said, "Please, Sir George, I wish to give notice. I was hired to drive and not to fly" … I think I am right in saying that I saw the said machine flown across the dale in 1852, when I was nine years old. At any rate it was very like it.'

Ahead of His Time

Apart from practical experiments such as these, Cayley's scientific papers were to have a profound influence on the expanding world of aeronautics. His most important work, entitled *On Aerial Navigation*, discussed the principles of aerodynamics and their practical application, and appeared in 1909–10 in a scientific publication called *Nicholson's Journal of Natural Philosophy, Chemistry and the Arts*. It was a long time, however – some 20 years after his death – before Cayley's writings reached a wider audience, his papers being published in England in 1876 and in France in 1877.

In one passage, Cayley stated that he was 'totally convinced that this noble art will soon be within man's competence and that we will eventually be able to travel with our families and baggage more safely than by sea … All that is needed is an engine which can produce more power per minute than can the human muscle system.' That, in essence, is the tragedy of Sir George Cayley: his designs were adequate enough to become airborne, but lacked the power to sustain them in the air. Had a suitable power source – such as the internal

Cayley's 1853 design for a man-carrying glider monoplane. This monoplane was probably the one in which his reluctant coachman made a short flight across a valley in Yorkshire.

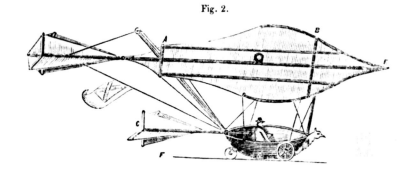

Mechanics' Magazine,

MUSEUM, REGISTER, JOURNAL, AND GAZETTE.

No. 1520.]   SATURDAY, SEPTEMBER 25, 1852.   [Price 3*d*., Stamped 4*d*.

Edited by J. C. Robertson, 166, Fleet-street.

SIR GEORGE CAYLEY'S GOVERNABLE PARACHUTES.

Fig. 2.

Fig. 1.

The British engineer William Samuel Henson patented a design for an Aerial Steam Carriage, which was the first ever concept of a fixed-wing aircraft along modern lines.

combustion engine – been available, it is virtually certain that one of Cayley's designs would have made a sustained and powered flight over the Yorkshire Dales of England in the latter half of the nineteenth century.

Steam Engine

There was one man who was profoundly influenced by the writings of Sir George Cayley who believed that the steam engine, heavy though it was, might provide a suitable power source for a flying machine. He was an engineer of Somerset, England, named William Samuel Henson, and in 1842 he designed and patented a flying machine which was to have an enormous influence on the subsequent development of heavier-than-air craft. Henson's design, the Aerial Steam Carriage, was the first ever concept of a fixed-wing aircraft along modern lines, comprising a boat-like fuselage surmounted by a conventional wing and with a tail unit attached. Such was Henson's enthusiasm for the project that he tried to set up an air freight business, the Aerial Steam Transit Company, in partnership with his friend John Stringfellow. In the event, the Aerial Steam Carriage was never built, Henson losing interest after tests with a scale model failed. He emigrated to the United States in 1848, and took no further interest in aviation.

When Henson became disillusioned with the project and emigrated, his colleague John Stringfellow set about improving the little steam engine his friend had built, and installed it in a new monoplane model which had a wingspan of about 3m (10ft). This was tested in 1848, but the results were disappointing. It was launched from a high cable at Chard, Somerset, but did not achieve sustained flight.

Stringfellow took a break from aeronautical design for the best part of 20 years, but in 1868 he produced another model, this time involving a triplane. He exhibited his design at the world's first aeronautical exhibition, which was held at London's Crystal Palace in that same year, and the

Samuel Henson became disillusioned with the Aerial Steam Carriage when a test model failed, but the concept was pursued by his colleague, John Stringfellow, who set about improving Henson's steam engine and designed a new monoplane.

John Stringfellow (above) may have been the first person to build and fly a powered aircraft, although his model (left) is not thought to have been capable of sustained flight.

innovative nature of his model triplane won him an award of £100, donated by the Aeronautical Society. In fact, the prize was awarded more in recognition of the efficiency of his little steam engine, which was found to have the best power-to-weight ratio of any tested. A contemporary description of this model exists in an Aeronautical Society journal:

'It consisted of three superposed surfaces aggregating 28 square feet [2.6 square metres] and a tail of 8 square feet [0.7 square metres] more. The weight was less than 12 pounds [5.5kg] and it was driven by a central propeller actuated by a steam engine overestimated at one-third of a horsepower. It ran suspended to a wire on its trials but failed of free flight, in consequence of defective equilibrium.'

According to one eyewitness account, Stringfellow continued to test his model after the Crystal Palace exhibition, on his return to Chard:

'When freed, it descended an incline with apparent lightness until caught in the canvas; but the impression conveyed was that had there been sufficient fall, it would have recovered itself … It was intended at the last to set this model free in the open country, when the requirements of the Exhibition were satisfied, but it was found that the engine, which had done much work, required repairs. Many months afterward, in the presence of the author (M. Brearey) an experiment was tried in a field at Chard, by means of a wire stretched across it. The engine was fed with methylated spirits, and during some portion of its run under the wire, the draft occasioned thereby invariably extinguished the flames, and so these interesting trials were rendered abortive.'

With this prize money, Stringfellow '… erected a building over 70 ft. [21m] long, in which to experiment with a view of ultimately constructing a large

Clement Ader rightly claimed to have been the first man to design an aircraft capable of flying under its own power, but his credibility was then damaged by his subsequent, fraudulent claims to be the first man actually to make sustained heavier-than-air flights.

machine to carry a person to guide and conduct it, his experience with models having evidently impressed him with the necessity for intelligent control of any aerial apparatus not possessing automatic stability; but he was already 69 years of age, his sight became impaired, and he died in 1883 without having accomplished any advance on his previous achievements.'

John Stringfellow's demise did not mean the end of the family name's involvement with aviation, for his son, F.J. Stringfellow, pursued his line of research, and in 1886 designed a steam-powered biplane model with twin propellers, but this also proved a failure. If the research carried out by the two Stringfellows proved anything, it was that steam was not the answer to the problem of achieving powered flight.

Steam Experiments Continue

Despite the Stringfellows' experiences, it was nevertheless a steam engine that was fitted to the world's first successful powered model plane. It was designed and flown in 1857 by a French naval officer, Félix du Temple de la Croix, and in 1874 he built a full-size version, the du Temple Monoplane. With a sailor whose name is not recorded sitting in the craft, it took off under power after a down-ramp run, and, although it did not achieve sustained flight, it became the first full-size powered plane to leave the ground.

In 1884, a plane powered by a British steam engine was built by a Russian engineer, Alexander Feodorovitch Mozhaiski, and tested at Krasnoye Selo, near St Petersburg. The machine, piloted by I.N. Golubev, made one take-off down a 'ski-jump' ramp, but did not achieve sustained flight. The aircaft's design was based on that of Henson's Aerial Steam Carriage, and the method of launching was based on his technique. During the Stalinist era, Soviet writers were eager to claim this as the world's first powered flight, which it was not, by any stretch of the imagination.

Unfortunately, fraudulent claims were by no means uncommon in the early years of aviation, such was the race to take to the air successfully. One of the saddest cases was that of Clement Ader, a talented French engineer who was assured of a place in aviation history as the man who designed the first aircraft to fly under its own power. Unfortunately, Ader's credibility was virtually destroyed by his subsequent claims to have been the first man to make sustained heavier-than-air flights, claims that were quickly and unequivocally disproved.

God of the Four Winds

Ader's steam-driven aircraft, a bat-shaped design named the *Eole* (after Aeolus, a Greek god who was custodian of the four winds) was completed in 1890, and on 9 October of that year Ader prepared

Right: Clement Ader testing his Avion III aircraft in 1897. The test was abandoned when the craft failed to leave the ground.

Below: Ader's Avion III pictured in France's Musée des Arts et Métiers. A previous aircraft, the Avion II, was never completed.

Samuel Pierpont Langley's Aerodrome mounted on top of a houseboat on the Potomac River. Langley was a leading figure in American nineteenth-century scientific research and designed a succession of model aircraft.

to make a test flight in the grounds of a friend's estate at the Château d'Armainvilliers, near Gretz in France. The steam engine was started, Ader positioned himself in the rudimentary cockpit, and at 4 p.m. the *Eole* got under way, taxiing a short distance, then rising into the air to make a hop of about 50m (160ft), skimming the ground. The brief flight was uncontrolled and could not be sustained by the unsuitable steam engine. Nevertheless, Ader had demonstrated, for the first time, that a heavier-than-air craft was capable of taking off from level ground under its own power.

With the help of a subsidy from the War Ministry, Ader set about modifying and enlarging the basic *Eole* design, and in 1892 he began constructing a machine he named Avion II. (The word *avion*, for plane, was Ader's invention, and remains the standard French word). It was never completed, but Ader then embarked on the design of another version, the Avion III, which was powered by two 15kW (20hp) steam engines driving contra-rotating tractor propellers. The machine was tested twice at Satory, south of Versailles, on 12 and 14 October 1897, but on neither occasion did it leave the ground. On the first occasion the Avion simply trundled along the track that had been laid out for it, and on the second occasion it jumped the track and rolled into a nearby field. Further testing was abandoned without the aircraft having flown.

In 1906, however, Ader claimed that

the Avion III had flown for a distance of 300m (985ft), and wrote an account of the flight that was pure fabrication. Apart from the rather sad nature of what became known as the 'Ader Affair', it was a pity that Ader had persisted in his study of the bat as the model for his flying machine. Had he based his design on the structure of a bird's wing, he might indeed have become the first man to make a controlled heavier-than-air flight; however, the Avion III, like the earlier *Eole*, was not fitted with an elevator or any other means of flight control. Clement Ader died in Toulouse, France, on 5 March 1926.

Samuel Pierpont Langley, a leading figure in American nineteenth-century scientific research, also devised his own name for a flying machine, and designed a succession of model aircraft all called the Aerodrome, a name that came to have an entirely different meaning in the world of aviation with the passage of time. After several failures with designs that were too fragile and underpowered to sustain themselves, Langley had his first genuine success on 6 May 1896, when his Aerodrome No. 5 made the first successful flight of an unpiloted engine-driven heavier-than-air craft of substantial size. It was launched from a spring-actuated catapult mounted on top of a houseboat on the Potomac River

Langley's Aerodrome 'A' shown breaking up in the air immediately after launching from a houseboat moored on the Potomac River, near Quantico, on 8 December 1903. This was the second of two attempted launches.

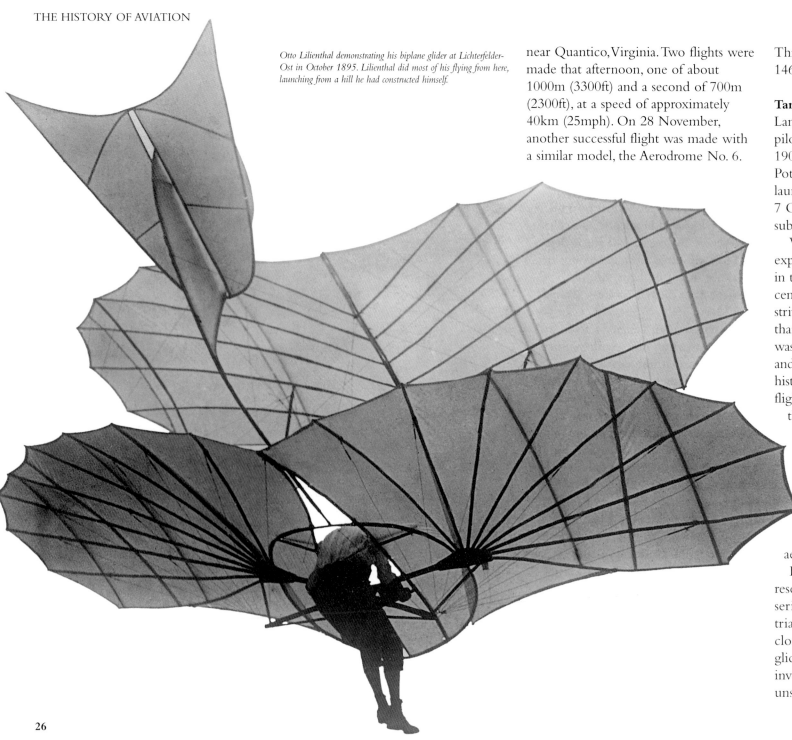

Otto Lilienthal demonstrating his biplane glider at Lichterfelder-Ost in October 1895. Lilienthal did most of his flying from here, launching from a hill he had constructed himself.

near Quantico, Virginia. Two flights were made that afternoon, one of about 1000m (3300ft) and a second of 700m (2300ft), at a speed of approximately 40km (25mph). On 28 November, another successful flight was made with a similar model, the Aerodrome No. 6.

This flew a distance of approximately 1460m (4790ft).

Tandem-Wing Monoplane

Langley went on to build a full-scale piloted tandem-wing monoplane in 1903; however, it it crashed into the Potomac in the course of two attempted launches from a converted houseboat on 7 October and 8 December, and was subsequently abandoned.

While Ader, Langley and the rest were experimenting with their powered designs in the latter years of the nineteenth century, one man above all others was striving to achieve perfection in heavier-than-air flight by the use of gliders. He was Otto Lilienthal, a German engineer and inventor who became the first man in history to take off and make a controlled flight. Lilienthal had become interested in the mechanics of flight while still a boy and, at the age of 14, he experimented with two rudimentary gliders. In the late 1860s, along with his brother Gustave, he began serious research into aeronautics, investigating the mechanics and aerodynamics of bird flight.

Between 1891 and 1896, he put his research into practice in the form of a series of highly successful full-size glider trials. During this period Lilienthal made close to 2000 brief flights in 16 different glider designs based on his aerodynamic investigations. His first two gliders were unsuccessful, but his third design, a monoplane with cruciform tailplane and fin, worked well, as did subsequent machines. Thanks to a circular shock absorber made out of willow, he survived a serious crash when his Glider No. 9 nosedived into the ground, he and went on to develop his 'standard' monoplane glider, the Lilienthal No. 11.

Lilienthal carried out most of his gliding from a hill he had constructed near his home at Gross-Lichterfelde, and from the hills surrounding the small village of Rhinow, about 80km (50 miles) from the city of Berlin. His best efforts with these gliders covered a distance of more than 300m (985ft) and were 12–15 seconds in duration.

In the summer of 1896, Lilienthal's aeronautical experiments came to an abrupt and tragic end. On 9 August, while he was soaring in one of his standard monoplane gliders, a strong gust of wind caused the craft to nose up sharply, stall and crash from an altitude of 15m (50ft). Lilienthal suffered a broken spine and died the following day in a Berlin hospital.

Pilcher's Gliders
Despite his fatal crash, Lilienthal efforts with his gliders provided the inspiration for other would-be aviators. One of them was a Scottish engineer named Percy Sinclair Pilcher, who visited Lilienthal twice and bought one of the German designer's machines. After gaining experience with this, Pilcher set about designing his own gliders, the first of which he built in 1895 and named the *Bat*. His next two gliders were unsuccessful, but in 1897 he set a distance record of 230m (750ft) in his latest design, the *Hawk*.

Pilcher was killed in 1899 when the *Hawk* suffered a structural failure. At the time of his death he was building a monoplane; the small oil engine that was to power it had already been completed and tested. In 2003, a replica of this aircraft was built by the School of Aeronautics at Cranfield University in the United Kingdom, and achieved a sustained controlled flight of 1 minute 26 seconds in still-air conditions, without the benefit of a headwind to help it become airborne. Percy Pilcher, then, might have become the first man to achieve a sustained powered flight, had it not been for his untimely death. Instead, that distinction would fall to two American brothers, who had been avidly following the efforts of Europe's embryo aviators from across the Atlantic.

One day in 1878, the brothers were given a present by their father. A model flying machine about 30cm (1ft) long, it was made of paper, bamboo and cork, and was fitted with twin blades that rotated by the tension of a rubber band. The boys played with it until it broke, then set about building one of their own. The boys' names were Wilbur and Orville Wright.

Lilienthal's No. 11 Monoplane Glider. It was while flying a glider of similar design that Lilienthal crashed on 9 August 1896 and sustained fatal injuries.

Pioneers of Powered Flight 1900–1914

Although would-be aviators were experimenting with various types of internal combustion engine in the latter years of the nineteenth century, it was the petrol-driven four-stroke engine, first demonstrated by Nikolaus von Otto in 1876, that was to precipitate the real technological revolution in manned flight.

The two Wright brothers, Orville and Wilbur, followed the sensible path of experimenting with kites and gliders before attempting to build a powered aircraft. Residents of Dayton, Ohio, they ran a bicycle design, repair and manufacturing company; its success enabled them to indulge their growing fascination with flight. They were greatly influenced by the articles that they read about Otto Lilienthal and his glider flights, and in 1896 three events appear to have combined to persuade them to build their own flying machines. The first was the successful flight of an unmanned steam-powered model plane built by Samuel Langley, Secretary of the Smithsonian Institution; the second was the work of a Chicago engineer named

A cameraman records one of the Wright brothers' early flights at Kitty Hawk. The Wrights were meticulous in their research, constructing several gliders before attempting a powered flight.

Orville Wright (left) and his brother Wilbur. The brothers were greatly influenced by articles they had read about Otto Lilienthal and his glider flights, and by Langley's experiments with models.

Octave Chanute, who tested various types of hang-glider on the south shore of Lake Michigan; and the third was the accidental death of Lilienthal.

The Wright brothers' first glider, built in 1899, was a biplane type, with a forward monoplane elevator and no tail surfaces. After consulting the Weather Bureau, they decided that the best place to test their machine was Kitty Hawk, in North Carolina, where a steady wind prevailed for most of the time. They flew it there in October 1900, mostly as a kite, while they took it in turns to get the 'feel' of what it was like to be airborne. Their

No. 2 glider, flown at the Kill Devil Hills, south of Kitty Hawk, in July and August 1901, was also a biplane with a forward monoplane elevator and no tail surfaces, but No. 3, flown in August 1902, had a fixed double rear fin. This was later replaced by a rear rudder, which was linked with the wing-warping (a method of achieving lateral control, later replaced by ailerons) to counteract warp drag.

A Scientific Approach

The Wrights approached their work scientifically. They even designed a wind tunnel equipped with balances for

measuring the magnitude and direction of forces on an aircraft's wing. They made useful measurements of lift and drag, and other factors affecting flight, and set them down in tabular form. The construction of their No. 3 glider was based on the results of these wind tunnel measurements, which they considered accurate enough to enable them to set about designing a powered aircraft.

The machine that gradually emerged on the drawing board was a biplane with a wingspan of 12.3m (40ft 6in), a length of 8.5m (28ft) and a height of 2.5m (8ft). It weighed 274kg (605lb). The wings were

The first Wright Flyer after it had been fitted with a wheeled undercarriage in 1909. The personnel in the photograph represent the entire flying branch of the US Signal Corps at the time.

constructed of spars and ribs covered on top and bottom with unbleached and untreated muslin. The outer wing extremities could be warped for lateral balance. Behind the wings were two propellers, rotating in opposite directions. They were made of two layers of spruce glued together, each layer 4.5cm (1¾in) thick. The ribs and undercarriage (a pair of skids) were of second-growth ash, and the spars and struts were of spruce. In front, mounted on outriggers, was the elevator, movable for vertical control, with 4.5 square metres (48 square feet) of fabric surfaces. In the rear was a rudder with a fabric area of 1.9 square metres (20 square feet). The pilot lay prone on the lower wing, operating the elevator by rocking a small lever with his left hand; he controlled the warping of the wings and the rudder, which were interconnected, by moving his body from side to side so as to shift the control cradle on which his hips lay. His position on the lower wing slightly to the left balanced the weight of the engine, which was attached to the wing beams.

As it was impossible to procure an engine from American manufacturers, the Wright brothers – who had already built an engine to power their tool shop – decided to build one of their own with the aid of Charles E. Taylor, a machinist in their employ. Their joint efforts produced a four-cylinder engine with a 10cm (4in) bore and stroke developing nearly 9kW (12hp).

In September 1903, the aircraft and its engine were shipped to Kitty Hawk. There were delays and problems with the equipment; however, on 14 December, everything was ready for a test flight. The aircraft, facing into the wind, was mounted on a dolly, which rode on an 18m (60ft) launching track laid out on level ground. The brothers tossed a coin to determine who would be the first to pilot the machine, and Wilbur won. Propellers turning, it moved down the track, gathering speed, and rose into the air – only to rise at too steep an angle, stall and crash, breaking a skid and other small parts, but leaving Wilbur unhurt.

Twelve-Second Flight

Repairs were quickly made, and on 17 December, a cold and windy day, the brothers tried again, this time with Orville at the controls. After travelling 12m (40ft), with Wilbur running alongside and holding on to a wingtip to steady the machine, the 'Flyer' rose into the air and flew a distance of 37m (120ft) into a wind gusting up to 43kph (27mph); the flight lasted just 12 seconds.

Three more flights were made that day, the brothers taking turns at the controls, and on the last flight Wilbur remained airborne for 59 seconds, covering a distance of 260m (852ft). The landing, unfortunately, was a rough one,

The Wright Flyer taking off on its historic 12-second flight at Kitty Hawk on 17 December 1903, with Orville at the controls. Three more flights were made that day.

Side view of the Wright Flyer, showing the position of the engine and arrangement of the crankshafts for driving the propellers. The Wright brothers' design showed a great deal of ingenuity.

First True Powered Aircraft
Wright Flyer

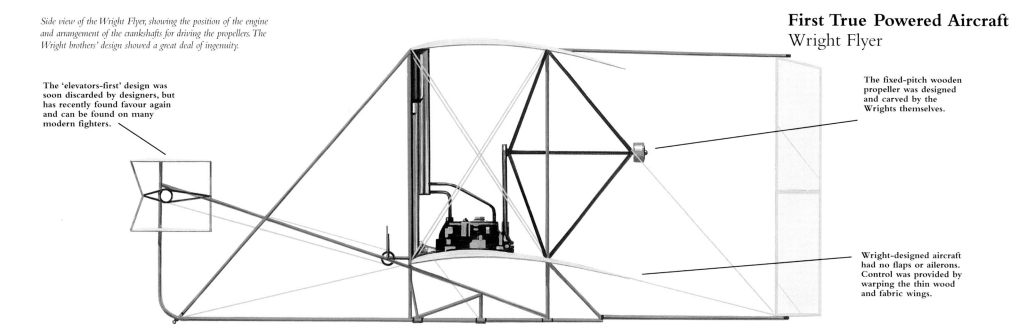

The 'elevators-first' design was soon discarded by designers, but has recently found favour again and can be found on many modern fighters.

The fixed-pitch wooden propeller was designed and carved by the Wrights themselves.

Wright-designed aircraft had no flaps or ailerons. Control was provided by warping the thin wood and fabric wings.

damaging the skids and the braces of the elevator, and while the Wrights were standing nearby discussing the flight, a sudden strong gust of wind caught the aircraft and turned it over several times, causing further damage. With no prospect of repairs being made on the spot, flights were discontinued at Kitty Hawk and the damaged machine was shipped back to Dayton, Ohio.

The Wright brothers' second biplane, or Flyer II, was flown for the first time on 23 May 1904, the flying site having now moved from Kill Devil Hills to the Huffmann Prairie near Dayton. Hitherto, the Flyer had been launched from a rail, the aircraft being tethered while the

engine was run up, then released; however, at Huffmann Prairie, take-off was assisted by a weight-and-derrick apparatus that was to be used successfully in hundreds of subsequent take-offs.

On 9 November 1904, after completing its first circuit flight, the Flyer II, powered by a 12kW (16hp) Wright engine, covered 4.5km (2.75 miles) in a flight lasting more than five minutes. In 1905, after being offered to – and rejected by – the US and British War departments, it was broken up, and various components used in the construction of the greatly improved Flyer III. This was the Wrights' first fully practical aircraft, and it had made some 50 flights by mid-October of that year.

By this time, the Wrights were a long way ahead of their counterparts in Europe. They had no serious rivals in the United States, although claims were made in later years that one Gustave Whitehead, an American-domiciled German who had changed his name from Gustav Weisskopf, had made a series of powered flights starting in 1901, including one of just over 11km (7 miles) over Long Island Sound on the eastern seaboard of the United States in 1912. The claims were dismissed as false. Although Whitehead did build and fly some gliders, his prototype powered aircraft never flew. A photograph of it shows a boat-like fuselage for the pilot

Wright Flyer

Type: experimenal biplane

Powerplant: one 9kW (12hp) Wright four-cylinder inline engine

Maximum speed: c.50km/h (31mph)

Weight: 340 kg (750lb)

Dimensions:		
	span	12.29m (40ft)
	length	6.43m (21ft)
	height	2.81m (9ft)
	wing area	c.35m² (510sq ft)

The Curtiss June Bug, *also called the Golden Flyer, was the first aircraft built by the US pioneer Glenn H. Curtiss. It was flown to victory in the* Scientific American *prize by making a 40-km (25-mile) flight in 1909.*

and engine, the latter driving two tractor propellers on outriggers, wings derived from a Lilienthal design, and a bird-like 'spreading' tail surface with no rudder.

Modified Version

The Wrights did not fly again until May 1908, when they demonstrated a modified version of the Flyer III. Meanwhile, in October 1907, an organization called the Aerial Experimental Association (AEA) had been founded and financed by Dr and Mrs Alexander Graham Bell. Its other members were F.W. 'Casey' Baldwin, J.A.D. McCurdy (both Canadians), Lieutenant T.E. Selfridge and Glenn H. Curtiss. The AEA was based in Beinn Bhreagh, Baddeck Bay, in Nova Scotia, Canada, and Hammondsport, on Lake Keuka, in New York State. The association's first design was a large kite-glider, which made two successful towed flights in December 1907; the second was a biplane hang-glider, which made some 50 flights early in 1908.

The AEA's first powered aircraft, flown twice in March 1908, was the *Red Wing*, fitted with a 30kW (40hp) engine designed by Glenn Curtiss. It was followed by the *White Wing*, flown in May 1908; this was the first American machine to have ailerons, which were fitted at the wingtips. The AEA's third aircraft was the *June Bug*,

In the first decade of the twentieth century, ailerons (seen here at the wingtips of this Levavasseur monoplane) were beginning to replace the well-tried technique of wing warping, used by the Wright brothers and other early designers.

The Channel Crosser
Blériot XI Monoplane

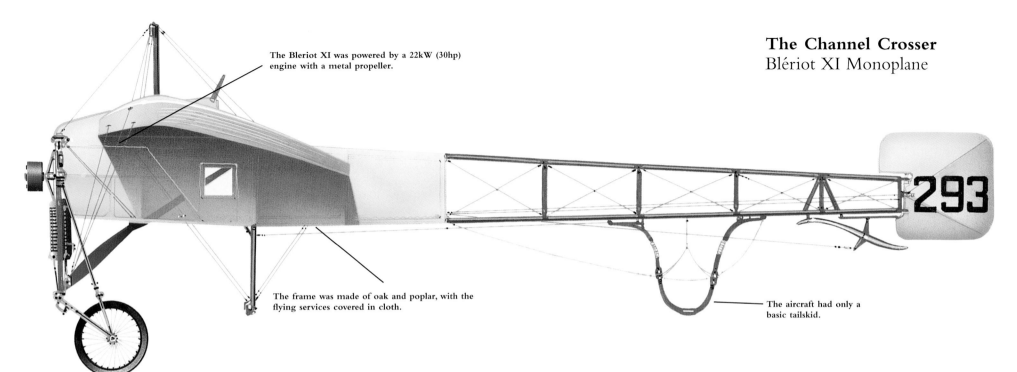

The Blériot XI was powered by a 22kW (30hp) engine with a metal propeller.

The frame was made of oak and poplar, with the flying services covered in cloth.

The aircraft had only a basic tailskid.

The Blériot monoplane, the first aircraft to fly over the English Channel, brought a new dimension to flying in general. The well-proven design was popular with civilian and military customers.

first flown at Hammondsport on 21 June 1908 powered by the *Red Wing*'s 30kW engine. It was designed by Glenn Curtiss, who had been a leading builder and racer of motorcycles before turning his attention to aviation. On 4 July it won a prize offered by the journal *Scientific American* for the first officially recorded flight in the United States of more than one kilometre (0.6 miles), even though the modified Wright Flyer III had flown five miles on 14 May with Wilbur at the

controls. Earlier that day, the Flyer III had made two flights carrying passengers – the first passenger flights in history.

The AEA's fourth and last aircraft was the *Silver Dart*, which was similar to the *June Bug*, but powered by a 37kW (50hp) water-cooled Curtiss engine mounted between the upper and lower mainplanes, with a chain-belt drive to two pusher propellers outboard of the rear fuselage framework. Built at Hammondsport, it was taken to ice-covered Baddeck Bay, where it was flown by Casey Baldwin and John McCurdy, who consequently became the first pilots to make flights in the British Empire outside Britain.

In Europe, the man who contributed the most to the development of aviation during this period was Léon Levavasseur, an engineer and former artist who, from 1903, produced a range of excellent engines, designed originally to power motor boats. He subsequently became chief designer of the Société Antoinette, named after Mlle Antoinette Gastimbide, daughter of the head of the company.

Down in the Sea
Levavasseur's designs were monoplanes. The first, a pusher type, was not completed; a second, the Gastimbide-Mengin I (Mengin was a member of the

Blériot XI Monoplane

Type: monoplane

Powerplant: 16.5–19kW (22-25hp) Anzani three-cylinder fan-type

Maximum speed: 75.6km/h (47mph)

Weight: 230kg (507lb)

Dimensions:		
span	7.79m (25ft 7in)	
length	7.62m (25ft)	
height	2.69m (8ft 10in)	
wing area	14m² (150sq ft)	

This Blériot XI monoplane is part of the Shuttleworth Collection at Old Warden, Biggleswade, England. It is in flying condition, but its displays are restricted to calm days.

company) appears to have made a few short hops before being wrecked. Rebuilt as the Antoinette II, it was successfully flown on 22 July 1908, and on 21 August it made the first circular flight by a monoplane. The Antoinette IV, first flown in October 1908, was the first 'standard' Antoinette. It was flown by pioneer aviator Hubert Latham (born in France, though of English ancestry), who attempted a crossing of the English Channel in it on 19 July 1909, and came down in the sea.

A week later, on 25 July 1909, the Channel was successfully crossed by French aviator Louis Blériot. In December 1908, Blériot – who had been building experimental aircraft since 1908 – exhibited three of his designs at the Salon de l'Automobile et de l'Aéronautique, Paris. Of these, the Blériot IX was a monoplane with a 75kW (100hp) Antoinette engine, which succeeded in making only a few brief hops, while the Blériot X, a pusher biplane, was never completed. It was the third machine, the Blériot XI, that was destined to make Blériot's reputation, and his fortune. A tractor monoplane type, the Blériot XI flew for the first time at Issy on 23 January 1909, powered by a 22kW (30hp) REP (Robert Esnault-Pelterie) engine fitted with a crude four-bladed metal propeller. When the aircraft was

Louis Blériot was born in Cambrai, France, on 1 July 1872, and studied engineering in Paris. Blériot displayed an early interest in aviation, and in 1900 he built a motor-powered ornithopter, which failed to work.

modified in April, the REP was replaced by a 19kW (25hp) Anzani engine with a more refined propeller. The aircraft used the wing-warping technique for lateral control, and was the first European aircraft to employ this system effectively.

After making several excellent flights in the spring and summer of 1909, including one of 50 minutes, Blériot took off in the Type XI from Le Baraques, near Calais, and landed in a field near Dover Castle, England, about half an hour later, so winning the prize of £1000 offered by Lord Northcliffe, proprietor of the London *Daily Mail*, to the first aviator to fly across the English

Channel from coast to coast in either direction. The exploit provided an enormous boost for the Type XI, which was soon in production for the French Aviation Militaire and other air arms.

Meanwhile, the Wright brothers had been demonstrating their commanding

Wilbur Wright's French tour of 1908 persuaded the English brothers Horace, Eustace and Oswald Short to take up aircraft manufacture. This is their biplane No 1.

lead in aviation development. In July 1907, their latest aircraft, the Wright A, was shipped to Le Havre, France. This was the first Wright design to be demonstrated in public, Wilbur Wright being the pilot, and spectators were amazed by his display of flight control. From August to December 1908, Wilbur made 113 flights, including 60 with passengers, at Hunaudières and Auvours, then moved to Pau, where the Wright A made a

further 68 flights, flown by Wilbur or his pupils. While these displays were in progress, a second Wright A was undergoing acceptance trials for the US Signal Corps, but this machine crashed on 17 September 1908, killing Lieutenant T.E. Selfridge and injuring Orville Wright. Despite this tragedy, a second machine was built and was accepted by the Signal Corps, becoming the world's first military plane. Ten more Wright As were built or assembled in Europe in 1909 for use by various customers.

It was Wilbur Wright's demonstration tour of France in 1908 that persuaded three brothers, Horace, Eustace and Oswald Short, to form the first company in Britain for the commercial production of aircraft. At the beginning of 1909, the Short brothers' reputation for excellent workmanship in balloon manufacture earned them a licence to build six Wright Flyers for British customers, but by this time Horace Short had already embarked on a design of his own. A pusher-type biplane, broadly based on the Wright design, it was built at the company's premises under the railway arches at

Battersea, London, and completed in the summer of 1909. It was powered by a 22kW (30hp) engine and several attempts were made to fly it, but it never left its launching rail. The next aircraft was more successful, and was first flown on 27 September 1909 by its owner, J.T.C. Moore-Brabazon, who on 1 March 1910 won the British Empire Michelin Cup with a flight of just over 30km (19 miles) in 31 minutes.

The Michelin Cup was one of a succession of trophies that gave enormous impetus to the development of flying in the early years of the twentieth century. Awarded by the Michelin Tyre Company for duration flying, it was open to all comers, and was first won by Wilbur Wright, who completed 56 laps of a 2.2km (1.37-mile) circuit in France on 31 December 1908, establishing at the same time world records for both duration and distance flown. Subsequent competitions, open only to British pilots flying all-British aircraft, were for the British Empire Michelin Cup numbers 1 and 2, and it was the first of these that was won by Moore-Brabazon.

One man above all others, perhaps, did his utmost to promote flying for sporting purposes. He was Alberto Santos-Dumont, a Brazilian expatriate who had settled in Paris and had played an important part in making

Alberto Santos-Dumont, who had achieved fame with his series of little airships, went on to produce powered aircraft designed primarily for sports flying.

39

Europe air-minded through his little sporting airship designs at the beginning of the twentieth century. He subsequently went on to produce a series of heavier-than-air craft which may be justifiably described as the world's first true light aircraft. The first of them was the 14-bis, which was tested in 1906 suspended under Santos-Dumont's Airship No. 14, and which later made a series of short powered 'hops'. Further designs led to a series of little single-seater aircraft known collectively by the name Demoiselle (Dragonfly), the first of which (Demoiselle No. 19) flew in 1907. In September 1909, Demoiselle No. 20, a much-modified

Alliot Verdon Roe's triplane. Verdon Roe went on to found Avro, one of the most famous aircraft manufacturers in the world. It would later produce magnificent aircraft such as the Lancaster bomber of World War II fame.

version with a more powerful engine flew for 16 minutes and covered about 18km (11 miles). The Demoiselle was the first aircraft to be produced for sporting purposes, between 10 and 15 being built for sale to aspiring aviators. Unfortunately, the Demoiselle was Santos-Dumont's first and last really successful design, as the onset of multiple sclerosis in 1910 compelled him to retire from an active life. He committed suicide in 1932.

Substantial Prize Money

Meanwhile, other aviators went in vigorous pursuit of the substantial prize money that was being offered for aviation achievement. One of them was Alliot Verdon Roe, the founder of Avro, the firm that was to play such a huge part in the development of aviation, who embarked on his career as an aircraft designer in 1907 with a canard pusher biplane design, the Roe No. 1. He entered the aircraft in a contest to be the first pilot to fly round the Brooklands racing circuit, which carried a £2500 prize, but was unsuccessful. Undeterred, he embarked on the design of a triplane, and on 23 July 1909, with Roe at the controls, the Triplane No. 1 became the first British aircraft, powered by a British-designed engine, to make a successful flight in England. A second aircraft, the Roe II Triplane, flew successfully at Brooklands. These early designs provided invaluable experience in developing A.V. Roe's first true success, the celebrated Avro 504.

Albert Santos-Dumont was the 'little man whom Paris loved'. Santos-Dumont described himself as the first 'sportsman of the air'. He started flying by hiring an experienced balloon pilot and took his first balloon rides as a passenger.

Pioneering Classic
Avro 504

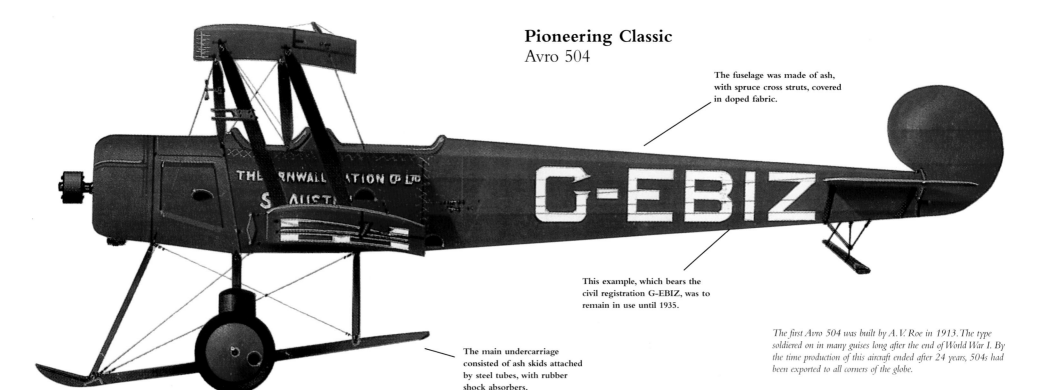

The fuselage was made of ash, with spruce cross struts, covered in doped fabric.

This example, which bears the civil registration G-EBIZ, was to remain in use until 1935.

The main undercarriage consisted of ash skids attached by steel tubes, with rubber shock absorbers.

The first Avro 504 was built by A.V. Roe in 1913. The type soldiered on in many guises long after the end of World War I. By the time production of this aircraft ended after 24 years, 504s had been exported to all corners of the globe.

Although the Short brothers were the first commercial aircraft manufacturers in Britain, it was two more brothers, Gabriel and Charles Voisin, who became the first in Europe, with the establishment of a factory at Billancourt early in 1906. The Voisin brothers went on to produce a series of unspectacular but safe biplanes for private customers. One of them was an aviator named Henry Farman, the son of an English newspaper correspondent working in Paris. Farman's early career in aviation was inextricably linked with the Voisins, who built an aircraft to his order in the summer of 1907. Farman made various modifications to it, and when the Voisin-Farman I first flew on 7 October it was a great success, reaching a height of 771m (2530 ft) in 52.6 seconds.

In 1909, Henry Farman set up his own factory and began producing his own designs; from then on the Henry Farman series of biplanes went from strength to strength, becoming the most reliable and widely used planes of the period, not only in Europe, but also in other parts of the world. In April 1910, Farman biplanes were used by aviators Claude Grahame-White and Louis Paulhan in a spectacular London to Manchester air race, the prize being £10,000 put up by the *Daily Mail* newspaper. Paulhan won the race, but the prize money was divided equally between the two competitors, as Graham-White had made a daring night flight – the first of its kind in England – in an attempt to make up lost ground.

Army Aeroplane No. 1
One man who rose to the pinnacle of British aviation during this pioneering era was an expatriate American, Samuel

Avro 504K

Type: two-seat elementary trainer

Powerplant: one 82kW (110hp) le Rhone rotary piston engine

Maximum speed: 153km/h (95mph)

Ferry range: 402km (250 miles)

Service ceiling: 4875m (16,000ft)

Weights: empty 558kg (1230lb); maximum take-off weight 830kg (1829lb)

Dimensions:

span	10.97m	(36ft)
length	8.97m	(29ft 5in)
height	3.17m	(10ft 5in)
wing area	30.66m²	(330sq ft)

Avro 504s showing their paces at an air display. Thousands of RAF, Commonwealth and foreign pilots were to learn to fly in the aircraft, which was also used in bombing, reconnaissance and night-fighting roles.

UNTY OF MIDDLESEX (B) SQUADRON AUXILIARY AIR FORCE

Many Allied airmen had their first taste of flight in the draughty cockpit of a Maurice Farman Shorthorn during World War I. It was a Shorthorn of the Royal Naval Air Service (RNAS) that made the first night bombing raid of the war.

44

Franklin Cody, who was employed as an observation kite instructor at the Royal Engineers Balloon Factory, Farnborough. Cody man-lifting kites were officially adopted by the British Army in 1906, and were used quite extensively. Cody, who became a British citizen in 1909, experimented with an unmanned powered kite in 1907, and in 1908 he built his first full-sized powered plane, the British Army Aeroplane No. 1. Based on a Wright design, it was a twin-propeller pusher biplane powered by a 37kW (50hp) Antoinette engine. The British Army Aeroplane No. 1 made its first fully authenticated take-off on 29 September 1908, when it made a 'hop' of 71.3m (234ft). On 16 October, at Farnborough, it made what is recognized officially as the first sustained powered flight in Great Britain by a heavier-than-air machine, covering 423.7m (1390ft) before crash-landing. On 8 September 1909, after undergoing many modifications, the aircraft made a sustained flight of more than an hour around Laffan's Plain (Farnborough), covering about 64km (40 miles).

After carrying out more than a year of test flights in his British Army Aeroplane No. 1, Cody built another biplane specifically to compete for the first Michelin Cup. This aircraft, named simply the Cody Michelin Cup Biplane, resembled his first machine, but had improved controls and used ailerons instead of the wing-warping technique. In this second biplane, Cody established

British records for endurance and distance, flying 152km (94.5 miles) in 2 hours 45 minutes. On 31 December 1910, he won the Michelin Cup and broke his own records, covering 298.47km (185.46 miles) in 4 hours 47 minutes.

The Short Brothers, meanwhile, in new premises at Eastchurch, had been turning their attention to meeting the requirements of the British Admiralty. Horace Short's first monoplane design was a 37kW (50hp) Gnome-engined aircraft built in January 1912. It was a Blériot type, and was test flown by a number of naval pilots before being abandoned. The second aircraft was built to an Admiralty order and was fitted with two 52kW (70hp) Gnome engines, one at each end of the two-man crew nacelle. The engines showered the occupants with castor oil, earning the aircraft the nickname of 'Double-Dirty'. It was flown on several occasions, but was not accepted for Naval service, although the Admiralty issued Short with a list of instructions, including folding wings, to suit it for shipboard stowage.

Later in 1912, Horace Short received an Admiralty contract to build two tractor biplanes with interchangeable landing gear so that they could be used from either land or water. The larger of the two, the S.41, flew for the first time

Air mechanics at work on Cody's Michelin Cup aeroplane, in which its designer and pilot established records for both endurance and distance. It was in effect a revised Army Aeroplane No. 1.

in April 1912 and was converted into a seaplane. On 3 May, after being ferried to Weymouth for the 1912 Naval Review, it was lowered overboard from the cruiser HMS *Hibernia* and flown to Portland by Commander C.R. Samson, who had piloted it on its first flight. Three days later, the same pilot flew the S.14 19km (12 miles) out to sea to rendezvous with the fleet and escorted the flagship into Weymouth Bay. The S.41, which made many more successful flights, was the forerunner of a series of successful tractor-engined seaplanes built by Short.

Firmly Established
The Short Brothers' long-standing involvement with maritime aviation really became firmly established in 1913, when Horace Short, in response to the earlier Admiralty requirement, developed a mechanism that enabled a seaplane's wings to be folded back to lie alongside the fuselage, so that it could easily be stored on board a warship. The Short Folder, as the new type was known, entered service with the Royal Naval Air Service in 1913, and on 28 July 1914 one of these aircraft, flown by Squadron Commander A.M. Longmore, air-dropped a torpedo for the first time in Britain.

By the end of the twentieth century's first decade, the plane was being viewed increasingly as a potential war machine.

Samuel F. Cody taking off in the British Army Aeroplane No. 1 to make the first powered flight in Great Britain, on 16 October 1908.

On 10 February 1910, the French Army took delivery of its first heavier-than-air machine, a Wright biplane, at Satory near Versailles. General Roques, in charge of military aviation, launched a campaign to recruit pilots; the artillery provided three men, the infantry four, and the cavalry rejected the request with disdain! In June that year, France's Aéronautique Militaire carried out its first operational mission when Lieutenant Féquant and his observer, Captain Marconnet, flew from Chalons to Vincennes and took aerial photographs from a two-seater Blériot.

In Britain, on 1 April 1911, the Air Battalion of the Royal Engineers was formed at Larkhill, Wiltshire, under the command of Major Sir Alexander Bannerman. It consisted of two companies: No. 1 (Airship, Balloon and Kite) and No. 2

(Aeroplanes). The establishment of the battalion was set at 14 officers and 176 men, but it was some time before full strength was attained. The battalion had three airships, the *Beta*, *Gamma* and *Delta*, and an assortment of aircraft described as 'an antique Wright which had originally belonged to C.S. Rolls; a somewhat antique and very dangerous Blériot; "The Paulhan", a type no longer sold by Paulhan; a de Havilland; a Henri Farman; four Bristols and a Howard Wright.'

On 10 September 1911, the French 6th and 7th Army Corps, each

supported by 25 aircraft, began a week of intensive military exercises on France's eastern frontier. Originally scheduled to take place in central France, the exercises were switched to the country's frontier with Germany following

The British Army Aeroplane No. 1 pictured after making the first powered and sustained flight in Britain on 16 October 1908. Although the flight ended in a crash-landing, the pilot escaped without injury.

a rise in political tension. It was the first time that aircraft had been used as part of a military show of strength.

War Situation

It was Italy, however, that became the first nation to use a plane in a war situation. It happened on 22 October 1911 when, following Italy's declaration of war on Turkey over a dispute involving the Italian occupation of Cyrenaica and Tripoliania (Libya), Captain Carlo Piazza, commanding the Italian Expeditionary Force's air flotilla, made a reconnaissance of Turkish positions between Tripoli and Azizzia in a Blériot XI.

But it was Britain's Royal Navy that first defined the role of its aviators in time of war. In December 1911, the Royal Navy's first flying school was established at Eastchurch, Kent, with six Short biplanes loaned by Frank McLean, a pioneer of the Royal Aero Club. The first four RN pilots had actually begun their flying training in March 1911. Their principal role would be reconnaissance, but they would also be required to search for submarines, locate minefields, 'ascend from a floating base' and act as spotters for naval guns.

On 13 April 1912, the Royal Flying Corps was formed. It became officially established a month later, absorbing the Royal Engineers Air Battalion and the

Glenn H. Curtiss (left) pictured with his Model E flying boat. Curtiss was second only to the Wright brothers in his work of pioneering powered flight in the United States. His first seaplane was flown in 1911.

Naval Air Organization. The new Royal Flying Corps included a Military Wing, a Naval Wing, a Central Flying School, a Reserve and the Royal (formerly Army) Aircraft Factory at Farnborough. The Military Wing (Captain F.M. Sykes) was to comprise a headquarters, seven plane squadrons, one airship and kite squadron, and a Flying Depot, Line of Communications (later renamed Aircraft Park). Nos. 1, 2 and 3 Squadrons formed on 13 May 1912, No. 4 in September 1912, No. 5 in August 1913, No. 6 in January 1914 and No. 7 in May 1914. The first four squadrons were equipped with a miscellany of the aircraft types then available.

In the United States, on 5 March 1913, the US Army Signal Corps' Aeronautical Division issued Field Order No. 1, establishing the First Aero Squadron at Galveston Bay, Texas City, under Captain Charles Chandler. The Aeronautical Division's sole Wright biplane was joined by a Curtiss D, a Burgess H and a Martin TT seaplane. During these formative years, aviation development in the United States did not keep pace with that in Europe, despite the early lead established by the Wright brothers. Yet US airmen were among the first in the world to experience combat, a detachment of US Navy pilots flying Curtiss floatplanes on observation duties during the Mexican crisis of early 1914. One of the aircraft was hit by small-arms fire over Mexican positions near Veracruz on 6 May.

In Germany – which, it must be remembered, had been a united nation for only 30 years – the emphasis at the dawn of the twentieth century was on creation of a powerful fleet to challenge Britain's dominance of the high seas, and pioneering aviation was mainly confined to building foreign types under licence

The Curtiss A1 was the subject of an order from the US Navy, beginning a long association with Glenn Curtiss. The aircraft was named Triad after the addition of retractable wheels to the main float.

during the first decade, with the military showing little interest. The firms that would make a real impact on German aviation, such as Albatros and Fokker, would not become established until 1912.

In one area, however – namely the development of the rigid airship for both commercial and military use – Germany would become renowned, and one man stood at the forefront of the field. His name was Count Ferdinand von Zeppelin.

Airships for Peace and War

By the second half of the nineteenth century, ballooning had become a well-established pastime of the wealthy. Not only that, but balloons had also proved that they could serve a military purpose, particularly in the American Civil War, where they were used for observation. Even as the ranks of those who had tasted the heady joy of flight grew steadily, however, there were those who would not be content. They knew that a man in a balloon could never truly be master of his new environment; he could rise beyond the clouds and he could come down again safely, but where he came down depended on the vagaries of the wind. Not until an aeronaut had some means of steering his balloon, of directing it in whatever path he chose, would the conquest of the air have begun in reality.

The first attempt to steer a balloon in flight was made on 2 March 1784, by a 31-year-old Norman Frenchman named Jean-Pierre Blanchard, a man of considerable inventive capability. By the age of 16 he had built a 'velocipede', an ancestor of the bicycle, and had later equipped it with four flapping wings driven by foot treadles and levers in an unsuccessful attempt to get the machine off the ground. Later, following the first balloon ascents, he decided to attach his steering apparatus to the car of a hydrogen balloon; with the problem of lift overcome, he reasoned that he would be free to concentrate on the steering.

The balloon was launched from the Champ de Mars in Paris. His mechanical wings flapping furiously, Blanchard tried to make the craft go in the direction he wished. Needless to say, he failed, as he did on two subsequent attempts later that year. Disappointed, he took his balloon to England, where his skill as a balloonist was quickly recognized. It was the beginning of a reputation that was to place him high in the ranks of the great aeronauts.

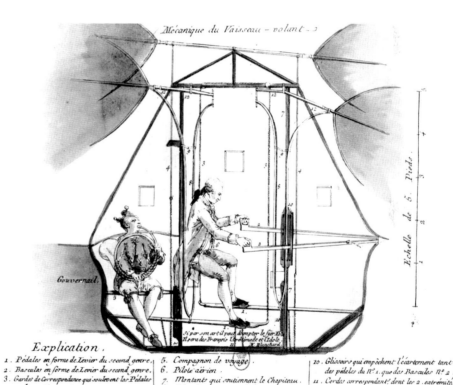

Left: Thaddeus Lowe's balloon Enterprise *at the Battle of Fairoaks, 1862. Lowe was the most important of the aeronauts to take part in the American Civil War, and was appointed Chief Aeronaut of the Army of the Potomac in 1861.*

Right: The first attempt to steer a balloon in flight was made by a Norman Frenchman, Jean-Pierre Blanchard, who invented a flapping wing system, as shown in this diagram. Predictably, Blanchard's system failed to work.

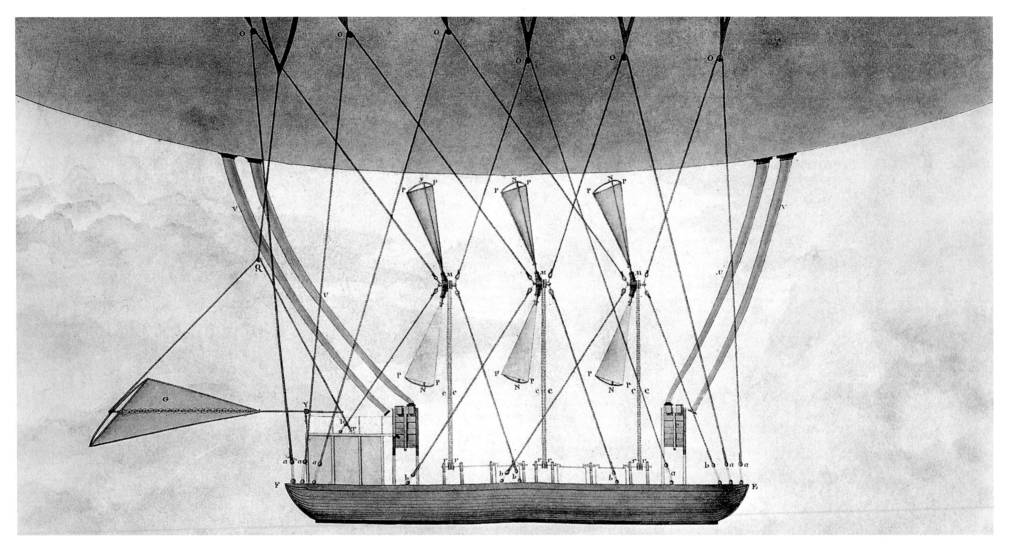

Dirigible Balloon

Although Blanchard's flapping wing arrangement was ingenious enough in its way, it was based on a fairly loose study of birds in flight and was not backed up by sound scientific knowledge. It was different in every way from another approach to the same problem, made by a young French army officer named Jean-Baptiste Meusnier. While Blanchard was busy flapping his ineffective wings, Meusnier was putting the finishing touches to the design of a dirigible balloon: a craft with a streamlined elongated envelope, which was to be pushed through the air by three screws hand-driven from its car.

Meusnier looked upon his dirigible balloon as a kind of ship, which would carve its way through the air as a conventional vessel under sail knifed

Jean-Baptiste Meusnier thought that his dirigible balloon would work in the same manner as a ship under sail, forging its way ahead through the air and turning by means of a rudder.

through the sea, turning with the aid of a rudder at the will of its pilot. Although his craft was destined never to fly, in the years to come, the sky would know its successors. It would be a hundred years before the airship became a practical proposition – a hundred years before the dream of guided flight became a reality. It was Meusnier who pointed the way, however, almost before the cheers of the crowds that watched the first balloon ascents died away. There would be no opportunity, though, for him to pursue his ideas further. In 1793, he was killed while fighting the Prussians at Mainz.

In the mid-nineteenth century, a leading British aeronaut Charles Green demonstrated an innovation which, in due course, was to revolutionize aviation.

Scientist Charles B. Mansfield described it in his book *Aerial Navigation*, which was published in 1877:

'In 1840 Mr Green exhibited at the Polytechnic Institution in London a miniature balloon armed with screw-propellers driven by a spring, for the purpose of showing that it was possible to move such a body at a certain slow rate horizontally up or down, for the purpose of seeking appropriate currents … The balloon, being filled with coal-gas, was then balanced, that is, a sufficient weight was placed in the car to keep it suspended in the air, without the capacity to rise, or the inclination to sink. Mr Green then touched a stop in the spring mechanism, which immediately communicated a rapid rotary motion to the fans, whereupon the machine rose steadily to the ceiling, from which it continued to rebound until the clockwork had run out. Deprived of this assistance [the machine] immediately fell.'

Cigar-like Shape

Several model airships were built and flown during the next few years, with varying degrees of success, powered by a clockwork motor driving a propeller. Possibly the best of them all was built in 1850 by a French clockmaker named

One man who witnessed the flights of model airships with great interest was Henri Giffard, who was inspired by a clockwork-driven model made by Pierre Jullien in 1850 and demonstrated at the Paris Hippodrome.

Pierre Jullien, of Villejuif. Long and slender, the model's cigar-like shape was maintained by a framework of light wire. Its gondola, together with elevators and rudder, was mounted well forwards under the envelope; the small clockwork motor drove two propellers, mounted one on each side. The model was demonstrated at the Paris Hippodrome, where it aroused enormous interest.

Charles Green, one of the leading aeronauts of his time, demonstrated how a balloon might be propelled through the air by means of an airscrew, an innovation that was shortly to revolutionize aviation.

One spectator was a man named Henri Giffard, who afterwards set to work to design a full-size steam-powered dirigible, with a hydrogen-filled envelope 12m (40ft) in diameter and 44m (144ft) long, tapering to a sharp point at each end. The whole envelope was covered by a net, from which the gondola, attached to a long wooden pole, was slung beneath the craft. The distance between the gondola and the envelope was some 12m (40ft), an insurance against a stray spark from the engine sending the whole ship up in flames. The powerplant drove a three-bladed propeller and weighed a total of 158kg (350lb), pushing the total weight of the ship up to a ton and a half.

The dirigible's maiden flight took place on 24 September 1852 from the Paris Hippodrome. Its motor hissing and pounding, the ship rose steadily in conditions of almost perfect calm and flew slowly away over the city. The average speed logged during the flight was 8km/h (5mph) and the craft made a safe landing at Trappes, 27km (17 miles) from its starting point. So ended man's first powered flight, and Giffard subsequently went on to make several

more in the same craft; on one flight, he demonstrated the effectiveness of the ship's triangular canvas rudder by describing a big circle over the rooftops of Paris. Giffard, however, was the first to admit that he had been exceptionally lucky. He knew that if even a moderate breeze had been blowing the power of his steam engine would not have been great enough to overcome it.

Strangely, the successful flight of Giffard's first steam-powered dirigible did not result in a sudden wave of interest, with other scientist-aeronauts trying to emulate it and improve on it, as might have been expected. In fact, for some 15 years interest in dirigible balloons (the word 'airship' had not yet been coined) actually appeared to

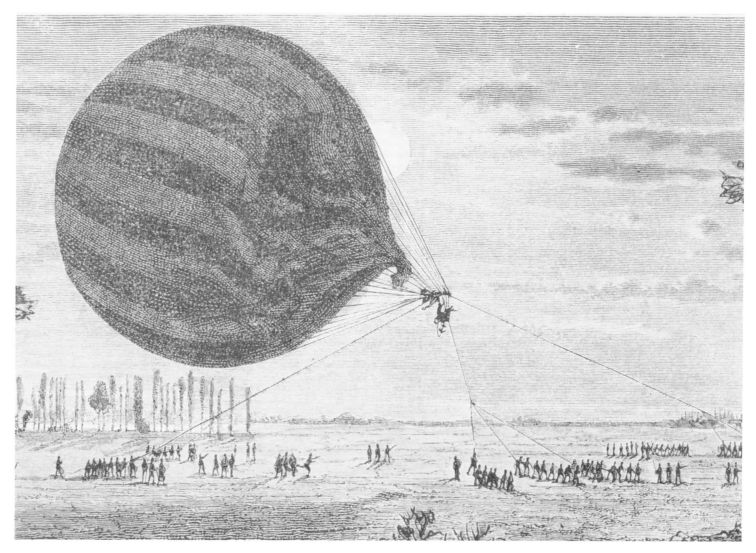

Left: Henri Giffard built the world's first successful airship and made the first ever powered flight in it on 24 September 1852. The dirigible was steam-powered, and covered a distance of 27km (17 miles) in its first flight.

Right: Balloons were used to carry passengers and mail from the city of Paris, besieged by Prussian forces, in 1870–71. It was the first airlift in history and underlined the need for a balloon that could be steered.

wane. Although a number of successful models were built and flown, the handful of full-scale craft that were tested produced disappointing results, offering no improvement over Giffard's design.

Then came the Franco-Prussian war, where balloons played a prominent part in the siege of Paris, and suddenly the whole sphere of aviation assumed a new importance. Between 23 September 1870 and 28 January 1871, 100 passengers succeeded in leaving the city in a total of 66 balloons, which also carried 400 pigeons and 10 tons of mail.

While the balloon flights out of Paris – the first airlift in history – had been something of an epic, it was clear that the venture would have enjoyed far greater success if the balloons had been dirigible. As a direct consequence, a marine engineer named Dupuy de Lôme received a contract to build a dirigible balloon for the French Government. Made of rubberized fabric, the balloon was equipped with a big four-bladed propeller, designed to be cranked by a crew of eight men. It made only one flight, with 15 on board, on 2 February 1872, and succeeded in making a short low-altitude cruise at an average speed of 8km/h (5mph). There was practically no directional control, however, and the project was abandoned.

Gas Engine

One man who had been inspired by the use of aviation during the Franco-Prussian war was an Austrian named Paul Haenlein, who had been giving serious thought to the problem of powering a dirigible balloon. In 1860, a Frenchman, Etienne Lenoir, had patented a gas engine – the forerunner of the internal combustion engine – which worked on the principle of admitting a mixture of gas and air to a cylinder in charges controlled by a valve, each charge then being ignited by an electric spark. The

Frenchman Etienne Lenoir patented the gas engine in 1860. It worked on the principle of admitting gas and air into a cylinder in controlled charges, which were ignited by an electric spark.

engine was a very primitive affair and in fact did not appear as promising as the latest type of steam engine, but at least it made the use of a boiler unnecessary, and Haenlein, who had followed Lenoir's work with keen interest, began to investigate the possibilities of using the gas engine to drive the propeller of a dirigible balloon.

The Franco-Prussian war convinced Haenlein that he ought to lose no time in putting his theories into practice, and he started work on the design of a dirigible in 1872. The craft was 50m (164ft) in length, with a capacity of 2400 cubic metres (85,000 cubic feet). Despite the fire risk there was very little clearance between the envelope and the gondola containing the gas engine. The latter drove a single propeller; unlike the propellers of earlier dirigible designs, Haenlein's was of the tractor type – in other words, it was designed to pull the ship through the air rather than push it. Fuel for the motor was obtained from the balloon itself, which was filled with coal gas instead of the lighter hydrogen. The balloon was equipped with a ballonet, into which air would be pumped by the aeronaut to maintain the envelope's shape as gas was progressively drawn off to feed the engine.

The balloon was tested for the first time at Brünn on 13 December 1872. It was a tethered flight, as was a second that took place on the following day. The results were disappointing: although the balloon attained speeds of up to 15 km/h (9mph) at the end of its ropes, it was

Brothers Albert and Gaston Tissandier demonstrated a model electric-powered airship in Paris in 1881, following it up with a full-size version that flew two years later, in October 1883.

obvious that the engine assembly was too heavy and the balloon too deficient in lift – because of the type of gas used – for a free flight to be attempted. Further development of the project, which might have resulted in considerable advances, as Haenlein was a talented engineer, was abandoned through shortage of funds.

It would be some time yet before the gas engine was sufficiently developed to provide an efficient power source. In the meantime, considerable interest was being aroused by another possibility: the electric motor. In 1881, two brothers, Albert and Gaston Tissandier, were to create a sensation when they built and demonstrated a model electric-powered airship in Paris. Several influential people were so impressed by the little craft's performance that they immediately offered to provide the necessary funds to build a full-size airship. The full-scale design was completed in 1883, and the airship was 28m (92ft) long, with a diameter of 9m (30ft). The powerplant used was a Siemens electric motor, driving a pusher-type paddle-bladed propeller situated immediately aft of the

Captain Charles Renard (1847–1905) began working on the design of an airship immediately after the end of the Franco-Prussian war, when he was employed at the French Army's Aeronautical Department.

Although famous for his pioneering airship work, Arthur Konstantin Krebs (1850–1935) also went on to design the first French submarine, and introduced many improvements in automobile design.

open-framework car. The ship, with the two brothers on board, made its first voyage on 8 October 1883, flying from Auteuil to Croissy-sur-Seine in 1 hour 15 minutes. A second flight of 24km (15 miles) was made on 26 November.

Although the performance of the Tissandier airship was better than anything that had preceded it, its success was strictly limited by the poor power-to-weight ratio of its electric motor. While the Tissandiers went ahead with their flight tests, however, the craft that was to go down in history as the world's first really successful airship was already under construction. Its designers were two engineer officers in the French army, Charles Renard and Arthur Krebs. Named *La France*, the airship had an envelope 1867 cubic metres (66,000

cubic feet) in capacity and nearly 52m (170ft) in length. Renard and Krebs designed their own electric motor to power it, but this was later replaced by a more effective unit.

Electric Flight

The ship was completed in June 1884, and her maiden flight was made from Chalais-Meudon on 9 August. At 4 p.m. that afternoon, with the two aeronauts on board, the craft left the ground in a steady ascent. Renard started the electric motor at 15m (50ft) and the ship began to move, cruising slowly to the south. Gently, Krebs tested the rudder and felt *La France* answer with a perceptible change in direction. The road leading from Choisy to Versailles crept past below, and Krebs brought the ship round in a slow turn to starboard, intending to fly west for a time. Then, on an impulse, he changed his mind and continued the turn through 180 degrees until the craft was heading back towards Chalais-Meudon, nosing into a northerly breeze. For the first time, aeronauts were defying the breeze; for the first time, an airship was truly dirigible. Twenty-three minutes after take-off the airship was once again directly over Chalais-Meudon, and the aeronauts brought her cautiously down

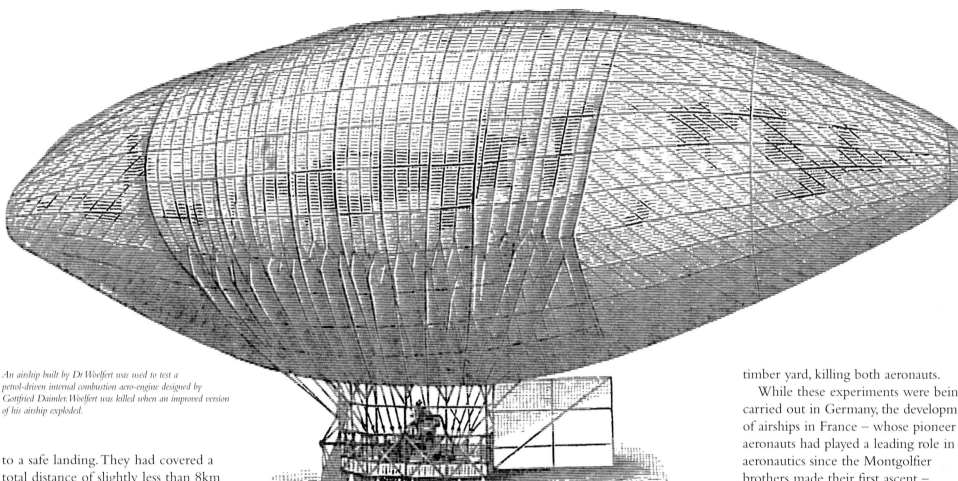

An airship built by Dr Woelfert was used to test a petrol-driven internal combustion aero-engine designed by Gottfried Daimler. Woelfert was killed when an improved version of his airship exploded.

to a safe landing. They had covered a total distance of slightly less than 8km (5 miles).

Internal Combustion Engine

In 1885, while Renard and Krebs were still trying to extract more power from their electric motor, a German engineer named Gottfried Daimler was putting the finish touches to a revolutionary development of the earlier four-stroke gas motor: a petrol-driven internal combustion engine. In 1888, it was tested

in an airship built by Dr Karl Woelfert; however, after this had made a short series of flights, Daimler turned the whole of his attention to perfecting the engine for use in the 'horseless carriage' and lost interest in the airship project. This was a severe blow to Woelfert, who had depended almost entirely on Daimler

for his financial support; nevertheless, he managed to scrape together enough money to build an improved version of his airship. On 12 June 1897, he took off on a test flight from Berlin-Tempelhof with his engineer, Robert Knabe. At an altitude of 9200m (3000ft) the airship exploded and plunged in flames into a

timber yard, killing both aeronauts.

While these experiments were being carried out in Germany, the development of airships in France – whose pioneer aeronauts had played a leading role in aeronautics since the Montgolfier brothers made their first ascent – remained at a standstill. Then a young Brazilian named Alberto Santos-Dumont arrived on the Parisian scene, possessing two attributes that were absolutely vital to any would-be aeronaut of the late nineteenth century: excellent mechanical ability and considerable wealth.

Right: Alberto Santos-Dumont's Airship No. 1 was to cause a sensation when it first flew over Paris in September 1898. Over the next few years, the Brazilian-born aeronaut went on to build a whole series of airships.

Santos-Dumont won substantial prize money in 1901 for taking off from Saint-Cloud, making a circuit of the Eiffel Tower and returning to his starting point. His airships were designed with 'sports flying' in mind.

Santos-Dumont flew his first airship, known simply as Dirigible No. 1, on 18 September 1898, and during the next two years he built three more, each one a slight improvement over its predecessor. Surviving a number of mishaps, he went on to build and fly 11 more dirigibles, his expertise bringing its reward. On 19 October 1901, he claimed a £30,000 prize (most of which he gave to various charities) offered by Henry Deutsch de la Meurthe, one of the leading members of the Paris Aero Club, to any aeronaut who successfully flew from Saint-Cloud, the site of the Aero Club, and returned to the starting point after making a circuit of the Eiffel Tower. The distance involved was 11km (7 miles), and the course had to be completed within 30 minutes. Santos-Dumont did it in twenty-nine and a half.

Some of the flights he made were adventurous; on 13 February 1902, for example, he was fished out of Monaco Bay after becoming the first pilot ever to 'ditch' a dirigible. On 27 June 1903, he achieved another first, albeit a more pleasant one, when he took a lady named Melle d'Acosta for a short flight in his Dirigible No. 8; she was the first woman to fly in

The Lebaudy No 1, seen here over the rooftops of Nantes, France, in 1903, made 29 flights and set up a number of distance records. Damaged in a forced landing, she was rebuilt as the Lebaudy II and went on to add to her successes.

an airship. The most famous of Santos-Dumont's airships was also the smallest: Dirigible No. 9, with a capacity of only 218 cubic metres (7710 cubic feet). Alberto used the little craft in exactly the same way that other people used carriages and automobiles. He would quite literally drop in at a café, tethering the ship to a lamp post or some convenient railings while he went in and enjoyed a leisurely drink.

Source of Inspiration

The exploits of Santos-Dumont – 'the little man that Paris loved' – were a source of inspiration to many other aeronauts at the turn of the century. Among them were Paul and Pierre Lebaudy, the owners of a large sugar refinery, who commissioned their chief engineer, Henri Julliot, to construct a dirigible. The craft, known as Lebaudy No. 1, was completed early in November 1902. It was 57m (187ft) long, with a diameter of 9.7m (32ft) and a capacity of 2547 cubic metres (90,000 cubic feet). The envelope of the ship was fixed to a floor made from steel tubing, running along slightly less than half the ship's

length, to which the gondola was attached. The ship's twin propellers were mounted on either side of the gondola and were powered by a Daimler engine developing 26kW (35hp).

Between its maiden flight, on 13 November 1902, and July 1903, the ship made a total of 29 flights from Moisson, near Nantes, setting up a number of distance records in the process. Damaged in a forced landing, it was rebuilt as the Lebaudy II, and went on to make many more successful flights, on one of which, in 1905, it remained airborne for 3 hours 21 minutes. This was achieved on 3 July 1905, on the last leg of a flight from Moisson to Cap de Chalons; in all, the ship was in the air for 6 hours 38 minutes that day, covering a total distance of 203km (126 miles).

Lebaudy II was subsequently acquired by the French army, in which she served until the middle of 1909. She was the first of a line of Lebaudy airships – highly successful craft which were used by several countries. At the dawn of the twentieth century, however, it was not the French who dominated the airship scene in Europe. Like a comet, the name of one man was climbing rapidly over the horizon to eclipse all others – a name that was to become inseparable from the word 'airship'.

Ferdinand von Zeppelin's first airship, the LZ.1, seen over Lake Constance. The LZ.1 was the first untethered rigid airship, making its first flight on 2 July 1900 with five passengers on board.

Ferdinand von Zeppelin was born in Konstanz, in what is now Germany, on 8 July 1838, the son of Count Frederick Zeppelin and his French-born wife, Amalie. In 1857, at the age of 19, Ferdinand was commissioned into the German army, and he embarked on a long military career. In 1870, during a visit to the

Count Ferdinand von Zeppelin seen in his younger days. A career soldier, he reached the rank of lieutenant general and had the reputation of being one of the best engineers in Germany.

United States, he made his first ascent in a military balloon.

Zeppelin's serious involvement with airship development really began in 1874, when he read a paper entitled *World Mail and Airship Travel* by the German Postmaster-General. Ten years later, when Renard and Krebs made their first flight in *La France*, Zeppelin began to feel a sense of urgency. He was not slow to realize the potential of the airship as a weapon, and his fear was that Germany would be left behind in the race to develop an 'air cruiser'.

By this time, Zeppelin had reached the rank of lieutenant general. He was a man of considerable influence, with the reputation of being one of the best engineers in Germany, and his proposals to put Germany on a sound aeronautical footing were being viewed approvingly in high quarters. The army was still his career, however, and his aeronautical work had to take second place to military duty. It was a situation which, had it endured, might have forced the name of Zeppelin into the ranks of forgotten pioneers.

Rigid Airship

The picture changed dramatically in 1889, when Zeppelin wrote a strongly worded letter to the German War Ministry, protesting that the state's army was being brought progressively under Prussian control. Forced to resign at the age of 52, he turned his whole attention to airship design and, in 1893, in collaboration with an engineer named

Theodore Kober, he submitted a design for a rigid airship to the War Ministry, which appointed a scientific commission to examine the proposal. This involved an airship 117m (384ft) long and 11m (36ft) in diameter, powered by two Daimler engines. Zeppelin envisaged a kind of aerial train, the main airship towing a series of unpowered rigid craft linked together like railway coaches and carrying the passengers and freight.

The scientific commission, however, pointed out many serious flaws in the design and in Zeppelin's performance estimates, recommending that no public money should be risked on the venture.

Undaunted, Zeppelin embarked on the design of a second airship and formed his own company to build it, sinking almost the whole of his personal fortune into the venture, the rest of the funds being raised by the Union of German Engineers. Construction of his first airship, the LZ.1 (Luftschiff Zeppelin

Above: French soldiers examining the car of Zeppelin LZ4. This airship made some notable flights, one of them to Zurich in Switzerland. The airship was destroyed, without loss of life, in a storm on 5 August 1908.

Right: Zeppelin L2 (LZ18) was built for the German Navy, and was the forerunner of a long line of Zeppelin airships to serve with the German Naval Airship Service. It exploded during an altitude test on 10 October 1913 with the loss of 27 lives.

No. 1), was begun in under a year from the date when the company was first formed, the structure gradually taking shape in a huge floating shed which Zeppelin had built at Manzell, near Friedrichshafen on Lake Constance.

The LZ.1 was completed in 1900, and the airship's maiden flight was made on

The LZ.3, seen here being manoeuvred into her floating dock on Lake Constance, was Zeppelin's first truly successful airship, making 45 flights up to 1908. She was later impressed into military service and renamed Z1.

2 July. After two more flights, it was clear that LZ.1 was unstable and a failure, so she was broken up, and Zeppelin, having raised more money, set about building a successor, the LZ.2, in 1905. She was almost identical to her predecessor, having a length of 126m (413ft), a diameter of 11.13m (36ft 8in) and a capacity of 10,400 cubic metres (367,500 cubic feet). Her two engines, however, represented an enormous improvement, developing 63kW (85hp) each compared with the 12kW (16hp) of the LZ.1's motors.

Unfortunately, it was the engines that let her down. On her maiden flight, on 30 November 1905, engine failure compelled her to land on Lake Constance, from which she was towed to safety; on her second flight, on 17 January 1906, engine failure brought her down to a crash landing 32km (20 miles) away from her base. That night, a fierce storm blew up, and she was completely wrecked.

Neither the state nor the public was willing to contribute any more money to what by this time were regarded as Count Zeppelin's crazy schemes. Nevertheless, by scraping together the last reserves of his fortune and by borrowing from a group of faithful friends, Zeppelin was able to begin construction of a third airship with the minimum of delay. The dimensions of the LZ.3 were similar to those of her two predecessors, and, like the LZ.2, she was equipped with two 63kW (85hp) engines. She was completed remarkably quickly, making her maiden voyage on 9 October 1906.

Endurance Record

This time, good fortune favoured the count; on her maiden flight, the LZ.3 flew 96km (60 miles) in two hours, returning to her base without difficulty. She went on to make several more successful flights during the months that followed, and, in September 1907, she set a new endurance record for airships by remaining airborne for eight hours.

Now that Zeppelin's designs were beginning to vindicate themselves, the authorities began to take an interest in his work, and he received a grant of half a million marks to carry out further development work. He used it to build a larger and better airship hangar and to construct a fourth Zeppelin, the LZ.4. She was of the same diameter as the LZ.3, but longer, measuring 136m (446ft) from stem to stern. She carried a small

passenger cabin amidships and was fitted with two engines, each of 78kW (105hp). LZ.4 first flew on 20 June 1908 and was being prepared to make a record-breaking 24-hour flight on 4 August when she came to grief while being moored in a thunderstorm, fortunately after her crew had disembarked.

Zeppelin now concentrated on rebuilding his remaining airship, the LZ.3. She was completed in October 1908 and taken over by the army as the Z.1 for use as a training airship. On 26 May 1909, while Z.1 was completing her military trials, Zeppelin's latest airship, the LZ.5, flew for the first time. On 29 May an attempt was made to fly to Berlin. The journey was frustrated by bad weather and she was forced to turn back; nevertheless, she made a record-breaking endurance flight of 37 hours 40 minutes, covering a distance of 970km (603 miles).

On 16 November 1909, the German Airship Transport Company – Deutsche Luftschiffharts-Aktien-Gesellschaft, or DELAG – was formed at Frankfurt. Ten days later, the world's first commercial airship, the LZ.7, was ordered. She was completed in May 1910, by which time the first crews had been trained. On 22 June the new airship, named the *Deutschland*, made a successful flight lasting 2 hours 30 minutes to Düsseldorf, with 32 people on board. On her sixth flight, however, the Zeppelin jinx struck again when one of her engines failed and she came down in the Teutoberg Forest and was totally wrecked, fortunately

Zeppelin LZ.5 pictured during military manoeuvres. Note the piled rifles and kitbags in the foreground. The LZ.5 proved that the airship was a practical proposition as a commercial transport.

without loss of life. Her replacement, the LZ.8 *Deutschland II*, had to be almost completely rebuilt after a ground handling accident in May 1911.

Zeppelin's next commercial airship, the *Schwaben*, was completed on 15 July 1911. She made her maiden flight five days later, flying from Friedrichshafen to Lucerne, with Hugo Eckener DELAG's

Director of Flight Operations in command. In 11 months, she made a total of 218 flights and carried 1553 passengers. Her career ended abruptly on 28 June 1912 when, after reaching Düsseldorf minutes ahead of a violent storm and unloading her passengers safely, she began to break up under the repeated blows of a gale-force wind and caught fire. The ship was a total loss, but no one was hurt.

Network of Routes

Meanwhile, another airship had entered DELAG service. She was the *Viktoria Luise* (LZ.11), and she made her maiden flight on 14 February 1912. Between that date and 31 October 1913, she made 384 flights, logging 838 hours of flying time, and carried 8135 passengers. During this period,

DELAG's network of routes continued to expand steadily, with services inaugurated to Hamburg, Fuhlsbüttel and Potsdam. Two more airships, the *Sachsen* and the *Hansa*, were added to the fleet, and in June 1913 Eckener captained the former on a flight to Vienna and back. In four years of service, up to August 1914, DELAG's ships had covered a total of 172,534 km (107,231 miles) on 1588 flights, carrying 10,197 passengers. Much of this passenger traffic was accounted for by pleasure flights, in the summer months. Twenty passengers were usually carried in comfort, and were treated to a sumptuous meal during the two-hour round trip.

During these pioneer years, Zeppelin had been able to continue his work in the rigid airship field with the knowledge that he had no rival. A number of airships had been built by other concerns, but these were of the non-rigid or semi-rigid type. It was not until 1911 that a serious competitor to Count Zeppelin in the design of rigid airships entered the field: the Luftschiffbau Schütte-Lanz of Mannheim Rheinau. Its first airship, the SL.1, flew on 17 October 1911.

Instead of aluminium, the ship's hull was constructed of laminated plywood girders, crossing each other in a diamond-shaped pattern. She was 128m (420ft) long and her two engines, developing a total of 403kW (540hp), gave her a top speed of 61km/h (38mph). Later Schütte-Lanz airships,

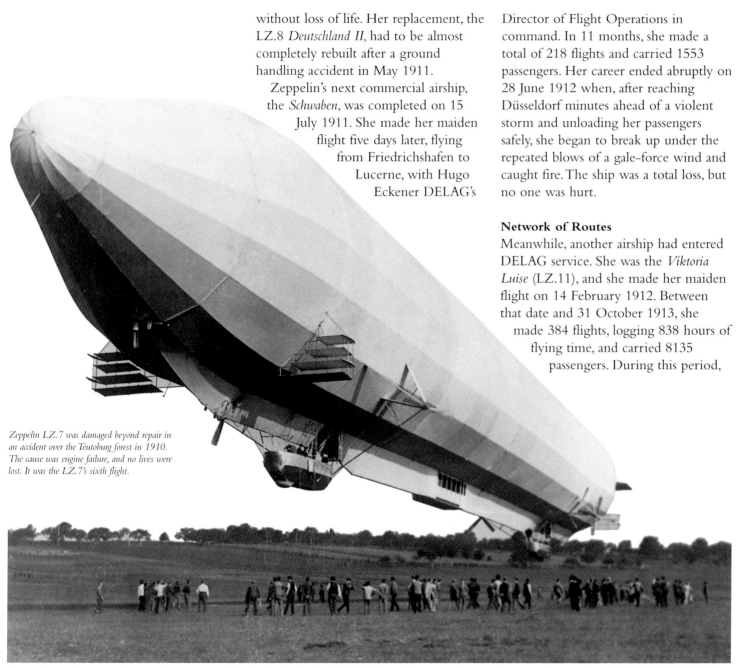

Zeppelin LZ.7 was damaged beyond repair in an accident over the Teutoburg forest in 1910. The cause was engine failure, and no lives were lost. It was the LZ.7's sixth flight.

The first Zeppelin to complete 1000 flights, commercial Zeppelin LZ.11 Viktoria Luise was taken over by the German military at the outbreak of World War I. She was destroyed in a mooring accident in 1915.

beginning with the SL.2, were powered by four Maybach engines. They were extremely advanced for their day, being beautifully streamlined and fitted with a simple, cruciform tail unit. The forward control car was completely enclosed, in contrast to the draughty, open gondolas of the Zeppelin airships (it was a long time before Count Zeppelin renounced his theory that an airship could be landed properly only if its pilot could feel the wind in his face).

Only a few Schütte-Lanz ships were built. In August 1914, the firm was taken over by the German government and absorbed into the Zeppelin organization. The airship was about to go to war.

The commercial Zeppelin LZ.13 Hansa pictured at Potsdam in January 1913. It was the airship that inaugurated the world's first international commercial passenger service, flying from Hamburg to Copenhagen, Denmark, and Malmö, Sweden, on 19 September 1912.

A Fall of Eagles: Aviation in World War I

In August 1914, the German Imperial Air Service comprised 246 aircraft, 254 pilots and 271 observers. There were 33 *Feldflieger Abteilungen* (field flight sections), each with six aircraft, and eight *Festungflieger Abteilungen* (fortress flight sections), each with four aircraft. The former came under the direct operational control of the army, one section being assigned to each individual army headquarters and one to each army corps, while the latter had the task of protecting fortified towns along Germany's frontiers. About half the aircraft were Etrich Taube (Dove) types, which in the years before the war were built in large numbers by several firms, including Albatros, Gotha, Rumpler and DFW. The unarmed Taube monoplane had a top speed of 96km/h (60mph). Other types in service, all biplanes, were the AEG B.II, Albatros B.II, Aviatik B.I and B.II, and the DFW B.I.

France's Aviation Militaire had at its disposal 132 aircraft, with a further 150 in reserve, the latter mostly assembled at Saint-Cyr. The first-line aircraft were divided between 24 escadrilles, each having six machines on average, although the number varied. Five were equipped with Maurice Farmans, four with Henry Farmans, two with Voisins, one with Caudrons, one with Bréguets, seven with Blériots, two with Deperdussins, one with REPs and one with Nieuports. All these units were tasked with reconnaissance and were assigned to the French field armies engaged on the Western Front.

Britain's Royal Flying Corps (RFC), at least on paper, had 180 aircraft of all types on its inventory, but many of these were elderly training types, and of the total only 84 could really be classed as airworthy. The five RFC squadrons formed at the start of hostilities operated a miscellany of aircraft that included Blériot XIs, Henry Farmans, Maurice Farmans, Royal Aircraft Factory BE.2s and 2as, Sopwith Tabloids, Avro 504s and BE.8s. The Royal Naval Air Service (RNAS) had 71 aircraft,

Left: French civilians examining an Etrich Taube (Dove) monoplane, brought down in French territory and mounted on a plinth. Germany had a large fleet of these aircraft.

Right: The Aviatik B.I was used for reconnaissance by Germany until the beginning of 1916.

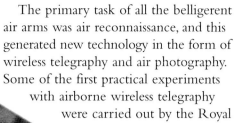

Left: The Avro 504 was a 'maid of all work', performing roles that varied from trainer to night fighter. It remained in service and civilian use long after World War I. This is a Canadian variant, the Avro 504Q seaplane.

First flight of the Sikorsky Ilya Murometz, the world's first four-engine bomber. It had an endurance of over five hours and established a number of aviation records.

The primary task of all the belligerent air arms was air reconnaissance, and this generated new technology in the form of wireless telegraphy and air photography. Some of the first practical experiments with airborne wireless telegraphy were carried out by the Royal Engineers during the British Army

of which 31 were seaplanes. The landplanes were a mixture of various types, but Short Brothers were becoming firmly established as the main seaplane suppliers, with 17 of their machines in service. The available aircraft were based at a series of air stations along the east coast of Britain, from the English Channel to Scotland. These stations were within flying distance of one another, enabling the RNAS to mount overlapping coastal patrols.

Poorly Equipped

The other main belligerents in August 1914, Russia and Austria, were poorly equipped in terms of aircraft. The Russian Imperial Air Service had 24 aircraft, 12 airships and 24 observation balloons in its possession. Most of the aircraft were of French origin. The most promising design in Russia at this time was the Ilya Murometz, by Igor Sikorsky. This, the world's first four-engined bomber, had flown early in 1914, and 10 examples were on order for the Air Service at the outbreak of war,

a number which was later increased to 80 aircraft.

The Austrian Air Service had 36 aircraft, one airship and 10 balloons in all. The aircraft were mostly Taube types. The small Austrian aviation industry did not really develop until the summer of 1915, when it underwent rapid expansion following Italy's entry into the war.

exercises of 1912, when the non-rigid airships Gamma and Delta transmitted signals that were received up to 56km (35 miles) away. The Naval Wing (later RNAS) had also been experimenting with wireless telegraphy and, by the outbreak of war, 16 of its seaplanes had been fitted with lightweight equipment of French design for communication with shore stations.

The radio traffic at this stage was one way, from air to ground; it would be some time before the difficulties of reception by aircraft were overcome. Early airborne wireless telegraphy equipment was bulky and unreliable, and visual signalling by strips, panels and other devices remained the primary means of communication between observation aircraft and artillery in the first months of World War I.

Pioneering Work

Much of the pioneering work in wireless telegraphy was carried out by No. 3 Squadron RFC, and this unit also pioneered aerial photography. A lack of funds meant that its officers had to buy their own cameras and adapt them for aerial work by trial and error. Just before the outbreak of war they succeeded in producing a complete set of photographs covering the defences of the Isle of

Aerial photography was a vital part of air operations during World War I. The specialist RFC unit in this field was No. 3 Squadron, whose personnel studied French photographic techniques and improved on them.

Wight and the Solent. The original cameras were of the folding type with bellows and loaded with plates. They were cumbersome to handle in the air, especially in cold weather, and produced poor results. In the autumn of 1914, Major W.G.H. Salmond made a study of the French photographic organization, which was more advanced than any other and, as a result of his report, an experimental photographic section was formed with Lieutenants J.T.C. Moore-Brabazon and C.D.M Campbell, Sergeant F.C.V. Laws and Second Air Mechanic W.D. Corse. These four men set about designing a new, effective air camera and completed their task in less than four months.

While they were doing so, the first successful photographic reconnaissance was carried out in January 1915, when pictures were taken of some brick stacks south of the La Bassée Canal. These revealed a new German trench and contributed greatly to the success of an Allied attack that went in on 6 January. From now on, aerial photography was to be a vital factor in operations on all fronts; its importance was such that the need to protect photographic reconnaissance aircraft brought about the requirement for fighter escorts, which in turn was to give enormous impetus to the development of the fighting as a whole.

The obvious solution to the problem of aircraft armament, right from the start, was the machine gun. Several problems had to be overcome, however, before the solution became a practical reality. First, machine guns could be fitted only to the sturdier of the types then in service; on other aircraft, the weight penalty was unacceptable. There was also the problem of aiming and firing any sort of gun, as pilot and observer were surrounded by a considerable wing area, with its attendant struts and bracing wires, and were seated either behind or in front of a large and vulnerable wooden propeller.

Nevertheless, both the RFC and RNAS quickly adopted the 12kg (27lb) American-designed Lewis gun as standard armament for their observation aircraft, particularly the pusher types in which the observer, who sat in front of the pilot, had a large cone of fire up, down and to either side. In the beginning the gun mounting was usually

Known by its nickname of 'Harry Tate' after a music hall comedian, the Royal Aircraft Factory RE.8 was only marginally better than the BE.2 series which it replaced, and had to operate with a strong fighter escort.

devised by the observer to suit himself. The French selected the Hotchkiss, which, like the Lewis, was air-cooled; a belt-fed weapon, it initially proved too inflexible for the observer, and so a drum feed was adopted. The Germans chose the lightweight Parabellum MG14, a modification of the water-cooled Maxim; this also had a drum magazine.

On 5 October 1914, a Voisin pusher biplane of Escadrille VB24, armed with a Hotchkiss machine gun and flown by Lieutenant Joseph Frantz (pilot) and Corporal Quénault (observer) shot down a German Aviatik two-seater near Reims in France. The crew of the Aviatik, both of whom were killed when their aircraft crashed in flames, were Wilhelm Schlichting (pilot) and Oberleutnant

Frizt von Zangen. Corporal Quénault fired 47 rounds at the Aviatik, which was the first aircraft in history to be shot down and destroyed by another, although a few weeks earlier, on 25 August, three BE.2s of No. 2 Squadron RFC had forced an enemy two-seater to land. One of the British pilots, Lieutenant H.D. Harvey-Kelly, landed nearby and, with his observer, chased the enemy crew into

a nearby wood before setting fire to the German aircraft and taking off again.

One of the most widely used Allied aircraft during the first year of the war was the Blériot XI, which served with at least eight escadrilles of the French Aviation Militaire, and with six squadrons of the Royal Flying Corps

Despite the structural soundness and good load-carrying capabilities of the Voisin types 8 and 10, they were inhibited by a poor maximum speed. This example is being used as a trainer by the US Air Service.

in France. When Italy entered the war in 1915, her air arm had six squadrons equipped with the Blériot XI.

The type also served with the Belgian Aviation Militaire. As well as performing the all-important reconnaissance role, some Blériots were used as nuisance bombers, carrying small hand-dropped bombs or flechettes (metal darts) in racks along the fuselage sides under the cockpit coaming. Flechettes were pointed and fluted steel darts about 13cm (5in) long, which were dropped from canisters containing about 500 from an optimum height of 1500m (5000ft) and attained the velocity of a rifle bullet by the time they reached the ground. They were intended to be effective against troop and cavalry concentrations, but in practice they were virtually useless.

Rifles or pistols were the only other form of armament carried by the crew. In a notable mission on 14 August 1914, Lieutenant Cesari and Corporal Prudhommeaux of the Aviation Militaire, flying a Blériot XI, bombed the German airship sheds at Metz-Frescaty, and during another similar mission on 18 August French aviators claimed to have destroyed three enemy aircraft and an airship on the ground, although this was unconfirmed. It was also in a Blériot XI that Captain Joubert de la Ferte of No. 3 Squadron made the Royal Flying Corp's first reconnaissance sortie of World War I, flying from Maueuge, Belgium, on 19 August 1914.

Basic Bombs

Aircraft were used for bombing from the outset of World War I, but the bombs available to both sides at the outbreak of hostilities were very rudimentary devices. The standard German bomb in the early months of the war was the so-called carbonite type; the smallest weight

The Blériot XI was one of the most widely used aircraft on the Allied side in 1914. Apart from observation and bombing missions, it also made the RFC's first reconnaissance flight of the conflict.

was 4.5kg (10lb) and the heaviest 50kg (110lb). They were pear-shaped, pointed and had a propeller-actuated pistol. Instead of fins, they were stabilized by a kind of inverted tin cap, which was attached to the tail of the bomb by stays. The Germans also used a hand-thrown grenade-type projectile, but this was too small to be effective.

Incendiary Bomb

The weapon initially available to the Royal Naval Air Service, which pioneered strategic bombing in its early raids on the Imperial German Navy's Zeppelin sheds, was the 9kg (20lb) Marten Hale bomb, which contained a 2kg (4.5lb) charge of Amatol, a mixture of TNT and ammonium nitrate, which exploded on impact. It was armed by a fusing mechanism activated by a small propeller behind the tail fins which started to revolve when the missile was dropped. The RNAS also used a small number of 45kg (100lb) bombs produced by the Royal Arsenal, Woolwich, but these were not provided with adequate safety devices and were dangerous to their users. Trials were also carried out with an incendiary bomb consisting of a light case

The first attempts at dropping bombs from aircraft were primitive in the extreme. This is a purpose-built bomb, but many early examples were simply artillery shells with fins added for stability.

Roland Garros and his machine gun, mounted to fire through the arc of the propeller. The bullets were deflected from the propeller blades by metal wedges, a somewhat dangerous arrangement.

machine was distinguished by pennants carried on the rear centre struts. Once the formation had made rendezvous well behind the lines, and out of the immediate sight of the enemy, the group commander fired off a series of signal flares, then set course for the target at optimum cruising speed, the rest of the aircraft formatting on him as closely as was practicable. Over the target, the formation made its bombing run downwind, increasing its ground speed and therefore minimizing the length of time spent in the defended area. Individual aircraft usually attacked from varying heights to make the task of the anti-aircraft gunners more difficult.

Apart from an understandable desire to get clear of the target area with the minimum delay, one reason for bombing downwind was the primitive nature of the bomb sights in use at the time, which had no mechanism for computing crosswind bombing angles. The Central Flying School Bomb Sight, used by the RFC and RNAS, was typical. Based on an earlier sight devised by an American, Lieutenant Riley Scott, it was developed by Lieutenant R.B. Bourdillon of the Central Flying School Experimental Flight and Lieutenant L.A. Strange. Known as the CFS 4B bomb sight, it had a timing scale which enabled the pilot or observer, with the aid of a

holding 9 litres (2 gallons) of petrol; this was fitted with a cartridge which detonated when the bomb was dropped and ignited the liquid. Such primitive bombs were used by the Royal Flying Corps, too, whose aircrews also employed flechettes.

The early bombs used by France's Aviation Militaire were little more than modified 75mm or 155mm artillery shells. The 75mm weapon, which weighed 9kg (20lb), proved reasonably effective as an anti-personnel missile and was usually released from a height of

2000m (6500ft). During 1915, the French formulated well-devised tactics for mounting large-scale bombing attacks on targets inside Germany. The first aircraft to take off was always that of the group commander, who led the formation throughout the mission; his

The BE.2c was the principal RFC observation aircraft at the outbreak of World War I. It was easy to fly, but its very stability was its undoing, as it lacked the manoeuvrability that was necessary to evade enemy fighters.

stopwatch, to measure his ground speed by taking two sights of one object. A movable foresight was then set on the timing scale to correspond with the time interval, recorded in seconds on the stopwatch between the two sightings, and this gave the correct angle for bomb release.

Step Forward

In 1915, a considerable step forward was taken in the science of air fighting when the French developed a device that enabled a machine gun to fire forwards through the propeller blades of the aircraft on which it was mounted. The device – which was extremely simple, although rather dangerous – consisted of triangular steel wedges, fitted to the nearside of each propeller blade so that any bullets that struck it would

be deflected. It was tested in action by Roland Garros, who had already achieved fame as one of France's pioneer aviators before the war; he shot down six enemy aircraft in three weeks before being forced down with engine trouble and taken prisoner.

Garros's captured aircraft, a Morane, was immediately flown to Berlin for examination by the Germans. One of the engineers summoned to look it over was Anthony Fokker, a young Dutchman who had been designing military aircraft for Germany since 1913. Fearing that the Allies would soon have hundreds of aircraft with forward-firing guns, the German High Command gave Fokker just 48 hours to design a comparable method of shooting through a whirling propeller disc.

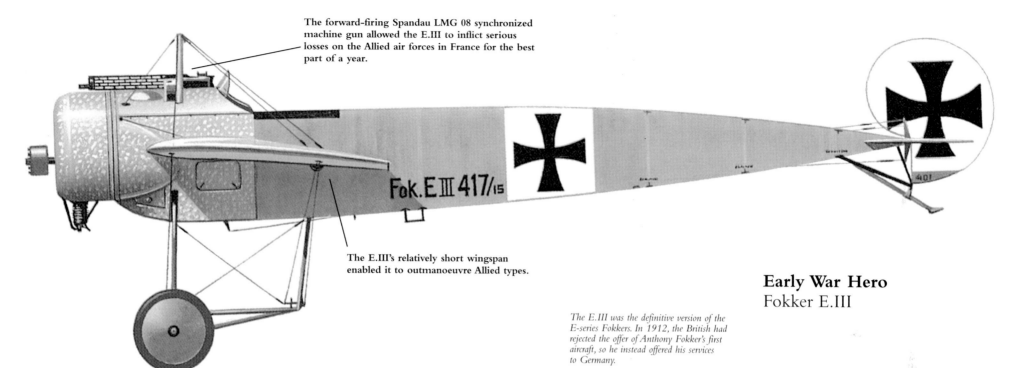

The forward-firing Spandau LMG 08 synchronized machine gun allowed the E.III to inflict serious losses on the Allied air forces in France for the best part of a year.

The E.III's relatively short wingspan enabled it to outmanoeuvre Allied types.

Early War Hero
Fokker E.III

The E.III was the definitive version of the E-series Fokkers. In 1912, the British had rejected the offer of Anthony Fokker's first aircraft, so he instead offered his services to Germany.

Fokker realized straight away that Garros's method was too primitive and dangerous: the force of the bullets striking the deflector plates would sooner or later shatter the propeller and shake the engine from its mounting. What was needed, Fokker reasoned, was some method whereby the propeller itself was geared to fire the machine gun, a synchronizing device so that every bullet passed between the revolving blades. He fitted a small knob to the propeller which struck a cam when it revolved; the cam was attached by a wire to the hammer of the gun. Fokker tested

the device, and it worked. After a few refinements, he was ready to demonstrate the technique to the General Staff. They were suitably impressed, and gave orders for Fokker's invention to be tested at the front.

After early trials, the device began to make its impact felt in the summer of 1915, with the service debut of the Fokker E.I monoplane, armed with a single Spandau machine gun firing through the propeller disc. This was a development that still eluded the Allies, whose only aircraft fitted with forward-firing machine guns were slow pusher

types. A few weeks later the German Imperial Air Service began to receive an improved model, the Fokker E.III, so beginning a martyrdom of Allied airmen that was to last for a year.

The German fighter pilots now held all the cards; cruising at altitude, they could select their target at leisure and make a diving attack on it, using their whole aircraft as an aiming platform, and, as their machine guns were belt-fed (as opposed to the drum-fed weapons used by the majority of British and French types), they were able to carry more ammunition and consequently

Fokker E.III

Type: single-seat fighting scout

Powerplant: one 75kW (100hp) Oberusel U.19-cylinder air-cooled rotary engine

Maximum speed: 134km/h (83mph)

Endurance: 2 hours 45 minutes

Service ceiling: 3500m (11,500ft)

Weights: empty 500kg (1100lb); loaded 635kg (1400lb)

Armament: one fixed forward-firing 7.92mm LMG O8/15 machine gun

Dimensions:
span	9.52m	(31ft 3 in)
length	7.3m	(23ft 11in)
height	3.12m	(9ft 6in)
wing area	16.05m²	(173sq ft)

deliver longer bursts of fire. The BE.2s suffered particularly heavy losses at the hands of the Fokkers, for the BE had a vulnerable blind spot under its belly, and the German pilots exploited this to the full, zooming up under their victims and firing as they went. The BEs' observers could retaliate only when the Fokkers climbed up into view, by which time it was usually too late.

German Air Aces

The autumn of 1915 marked the ascendancy of the first German air aces, Max Immelmann and Oswald Boelcke, whose scores mounted steadily towards the end of the year. The word 'ace' was coined by the French to describe fighter pilots of prowess, and was adopted by the Germans amid much publicity. The Royal Flying Corps, on the other hand, refused to countenance the notion, although outstanding British fighter pilots inevitably received their share of publicity, too.

Oswald Boelcke was the leading German air fighter of this period, gaining 40 official victories between 6 July 1915 and 26 October 1916. Thirty-one of these were two-seaters. Boelcke was killed in an air collision with one of his own pilots, Lieutenant Erwin Böhme; the latter went on to become one of

Fighting the Fokker
Airco D.H.2

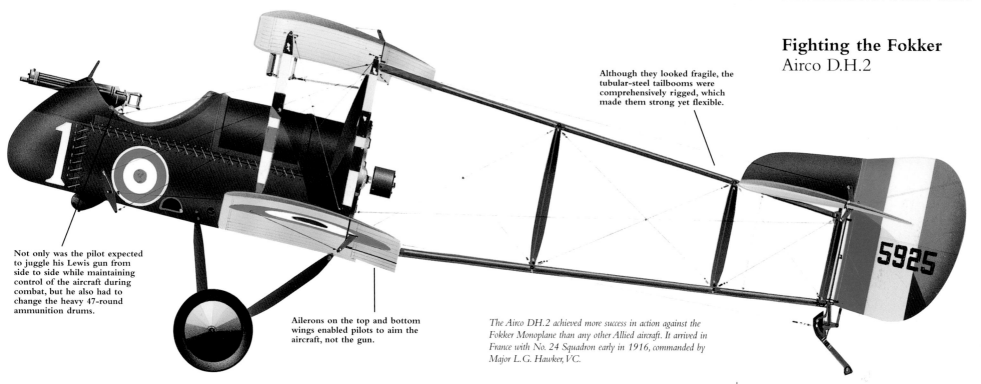

Although they looked fragile, the tubular-steel tailbooms were comprehensively rigged, which made them strong yet flexible.

Not only was the pilot expected to juggle his Lewis gun from side to side while maintaining control of the aircraft during combat, but he also had to change the heavy 47-round ammunition drums.

Ailerons on the top and bottom wings enabled pilots to aim the aircraft, not the gun.

The Airco DH.2 achieved more success in action against the Fokker Monoplane than any other Allied aircraft. It arrived in France with No. 24 Squadron early in 1916, commanded by Major L.G. Hawker, VC.

Germany's leading fighter aces, scoring 24 victories before being shot down by Captain John A. Pattern of No. 10 Squadron RFC on 29 November 1917.

The other of Germany's two initial air aces, Max Immelmann, was credited with 13 victories before he crashed to his death on 18 June 1916 under somewhat mysterious circumstances. According to one version he was shot down by Corporal J.H. Waller, the observer of a No. 25 Squadron FE.2b; however, another theory is that Fokker's synchronization gear failed to work properly and he shot off his own propeller, causing the engine to break

away from its mountings and leading to the disintegration of the whole aircraft.

The success of the 'Fokker Scourge' towards the end of 1915 led to a revision of the RFC's tactics. Various battle formations were tried out, with mixed success. In a typical arrangement, the formation was led by a reconnaissance aircraft, with a close escort 150m (500ft) above on either quarter and a third escort 300m (1000ft) above and to the rear. To achieve this, however, aircraft had to be drawn from other duties such as army cooperation work. This proved a serious disadvantage at the beginning of 1916, with the Allies planning a series

of major offensives and aircraft proving an even more valuable resource.

Constant Patrols

The real solution was to introduce fighter aircraft that were at least a match for the Fokkers, machines that could maintain constant patrols over the front and challenge the German aircraft in combat whenever they appeared. The tragic fact was that Britain had possessed such an aircraft, the FE.2, since 1913, but it had been a year before the first 12 were ordered from the Royal Aircraft Factory, and it was May 1915 before the first few production examples arrived in

Airco D.H.2

Type: single-seat scout fighter biplane

Powerplant: one 75kW (100hp) Gnome Monosoupape rotary piston engine; later examples had 82kW (110hp) Le Rhône rotary

Maximum speed: 150km/h (93mph)

Endurance: 2 hours 45 minutes

Service ceiling: 1300m (4265ft)

Weights: empty 428kg (943lb); maximum take-off weight 654kg (1441lb)

Armament: one forward-firing .303in Lewis gun on flexible mounting

Dimensions:

span	8.61m	(28ft 3in)
length	7.68m	(25ft 2in)
height	2.91m	(9ft 6½in)
wing area	23.13m²	(249sq ft)

Rittmeister Freiherr Manfred von Richthofen, on the right, with his brother Lothar. Von Richthofen. Manfred von Richthofen was the leading air ace of World War I, with 80 confirmed victories before his death on 21 April 1918.

France. A two-seat pusher type powered by an 89kW (120hp) Beardmore engine and armed with a Lewis gun in the front cockpit and a second on a telescopic mounting firing upwards over the wing centre-section, the FE.2b was slightly slower than the Fokker E.III, but a match in manoeuvrability.

The first RFC squadron to be entirely equipped with the FE.2b was No. 20, which arrived in France in January 1916. It was followed in February by No. 24 Squadron, which was equipped with Airco DH.2s. The DH.2 was a single-seat pusher type powered by a 75kW (100hp) Monosoupape engine and mounting a single Lewis gun installed on a pivot at the port side of the cockpit. Rugged and highly manoeuvrable, the DH.2 – designed by Geoffrey de Havilland – was to achieve more success in action against the Fokkers than any other Allied type.

No. 24 Squadron, commanded by Major L.G. Hawker, VC, soon became one of the best-known Allied air units. It scored its first victory on 2 April 1916, and from then on the squadron's tally rose steadily. In June 1916, its pilots destroyed 17 enemy aircraft, followed by 23 in July, 15 in August, 15 in September and 10 in November. On 23 November 1916, Major Hawker was shot down by an up-and-coming German pilot after a 35-minute duel over Bapaume. A lucky

The Nieuport 11 had an excellent performance and was immensely popular with its pilots. Many of the leading Allied air aces gained their first victories while flying this little fighter.

shot grazed Hawker's head, knocking him unconscious, and he crashed out of control. The name of the German pilot was Manfred von Richthofen, who later admitted that Hawker had given him the hardest fight of his outstanding career. Had it not been for that single bullet, the legend of the 'Red Baron' might never have been born.

Fokker Menace

New types of combat aircraft continued to appear in the air units of both sides during the spring and summer of 1916. From the spring of that year the task of overcoming the Fokker menace was shared, alongside the FE.2b and the DH.2, by the Nieuport 11 single-seat fighter biplane, a type on which several British and French air aces gained their early victories. Armed with a single Lewis gun mounted on the top wing and firing over the propeller arc, the Nieuport possessed an excellent rate of climb, although its maximum speed of 154km/h (96mph) left something to be desired, and it also had a tendency to suffer structural damage during violent manoeuvres.

By the summer of 1916, the Allied fighter squadrons were beginning to hold their own against the Fokkers. Germany's hopes for restoring air superiority now lay with the Albatros D.I, which – armed with twin 7.92mm Spandau guns and powered by a 119kW (160hp) Mercedes engine – made its appearance over the front in September 1916. It was the first German fighter to carry a two-gun armament without suffering a loss of performance, and, although it was less manoeuvrable than the Fokker types, it had better speed, rate of climb and firepower. In October 1916, an improved version, the Albatros D.II, also entered service at the front.

Some intense air battles took place in the summer of 1916, during the opening phase of the Battle of the Somme. In all, 27 RFC squadrons, comprising 421 aircraft, and four kite balloon squadrons with 14 balloons, were assigned to support the various British Army Corps

The Sopwith One-and-a-Half Strutter was the first operational British aircraft to feature a machine gun firing through the propeller arc. The aircraft's rather curious name was derived from the arrangement of its wing struts.

The Albatros D.III began to serve operationally with frontline units early in 1917 and had its heyday in April that year, when it took a heavy toll of Allied aircraft, especially the RFC's BE.2c observation aircraft.

committed to the battle. Most of the observation squadrons were equipped with BE.2cs, which were escorted by FE.2bs and DH.2s as they performed their difficult and dangerous task. The battle saw the operational debut of the Sopwith One-and-a-Half Strutter, the first British operational aircraft with a machine gun firing through the propeller. A two-seater, it also had a

Left: The complex latticework structure of a Zeppelin is well illustrated in this photograph of an airship under construction. In the beginning, Zeppelins were very difficult to intercept, being able to outclimb defending fighters.

Below: An extremely versatile aircraft, the Airco DH.4 has been described as the 'Mosquito' of World War I. Just like the later de Havilland aircraft of this name, it undertook a variety of combat roles with great success.

Lewis gun mounted in the rear cockpit.

The Aviation Militaire's main commitment to the battle, in support of General Fayolle's Sixth Army, comprised seven escadrilles, all of which were equipped with Nieuport Scouts. The Allies succeeded in establishing air superiority over the battleground with their new aircraft types and, to counter this, the German High Command ordered the formation of Jagdstaffeln – fighter squadrons – which were to be stationed on the most active areas of the front. The Jagdstaffeln, which on average were equipped with 14 fighter aircraft each, were the brainchild of the brilliant German tactician Oswald Boelcke. By the end of August 1916, seven

squadrons of this type were in operation; this number increased to 15 in September and 33 by the end of the same year. The Jagdstaffeln, or Jastas for short, were equipped initially with the Fokker E.III Monoplane, and later in 1916 received Albatros D.Is and D.IIIs and Halberstadt D.IIs.

Air Offensive

Boelcke's Jagdstaffel 2 sustained the renewed German air offensive virtually single-handed until more Jagdstaffeln reached the front during the first week of October and accounted for a large proportion of the 123 Allied

aircraft, most of them British, destroyed over the Somme during September. The Germans lost only 27 of their own aircraft during this period, and in October they destroyed a further 88 machines for the loss of 12 of their own. Boelcke himself destroyed 20 Allied machines during those two months, before his death late in October.

While air battles raged over the Somme, some RFC and RNAS pilots were fighting a war of a very different kind, against the Zeppelin night raiders. The Imperial German Navy's Airship Division had made its first successful

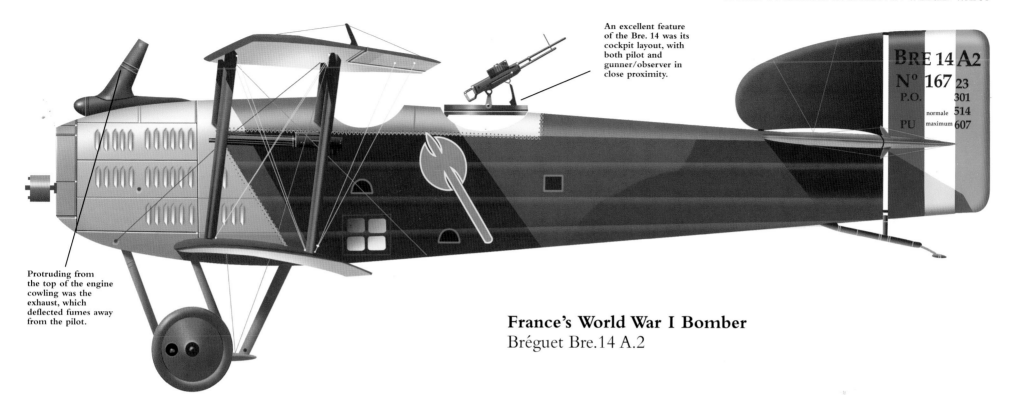

An excellent feature of the Bre. 14 was its cockpit layout, with both pilot and gunner/observer in close proximity.

Protruding from the top of the engine cowling was the exhaust, which deflected fumes away from the pilot.

BRE 14 A2
Nº 167 23
P.O. 301
normale 514
PU maximum 607

France's World War I Bomber
Bréguet Bre.14 A.2

attack on the British Isles on the night of 19 January 1915, when three airships, the L.3, L.4 and L.6, took off from Nordholz and Fuhlsbüttel. L.6 turned back with engine trouble, but the other two crossed the Norfolk coast. Nine bombs were

Above: The Bréguet XIV was arguably the best light bomber of World War I. The French certainly developed excellent tactics with this aircraft, sending out formations to attack targets in western Germany.

Left: A Friedrichshafen G.IIIa bomber. The G.IIIa differed mainly from the earlier G.III in that it had a compound tail unit instead of a single fin. The photograph shows a captured aircraft, with French markings applied to tail surfaces and fuselage sides.

dropped in the Great Yarmouth area by L.3, killing two people and injuring three others. L.4 bombed several targets in Norfolk, including King's Lynn, where it dropped seven high-explosive bombs and an incendiary, killing two people and injuring 13. The RFC flew its first ever night defence sorties against the raiders, but the two aircraft involved, both Vickers FB.5s, failed to intercept. As a result of this raid, a small number of RFC airfields around London remained at readiness to combat night attacks; the RNAS already had an air defence scheme, with a screen of aircraft between Grimsby and London

to intercept airships flying from northern Germany, and between London and Dungeness to cope with aircraft flying from Belgian bases.

Such was the weight of propaganda surrounding the German airship raids on Britain that it is for this type of operation that the Zeppelin is best remembered. Throughout the war, however, the primary task of the Naval Airship Division was reconnaissance. Far more could undoubtedly have been achieved if the German navy had exploited its airships to the full. Capable of remaining airborne for 100 hours,

Bréguet Bre.14 A.2

Type: two-seat reconnaisance/light bomber biplane

Powerplant: one 224kW (300hp) Renault 12Fe inline piston engine

Maximum speed: 184km/h (114mph)

Endurance: 3 hours

Service ceiling: 6000m (19,690ft)

Weights: empty 1030kg (2271lb); maximum take-off weight 1565kg (3450lb)

Armament: one fixed forward-firing .303 machine gun; twin .303in Lewis machine guns; underwing racks for up to 40kg (88lb) of bombs

Dimensions:

span	14.36m	(47ft 1in)
length	8.87m	(29ft 1in)
height	3.3m	(10ft 10in)
wing area	47.50m²	(530 sq ft)

Gotha's Giant Bombers
Gotha G.IV

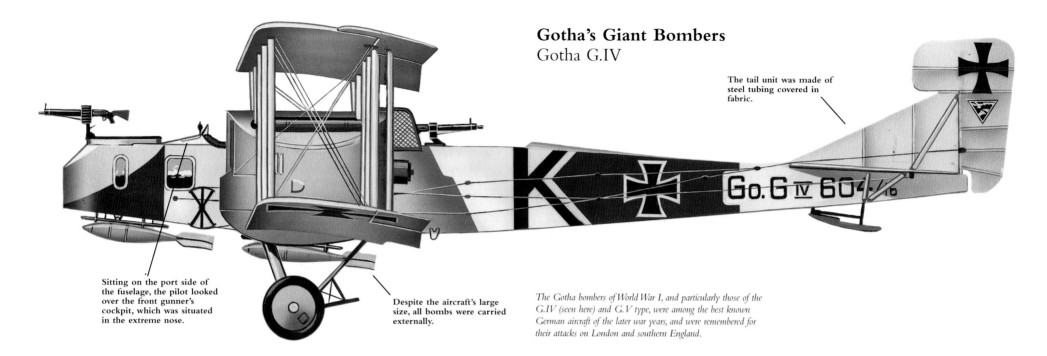

The tail unit was made of steel tubing covered in fabric.

Sitting on the port side of the fuselage, the pilot looked over the front gunner's cockpit, which was situated in the extreme nose.

Despite the aircraft's large size, all bombs were carried externally.

The Gotha bombers of World War I, and particularly those of the G.IV (seen here) and G.V type, were among the best known German aircraft of the later war years, and were remembered for their attacks on London and southern England.

Gotha G.V

Type: twin-engined long-range day or night bomber

Powerplant: two 194kW (260hp) Mercedes D Va six-cylinder in-line piston engines

Maximum speed: 140km/h (87mph) at 3660m (12,000ft)

Ferry range: 491km (300 miles)

Service ceiling: 6500m (21,300ft)

Weights: empty 2740kg (6,028lb); loaded 3975kg (8,745lb)

Armament: single manually operated 7.92mm Parabellum machine guns in nose and rear cockpits plus up to 500kg (1100lb) of bombs

Dimensions:
span	23.70m	(77ft 9in)
length	11.86m	(38ft 11in)
height	4.30m	(14ft 1in)
wing area	89.5m²	(963sq ft)

with a range of 4800km (3000 miles), the airships might have wrought havoc on Allied convoys in the North Atlantic had they been used for scouting in conjunction with submarines. Zeppelin tactics over the British Isles usually involved climbing to a height where the airship could exploit favourable easterly winds as it crossed the coastline. The Zeppelins could fly only in good weather and at night provided there was little or no moonlight. The engines would be switched off as the airship approached the target area, making it virtually impossible to detect from the ground unless illuminated by searchlights.

The Zeppelins were not invincible. On 7 June 1915, German Army Zeppelin LZ.37 was attacked by Flight Sub-Lt R.A.J. Warneford of No. 1 Squadron RNAS, flying a Morane Parasol from Dunkirk. The airship, together with LZ.38 and LZ.39, had set out from Bruges to bomb London. Warneford shadowed LZ.37 from Ostend to Ghent, being kept at bay by heavy defensive fire, then made a single pass over the airship and dropped six 9kg (20lb) bombs on it. The airship exploded in flames and fell on a convent, killing two nuns and two children. Warneford was awarded the Victoria Cross, only to be killed in a crash a few days later.

Of the 115 Zeppelin airships built by

the war's end, 22 were broken up at the end of their useful lives; nine were handed over to the Allies after the Armistice; seven were sabotaged by their own crews; 17 were destroyed in the air by aircraft or by anti-aircraft (AA) guns; 19 were damaged in the air and wrecked on landing; seven landed in enemy or neutral territory; eight were destroyed in their sheds by air attack; and 26 were lost in accidents. Some 380 air crew – about 40 per cent – were killed on active service.

The Bristol F2B Fighter was a superb combat aircraft when flown aggressively, like a single-seater. Although German pilots were contemptuous of the Bristol at first, they were soon forced to change their opinion.

Saviour of the Flying Corps
Royal Aircraft Factory S.E.5A

The S.E.5a was unusual in having only a single fixed forward-firing weapon. The Vickers machine gun was mounted above the engine on the starboard side, synchronized to fire through the propeller.

The S.E.5's wood and fabric construction meant that the aircraft was as much of a death trap as its contemporaries if it caught fire, but it did possess exceptional structural strength.

The Royal Aircraft Factory SE.5A was without doubt one of the best fighter designs to emerge from World War I. It was rugged, and pilots praised its excellent rate of climb, which often gave it an advantage in combat.

The hardships and losses suffered by the naval airship crews were overshadowed by those experienced in the Army Airship Service, at least in the early part of the war. Many of the missions they flew were suicidal, the airships operating at low level over enemy troop concentrations despite the hideous vulnerability of the hydrogen-filled gas cells to small-arms fire. The German army made extensive use of Schütte-Lanz airships, mostly on the Eastern Front; the German navy, by contrast, despised them because of the vulnerability of their plywood structures and their poor performance.

Giant Bomber
The year 1917 saw big strides in the development of bomber aircraft. Imperial Russia, with its giant Ilya Murometz series of aircraft, was the first of the belligerents to recognize the potential of the heavy bomber. Heavily armed with up to eight defensive machine guns, the four-engine IMs flew 450 missions and dropped 65 tons of bombs for the loss of only three aircraft in three years of operational flying before the October Revolution of 1917 brought an end to their activities.

Royal Aircraft Factory S.E.5a

Type: single-seat fighting scout

Powerplant: one 149kW (200hp) Wolseley (licence-built) Hispano-Suiza 8a eight-cylinder Vee piston engine

Maximum speed: 222km/h (138mph)

Ferry range: 483km (300 miles)

Service ceiling: 5185m (17,000ft)

Weights: empty 639kg (1410lb); maximum take-off weight 902kg (1988lb)

Armament: one fixed forward-firing .303in Vickers machine gun; one .303in Lewis machine gun on Foster mount on upper wing

Dimensions:		
span	8.11m	(26ft 7in)
length	6.38m	(20ft 11in)
height	2.89m	(9ft 6in)
wing area	22.67m²	(444 sq ft)

Sopwith's Finest Fighting Scout
Camel 2F.I

The Camel got its (unofficial) name from the small 'hump' fairing over the twin Vickers guns.

The outer fuselage skin was aluminium around the engine, plywood around the centre-section and fabric around the rear section.

Pictured here is a Sopwith Camel 2F.1 flown by Canadian ace Bill Alexander, with 'A' Flight, No. 10 (Naval) Squadron RNAS at Treizennes. This unit became No. 210 Squadron RAF on 1 April 1918.

Sopwith Camel F.1

Type: single-seat fighting scout

Powerplant: one 130hp (97kW) Clerget rotary piston engine

Maximum speed: 185km/h (115mph)

Endurance: 2 hours 30 minutes

Service ceiling: 5790m (19,000ft)

Weights: empty 421kg (929lb); maximum take-off weight 659kg (1453lb)

Armament: two fixed forward-firing .303in Vickers machine guns plus up to four 11.3kg (25lb) bombs carried on the fuselage sides

Dimensions:

span	8.2m	(26ft 11in)
tail length	5.72m	(18ft 9in)
height	2.59m	(8ft 6in)
wing area	21.46m²	(231sq ft)

Italy was the next country to introduce heavy bombers, and by 1917 the standard type was the Caproni Ca 33, a three-engine design which had an endurance of three and a half hours and could carry a 450kg (1000lb) bomb load. These aircraft carried out many strategic operations against targets on the Adriatic coast, including the city and seaport of Trieste. Strategic operations virtually ceased early in November 1917, when the Austrians overran the Capronis' main base at Pordenone following the Italian defeat at Caporetto.

France's efforts in 1917 concentrated on the production of the excellent Bréguet 14 medium bomber, broadly the equivalent of Britain's Airco DH.4. The British also set about building up an effective heavy bomber force, with the Handley Page 0/100 of 1916 being joined in the following year by an improved version, the 0/400. For the duration of the war these two types mounted what was virtually a round-the-clock offensive against enemy targets, with the Handley Page 0/100s switching to night attacks, while the higher performance 0/400s carried out more hazardous daylight raids.

In 1917, the Germans had several formidable heavy bombers at their disposal, notably the Gotha G.IV and G.V and the Friedrichshafen G.III. In the summer of 1917, the latter joined the Gotha G.V in carrying out a series of night air attacks on British depots and installations in the Dunkirk area, inflicting substantial damage. It was for their air raids on Britain, however, that the Gothas achieved notoriety, and at the end of the year they were joined by a still more formidable heavy bomber, the four-engine Zeppelin Staaken R.IV. In 1917–18, raids by these aircraft had a profound psychological effect on the civil population of southern England. Moreover, they compelled the British air defences – by now enjoying growing success against the Zeppelin airships – to revise their tactics almost completely.

Meanwhile, the fierce air fighting over the Western Front continued. During the first week of April 1917, a month that was to go down in history as 'Bloody April', the RFC lost 75 aircraft in action. The aircraft and tactics of the German Jagdstaffeln were superior, and new RFC pilots were being sent to the front with as little as 17 hours' flying experience. By the middle of 'Bloody April' the average life expectancy of an RFC pilot in France had dropped to two months. The fierce air battles of early April preceded the Battle of Arras, which began on 9 April. By the end of the month, the RFC and RNAS had lost more than 150 aircraft, while the French and Belgians had lost 200. The Germans lost 370 aircraft along the whole front, 260 of them in the British sectors.

A New Dimension

New aircraft types that would bring with them a new dimension to air fighting began to make their appearance in 1917. The first was the Bristol F.2A fighter. First flown on 19 September 1916, the Bristol F.2A two-seat fighter made its operational debut during the Allied spring offensive of 1917. Fifty F.2As were built, powered by 142kW (190hp) Rolls-Royce Falcon engines The first F.2As arrived in France with No. 48 Squadron RFC in March 1917 and were rushed into action before their crews were able to develop proper tactics. At first they were flown like earlier two-seaters, orientated around the observer's gun as the primary weapon, and losses were heavy. When flown offensively, in the same way as a single-seat fighter, the Bristol Fighter proved to be a superb weapon and went on to log a formidable record of success in action. The F.2A was succeeded by the F.2B, with an uprated Falcon engine, wide-span tailplane, modified lower wing centre-section and an improved view from the front cockpit. The F.2B equipped six RFC squadrons on the Western Front, four in the United Kingdom and one in Italy.

Appearing at about the same time as the Bristol Fighter was the Royal Aircraft Factory SE.5, which also entered service in the spring of 1917. Although less manoeuvrable than the French-built Nieuports and SPADs, the SE.5 was faster and had an excellent rate of climb, enabling it to hold its own in combat with the latest German fighter types. The original SE.5 was followed into service, in June 1917, by the SE.5a, with a 149kW (200hp) Hispano-Suiza engine. Deliveries were slowed by an acute shortage of engines, but the pilots of the units that did receive the SE.5a were full of praise for the aircraft's fine flying qualities, its physical strength and its performance. and it is probably no exaggeration to say that, in most respects, the SE.5a was the Spitfire of World War I. At the end of the war, some 2700 SE.5as were on RAF charge, the type having served with 24 British, two American and one Australian squadrons.

Shipboard Operation

Perhaps the most celebrated British fighter to join the battle in 1917,

Left: Squadron Commander E.H. Dunning touches down on HMS Furious in his Sopwith Pup, 2 August 1917, to make the first ever landing by an aircraft on a ship under way. Five days later Dunning was killed attempting to repeat the exploit.

Right: Although not the best dogfighter of all time, the Royal Aircraft Factory SE.5a was the preferred mount of many aces, mainly due to its speed. This preserved example is based at the Shuttleworth Collection at Old Warden, Bedfordshire, England.

Biggest and Fastest SPAD
SPAD S.XIII

The Lafayette Escadrille was an American-staffed squadron consisting of volunteer pilots fighting for the French air force. The unit included aces such as Raoul Lufbery, who shot down 17 enemy aircraft.

Like the S.VII, the S.XIII had a long, sloping fin with a ribbed trailing edge. The aircraft had large, powerful rudder and elevator surfaces.

A SPAD S.XIII in the colours of the Lafayette Escadrille, a French fighter unit composed mainly of American volunteers. The squadron was formed in April 1916 as the Escadrille Américaine prior to the United States' entry into the war.

Oberleutnant Werner Voss taxies out in his Fokker Triplane. Known as the 'Hussar of Krefeld', the German air ace, with 48 victories, was shot down and killed by Lieutenant Rhys-Davids of No. 56 Squadron RFC.

however, was the Sopwith Camel. Although it had a number of vicious tendencies, the Sopwith Camel – first issued to No. 4 Squadron RNAS and No. 70 Squadron RFC on the Western Front in July 1917 – was a superb fighting machine in the hands of a skilled pilot, and by November 1918 the many squadrons operating it had claimed the destruction of at least 3000 enemy aircraft, more than any other type. Total

production of the Camel reached 5490, many serving with foreign air arms.

Early production Camel F.1s were powered either by the 97kW (130hp) Clerget 9B or the 112kW (150hp) Bentley BR.1 rotary engine, but subsequent aircraft were fitted with either the Clerget or the 82kW (110hp) Le Rhone 9J. In addition to serving overseas, the Camel F.1 also equipped a number of Home Defence squadrons, the night-fighter version being equipped with a pair of Lewis guns mounted on the upper wing centre-section. The final production version was the Camel 2F.1, designed for shipboard operation. As well

as being flown from the aircraft carriers HMS *Furious* and HMS *Pegasus*, the 2F.1 could also be catapulted from platforms erected on the gun turrets and forecastles of other capital ships, or launched from a lighter towed behind a destroyer. In fact, the development of naval air power was an important step forward in 1917.

At this time the Royal Navy was a long way ahead of the rest of the world in the development of vessels that could truly be described as aircraft carriers – in other words, fitted with flight decks from which landplanes were able to operate. The first such ship was the light battlecruiser HMS *Furious*, laid down shortly after the

SPAD S.XIII

Type: single-seat fighting scout

Powerplant: one 164kW (220hp) Hispano-Suiza 88Ec eight-cylinder Vee piston engine

Maximum speed: 224km/h (139mph)

Service ceiling: 6650m (21,815ft)

Weights: maximum take-off weight 845kg (1863lb)

Armament: two fixed forward-firing .303in Vickers machine guns

Dimensions:		
span	8.1m	(26ft 7in)
length	6.3m	(20ft 8in)
height	2.35m	(7ft 8in)
wing area	20.00m²	(199sq ft)

outbreak of war. Launched on 15 August 1916, she was fitted initially with a flight deck forward of her superstructure, but was eventually completed with a continuous flight deck and hangar accommodation for 14 Sopwith One-and-a-Half Strutters and two Sopwith Pups, although by early 1918 she had been re-equipped with Sopwith Camels. She was also fitted with workshops, electrically operated lifts from her hangar to the flight deck and a primitive form of arrester gear comprising strong rope nets suspended from crosspieces.

On 17 July 1918, two flights of Sopwith Camels led by Captain W.D. Jackson and Captain B.A. Smart took off from the *Furious* to attack the Zeppelin sheds at Tondern. All six aircraft, each of which carried two 50lb (22kg) bombs, made successful attacks. Two sheds and an ammunition dump were hit and set on fire, and Zeppelins L.54 and L.60 were destroyed. Two British pilots regained the carrier; three more landed in Denmark in bad weather, and the other crashed in the sea and drowned.

Brief Foray

A similarly equipped vessel, HMS *Cavendish*, was commissioned in October 1918 and renamed HMS *Vindictive*, but her operational career was limited to a brief foray in support of the Allied Intervention Force in North Russia and the Baltic in 1918–20. The most important development was centred on three new carriers, all fitted with

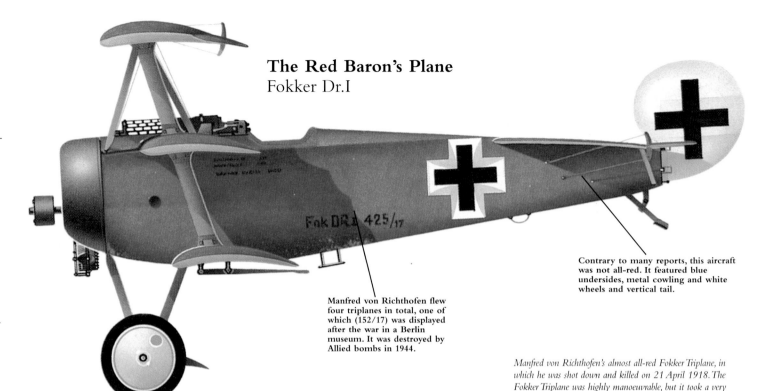

The Red Baron's Plane
Fokker Dr.I

Manfred von Richthofen flew four triplanes in total, one of which (152/17) was displayed after the war in a Berlin museum. It was destroyed by Allied bombs in 1944.

Contrary to many reports, this aircraft was not all-red. It featured blue undersides, metal cowling and white wheels and vertical tail.

Manfred von Richthofen's almost all-red Fokker Triplane, in which he was shot down and killed on 21 April 1918. The Fokker Triplane was highly manoeuvrable, but it took a very skilled pilot to get the best out of it.

unbroken flight decks: the 10,850-ton (11,023-tonne) HMS *Hermes*, HMS *Argus* and HMS *Eagle*. Of the three, only HMS *Argus* joined the fleet before the end of hostilities.

In May 1917, the French Escadrilles de Chasse began to standardize on a new type, the SPAD XIII. Like its predecessor, the SPAD VII, it was an excellent gun platform and was extremely strong, although it was tricky to fly at low speeds. Powered by a Hispano-Suiza 8Ba engine and armed with two forward-firing Vickers guns, it had a maximum speed of nearly 225km/h (140mph) –

quite exceptional for that time – and could climb to 6710m (22,000ft). The SPAD XIII subsequently equipped more than 80 escadrilles, and 8472 were built. The type also equipped 16 squadrons of the American Expeditionary Force, which became operational on the Western Front in April 1918, and it was supplied to Italy as well, which still had 100 in service in 1923.

On the German side, the rotary-engine Dr.I triplane, made famous as the red-painted mount of Baron Manfred von Richthofen at the time of his death in April 1918, was introduced into

Fokker Dr.I

Type: single-seat fighting scout

Powerplant: one 82kW (110hp) Oberusel Ur.II 9-cylinder rotary piston engine.

Maximum speed: 185km/h (115mph)

Endurance: 1 hr 30 mins

Service ceiling: 6100m (20,015ft)

Weights: empty 406kg (894lb); maximum take-off weight 586kg (1291lb)

Armament: two fixed forward-firing 7.92mm LMG 08/15 machine guns

Dimensions: span 7.19m (23ft 7in)
length 5.77m (18ft 11in)
height 2.95m (9ft 8in)
wing area 18.66m² (201sq ft)

Fokker's Finest Biplane Fighter
Fokker D.VII

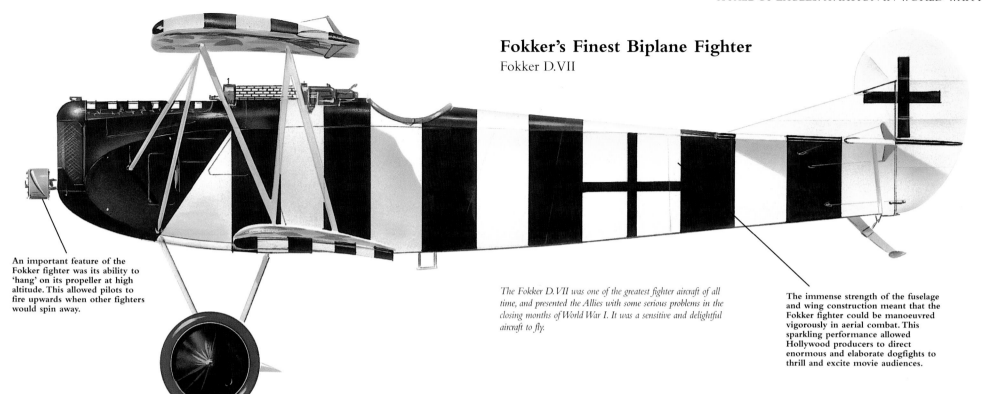

An important feature of the Fokker fighter was its ability to 'hang' on its propeller at high altitude. This allowed pilots to fire upwards when other fighters would spin away.

The Fokker D.VII was one of the greatest fighter aircraft of all time, and presented the Allies with some serious problems in the closing months of World War I. It was a sensitive and delightful aircraft to fly.

The immense strength of the fuselage and wing construction meant that the Fokker fighter could be manoeuvred vigorously in aerial combat. This sparkling performance allowed Hollywood producers to direct enormous and elaborate dogfights to thrill and excite movie audiences.

service in October 1917, but, although it was a supremely manoeuvrable fighter, it was already being outclassed by a new generation of fighting scouts. Its early career was marred by a series of fatal crashes. The fact that it received many accolades – at which Anthony Fokker himself expressed surprise – was due in the main to the skilled men who flew it, air aces such as Richthofen and Werner Voss. It was never used in very large numbers. Another Fokker design, the D.VII, was a very different aircraft. Without doubt the best fighter of World

War I to be produced in any numbers, the Fokker D.VII had its origins late in 1917, at a time when the German Flying Corps was beginning to lose the ascendancy and technical superiority it had enjoyed for nearly three years. The German High Command considered the situation so serious that it ordered German aircraft manufacturers to give top priority to the development of new fighters; the prototypes of the various designs would take part in a competitive fly-off. The Fokker D.VII proved to be by far the best all-round contender and

won by a handsome margin, and Fokker received an initial contract for 400 aircraft. (Up to that time, the largest order Fokker had received for any of his fighter designs had been for 60 Dr.I triplanes.) The first examples were delivered to Jagdgeschwader (JG) 1, and about 1000 had been completed by the time of the Armistice in November 1918.

Such were the aircraft that fought the final battles over France in the summer and autumn of 1918, until the Armistice of 11 November brought history's first air war to an end.

Fokker D.VII

Type: monoplane

Powerplant: one 138kW (185hp) B.M.W III six-cylinder inline piston engine

Maximum speed: 200km/h (124mph)

Endurance: 1 hour 30 minutes

Service ceiling: 7000m (22,965ft)

Weights: empty 735kg (1620lb); maximum take-off weight 880kg (1940lb)

Armament: two fixed forward-firing 7.92mm LMG O8/15 machine guns

Dimensions:		
	length	6.95m (22ft 9in)
	span	8.9m (29ft 2in)
	height	2.75m (9ft)
	wing area	20.5m² (221sq ft)

Ring Around the World

At 1.54 p.m. GMT on 6 July 1919, the British rigid airship R.34 nosed down to her moorings at Mineola Airfield, New York, at the close of the first ever flight from east to west across the Atlantic. She had left East Fortune, Scotland, 108 hours and 12 minutes earlier, under the command of Major G.H. Scott, AFC. On board her were Brigadier General E.M. Maitland, officer commanding the British Military Airship Service, a kitten and a stowaway, an airman named Ballantyne. She arrived at her destination unheralded, and, on 10 July, after three days of receptions and press interviews, she slipped away on the return flight. At 6.56 A.M. on 17 July, after a flight of 75 hours and 2 minutes, she reached Pulham in Norfolk, England, having completed the first round trip of the Atlantic by air.

The R.34 was not the first to make a successful Atlantic air crossing, but she was the last of the first. There had been several gallant failures in 1919, as brave men sought to tackle and overcome one of the greatest natural obstacles in the path of aviation, and the two big successes had been well publicized. First of all, a Curtiss NC-4 flying boat – one of a team of three, belonging to the US Navy's Seaplane Division One – had reached Lisbon, Portugal, on 27 May, after flying from Newfoundland in Canada, via the Azores; her two companion aircraft, the NC-1 and NC-3, had both landed short of their goal. The successful machine,

Left: The British rigid airship R34 approaching to land at Mineola, New York, at the end of the first flight from west to east across the Atlantic. She returned to her base at Pulham, England, on 17 July 1919.

Right: The US Navy NC-4 flying boat is seen here in Lisbon harbour, Portugal, on 27 May 1919, after completing the first transatlantic crossing by air. The aircraft flew from Newfoundland, Canada, via the Azores.

Strategic Reach for the RAF
Vickers Vimy Mk II

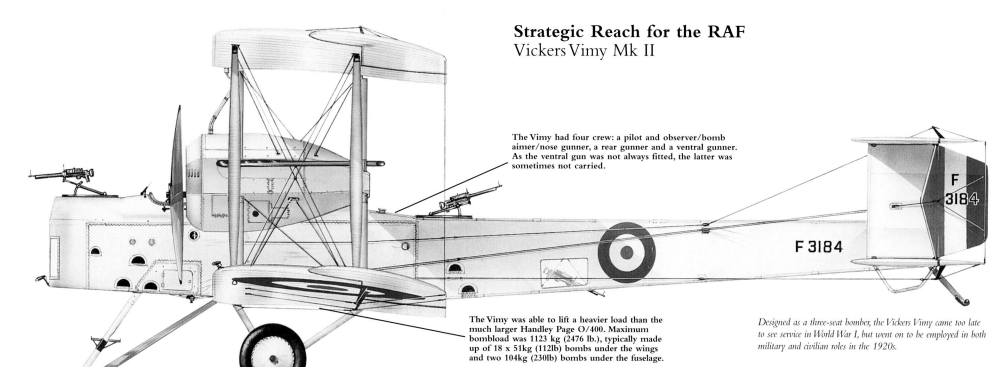

The Vimy had four crew: a pilot and observer/bomb aimer/nose gunner, a rear gunner and a ventral gunner. As the ventral gun was not always fitted, the latter was sometimes not carried.

The Vimy was able to lift a heavier load than the much larger Handley Page O/400. Maximum bombload was 1123 kg (2476 lb.), typically made up of 18 x 51kg (112lb) bombs under the wings and two 104kg (230lb) bombs under the fuselage.

Designed as a three-seat bomber, the Vickers Vimy came too late to see service in World War I, but went on to be employed in both military and civilian roles in the 1920s.

commanded by Lieutenant Commander A.C. Read, spent 10 days in Lisbon before flying on to Plymouth, England.

Then, just under three weeks later had come the most sensational flight so far: the first nonstop crossing of the Atlantic, from Lester's Field, Newfoundland, to Clifden in Galway, Ireland, by a converted Vickers Vimy flown by Captain John Alcock and navigated by Lieutenant Arthur Whitten Brown. To them went a *Daily Mail* prize of £10,000, knighthoods, the acclaim of the world and a coveted place in aviation history.

It might have been thought that these flights, and that of the R.34 after them, would have broken the dam and released a wave of aerial exploration over the Atlantic; however, such was not the case. A year after the R.34 made her flight, the airship remained the

Captain John Alcock (left) and Lieutenant Arthur Whitten Brown made the first crossing of the Atlantic in 1919. The flight ended rather ignominiously with their aircraft nose-down in an Irish peat bog.

Vickers Vimy Mk II

Type: heavy bomber

Powerplant: two 269kW (360hp) Rolls-Royce Eagle VIII 12-cylinder Vee piston engines

Maximum speed: 166km/h (103mph)

Ferry range: 1464km (910 miles)

Service ceiling: 2135m (7000ft)

Weights: empty 3221kg (7101lb); maximum take-off weight 5670kg (12,500lb)

Armament: three .303in Lewis Mk III machine guns on pivoted mounts: in nose, in dorsal position and in ventral positions; internal bomb cells and underwing racks with provision for up to 2179kg (480lb) of bombs

Dimensions:
span	20.75m (68ft 1in)
length	13.27m (43ft 6in)
height	4.76m (15ft 7in)
wing area	123.56m² (1330 sq ft)

Alcock and Brown taking off from St John's, Newfoundland, Canada, in their Vickers Vimy. They came down at Clifden, County Galway, Ireland, 16 hours and 27 minutes later. Both men were knighted for their achievement.

Triumphant Flying Boat
Savoia-Marchetti S.55SA

The twin engines were carried on a pylon above the cantilever wing, itself carried at shoulder height on the twin-hulls.

The Savoia S.55 flying boat was widely used by the Italians on voyages of exploration in the 1920s. Savoia was Italy's principal flying boat manufacturer, the firm producing both civil and military aircraft.

only vehicle capable of carrying a substantial number of people, or a cargo of reasonable size, across the Atlantic by air. There remained only the adventurers, and in the early 1920s the adventurers were looking to other challenges – a flight to Australia, for example, or across Asia. Although there were several crossings of the Atlantic in stages, it was 1924 before another nonstop crossing was made, and the vehicle was the German Zeppelin LZ.126, which crossed the ocean on a delivery flight to the US Navy.

Atlantic Exploration
It was not until 1927 that the tempo of Atlantic exploration picked up dramatically. On 8 February, a trio of Italians – de

Pinedo, del Prete and Zacchetti – set out to make the first flight around the periphery of the Atlantic in a Savoia S.55 seaplane named *Santa Maria*. They reached Rio de Janeiro, Brazil, on 26 February, after a relatively uneventful Atlantic crossing via Sierra Leone and the Cape Verde Islands; a month later they arrived in Cuba after a leisurely flag-showing northerly flight. Then, on 6 April, disaster struck when the aircraft caught fire at Roosevelt, Texas, and burned out; it was another month before a replacement machine, the *Santa Maria II*, could be made available, and they continued their flight to New York in this on 8 May.

On 18 May their tour brought them to Chicago, and on 20 May they reached

Newfoundland, Canada, in readiness for their eastbound flight across the North Atlantic. They took off on 23 May, and after a flight of 2413km (1500 miles) they touched down on the sea 290km (180 miles) northwest of Horta, in the Azores. A recovery ship came to their rescue, and, their fuel exhausted, the group reached Horta on 26 May, after spending three uncomfortable days under tow. On 10 June, after a much-needed rest, the trio then flew on to Ponta Delgada, and from there to Lisbon in Portugal and finally to Rome in Italy, their destination. Altogether, between 8 February and 16 June 1927, they had covered a distance of more than 40,707km (25,300 miles).

Savoia-Marchetti S.55SA

Type: (S.55X) long-range bomber-reconnaissance flying-boat

Powerplant: two 880hp (656kW) Isotta-Fraschini Asso 750 Vee piston engines

Maximum speed: 279km/h (173mph)

Ferry range: 3500km (2175miles)

Service ceiling: 5000m (16,405ft)

Weights: empty 5750kg (12,677lb); maximum take-off weight 8260kg (18,210lb)

Armament: two 7.7mm machine guns in nose position in each hull, plus one torpedo or 2000kg (4409lb) of bombs

Dimensions: span   24m (78ft 9in)
              length 16.75m (54ft 11in)
              Height   5m (16ft 5in)
              Wing area 93m2 (1001sq ft)

In the spring of 1927, there were plenty of incentives to rekindle interest in transatlantic flying. The main carrot that dangled temptingly before the noses of aviators was a prize of $25,000, which was put up by the New York hotel owner Raymond Orteig, for the first nonstop flight between New York and Paris, or vice versa. The difficulties involved in this undertaking were enormous. While engines were a little more reliable than when Alcock and

Brown had made their crossing eight years earlier, there were still no adequate methods of forecasting the unpredictable Atlantic weather, no blind flying instruments to help a pilot out of trouble if he was forced to fly through cloud, and no real aids to long-distance navigation over nearly two thousand miles of featureless sea. Last of all, but by no means least, was the prohibitive cost of fitting out an aircraft for a transatlantic attempt. No pilot could hope to do it without heavy sponsorship, and sponsors required a virtual guarantee of success before showing any willingness to commit.

The French, to their everlasting credit, tried hard and valiantly, despite a succession of tragedies. In 1927, two came in quick succession. In the first, a Farman Goliath left St Louis-du-Sénégal on 5 May and headed out over the Atlantic; neither it nor its crew was ever seen again. Then, only three days later, came another blow that shocked and saddened the whole of France. On 8 May, Charles Nungesser, one of the leading French air aces with 45 victories, and his navigator, Francois Coli, took off from Paris in a Levasseur aircraft named *L'Oiseau Blanc* (White Bird). The aircraft took

off safely, and as soon as it was airborne Nungesser jettisoned its undercarriage – a measure designed to save weight and cut down drag, for the Levasseur would have to contend with the prevailing westerly wind. A small fleet of aircraft accompanied it as far as the English Channel, before it continued on its way alone.

The aircraft vanished without trace, somewhere over the grey Atlantic wastes. All that remained of *L'Oiseau Blanc* was its undercarriage, preserved today in France's Musée de l'Air.

Lindbergh's Triumph

Thirteen days later, on 21 May, a Ryan Monoplane named *Spirit of St Louis* landed in the darkness at Le Bourget, Paris. It had flown from New York to Paris at an average speed of 173.6km/h (107.9mph), and its shy and serious-looking young pilot, Charles Lindbergh, had flown into the pages of history. That historic flight, its drama told and retold so many times, needs no repetition here. For Lindbergh, the solo transatlantic crossing was only the beginning of an eventful career that encompassed fame and tragedy alike.

In the early days, the US Navy was at the forefront of range and endurance flying, and it was the US Navy which, in

Charles Lindbergh (second left) pictured just before taking off on the first successful solo flight across the Atlantic. Several other aviators had previously died in the attempt, including the French air ace Charles Nungesser.

1924, successfully completed the first round-the-world flight, albeit with many stops en route, using Douglas DT-2 biplanes which were externally similar to those in service as torpedo-bombers.

Apart from bringing well-deserved honour to the crews, and praise for their flying and navigational skills, this epic voyage brought home a number of lessons which were to make their mark on the design of future aircraft and equipment. One such lesson was that wood and fabric were far from suitable materials for use in wing and float structures under hot and humid conditions; another was that the flight would not have been possible without massive support and organization, with US warships carrying spares, fuel and technicians positioned along the route. Logistical support of long-range air operations was something at which the Americans, over the next 20 years, would come to excel.

Remarkable Airship
Several other round-the-world attempts during the 1920s ended in failure, either because the aircraft and engines involved

were not up to the stresses imposed upon them or because adverse weather conditions resulted in mishap. Other attempts were not true round-the-globe flights because the aircraft were carried part of the way on ships. In fact, it was not until 1929 that the world was truly circumnavigated by air, and it was achieved by a remarkable airship, the *Graf Zeppelin*.

During World War I, some of the later types of Zeppelin had demonstrated astounding feats of endurance. In November 1917, for example, the L.59 had made a long-range flight to East Africa from Bulgaria. Recalled just past Khartoum, she returned to Bulgaria after 95 hours 35 minutes in the air, having covered a record distance of 6720km (4200 miles). Now, on 8 August 1929, the L.59's commercial descendant, the *Graf Zeppelin* – which made her first transatlantic flight

Left: A Douglas DT-2 World Cruiser, the aircraft that made the first world tour between 6 April and 28 September 1924. Four DWCs set out from Seattle, Washington, but two came to grief.

Right: The commercial airship Graf Zeppelin *and her sister craft, the* Hindenburg, *were highly successful, but there was an element of danger from their flammable hydrogen gas, which ultimately destroyed the* Hindenburg.

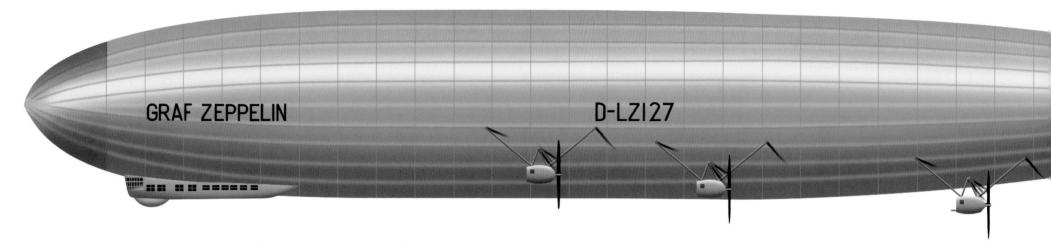

GRAF ZEPPELIN

D-LZI27

The LZ127 Graf Zeppelin. The airship circumnavigated the world with only three stops, bringing enormous prestige to her designer, but the flight was not without its problems and dangers.

Graf Zeppelin LZ127

Type: airship

Powerplant: five Maybach 410kW (550hp) engines

Maximum speed: 131km/h (81mph)

Dimensions: length   245m (804ft)
           Max diameter   41.2m (135ft)
           volume 105,000m³ (3,708,040cu ft)

on 11 October 1928, carrying 37 crew, 20 passengers, 62,000 letters and 100 specially franked postcards – set out from Lakehurst, New Jersey, and after crossing the Atlantic from west to east arrived at Friedrichshafen on 10 August.

Setting out once more five days later, she flew over Berlin, Stettin and Danzig, heading out over the Baltic towards Russia. Early on 16 August, she passed over the city of Vologda and cruised on towards the Ural Mountains, which she crossed north of Perm. On 17 and 18 August, she was over the vast wastes of Siberia, the crew eventually picking up the Yenisei River. The worst part of the voyage across Siberia was the flight over the uncharted Stanovoi Mountains, running parallel to the east coast and plunging into the Sea of Okhotsk. Hugo Eckener, the airship's commander, negotiated them by flying through a narrow valley in gusty wind conditions that threatened to hurl the craft against

the jagged rocks on several occasions. But Eckener's skill brought her through safely, and she scraped over the ridge that ran along the crest of the mountains with only feet to spare. Ahead of her now lay the Sea of Okhotsk, and beyond it Japan; the airship had just completed the first nonstop flight across the length of Russia.

The *Graf Zeppelin* had enough fuel and supplies to take her directly to Los Angeles, but for political reasons she was scheduled to make a call at Tokyo. She reached the Japanese capital on 19 August, having covered 11,263km (7000 miles) in 101 hours 44 minutes. Apart from running through severe turbulence in cloud over Siberia, and skirting the fringes of a typhoon off Sakhalin, she had encountered kindly weather.

Significant Flight

The *Graf Zeppelin* left Tokyo on 23 August and set course east–southeast over the Pacific, using the winds that

raced across the sky in the wake of a typhoon to help her along. Later, she had to nose her way through dense fog for 24 hours, but on the third day of her Pacific crossing she emerged into clear weather again and, at sunset on 25 August, she cruised over San Francisco, welcomed by dozens of aircraft. Then she flew on to Los Angeles for a dawn landing that proved extremely tricky because of a temperature inversion; as the airship descended into the cooler layers of air she became lighter, and the crew had to valve off a large amount of gas before she could be safely moored. When she cast off again the following evening, the opposite applied; quantities of gas had been automatically valved off during the day when the sun heated the ship's envelope and she was dangerously heavy. As there were no more supplies of hydrogen to top up her gas cells, Eckener had to make a long, slow take-off, nosing up gradually into the warmer layers of

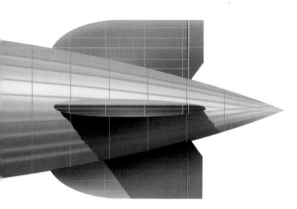

world in less than 10 days. They got off to a fine start by crossing the North Atlantic from Harbour Grace in Newfoundland, to Chester, England, in 16 hours 17 minutes. They were back in New York on 1 July, having successfully made the first round-the-world flight by a commercial aircraft (as distinct from an airship) in 8 days, 15 hours and 51 minutes, which earned them a prize of $10,000. Their total flying time was 107 hours 2 minutes.

In 1933, Wiley Post broke his own record with a solo flight around the world in the same aircraft, with some modifications. Setting out on 15 July, he flew from New York to Berlin in 25 hours 45 minutes, and from there his route took him through Königsberg, Moscow, Novosibirsk, Irkutsk, Khabarovsk, Flat (in Alaska), Fairbanks

air. She bounced several times as her tail struck the ground and only just cleared some high-tension cables, but she gained height and flew on to Lakehurst, New Jersey, where she moored on 29 August after a round-the-world voyage of 21 days, 7 hours and 34 minutes, of which a week had been spent on the ground at her ports of call. From Lakehurst, she flew home across the Atlantic.

The *Graf Zeppelin* had circumvented the world with only three stops, a remarkable achievement. But a far more significant flight was made some two years later, when Americans Wiley Post and Harold Gatty left New York in a Lockheed Vega monoplane named *Winnie Mae of Oklahoma* on 23 June 1931, in an attempt to fly around the

Wiley Post pictured with the Winnie Mae of Oklahoma *on 22 July 1933 after making his second round-the-world flight, this time solo, in which he cut almost a day off the time for the earlier flight he and Harold Gatty had made in 1931.*

and Edmonton, back to his start point. He made the journey in 7 days, 18 hours and 50 minutes, including 115 hours 54 minutes' flying time.

Men had flown around the world, both solo and in crews, and so had a woman, Lady Drummond Hay, aboard the *Graf Zeppelin* in 1929. But a woman had yet to make a round-the-world flight as pilot in command of an aircraft, and in 1937 Amelia Earhart determined that she would be the first. An initial attempt, in March 1937, ended in disaster when her Lockheed Electra ground-looped on take-off from Honolulu, shearing off the right mainwheel and damaging a wing.

Navigational Problems
The aircraft was repaired, and she tried again three months later. With Fred Noonan as her navigator, she planned to follow a route around the equator – the first time this would have been done – flying from west to east. Taking off from Miami, Florida, on 1 June, she flew to San Juan in Puerto Rico, then on to Caripito in Venezuela, Paramaribo in Dutch Guiana and Natal in South Africa, jumping-off point for the transatlantic

Left: Americans Wiley Post and Harold Gatty made the first successful round-the-world flight by a commercial aircraft in the Lockheed Vega Winnie Mae. *The flight lasted from 23 June to 1 July 1931.*

Right: Amelia Earhart and her Lockheed Vega at Londonderry, Northern Ireland, on 21 May 1932. Earhart had just become the first woman pilot to make a solo crossing of the Atlantic in an aircraft.

flight to Dakar. Haze over the coast of West Africa caused some navigational problems for Noonan, and in fact they landed at St Louis-du-Sénégal on 8 June, flying on to Dakar the next day.

From Dakar they went on via Gao and Fort Lamy to El Fasher, in the Anglo-Egyptian Sudan, then on through Khartoum to Massawa on the Red Sea. From there, they flew to Assab on the coast of Eritrea, the last staging point before a nonstop flight to Karachi that took 13 hours 10 minutes. At Karachi, Imperial Airways and Royal Air Force mechanics checked the Electra thoroughly while Amelia and Noonan enjoyed a two-day rest; they resumed their flight on 17 June, following the Imperial Airways route to Calcutta, India, 2236km (1390 miles) away.

They landed at Calcutta's Dum Dum Airport to find the field waterlogged. The weather was now giving them cause for concern, for the monsoon was about to break and it was important to press on as quickly as possible. The next leg of the flight, from Calcutta to Akyab, in Burma, was uneventful, but between Akyab and Rangoon the Electra was battered by storm-force winds and monsoon rain, lashing head-on from the southeast with

such force that it stripped paint from the leading edges of the aircraft's wings. It was impossible to find a way through the massive clouds, so they turned round and flew back to Akyab.

They managed to reach Rangoon on 19 June, and the following day they flew on to Bangkok and Singapore, hoping to make up some lost time. They seemed to have left the bad weather behind them, and they flew the next leg from Singapore to Bandung, Java, in excellent visibility. At Bandung, KLM technicians checked over the aircraft, then, on 27 June, the flight continued to Port Darwin, Australia, with one stop en route at Timor.

The next stretch, over 1930km (1200 miles) of water between Port Darwin and Lae, New Guinea, was difficult. The trip took eight hours, the aircraft having to fight its way through strong headwinds and turbulence, and by this time both pilots were feeling the strain of having flown 35,400km (22,000 miles).

On 2 July 1937, they took off from Lae on the 4113-km (2556-mile) jump to Howland Island

Right: Amelia Earhart and her Lockheed Electra. The aviatrix and her navigator vanished on the Pacific leg of a round-the-world flight in 1937, and to this day their fate remains a mystery.

Opposite: The Lockheed Model 14 was a scaled-up version of the Model 10 Electra. Produced in three main versions for airlines around the world, it also established some impressive endurance records in the hands of pilots such as Howard Hughes.

in the central Pacific – the last port of call before Oakland, California. They would actually land on 1 July, gaining a day when they crossed the International Date Line.

Unsolved Mystery

But they never reached Howland. Apart from a few fragmentary radio messages, nothing was seen or heard of them again. Despite a massive search that encompassed half the Pacific and a dozen nations, their disappearance remains one of aviation's great unsolved mysteries.

They vanished just when Pan American and Imperial

Airways were establishing routine round-the-world air services. 'One plane missing,' a newspaper editorial on the disappearance remarked, 'far out over the lonely Pacific. Another plane heading into the dawn, half a world away. And the day of the ocean pioneers is closed.'

But not quite. On 10 July 1938, a Lockheed 14 – an improved version of the Electra – took off from New York and flew around the world in just under four days; to be exact, in 91 hours 24 minutes. The main who captained the Lockheed 14 was one of the wealthiest and most controversial

figures of all time. He was also one whose contribution to aviation was immense. His name was Howard Hughes.

One factor above all others that gave impetus to the development of commercial aviation in the years between the two world wars was the requirement for fast mail services, and nowhere was this need more imperative than in the far-flung British Empire. Much of the pioneering work was done by the Royal Air Force, which laid the foundation of a network of air routes

across the empire and established some impressive records in the process.

The year 1924 saw the formation of Imperial Airways, a national airline that incorporated the many small air companies that had sprung into existence immediately

Handley Page foresaw the need for a purpose-built commercial transport at an early stage, and soon after the end of World War I initiated the design of such an aircraft, the W.8, which flew for the first time in December 1919.

after the war. Operations began in May, with Handley Page W8bs and de Havilland DH.34s flying the routes set up by the earlier companies, but Britain's preoccupation with her empire meant that the European routes always took

second place behind long-range routes to the Middle and Far East and to South Africa. Aircraft procurement, too, was dictated by the longer routes. It was not until 1928 that Imperial Airways invited tenders from all British manufacturers for new 40-seat, multi-engine airliners for service on the continental routes.

The Short S.17 G-ACJK Syrinx was one of two Short Scylla airliners to serve with Imperial Airways. Badly damaged in gale at Brussels, Syrinx was repaired and went on to serve with the RAF on transport duties in World War II.

A de Havilland DH89 Dragon Rapide in the colours of British European Airways. Production of the aircraft continued right up to the outbreak of World War II, by whch time 205 had been built. Many were impressed for service with the RAF.

Flying Imperial Routes
Handley Page H.P.42W

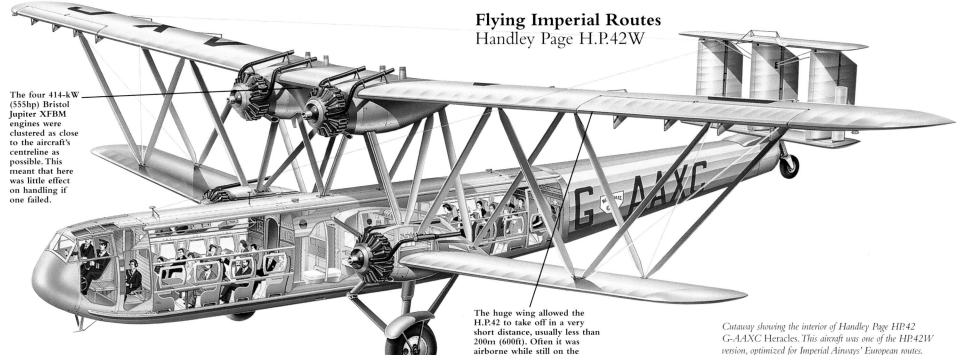

The four 414-kW (555hp) Bristol Jupiter XFBM engines were clustered as close to the aircraft's centreline as possible. This meant that here was little effect on handling if one failed.

The huge wing allowed the H.P.42 to take off in a very short distance, usually less than 200m (600ft). Often it was airborne while still on the taxiway and long before it reached the runway.

Cutaway showing the interior of Handley Page HP.42 G-AAXC Heracles. This aircraft was one of the HP.42W version, optimized for Imperial Airways' European routes. The HP.42E aircraft were based at Cairo in Egypt.

The design selected was the Handley Page HP.42, which had the added attraction that it could also be used on the British Empire routes overseas. The first proving flight from London to Paris was not made until 9 June 1931, however. and in the meantime Imperial Airways' European services were maintained by its fleet of Armstrong Whitworth Argosy and Handley Page W.8 aircraft.

The introduction of the HP.42 brought a new air of organization and efficiency to Imperial Airways' continental routes. It would never be relinquished, but, in the spring of 1933,

following several accidents and a sudden growth of traffic demands, the airline found itself desperately short of landplanes. Short Brothers filled the gap by building a landplane version of their Kent flying boat; two examples were produced, named *Scylla* and *Syrinx*, and both went into service in 1934 on Imperial Airways' summer schedules from Croydon to Paris, Brussels, Basle and Zurich, supplementing the HP.42s.

British Commercial Aviation
Meanwhile, during the early 1930s, a spate of small charter and air taxi

companies had burst out over the British commercial aviation scene, equipped with a wide variety of aircraft. They included Highland Airways, Hillman's Airways, Jersey Airways, Railway Air Services and London, Scottish and Provincial Airways. From 1933, these small concerns began to standardize on a new and commercially successful feeder liner, the de Havilland DH.84 Dragon. The DH.89 Dragon Rapide was an uprated version, while another de Havilland machine – the DH.86 – was evolved in 1934 to meet an original requirement for an aircraft capable of

Handley Page H.P.42W

Type: civil transport aircraft

Powerplant: four 414kW (555hp) Bristol Jupiter XFBM nine-cylinder radial engines

Maximum speed: 204km/h (125mph)

Ferry range: 805km (500 miles)

Service ceiling: n/a

Weights: empty 8047kg (17,740lb); maximum take-off weight 12,701kg (28,000lb)

Dimensions:
span	39.62m (130ft)
length	28.09m (92ft 2in)
height	8.23m (27ft)
wing area	277.68m² (2989sq ft)

Middle East Mailplane
de Havilland DH.66 Hercules

Two pilots flew the Hercules, and the cabin could hold a wireless operator, seven passengers and up to 13.2 m³ (466 cu ft) of mail. Australian DH.66s had sufficient seating for 14 passengers.

In light of experience in hotter climates, Imperial Airways' standard colour scheme was changed from dark blue to a less heat-absorbent all-over silver dope finish.

operating between Singapore and Brisbane, Australia. The DH.86 was used by Imperial Airways on some of its continental services and also equipped two new companies, British Airways and United Airways, both registered in 1935.

Since the late 1920s, Imperial Airways had gradually been taking over responsibility for the British Empire air routes pioneered by the RAF. It was able to do this thanks to the advent of a new aircraft, the de Havilland DH.66 Hercules, specifically designed for long-range operations. The three-engine Hercules carried a three-man crew – two pilots and a wireless operator – and there was accommodation for seven passengers, with two separate cargo compartments for baggage and mail.

Surplus Machines
In the United States, after the end of the 1914–18 war, aviation – military and civil alike – had slipped into the doldrums, mainly because of a steadfast refusal by Congress, under President Coolidge, to budget any funds for its development. Besides, there was not much incentive to develop new types of aircraft, as the market was flooded with thousands of surplus military machines, most of them in mint condition, and they were sold off to anyone who wanted them at ridiculously cheap prices.

As was also the case in Europe, the key to development in civil aviation in the United States during this period was mail. In 1925, Congress passed the Air Mail Act, which turned over the carriage of airmail to private contractors. There was already a coast-to-coast airmail route, which was flown by military aircraft on charter to the US Post Office, but under the new Act bids were authorized for certain connections to this route. The most profitable and potentially worthwhile of these was the New York–Boston connection, for which there were two serious bidders; one was Eastern Air Transport, founded in September 1925 by Juan Trippe, and the other was Colonial Airlines, which was run by a consortium of influential investors. The two companies merged and became Colonial Air Transport, which was duly awarded the contract. Initially, the route was flown by Fokker Universal aircraft.

de Havilland DH.66 Hercules

Type: seven-seat commercial transport biplane

Powerplant: three 313kW (420hp) Bristol Jupiter VI radial piston engines

Maximum speed: 206km/h (128mph)

Ferry range: 845km (525 miles)

Service ceiling: 3960m (13,000ft)

Weights: empty 4110kg (9060lb); maximum take-off weight 7076kg (15,600lb)

Dimensions:
span	24.23m	(79ft 6in)
tail length	16.92m	(55ft 6in)
height	5.56m	(18ft 3in)
wing area	143.72m²	(1547sq ft)

Meanwhile, in November 1925, another company, called Western Air Express, had been awarded a contract to carry mail between Los Angeles and Salt Lake City, Utahm beginning operations in April 1926 with six Douglas M-2 biplanes, conversions of military observation aircraft. In May 1926, Western Air Express began to carry passengers whenever the mail load permitted, the trip costing $90.

In the east, Juan Trippe had left Colonial Air Transport and was busy founding a new company called Pan American Airways, Inc. Its purpose was to exploit the Caribbean routes, operating from Key West in Florida to Havana, Cuba, across the Yucatán peninsulain Mexico, then down through British Honduras and Nicaragua to Panama. A mail contract for operations in these routes was awarded to Pan American on 16 July 1927, and under its terms the service had to start by 19 October. The problem was that Pan American had no aircraft. Before Trippe had left Colonial, however, he had ordered several Fokker Tri-motors; Colonial had not wanted these, which was one of the reasons why Trippe had split with the company, but the first two were nearing completion. On 13 October 1927, Juan Trippe was elected president and general manager of Pan American, and on 28 October the new company's first Fokker Tri-motor made the inaugural flight from Key West to Havana, carrying 350kg (772lb) of mail.

Rapid Expansion

From then on, expansion was rapid. A new base was set up in Miami, and later in the year a new service was started to Nassau, in the Bahamas. Trippe's plan was now to encircle the whole of the Caribbean, forming a route that would pass through Mexico and into Texas. To achieve this, Pan American needed an amphibian, and Trippe ordered the eight-passenger S-38, which entered service with the airline in October 1928. Before that, in July, Trippe had bought out a rival company which stood in the way

Pan American Airways' Fokker F.VII pictured before its inaugural flight to Havana, Cuba, from Key West, Florida, on 28 October 1927. The photograph encompasses just about all of Pan Am's air and ground staff at the time.

of Pan American's ambitions; this was the West Indian Aerial Express, which had begun services between Port au Prince, Haiti, and San Juan in Puerto Rico in December 1927, using Fairchild FC-2 floatplanes. In January 1929, Trippe also purchased the Mexican airline Compañia Mexicana de Aviación, which had been operating since 1924 and which, five years later, was equipped with Ford Tri-motors, Fokker F-10s and Fairchild 71s.

By May 1930, Pan American's circle around the Caribbean was complete, and the airline now owned 110 aircraft, comprising 38 Sikorsky S.38s, 29 Ford Tri-motors, 12 Fokker F.10s and 31 Fairchild 71s and FC-2s. It was an impressive foundation on which to base what was to become the greatest civil aviation enterprise in the world.

Pam American also played a leading part in opening up the Pacific air routes. Prior to 1927 the only trans-Pacific flight from the United States to Asia had been made via Alaska, the Aleutian Islands, Kamchatka, the Kuriles and Japan; that had been early in 1924, when the US round-the-world team had made the trip in their Douglas DT-2 biplanes. Not until the advent of improved versions of the Fokker F.VII, the first aircraft with anything like a long-range capability, did long overwater flights become feasible; it

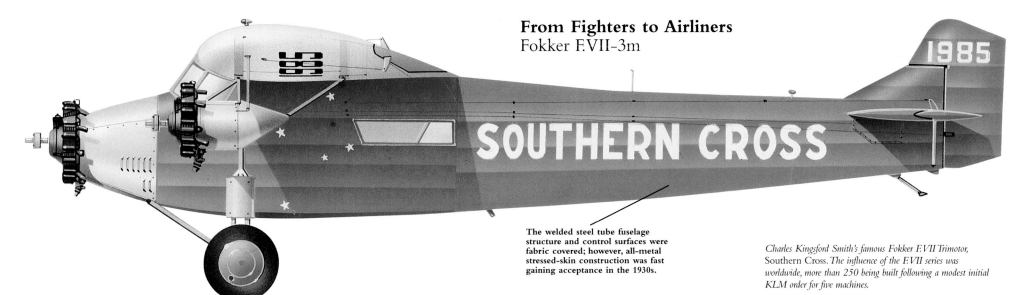

From Fighters to Airliners
Fokker F.VII-3m

The welded steel tube fuselage structure and control surfaces were fabric covered; however, all-metal stressed-skin construction was fast gaining acceptance in the 1930s.

Charles Kingsford Smith's famous Fokker F.VII Trimotor, Southern Cross. The influence of the F.VII series was worldwide, more than 250 being built following a modest initial KLM order for five machines.

should be remembered that the distance from North America to the Pacific's midway point was greater than that from Newfoundland to Ireland.

Lost at Sea
It was in an F.VII-3m that two Americans, Lieutenants Maitland (pilot) and Hagenberger (navigator), made the first Pacific crossing from San Francisco to Honolulu. Taking off at 4.09 p.m. on 28 June 1927, they landed at Honolulu the following day after a flight of 25 hours, 49 minutes and 30 seconds, during which they covered a distance of 3910km (2430 miles). Other attempts to cross the Pacific later that year, however, met with disaster. When an American millionaire named John Dole put up a prize of $35,000, to be divided between

the first two crews who made the San Francisco-Honolulu flight in a properly organized contest, 10 crews responded. Of these, three were killed in test flights, one was eliminated when the judges decided that its aircraft could not carry sufficient fuel, and two aborted because of mechanical trouble. Of the four crews that did take part, two were lost at sea; one of the crews who had not been able to take part in the race set off to search for them and never returned.

The first complete crossing of the Pacific was made in the following year and was a joint Australian–American venture. The aircraft was a Fokker F.VIIB-3m named *Southern Cross*; the pilot and commander was Charles Kingsford Smith, his second pilot was C.T.P. Ulm, his wireless operator James Warner – both

Australians – and his supremely skilled navigator was an American, Harry Lyon.

The *Southern Cross* left Oakland, California, on 31 May 1928 and arrived at Honolulu without incident on 1 June, after a flight lasting 27 hours 27 minutes. From Honolulu, Kingsford-Smith flew to Kaoui Island, 177km (110 miles) away, where there was a longer airstrip; from there, on 2 June, he took off for Fiji, laden with fuel. This was the most difficult part of the flight, for the aircraft encountered violent rainstorms as it crossed the equator, and it was a tribute to Harry Lyon's navigation that they reached Suva on 4 June after covering 5121km (3183 miles) in 34 hours 33 minutes.

The aircraft left Suva on 8 June. Violent electrical storms en route and also a strong headwind meant that the aircraft

Fokker F.VII-3m
Southern Cross

Type:

Powerplant: three 179kW (240hp) Wright Whirlwind radials

Cruising speed: 170km/h (106mph)

Ferry range: 2600km (1616 miles) with extra fuel

Service ceiling: 4700m (15,420ft)

Weight: loaded 3986kg (8788lb)

Dimensions:
span	19.31m (63ft 4in)
tail length	14.57m (47ft 10in)
height	3.9m (12ft 10in)

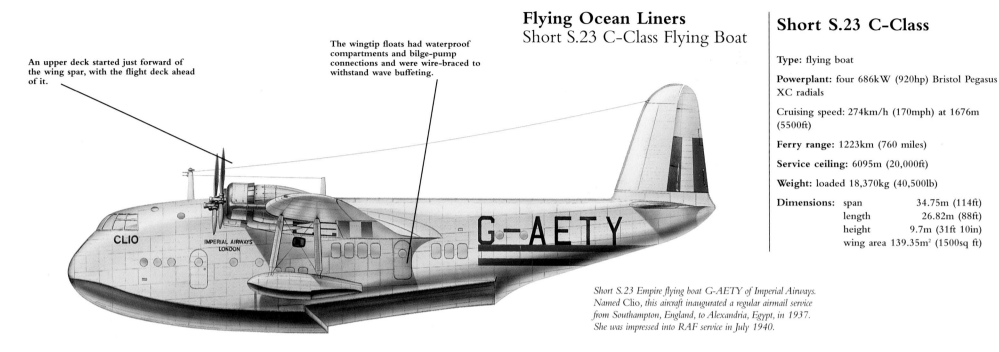

An upper deck started just forward of the wing spar, with the flight deck ahead of it.

The wingtip floats had waterproof compartments and bilge-pump connections and were wire-braced to withstand wave buffeting.

Flying Ocean Liners
Short S.23 C-Class Flying Boat

CLIO

IMPERIAL AIRWAYS LONDON

G-AETY

Short S.23 Empire flying boat G-AETY of Imperial Airways. Named Clio, this aircraft inaugurated a regular airmail service from Southampton, England, to Alexandria, Egypt, in 1937. She was impressed into RAF service in July 1940.

Short S.23 C-Class

Type: flying boat

Powerplant: four 686kW (920hp) Bristol Pegasus XC radials

Cruising speed: 274km/h (170mph) at 1676m (5500ft)

Ferry range: 1223km (760 miles)

Service ceiling: 6095m (20,000ft)

Weight: loaded 18,370kg (40,500lb)

Dimensions: span 34.75m (114ft)
length 26.82m (88ft)
height 9.7m (31ft 10in)
wing area 139.35m² (1500sq ft)

made slow progress, taking 21 hours 35 minutes to cover the 2896km (1800-mile) leg, and matters were further complicated by the erratic behaviour of Lyon's compasses. Nevertheless, landfall was made at Eagle Farm, Brisbane, some 145km (90 miles) off the intended track, the *Southern Cross* having covered a distance of 11,890km (7389 miles) in an elapsed time of 83 hours 38 minutes.

Vanished without Trace
After a series of preliminary surveys, Pan American began scheduled services across the Pacific in the mid-1930s, using two types of flying boat, the Sikorsky S-42 and the Martin M-130, both large four-

engine aircraft. A service to the mainland of Asia was officially inaugurated on 21 October 1936, the trip taking five days and involving an elapsed time of 60 hours. In fact, early passenger flights only went as far as Manila in the Philippines; it was not until 1937 that the route was extended to Hong Kong to link up with Chinese internal routes.

These operations were not without their share of tragedies. In December 1937, a Sikorsky S-42 on a proving flight to New Zealand exploded in midair, with the loss of its six crew; six months later a Martin M-130 with nine crew and six passengers vanished without trace while on a flight from Guam to Manila.

Flying boats were also essential to the expansion of the British Empire air routes during the 1930s. In this respect, Imperial Airways relied on the excellent Short C-Class flying boat, designed in 1935 specifically to meet the Empire Air Mail Scheme's requirements. Two versions were produced: the S.30 for transatlantic operations, nine of which were built, and the earlier S.23, which had insufficient range for transatlantic flying but proved highly successful on the England–Australia mail service. Forty-two 'Empire' boats were built in total; one of them, *Caledonia*, surveyed the first leg of the proposed transatlantic route, flying from Hythe to the Azores via Lisbon on 5 July 1937.

But it was an American flying boat that really conquered the Atlantic. The large Boeing 314 represented a major stride in flying boat technology. Pan American Airways ordered six, and, on 20 May 1939, one of them, named *Yankee Clipper* (which was to become Pan American's celebrated callsign), inaugurated a mail service between New York and Marseille, France. On 28 June, a second aircraft, *Dixie Clipper*, opened a new passenger service between New York and Marseille via Lisbon, Portugal, and, on 8 July, a passenger service was begun between New York and Southampton, England, with *Yankee Clipper*. In all, 12 aircraft were built, the

The Boeing 314 represented a major advance in commercial flying-boat technology. This aircraft inaugurated regular transatlantic passenger and freight services, and continued to operate throughout World War II.

Only two examples of the huge Junkers G 38 were built. The original aircraft, D-AZUR, was lost in a take-off crash in 1936, but the second, D-APIS, was taken over by the Luftwaffe for use as a transport in September 1939.

original six being followed by six of a more powerful variant, the Boeing 314A.

Meanwhile, French, Italian and Belgian aviators had gradually been opening up the continent of Africa. Aerial surveys began in 1919, using war-surplus aircraft such as the Bréguet XIV; by the end of the 1920s, the French had established an airmail network throughout their African colonies. Belgian services began in 1931, when a Fokker F.VII of the Belgian airline SABENA inaugurated a regular passenger service from Brussels to the Congo, although a number of proving flights had been made prior to that, the Belgians using British aircraft such as the Handley Page W.8e.

National Airline

April 1926 saw the creation of a new national airline in Germany. This was Deutsche Luft Hansa AG ('Lufthansa' was a later spelling), which initially began operations over eight routes. During the next three years, Luft Hansa airliners operated regular services to Denmark, Czechoslovakia, Norway, Italy, Spain, Russia, Great Britain and France, and, in 1930, a regular airmail service was opened between Vienna and Istanbul via Budapest, Belgrade and Sofia. In the following year, the world's biggest landplane, the Junkers G.38, made its debut on the Berlin–Amsterdam–London route; it was the forerunner of a whole range of new types that would put Luft Hansa at the forefront of European commercial aviation.

The most famous of these was the Junkers Ju 52 Tri-Motor, which entered Luft Hansa service in 1932; no fewer than 231 eventually passed through the airline's hands, although most of these would be operated on behalf of the Luftwaffe between 1939 and 1945. Thirty-eight were in service by the end of 1934, the year in which Luft Hansa began a scheduled service to Warsaw.

Yet within two years, an aircraft would make its appearance and overshadow all others in its class, thrusting the world of commercial aviation into a new era. It was the Douglas DC-3.

The Junkers Ju 52/3m was one of the most reliable aircraft in the world in the 1930s. As well as its commercial airline service, it made some prestige flights, including flying the Olympic torch from Greece to Berlin for the 1936 Olympic Games.

The Power to Fly

In the two decades following the end of World War I, the development of progressively more powerful engines enabled the major air arms of the world to take part in record-breaking exercises that pushed range, endurance, altitude and speed to the limits of known technology. Such exercises were to have a profound effect on the development of future military and civil aircraft, some of which were directly descended from machines produced specifically for record-breaking purposes. As far as long-range flying was concerned, the Royal Air Force led the field during this period. From the mid-1920s, RAF operations overseas were characterized by a series of record-breaking long-distance flights, which enabled the aircrew involved to acquire a vast amount of navigational experience over difficult terrain.

The Fairey Long Range Monoplane was a two-seater in which every available space was crammed with fuel. It failed in an attempt to make a nonstop flight around the world, but set up other distance records.

A lthough individual RAF crews and aircraft took part in many of the long-distance record attempts that were a feature of aviation development in the 1920s and 1930s, most truly significant long-range operations were mounted to develop navigational

Left: The Supermarine Southampton entered service with a coastal reconnaissance flight of the RAF in September 1925. Most of the 78 Southamptons built were Mk IIs with lightened duralumin hulls.

techniques or to test new equipment under arduous conditions. On 17 October

1927, for example, four Supermarine Southampton flying boats of the RAF's Far East Flight (later to become No. 205 Squadron) left Felixstowe on the first leg of a long-range flight that was intended primarily to test the strength of the Southampton's hull under prolonged operational conditions. On 15 December, the flying boats reached Bombay after 16 stages; on 27 December, they set off for Singapore, arriving on 28 February 1928 after 13 stops en route. Between 21 May and 15 September 1928, the four Southamptons, still in formation, made the Singapore–Sydney round trip in 29 stages. Finally, from 1 November to 10 December, they made a tour of various points in the Far East, including Manila, Hong Kong, Tourane and Bangkok, before returning to their base at Singapore. During the whole of the journey, since leaving England, they had covered 44,443km (27,000 miles).

From 1929, the RAF was much preoccupied with the development of nonstop long-range flying, and to this end the Fairey Aviation Company designed a special Long Range Monoplane, a two-seater in which every available space was crammed with fuel. In this machine, on 24 April 1929, Squadron Leader A.G. Jones-Williams and Flight Lieutenant N.H. Jenkins set out from RAF Cranwell in Lincolnshire in a bid to establish a world nonstop flight record. They failed, but landed at Karachi on 26 April after covering a distance of 6688km (4156 miles) in 50 hours 48 minutes.

Three years later, these two airmen were to lose their lives in a tragic accident when their Fairey Monoplane crashed in the Atlas Mountains near Tunis on another long-range flight.

Endurance Records

In 1930, Britain seemed on the verge of setting up some endurance records with the use of two airships, the R.100, built by Vickers and designed by a talented young engineer called Barnes Wallis, and the R.101, built by the Air Ministry. The R.100 was a good design; the R.101 was a disaster, and on 5 October 1930 it crashed into a hillside near Beauvais, France, on the first leg of a flight to India, with the loss of 38 lives. After this accident, the R.100 was grounded and never flew again. The era of the big rigid commercial airships lived on for a while in Germany's *Graf Zeppelin* and her sister ship, *Hindenburg*, but that, too, ended abruptly on 6 May 1936 when *Hindenburg* exploded and burned at her mooring mast at Lakehurst, New Jersey, with the loss of 35 lives. It was a miracle that 62 people survived.

The distance record that Jones-Williams and Jenkins had set out to beat in 1929 had then been held by Charles Lindbergh; this was beaten in July 1931 by two more Americans,

Unlike the Vickers-designed R.100, the R.101, a government venture, was ill-conceived from the start, and should never have been permitted to embark on its ill-fated flight to India.

Russell Boardman and John Polando, who set up a nonstop record of just over 8000km (5000 miles) on a flight from New York to Istanbul. On 6 February 1933, the RAF set out to better this; the aircraft, once again, was a Fairey Long Range Monoplane, and the crew consisted of Squadron Leader O.R. Gayford and Flight Lieutenant E. Nicholetts. Their aircraft, K1991, was

equipped with three altimeters, an autopilot which had been tested by various RAF units – particularly No. 7 Squadron, which operated Vickers Virginias in the long-range bombing role – and roller bearings on the wheels to assist take-off at an all-up weight of 7700kg (17,000lb). Extra 3780-litre (1000-gallon) fuel tanks had also been fitted into the wings.

K1991 left Cranwell and touched down at Walvis Bay, southwest Africa, on 8 February after a nonstop flight of 57 hours 25 minutes, having covered a distance of 8544.16km (5309.24 miles) at an average speed of 150km/h (93mph). On 12 February, the aircraft flew on to Cape Town, where a new Napier Lion engine was fitted before the flight back to England.

The nonstop distance record set up by Gayford and Nicholetts stood until

Right: The R.101's prestige flight to India ended in disaster and tangled wreckage on a hillside near Beauvais, France. That accident cost the lives of 38 people and was to bring an end to airship development in Britain.

1938, when it was beaten by two Vickers Wellesley long-range bombers of the RAF Long Range Development Flight. In July 1938, a detachment of four aircraft under the command of Squadron Leader R.G. Kellett flew from Cranwell in Lincolnshire to Ismailia in Egypt via the Persian Gulf, in preparation for an attempt on the world record for the greatest distance flown in a straight line. On 5 November, three of the aircraft took off from Ismailia to fly direct to Australia. One was obliged to land at Keopang, in the island of Timor in the Netherlands East Indies, but the other

two aircraft flew on in deteriorating weather to reach Darwin after covering a straight-line distance of 11,526km (7162 miles) in 48 hours.

High-Altitude Flight

The RAF also succeeded in establishing a number of altitude records in the 1930s, a High Altitude Flight having been established at Farnborough. One of its objectives was to assess the ability of a pilot to withstand prolonged high-altitude flight with a view to future reconnaissance tasks. The aircraft involved was

the Bristol Type 138A, which had been specially developed for the task; the pilot who set out to establish a new altitude record in it was Squadron Leader F.R.D. Swain. Taking off from Farnborough, Hampshire, on 28 September 1936, and fitted with a special pressure suit made of rubberized fabric and a helmet with a large double plastic faceplate, Swain

succeeded in reaching a record height of 15,223m (49,944ft). The Italians captured the altitude record in 1937, only to lose it again when the 138A reached a new altitude of 16,440m (53,937ft) on 30 June that year, the pilot on this occasion being Flight Lieutenant M.J. Adam.

Left: The prototype Vickers Wellesley, built as a private venture, first flew on 19 June 1935. Its most important feature was its geodetic construction, a method first developed by Barnes Wallis for the R-100 airship.

Right: The Bristol 138A monoplane was specifically developed for high-altitude research, the aim being to assess a pilot's ability to withstand lengthy flights at extreme altitudes in order to carry out reconnaissance tasks.

The evolution of high-performance engines in Britain, the United States, France and Italy during the 1920s and early 1930s was synonymous with record-breaking and trophy-capturing attempts. In Britain, while Rolls-Royce and Napier were eventually to emerge as the principal runners in the field, it was the Fairey Aviation Company which, at least in the early days, was the quickest to appreciate the advantages of marrying a high-performance powerplant to a very clean airframe. In September 1923, Richard Fairey watched a US Navy pilot, David Rittenhouse, capture the Schneider Trophy at Bournemouth in a Curtiss CR-3 biplane, with another CR-3 coming in second. Both aircraft were equipped with 298kW (400hp) Curtiss D-12 engines, and in 1924 Fairey went to the United States to inspect this powerplant. He was impressed enough to buy a batch, and at once set about designing an aircraft to fit the engine.

The Curtiss CR-3 racing seaplane won the 1923 Schneider Trophy, another CR-3 taking second place. Their victory gave the impetus for the development of powerful British aero-engines.

The result was the Fairey Fox, which was the cleanest light bomber of its day and was at least 80km/h (50mph) faster than contemporary fighters.

The Supermarine S.5 was powered by a Napier Lion engine. It is seen here with Flight Lieutenant S.N. Webster AFC, who flew it to victory in the 1927 Schneider Trophy contest, which was held in Venice.

The Schneider Trophy contest provided huge impetus to aero-engine development. The trophy – or La Coupe d'Aviation Maritime Jacques Schneider, to give it its correct title – had originated in 1912, when Schneider first offered the 25,000 franc trophy, together with a similar sum of money, to be competed for by seaplanes of any nationality over a course of at least 150 nautical miles (277.8km) in length.

Seaplane Speed Record
In 1927, for the first time, the British entry in the contest was an all-RAF affair, and a unit known as the High Speed Flight was formed for the occasion, although this did not achieve official status until April 1928. Meanwhile, two Supermarine S.5 floatplanes had been shipped to Venice, where the 1927 contest was to be held; the aircraft differed slightly from one another in that one, N219 – which was to be flown by Flight Lieutenant O.E. Worsley – had a direct-drive Napier Lion VIIB engine, while the other, N220 (Flight Lieutenant S.N. Webster) had a geared version of this powerplant. In the event, it was Webster's S.5 that won the race with an

Powered by a Rolls-Royce 'R' engine, the Supermarine S.6B captured the Schneider Trophy for Britain for all time on 13 September 1932, piloted by Flight Lieutenant J.W. Boothman.

powered by a 1417kW (1900hp) Rolls-Royce 'R' racing engine, while the Gloster Aircraft Company produced the Gloster–Napier VI, powered by a 1044kW (1400hp) Lion VIID engine. In the event, the Gloster aircraft were withdrawn because of engine problems, and it was one of the S.6s, flown by Flying Officer H.R.D. Waghorn, that went on to win the contest with a speed of 528.86km/h (328.63mph). On 12 September, one of the other High Speed Flight pilots, Squadron Leader A.H. Orlebar, flew this aircraft (N247) to a new world seaplane record speed of 575.65km/h (357.7mph).

A Permanent Tropy

The Schneider Trophy contest was now held every two years, and early in 1931 the British government announced that it was not prepared to subsidize RAF participation on grounds of cost. The news was received bitterly by everyone involved because Britain had won two consecutive contests; if she won a third, she would keep the trophy permanently. In the end, it was that great patriot Lady Houston who stepped into the breach with an offer of £100,000. Time was short so, instead of initiating a new design, Mitchell modified the two existing S.6s by fitting them with enlarged floats and redesignating them S.6As, then building

average speed of 453km/h (281.49mph), with Worsley's aircraft coming second. None of the other competitors completed the course. During the contest, which was held on 26 September, Webster also set up a 100km (62-mile) closed circuit world seaplane speed record of 456.49km/h (283.66mph).

There was no contest in 1928, but high-speed development work was carried on at Felixstowe, Suffolk, by the High Speed Flight under Flight Lieutenant D. d'Arcy Greig. It was he who, in the course of the year, set up a new British seaplane speed record of 514.28km/h (319.57mph) in one of the S.5s. Then, in

February 1929, the Air Ministry once again decided to field a team for that year's Schneider Trophy race. At the Supermarine Aviation Works, the design team under a talented young engineer called Reginald Mitchell set about developing a new aircraft, the S.6, which was somewhat larger than the S.5 and

two new machines, based on the existing airframe but incorporating much more powerful 1752kW (2350hp) Rolls-Royce 'R' engines. The new aircraft were designated S.6B.

Suddenly, the British found themselves with no competitors. The Italians could

not produce an aircraft in time, and the French entry had crashed during trials, killing its pilot. Nevertheless, Britain allowed the 'race' to go ahead, and, on 13 September 1932, Flight Lieutenant J.W. Boothman flew S.6B over the seven laps of the 50km

The Bristol Bulldog was adopted in 1929 as the RAF's standard day and night fighter. This example is a production Mk IIA powered by a Bristol Jupiter IIIF engine.

(31-mile) course at an average speed of 547.3km/h (340.08mph). That same afternoon, Flight Lieutenant G.H. Stainforth set up a new world speed record of 610km/h (379.05mph) in the other S.6B, S1596. Later, on 29 September, Stainforth pushed the absolute world speed record to 655.78km/h (407.5mph).

The combination of Reginald Mitchell's design and a superb aero-engine had brought the Schneider Trophy back to Britain for all time, and Supermarine's racing seaplanes contributed to the development of high-speed aerodynamics and high-powered engines that, within

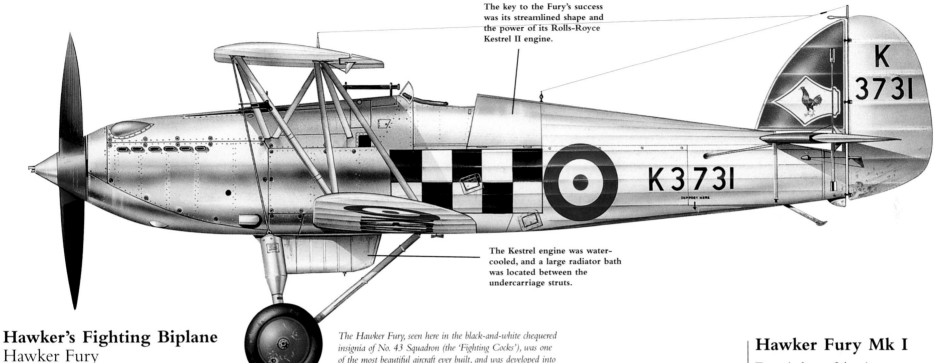

The key to the Fury's success was its streamlined shape and the power of its Rolls-Royce Kestrel II engine.

The Kestrel engine was water-cooled, and a large radiator bath was located between the undercarriage struts.

Hawker's Fighting Biplane
Hawker Fury

The Hawker Fury, seen here in the black-and-white chequered insignia of No. 43 Squadron (the 'Fighting Cocks'), was one of the most beautiful aircraft ever built, and was developed into the Hurricane monoplane.

a decade, would help the nation to survive her hour of greatest peril.

During the first three years of the 1930s, the RAF's principal fighter type was the Bristol Bulldog, which equipped 10 squadrons and which, with a top speed of 290km/h (180mph), was a good deal faster than the fighters it replaced. Its contemporary was the Hawker Fury,

A Gloster Gauntlet in the markings of the Royal Danish Air Force. A number of Gauntlet Mk IIs were licence-built in Denmark during 1936–38. The RAF's Gauntlets were used as trainers from 1940.

the epitome of British fighter biplane design and probably the most beautiful aircraft of its day. The Bulldog was replaced in RAF service by the Gloster Gauntlet, the last of the RAF's open-cockpit fighter biplanes. By the time it entered squadron service in 1935, radical changes in fighter design were already being implemented as a result of the development of new monoplane types, powered by the new Rolls-Royce Merlin engine and given an unprecedented armament of eight Colt-Browning .303in machine guns. The adoption of

this armament was a consequence of a vigorous campaign conducted by Squadron leader Ralph Sorley of Flying Operations 1 (FO1) in the Air Ministry, who wrote later:

'The choice lay between the 0.303 gun, the 0.50 gun and a new 20mm Hispano gun which was attracting the attention of the French, and in fact of other countries in Europe who could obtain knowledge of it from them. During 1934 this gun was experimental and details of its performance were hard to establish. On the other hand, designs

Hawker Fury Mk I

Type: single-seat fighter interceptor

Powerplant: one 392kW (525hp) Rolls-Royce Kestrel IIS 12-cylinder Vee piston engine

Maximum speed: 333km/h (207mph)

Ferry range: 491km (305 miles)

Service ceiling: 8535m (28,000ft)

Weights: empty 1190kg (2623lb); maximum take-off weight 1583kg (3490lb)

Armament: two fixed forward-firing .303in Vickers Mk III machine guns

Dimensions:		
span		9.14m (30ft)
length		8.13m (26ft 8in)
height		3.1m (10 ft 2in)
wing area		23.41m² (252sq ft)

K6132 was one of the first four production Gladiators to be
issued to the RAF, joining No. 72 Squadron at Church
Fenton, Yorkshire, on 22 February 1937. The squadron
continued to use Gladiators until April 1939.

'Hurribombers' and Tank Busters
Hawker Hurricane

Unlike contemporaries such as the Spitfire, the Hurricane had a fabric-covered rear fuselage, which it retained throughout its production history.

Although outclassed as an interceptor by 1941, the Rolls-Royce Merlin-powered Hurricane served as a valuable fighter-bomber in Europe, Asia and Africa.

of better 0.303 guns than the Vickers had been tested over the preceding years with the result that the American Browning from the Colt Automatic Weapon Corporation appeared to offer the best possibilities from the point of view of rate of fire.

'Our own development of guns of this calibre had been thorough but slow, since we were in the throes of economizing, and considerable stocks of old Vickers guns still remained from the First War. The acceptance of a new gun in the numbers likely to be required was a heavy financial and manufacturing

commitment. The 0.50-inch on the other hand had developed little, and although it possessed a better hitting power the rate of fire was slow and it was a heavy item, together with its ammunition, in respect of installed weight. The controversy was something of a nightmare during 1933–34. It was a choice on which the whole concept of the fighter would depend, but a trial staged on the ground with eight 0.303s was sufficiently convincing and satisfying to enable them to carry the day.'

Inadequate Armament
It was just as well, for otherwise the new generation of RAF monoplane fighters might have gone to war with a wholly inadequate armament of four machine

guns. One type in fact did so, but it was a biplane, the Gloster Gladiator, which entered service in February 1937 and went on to give gallant service during the early months of World War II in both Europe and North Africa.

The first of the monoplane designs, the Hawker Hurricane, evolved under the leadership of Sydney Camm to meet Air Ministry Specification F.36/34; the prototype flew on 6 November 1935, powered by a Merlin 'C' engine of 738kW (990hp), and began service trials at Martlesham Heath in March 1936. Hawker, confident of its design's success, began preparations for the production of 1000 examples before the first Air Ministry order was forthcoming. An order for 600 machines materialized in June 1936. The

Hawker Hurricane Mark I

Type: single-seat fighter

Powerplant: one 768kW (1030hp) Rolls-Royce Merlin III 12-cylinder Vee engine

Maximum speed: 521km/h (324mph)

Ferry range: 716km (445 miles)

Service ceiling: 10,120m (33,200 ft)

Weights: empty 2308kg (5085lb); maximum take-off 3024kg (6661lb)

Armament: eight .303in fixed forward-firing machine guns in the leading edges of the wing

Dimensions:		
span	12.19m	(40ft)
length	9.55m	(31ft 4in)
height	4.07m	(13ft 4.5in)
wing area	23.97m²	(258sq ft)

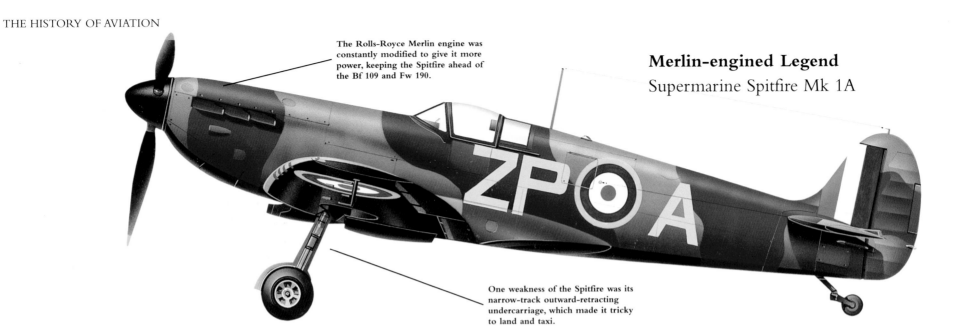

The Rolls-Royce Merlin engine was constantly modified to give it more power, keeping the Spitfire ahead of the Bf 109 and Fw 190.

Merlin-engined Legend
Supermarine Spitfire Mk 1A

One weakness of the Spitfire was its narrow-track outward-retracting undercarriage, which made it tricky to land and taxi.

Supermarine Spitfire Mk.VA

Type: single-seat fighter/interceptor

Powerplant: one 1103kW (1440hp) Rolls-Royce Merlin 45 Vee piston engine

Maximum speed: 594km/h (374mph) at 5945m (13,000ft)

Ferry range: 1827km (1135 miles)

Service ceiling: 11,125m (37,000ft)

Weights: empty 2267kg (5,000lb); loaded 2911kg (6,400lb)

Armament: eight .303in Browning machine guns with 350 rounds per gun

Dimensions:
length	9.12m	(29ft 11in)
span	11.23m	(36ft 10in)
height	3.02m	(11ft 5in)
wing area	22.48m²	(242sq ft)

first of these – after some delay caused by the decision to install the Merlin II engine – flew on 12 October 1937, an initial batch being delivered to No. 111 Squadron at Northolt in November.

The other eight-gun monoplane type, the Supermarine Spitfire, was designed by a team under the direction of Reginald Mitchell, and traced its ancestry to the S.6 series of Schneider Trophy racing seaplanes. The prototype made its first flight on 5 March 1936 and, like the Hurricane, was powered by a Rolls-Royce Merlin 'C' engine. A contract for the production of 310 Spitfires was issued by the Air Ministry in June 1936, at the same time as the Hurricane contract, and the first examples were delivered to No. 19 Squadron at Duxford in August 1938. Eight other squadrons had rearmed with

Spitfires by September 1939, and two auxiliary units (Nos. 603 and 609) were undergoing operational training.

In the United States, despite the success of the liquid-cooled Curtiss D.12, aero-engine manufacturers – notably Wright and Pratt & Whitney – concentrated on the development of radial engines for the future generation of combat aircraft. Both firms were to make outstanding contributions to military aviation in World War II, producing engines that achieved a remarkable reputation for reliability – a vital factor in the Pacific theatre, where operations involved long hours of overwater flying. On the other hand, the US in-line engine that was in production at the end of 1939 – the Allison V-1710, which powered the Curtiss P-40 and early variants of the North American P-51

Mustang – was unreliable. In fact, it was replaced in later versions of the Mustang by the Packard-built Rolls-Royce Merlin. The result was an exceptional combination of engine and airframe.

In Germany, aero-engine development progressed rapidly during the early 1930s, with four main companies involved: Daimler-Benz, Junkers, BMW and Siemens-Halske. The first two built inverted 12-cylinder liquid-cooled engines and the other two air-cooled radials. The Daimler-Benz engine was also designed to take a 20mm gun fitted in the V formed by the cylinder blocks and firing through the hollow shaft of the propeller reduction gear. This arrangement produced an unexpected spin-off in that the supercharger had to be repositioned, and it proved

The Shark-mouthed Hawks
Curtiss P-40 Tomahawk Mk IIB

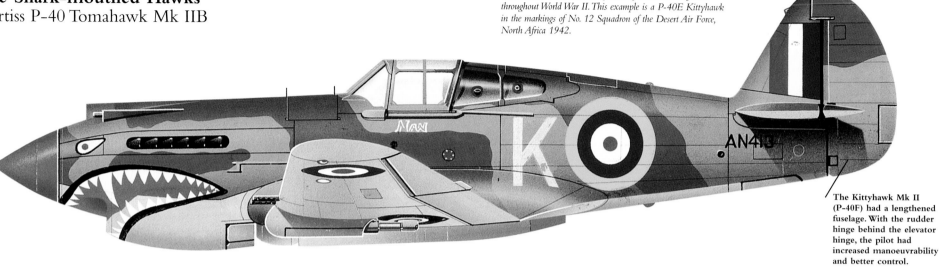

The Curtiss P-40 was widely used by the Allied air forces throughout World War II. This example is a P-40E Kittyhawk in the markings of No. 12 Squadron of the Desert Air Force, North Africa 1942.

The Kittyhawk Mk II (P-40F) had a lengthened fuselage. With the rudder hinge behind the elevator hinge, the pilot had increased manoeuvrability and better control.

impracticable to fit the carburettor to it in the normal way. The designers tried several variations, but in the end they dispensed with the carburettor altogether and instead used a multi-point fuel injection system spraying directly on to the cylinders. The result was that the Daimler engine continued to perform well during all combat manoeuvres – unlike the Rolls-Royce Merlin, which tended to cut out because of a negative *g* effect on the carburettor when the aircraft was inverted or when the pilot put the nose down to dive on an enemy.

Modern Air Arm
Since 1922, German rearmament had been progressing in secret, with the assistance of the Soviet Union. A steady flow of German officer cadets entered various military training establishments in the USSR; many went to a flying school that had been set up at Lipetsk and was entirely under German control. When Adolf Hitler and the Nazi Party rose to power in Germany in 1933, and embarked on an open programme of rearmament, the first problem they had to consider – as far as the creation of a modern air arm was concerned – was that Germany was still disarmed and vulnerable and therefore faced with the prospect of a preventive war, waged by the surrounding countries to stop her resurrection as a military power. France was Hitler's greatest fear, and France had a large army. The Germans, therefore, had no real choice in deciding whether their air force was to be built around a nucleus of strategic bomber aircraft, as was

Britain's, or a nucleus of tactical ground support aircraft protected by an umbrella of fighters, as was France's.

The designer Ernst Heinkel rapidly moved into a leading position, thanks to his willingness to design and build every type of aircraft required by the crash re-equipment programme. He produced the He 51 fighter, which evolved through a series of small, streamlined biplane fighter prototypes, culminating in the He 51 that first flew in mid-1933. In all, 700 He 51 production aircraft were built. The type was succeeded in Luftwaffe service by the Arado Ar 68 biplane fighter, which appeared in prototype form in the summer of 1934.

Heinkel proposed a monoplane fighter, the He 100, but it was rejected, and it is for his Heinkel He 111 bomber that he

Curtiss P-40N Warhawk

Type: single-seat interceptor and fighter bomber

Powerplant: one 1015kW (1360hp) Allison V-1710-81 inline piston engine

Maximum speed: 609km/h (378mph) at 3210m (10,500ft)

Ferry range: 386km (240 miles)

Service ceiling: 11,630m (38,160ft)

Weights: empty 2724kg (6045lb); loaded 4018kg (8858lb)

Armament: six 12.7mm (.50cal.) machine guns in wing; provision for 227kg (500lb) bomb or 197-litre (US 52-gallon) droptank under fuselage

Dimensions:

span	11.42m	(37ft 6in)
length	10.20m	(33ft 6in)
height	3.77m	(12ft 4in)
wing area	21.95m²	(236sq ft)

is best remembered. The Heinkel He 111 was designed early in 1934 as a high-speed transport and as a bomber for the still-secret Luftwaffe. The first prototype, the He 111a (later redesignated He 111 V1), flew for the first time on 24 February 1935, powered by two 492kW (660hp) BMW VI engines, and was followed by the V2, which made its maiden flight on 12 March 1935. This aircraft, D-ALIX, was a transport version with a reduced span and a straight trailing edge; it was delivered to Luft Hansa and named *Rostock*, and was later used for clandestine reconnaissance missions. The He 111 V3, D-ALES, was a bomber with a further

reduced wingspan, and was forerunner of the He 111A production model.

Heinkel's He 100 fighter was rejected by the German Air Ministry in favour of a fighter designed by his rival, Willi Messerschmitt. Development of the famous Bf 109 fighter (the prefix 'Bf', incidentally, is a company designation denoting Bayerische Flugzeugwerke, the Bavarian Aircraft Factory where the type was first manufactured) began in 1933, when the Reichsluftministerium

The Heinkel He 51 was one of the Luftwaffe's first standard fighters, the other being the Arado Ar 68. The He 51 was widely used in the Spanish Civil War, and many of the Luftwaffe's aces gained their first victories while flying it.

(RLM) issued a requirement for a new monoplane fighter. When the prototype Bf 109V-1 flew for the first time in September 1935, it was powered rather ironically by a 518kW (695hp) Rolls-Royce Kestrel engine, as

the 455kW (610hp) Junkers Jumo 210A which was intended for it was not yet available. It was installed in the second prototype, which flew in January 1936.

Fighter Tactics

Professor Willi Messerschmitt originally intended the 109's thin, frail wings to be left free of guns, but when the Luftwaffe High Command learned that the Spitfire and Hurricane were to be fitted with eight machine guns it insisted that the

The third Heinkel He 111 prototype, D-ALES, was the first bomber variant and was the forerunner of the first production model. The He 111 was an orthodox cantilever low-wing monoplane with a fully retractable undercarriage.

The Spitfire Challenged
Messerschmitt BF 109

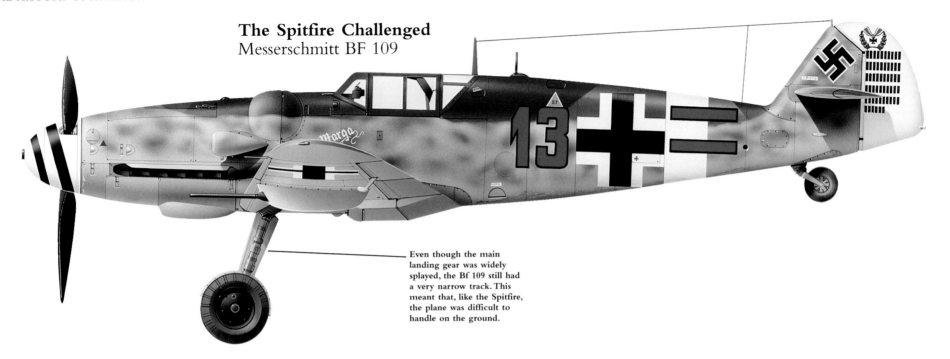

Even though the main landing gear was widely splayed, the Bf 109 still had a very narrow track. This meant that, like the Spitfire, the plane was difficult to handle on the ground.

Messerschmitt Bf 109G-6

Type: single-seat fighter and fighter-bomber

Powerplant: one 1100kW (1474hp) Daimler-Benz DB 605AM 12-cylinder inverted-Vee engine

Maximum speed: 621km/h (386mph); climb to 5700m (18,700ft) in 6 minutes

Ferry range: 1000km (621 miles)

Service ceiling: 11,550m (37,890ft)

Weights: empty 2673kg (5893lb); maximum take-off weight 3400kg (7496lb)

Armament: one 20mm/30mm fixed forward-firing cannon in engine installation; two 13mm fixed forward-firing machine guns in forward fuselage, external bomb load 250kg (551lb)

Dimensions: span   9.92m (32ft 6.5in)
            length   8.85m (29ft 0.5in)
            height   2.5m (8ft 2.5in)
            wing area 16.40 m² (173.3sq ft)

Bf 109 carry wing-mounted guns, too. Messerschmitt was therefore forced to design a new wing, with bulges for the ammunition boxes of the 20mm cannon mounted on each side. Three of the Bf 109 prototypes were evaluated in Spain in February and March 1937, and were followed by 24 Bf 109B-2s, which immediately proved superior to any other fighter engaged in the Spanish Civil War. It was the use of the Bf 109 in Spain that enabled the Luftwaffe to develop the fighter tactics that enabled it to wreak havoc among its opponents in the early years of World War II.

In the spring of 1939, the Nazi propaganda machine spread the word that a derivative of the Bf 109, the 109R, had captured the world air speed record. It was a blatant lie; the aircraft involved was a new design, the Me 209, built specifically to capture the world air speed record, which it did by logging a speed of 755.138km/h (469.22mph) on 26 April 1939. This record for a piston-engine type was to stand for more than 30 years, until it was beaten by a Grumman F8F Bearcat in August 1969. An ugly little machine, and one described by its pilots as a brute to fly, the Me 209 first flew on 1 August 1938. Four Me 209s were built, the second being destroyed in a crash.

Germany was a principal player in the Spanish Civil War (1936–39), providing weapons and volunteers to the Nationalists. On the opposite (Loyalist/Republican) side, and emerging from it with far less expertise, was the Soviet Union. Aviation development in the USSR was slow in the chaotic aftermath of the civil war, and it was only in the 1930s that real technological strides began to be made. On 25 February 1932, all civil aviation activities came under the control of the Chief Directorate of the Civil Air Fleet, and on 25 March the State airline was renamed Aeroflot. New transport aircraft of indigenous design were progressively introduced on Aeroflot's internal routes, but there were still no international services in 1939 other than those to Mongolia and Afghanistan. Nevertheless, Soviet aviators and aircraft carried out important pioneering long-range work

Difficult, Dangerous, but Fast
Messerschmitt Me 209

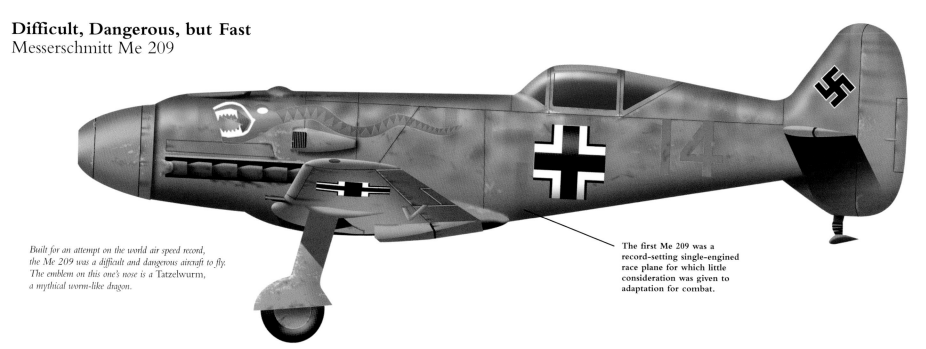

Built for an attempt on the world air speed record, the Me 209 was a difficult and dangerous aircraft to fly. The emblem on this one's nose is a Tatzelwurm, *a mythical worm-like dragon.*

The first Me 209 was a record-setting single-engined race plane for which little consideration was given to adaptation for combat.

over the Arctic, establishing a number of long-distance records in the process. Only World War II brought a halt to plans for a transpolar service to the United States.

Considerable Strides

In the military aviation field, the USSR made considerable strides in the 1930s. In 1933, the Polikarpov Design Bureau produced the I-13 biplane, forerunner of the famous I-15, which made its first flight in October of that year. The I-15 was a biplane with a fixed undercarriage; the upper wing was gull-shaped, giving an excellent view forwards and upwards. It was fitted with a 559kW (750hp) M-25 engine (the licence-built version of the American Wright Cyclone), which gave

it a top speed of 354km/h (220 mph). It was armed with four .303in machine guns, and there was provision for light bombs in racks under the wings. In 1934, the I-15 was followed by the I-15bis, with an improved M-25V engine that raised its top speed to 370km/h (230mph). In a bid to raise the speed still further, Polikarpov then produced the I-153, featuring a retractable undercarriage, but the maximum speed of the early I-153s (386km/h, or 240mph) was still insufficient when compared with that of the new fighter aircraft that were beginning to enter service with the principal European air forces. The I-153, dubbed Chaika (Seagull) because of its distinctive wing

shape, was a first-rate combat aircraft and subsequently proved its worth in air fighting, being able to out-turn almost every aircraft that opposed it in action. It was the last single-seat fighter biplane to be series-produced in the USSR.

On 31 December 1933, two months after the appearance of the I-15 biplane, a new Polikarpov fighter made its first flight. This was the I-16, a low-wing monoplane with two wing-mounted .303in guns and a large 358kW (480hp) M-22 engine. The I-16 was the first production monoplane in the world to feature a retractable undercarriage. In 1938, the I-16 Type 17 was tested, armed with two wing-mounted cannon. This version was produced in large numbers.

Messerschmitt Me 209

Type: piston-engined racer/experimental fighter

Powerplant: one 1397kW (1900hp) Daimler-Benz 603G liquid-cooled in-line engine

Maximum speed: 678km/h (423mph)

Service ceiling: 11,000m (36,080ft)

Weights: empty 3339kg (7346lb); loaded 4085kg (8987lb)

Armament: (fighter variant) one 30mm MK 108 cannon; two 13mm MG 131 machine guns

Dimensions: span   10.95m (35ft 11in)
          length   9.74m (31ft 11in)
          height   4.00m (13ft 1in)
          wing area 17.2m² (185sq ft)

Altogether, 6555 I-16s were built before production ended in 1940.

The I-16 was to see considerable action during its career, starting with the Spanish Civil War. The first machines to arrive in Spain went into battle on 15 November 1936, when they provided air cover for a Republican offensive against Nationalist forces which were advancing on Valdemoro, Sesena and Equivias. The I-16 – nicknamed Mosca (Fly) by the Republicans and Rata (Rat) by the Nationalists – proved markedly superior to the Heinkel He 51. It was also faster than its most numerous Nationalist opponent, the Fiat CR.32, although the Italian fighter was slightly more manoeuvrable and provided a better gun platform.

Another Soviet type to see action in the Spanish Civil War was the Tupolev SB-2, which was almost certainly the most capable light bomber in service anywhere in the world in the mid-1930s. It was the first aircraft of modern stressed-skin construction to be produced in the USSR, and in numerical terms was also the most important bomber of its day. The story of the SB-2 (the initials stand for Skorostnoy Bombardirovshchik, or

Right: First flown in 1933, the Fiat CR.32 was a development of the CR.30, which it closely resembled, although it was considerably faster. The CR.32 saw widespread service with the Nationalist air arm during the Spanish Civil War.

Below: The Polikarpov I-15Bis (I-152) version of the I-15 had improved pilot visibility. Mass-produced from 1937, the aircraft had a redesigned upper wing of increased span. Its wheel spats were usually discarded.

high-speed bomber) began in the early 1930s, when Andrei N. Tupolev embarked on design studies of a fast tactical bomber. Considering the official requirement to be inadequate, he built two prototypes according to the Air Force Technical Office specification, and a third according to his own. All three prototypes, designated ANT-40, ANT-40-1 and ANT-40-2, flew in 1934, and Tupolev's version, the ANT-40-2, proved the best. The type was ordered into production, entering service in 1936, and 6967 aircraft were built before production ended in 1941.

Japanese Advances

In both the USSR and Japan, development of monoplane fighters and bombers proceeded on more or less parallel lines in the early 1930s, although there were separate requirements for the Imperial Japanese Navy and Army. These resulted, respectively, in the Mitsubishi A5M and the Nakajima Ki-27, both of which were powered by radial engines

and had fixed undercarriages. Both types had been in service for only a short time when their merits were put to the test in combat. In July 1937, the Japanese launched a full-scale invasion of China, quickly capturing urban centres along the Chinese coast and pushing rapidly along the Yangtse River as Chinese forces retreated westwards. During the initial period of operations, the Imperial Japanese Army left the brunt of the air fighting to the navy, limiting its activity to air support of ground operations along the Manchurian border while new units were formed. The Imperial Japanese Navy was well placed to conduct offensive air

The first production Dewoitine D.510, seen here, differed only slightly from the D.500 prototype, which flew for the first time on 18 June 1932. It represented a big leap forward in French fighter design.

operations. Its first-line fighter squadrons were now equipped with Mitsubishi A5Ms, its carrier-based attack squadrons with the Yokosuka B4Y bomber and its land-based bomber squadrons with the twin-engined Mitsubishi G3M.

French Designs

France, which had played such a vibrant role in the development of aviation since the Montgolfier brothers launched their first balloon, lay in the doldrums in the

1930s, its aviation industry becalmed in a sea of political indecision and industrial unrest. France's first cantilever low-wing monoplanes were those of the handsome all-metal D.500 series, which was evolved in response to a 1930 requirement for a machine to replace the biplanes and parasol monoplanes then in service. The prototype D.500 flew on 18 June 1932, and development culminated in the D.510, which first flew in August 1934. The first French monoplane fighter with a retractable undercarriage and enclosed cockpit was the Morane-Saulnier MS.405, the production version of which, the MS.406, flew in January 1939. The MS.406 was a rugged cannon-armed fighter, and 225 had been delivered by August 1939, equipping four Escadres de Chasse (fighter wings). In terms of all-round performance, the Morane was inferior to its British and German

counterparts, the Hawker Hurricane and Messerschmitt Bf 109E. France's other first-line fighter was an American type, the Curtiss Hawk 75A. An initial order for 100 of these machines had been placed in May 1938, and in 1939 – when it was at last obvious that the French industry was in no position to match German fighter production – follow-on orders were placed for a further 100 Hawk 75A-2s and 135 Hawk A-3s. Two French fighter units began conversion to the type in March 1939, and, by the end of August, 100 Hawks were operational. Bomber development lagged behind, and although some superlative types – such as the Lioré et

Right: Italy's main bomber type during World War II, the Savoia-Marchetti SM.79 Sparviero (Sparrowhawk), performed extremely well, especially as a torpedo-bomber against Allied convoys.

Left: A Boeing P-26C of the 19th Pursuit Squadron, 18th Pursuit Group, USAAC, pictured over Oahu, Hawaii, in 1939. Known as the 'Peashooter', the P-26 saw some action in the Philippines early in 1942.

Below: The Martin B-10, a smooth, sleek monoplane with a fully enclosed bomb bay and retractable main undercarriage, was a good example of what a designer could achieve when not limited by an official specification.

Olivier LeO 45 – were on the point of entering service, it would be some time before they were available in any numbers.

Inspired by dreams of creating a new Roman empire, Benito Mussolini wanted to build Italy's military forces to formidable strength. In fact, Italy was the first of the European powers to launch a determined policy of rearmament, and the aviation industry, building on the lessons of World War I, produced a number of practical combat aircraft designs, which were to give excellent service. In the early 1930s, the Italian Air Force's principal fighter type was the Fiat CR.30, designed in response to a requirement issued by Air Minister Italo Balbo for a 'super fighter'. It first flew on 5 March 1932. The first of 121 CR.30s was delivered in spring 1934, but the type was soon superseded by the more refined CR.32, which appeared in 1933. Considerably faster than the CR.30 and more manoeuvrable, it saw a great deal of action in the Spanish Civil War. It was succeeded by another biplane, the Fiat CR.42.

Castles in the Sky
Boeing B-17F

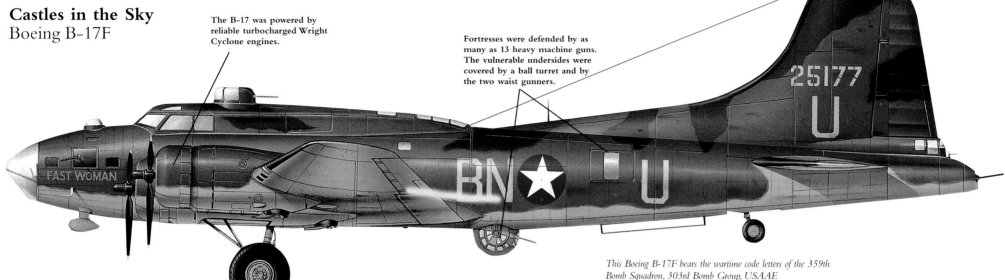

The B-17 was powered by reliable turbocharged Wright Cyclone engines.

Fortresses were defended by as many as 13 heavy machine guns. The vulnerable undersides were covered by a ball turret and by the two waist gunners.

This Boeing B-17F bears the wartime code letters of the 359th Bomb Squadron, 303rd Bomb Group, USAAF.

Boeing B-17G Flying Fortress

Type: 10-seat heavy bomber

Powerplant: four 895kW (1200hp) Wright R-1820-97 nine-cylinder radial engines

Maximum speed: 486km/h (302mph); climb to 6095m (20,000ft) in 37 minutes

Ferry range: 2897km (1800 miles)

Service ceiling: 10,850m (35,600ft)

Weights: empty 20,212kg (44,560lb); maximum take-off weight 32,659kg (72,000lb)

Armament: 10 0.5in machine guns in chin turret, each cheek position, in dorsal turret, in roof position, in ventral turret; in waist; in tail; and bomb load of 7983kg (17,600lb)

Dimensions: span   31.63m (103ft 9.4in)
            length   22.78m (74ft 9in)
            height   5.82m (19ft 1in)
            wing area 131.91m² (1420sq ft)

Although it was effective in the limited wars in which Italy was involved in the 1930s, the Regia Aeronautica's bomber force never matched that of the opposing Allied air forces during World War II, either in quality of the aircraft types used or in numbers. Typical examples of the bombers forming the backbone of the Regia Aeronautica were the three-engine machines produced by Savoia-Marchetti, a firm with considerable experience in the field of commercial aircraft design. One such design was the SM.73, an 18-passenger airliner with a tapered cantilever low wing and a fixed undercarriage; the military version was the SM.81 Pipistrello (Bat), a tri-motor which, when it made its service debut in 1935, represented a considerable advance over the Regia Aeronautica's existing bomber types. Fast, well armed and with a good range, it was used to good effect during the Italian campaign in Abyssinia, which began in October 1935; from August 1936 it was also used operationally during the Spanish Civil War. Another of Savoia-Marchetti's bombers that was developed from an airliner was the SM.79, which was also a tri-motor.

Monoplane Fighter
The United States, the nation that produced France's Curtiss Hawks, took its first step on the road of monoplane fighter design with the Boeing P-26, which first flew in March 1932. Deliveries of production P-26As to the US Army Air Corps began at the end of 1933. Pilots soon gave the little fighter the affectionate nickname 'Peashooter'.

The first modern fighter aircraft used by the US Army Air Corps was the Seversky P-35, development of which originated in 1935. Designed by Alexander Kartveli, it first flew in August 1935 and an order for 76 production models was placed by the Air Corps in June 1936, delivery taking place between July 1937 and August 1938. From the Curtiss stable came the P-40 Warhawk, the prototype of which flew in October 1938.

Contemporary with the P-40 was the Bell P-39 Airacobra, which flew in its original form in April 1938. The P-39 featured a 37mm cannon installed in the extreme nose and firing through the hub of the propeller shaft, the engine being positioned behind the pilot. Another feature, novel for its time, was a tricycle undercarriage. The P-39 underwent numerous modifications, not all of them for the better, before it was ordered into mass production in August 1939.

In the mid-1930s the standard US Army Air Corps bomber was the Martin B-10. Although it quickly became obsolete in comparison with the bombers then being produced in Europe, the B-10 was a very advanced aircraft when it first appeared in 1932. It was the first US bomber of all-metal construction to enter large-scale production, the first US warplane with turreted armament, and the first US Army Air Corps cantilever low-wing monoplane. The USAAC took delivery of 151 B-10s and a slightly improved version, the B-12.

Great improvements were on the horizon. In 1934, the USAAC issued a requirement for a long-range high-altitude daylight bomber. The prototype, with the designation Boeing Model 299, was powered by four 559kW (750hp) Pratt & Whitney Hornet engines and flew for the first time on 28 July 1935. Although it was later destroyed in an accident, the cause was attributed to human error and the project went ahead. It would emerge as one of the most famous bombers of all time, the B-17 Flying Fortress. Its rival was the Consolidated B-24, later named the Liberator. Produced in a number of variants for a host of operational and training tasks, the Consolidated B-24 Liberator was built in larger numbers

Poland's Gull-winged Fighter
PZL P.11

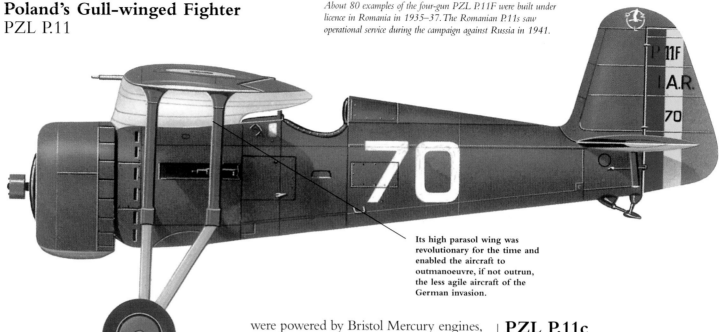

About 80 examples of the four-gun PZL P.11F were built under licence in Romania in 1935–37. The Romanian P.11s saw operational service during the campaign against Russia in 1941.

Its high parasol wing was revolutionary for the time and enabled the aircraft to outmanoeuvre, if not outrun, the less agile aircraft of the German invasion.

than any other US warplane of World War II, with 18,431 produced in total, and was delivered in greater quantities than any other bomber in aviation history.

German Onslaught
As the 1930s drew to a close, the eyes of the world became focused on Poland, sandwiched between Nazi Germany and the Soviet Union. At the end of August 1939, the Polish Air Force had some 436 operational aircraft. Poland's fighter squadrons were equipped with the PZL P.11, first delivered in 1934. Most P-11s

were powered by Bristol Mercury engines, built under licence by Skoda; the definitive version of the fighter was the P-11c, of which 175 were built. The P-11 was to have been replaced by a low-wing fighter monoplane, the P-50 Jastrzeb (Hawk), as part of a major expansion scheme, but military budget cuts resulted in the cancellation of an order for 300 P-50s, and more P-11s were purchased instead. A similar fate befell the twin-engine Wilk (Wolf), which was to have had the dual role of heavy long-range fighter and dive-bomber. One modern bomber type, the PZL P-37 Los (Elk), was in service, but there were only 60 of them.

It was not enough to stem the German onslaught that fell upon Poland at dawn on 1 September 1939.

PZL P.11c

Type: single-seat monoplane interceptor and light-attack fighter

Powerplant: one 373kW (500hp) Skoda-built Bristol Mercury VIS.2 radial piston engine

Maximum speed: 390km/h (242mph) at 5500m (18,000ft)

Initial climb rate: 5000m (16,400ft) in 6 minutes

Combat radius: maximum loaded range 700 km (435 mi.)

Service ceiling: 8000m (26,250ft)

Weights: maximum take-off weight 1800kg (3,960lb)

Armament: two .303 cal. machine guns

Dimensions:

span	10.72m (35ft 2in)
length	7.55 m (24ft 9in)
height	2.85 m (9ft 4in)
wing area	17.9 m² (167sq ft)

Handley Page Hampden of No. 455 Squadron, Royal Australian Air Force. Originally a Bomber Command unit, this unit was later transferred to Coastal Command and operated in the torpedo-bomber role.

Aviation in World War II: Blitzkrieg to the Bomb

By March 1939, with Germany dismembering Czechoslovakia, it was clear to both the British and French governments that their policy of appeasing Nazi Germany no longer held good. Somewhat belatedly, the British and French general staffs met to work out a common defensive policy against the Axis powers, which then comprised Germany and Italy. Germany's absorption of Czechoslovakia had been followed rapidly by the German invasion of Albania in April 1939, and the probability that Britain and France would be drawn into war if Germany attacked Poland now loomed large.

It was decided that a British Expeditionary Force (BEF), together with an Air Component and an Advanced Air Striking Force (AASF) of Bomber Command squadrons, with supporting fighters, should be sent to France; the British squadrons would be given full facilities on French airfields provided that their aircraft would not be used for the unrestricted bombing of German targets from these bases. There followed months of disagreement between the British and French on how the RAF squadrons were to be best employed.

The problems still had not been resolved when, at 0400 on 1 September 1939, a code word flashed out over the military communications network of the Luftwaffe High Command in Berlin to a score of airfields in eastern Germany. The code word – Ostmarkflug – was the signal to launch the air onslaught preceding the German invasion of Poland. At 0445, 15 minutes before the German armies rolled across the frontier, three Junkers Ju 87 Stuka dive-bombers attacked the railway line near the bridge at Dirschau, severing demolition cables and paving the way for the capture of this vital river crossing by an army task force.

The tactics used in the German assault on Poland involved, first of all, large-scale air attacks on Polish airfields and strategic positions, followed by armoured thrusts deep into enemy territory. Ahead of these armoured spearheads would go the dive-bombers, clearing the way for the tanks and attacking lines of

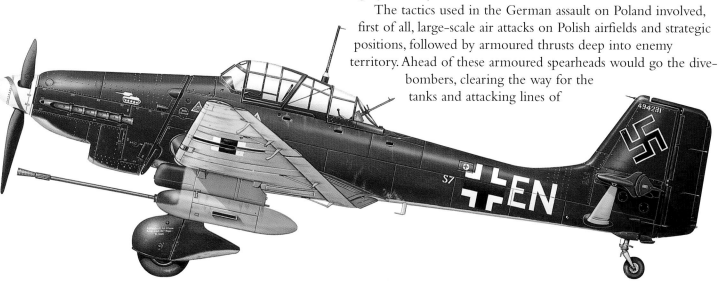

The Junkers Ju 87 Stuka was a formidable fighting machine when it first made its appearance, but it proved extremely vulnerable to fighter attack, which was its eventual downfall.

communication, while overhead the Luftwaffe's fighters would deal with what was left of the Polish Air Force. Such was Germany's concept of modern warfare. It was a concept that had a name: Blitzkrieg, or 'lightning war'. It had already been tested and proved under operational conditions, on the battlefields of the Spanish Civil War.

Finger Four

At this time the world's air forces generally employed close wingtip-to-wingtip battle formations, and the Luftwaffe fighter pilots soon found that these were totally unsuited to combat because they hampered free manoeuvring. They therefore evolved a combat formation based on a pair of fighters, separated by about 180m (200 yards), with the number two aircraft covering the leader's tail. Two pairs made up a Schwarm, to be known as a 'finger four' by the Allies because the four aircraft formed a similar pattern to the spread-out fingertips of the right hand, palm downwards, and a squadron formation was made up of these sections of four, deployed down-sun at staggered altitudes so that all quarters of the sky were covered.

The Polish Air Force could do little to oppose the Luftwaffe's might. On the outbreak of hostilities, it possessed about 450 aircraft of all types, including 140 fighters; however, these were mostly obsolescent PZL P.11s, which were outclassed by the Messerschmitts. By 17 September, although its fighters

claimed the destruction of 126 enemy aircraft, the Polish Air Force had lost 83 per cent of its machines and had practically ceased to exist as a fighting force. Moreover, Soviet forces, by agreement with the Germans, had just invaded the eastern part of the country.

The Luftwaffe was now able to roam unopposed across the sky, and, on 25 September, wave after wave of German bombers systematically pounded the Polish capital, Warsaw, into rubble. Two days later, with no hope left, Poland capitulated. Yet the Polish contribution to

Bristol Blenheim Mk IV bombers in formation. The Mk IV had a redesigned nose. Committed to almost suicidal daylight missions in the early months of World War II, it suffered massive casualties.

the fight against Nazi Germany was only just beginning, for thousands of Polish soldiers and airmen who escaped before the final collapse fought on valiantly in the Allied cause until the end of the war.

One aircraft in particular made an enormous contribution to the swift German victory: the Junkers Ju 87 Stuka. Although the word Stuka – an abbreviation of *Sturzkampfflugzeug*, which literally translates as 'diving combat aircraft' – was applied to all German bomber aircraft with a dive-bombing capability during World War II, it will forever be associated with the Junkers Ju 87, with its ugly lines, inverted gull-wing and, above all, the banshee howl of its wing-mounted sirens as it plummeted towards its target.

Comparative Trials

Designed in response to a 1933 Luftwaffe requirement for a dive-bomber, the Ju 87 was developed from the K-47, a two-seat high-performance monoplane fighter of 1928. In March 1937, the Ju 87V2 was sent to the Luftwaffe test centre at Rechlin for comparative trials, and was chosen in preference to the other three contenders. Production began with the pre-series Ju 87A-0, powered by the Jumo 210Da engine, and continued with the Ju 87A-1, first deliveries of which were made to I/St.G 162 Immelmann, the unit tasked with developing operational tactics, in 1937. The early-model Stuka had been mainly relegated to training duties by the outbreak of World War II in September 1939, and was succeeded on the production line in 1938 by an extensively modified version, the Ju 87B, which used the more powerful 820kW (1100hp) Jumo 211Da.

The Vickers Wellington was one of the most popular aircraft used by RAF Bomber Command, despite its lack of range. Its self-supporting geodetic construction allowed it to absorb a great deal of damage and remain airworthy.

After the collapse of Poland, while the Allied and German armies faced one another along the Franco–German frontier in the autumn and winter of 1939 and their air forces skirmished for the first time over the Maginot Line, the Royal Air Force and the Luftwaffe launched tentative bombing attacks against their respective navies. The RAF's first such mission was flown on 4 September, the day after Britain declared war on Germany, when 10 Bristol Blenheims set out to attack enemy shipping off Wilhelmshaven.

A few years earlier, the Blenheim had been as fast as any fighter in service anywhere. It was developed from the Bristol Type 142, an eight-seat fast passenger aircraft, and in September 1935 the Air Ministry had placed an initial order for 150 aircraft under the service designation Blenheim Mk I, a second order for 434 aircraft following on completion of trials in December 1936.

Above: The Armstrong Whitworth Whitley was one of the RAF's principal heavy bomber types at World War II's outbreak. Its very long range made it useful for special duties, such as dropping agents.

Left: The Bristol Blenheim, seen here in prototype form, was developed from the Bristol 142 'Britain First', designed as a fast VIP transport for the newspaper proprietor Lord Rothermere. The Blenheim Mk I first flew in June 1936.

The first Blenheims were delivered to No. 114 Squadron in March 1937. By the time war broke out, most of the Mk I bombers were serving in the Middle and Far East, the home-based squadrons having rearmed with the improved Blenheim Mk IV.

Geodetic Construction
The other main RAF bomber type used in these early attacks was the Vickers Wellington. The Wellington was designed by Barnes Wallis, who had been responsible for the R.100 airship and who was later to conceive the mines that destroyed the Ruhr dams. Like its predecessor, the Vickers Wellesley, the aircraft featured geodetic construction, a 'basket weave' construction system producing a self-stabilizing framework in which loads in any direction were automatically equalized by forces in the intersecting set of frames, producing high strength for low weight. It was a system that enabled the Wellington to absorb a tremendous amount of battle damage and still survive. The first Wellington Mk I flew on 23 December 1937, powered by two Pegasus XX engines, and the first Bomber Command squadron to rearm, No. 9, began receiving its aircraft in December 1938. The Wellingtons in RAF service at the outbreak of World War II were the Pegasus-engined Mks I and IA.

Two further bombers, the Handley Page Hampden and the Armstrong

Mainstay of the Luftwaffe
Junkers Ju 88

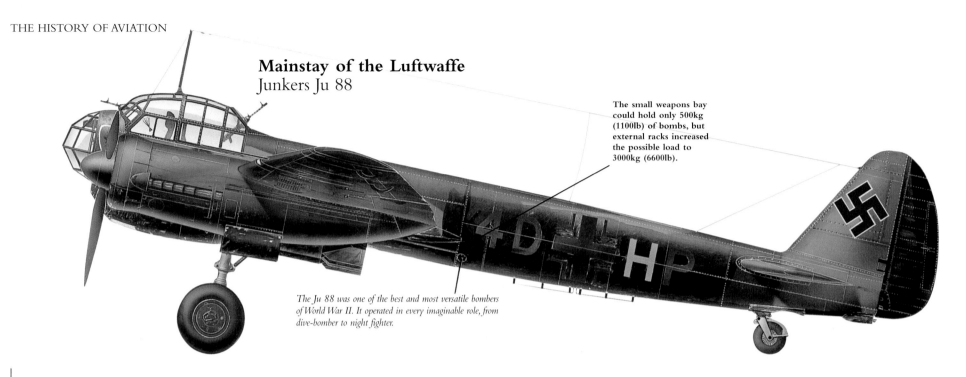

The small weapons bay could hold only 500kg (1100lb) of bombs, but external racks increased the possible load to 3000kg (6600lb).

The Ju 88 was one of the best and most versatile bombers of World War II. It operated in every imaginable role, from dive-bomber to night fighter.

Junkers Ju 88A-4

Type: four-seat medium and dive bomber

Powerplant: two 1000kW (1200hp) Junkers Jumo 211J 12-cylinder liquid-cooled engines

Maximum speed: 440km/h (280mph)

Ferry range: 1800km (1200 miles)

Service ceiling: 8200m (27,000ft)

Weights: empty 8000kg (17,600lb); loaded 14,000kg (31,000lb)

Armament: two 13mm machine guns, four 7.92mm machine guns and 3000kg (6600lb) of bombs

Dimensions:
span	20.13m	(60ft 3in)
length	14.40m	(47ft 1in)
height	4.85m	(17ft 6in)
wing area	54.50m²	(587sq ft)

Whitworth Whitley, completed RAF Bomber Command's strategic bombing force at this stage of the war. One of the RAF's most important medium bombers at the outbreak of World War II, the highly manoeuvrable but badly underarmed Hampden, first flew in June 1937, the first of 1430 Hampden Mk Is being delivered in September 1938. The prototype Whitley flew on 17 March 1936 was followed by a production batch of 34 Whitley Mk Is, with first deliveries of the aircraft being made to No. 10 Squadron in March 1937. The main wartime version of the Whitley was the Mk V, of which 1466 were produced. The RAF had 207 Whitleys on strength at the outbreak of World War II, and they were initially used for leaflet-dropping

operations over Germany because of their long range.

The Blenheim and Wellington squadrons suffered heavy losses in their early daylight raids on the north German harbours, which led to Bomber Command switching to a night-time offensive. The Germans persisted with daylight attacks, their first raids against Royal Navy bases in Scotland being carried out by the Luftwaffe's newest bomber, the Junkers Ju 88. One of the most versatile and effective combat aircraft ever produced, the Junkers Ju 88 was to remain of vital importance to the Luftwaffe throughout World War II, serving as a bomber, dive-bomber, night fighter, close support aircraft, long-range heavy fighter, reconnaissance aircraft and

torpedo-bomber. The prototype Ju 88 flew for the first time on 21 December 1936, powered by two 1000hp DB 600A in-line engines; the second prototype was essentially similar, except that it was fitted with Jumo 211A radials, the engines that were to power the aircraft throughout most of its career. A pre-series batch of Ju 88A-0s was completed during the summer of 1939, the first production Ju 88A-1s being delivered to a test unit, Erprobungskommando 88. In August 1939, this unit was redesignated I/KG 25, and soon afterwards it became I/KG 30, carrying out its first operational mission – an attack on British warships in the Firth of Forth – in September. About 60 operational aircraft were in service by the end of the year.

The Fairey Battle light bomber was underpowered and underarmed. It formed the main element of the RAF's Advanced Air Striking Force in France, and suffered terrible losses to both flak and fighters.

In April 1940, the Germans invaded Denmark and Norway, and, on 10 May, while the struggle for Norway was still in progress, they invaded France and the Low Countries. Between dawn and dusk on this fateful day, German bombers attacked 72 Allied airfields in the Netherlands, Belgium and France. During the first three days of the invasion, the British and French air forces carried out a series of desperate attacks on the enemy armoured columns advancing through the Ardennes and across the Meuse bridges at Maastricht and Tongeren.

Fearful Losses

Allied losses were fearful. On the first day alone, the squadrons of the RAF Advanced Air Striking Force (AASF) in France, equipped with Fairey Battle light bombers, lost 23 aircraft out of the 64 sent into action; by the end of the second day, the AASF's two squadrons of Blenheim bombers had also been wiped out. On 12 May, five Battles of No. 12 Squadron made a suicidal attack on the bridges at Maastricht; all were shot down by the German anti-aircraft guns, known as 'flak', or the Messerschmitts.

On 14 May, the Germans forced a crossing of the Meuse near Sedan, and the AASF was asked to mount an attack on the enemy bridgeheads using every available aircraft. Sixty-three Fairey Battles were thrown into the cauldron;

35 failed to return. The French day-bomber force, too, suffered heavy casualties, and by the end of May was in no position to carry out further attacks.

After the breakthrough at Sedan, the German Panzer columns raced across Belgium and northern France with shattering speed, driving for the Channel coast; by 23 May, it was clear that the Allied armies in Flanders were hopelessly trapped, with the British Expeditionary Force beginning its retreat to Dunkirk. On this day, the Panzers reached the Channel coast at Gravelines and swung northwards.

Twenty-four hours later, the Panzers halted – partly because they had accomplished the major part of their mission and badly needed a rest and partly because Herman Göring, the Luftwaffe Commander in Chief, had indicated that his airmen alone were capable of eliminating Allied resistance in and around the main evacuation ports.

The Luftwaffe was in fact in no position to do anything of the kind. The Stukas of Fliegerkorps VIII, which had supported the German armour in its dash through Belgium and France, were already badly overworked, and a large part of the Luftwaffe's medium-bomber and fighter force was still operating from bases inside Germany. As

Supermarine Spitfire Mk I of No. 603 'City of Edinburgh' Squadron, an Auxiliary Air Force unit that destroyed some of the first enemy aircraft at the beginning of World War II.

Dunkirk and the other ports were within easy reach of fighter bases in southern England, the Stukas could expect strong opposition.

Daily Patrols

The Stukas had a taste of things to come on 25 May, when 15 of them were attacked by Spitfires over Calais and four were shot down. The day after that, the Luftwaffe mounted its first major attacks on Dunkirk. RAF Fighter Command maintained regular daily patrols by 16 Spitfire and Hurricane squadrons. In the air battles that raged over and around the beaches during the nine days of the Dunkirk evacuation, the RAF lost 177 aircraft, and the Luftwaffe suffered a

comparable loss. Although the losses were roughly similar, the fact remained that the Luftwaffe had, for the first time, lost the air superiority it had enjoyed since its attack on Poland the year before, and at the hands of RAF Fighter Command had suffered a psychological wound which, before long, was to be made deeper and more damaging in the skies over southern England.

After Dunkirk, the Luftwaffe was heavily engaged in support of the German offensive across the river Somme against the French armies in the south, who fought on for another three weeks before the final collapse. The French air force, supported by naval air units, battled on gallantly until the last, its efforts crippled by shortages of fuel, ammunition and spares, and the continual need to withdraw before the Germans overran its airfields. After the armistice was signed on 22 June 1940, many French airmen made their escape to North Africa, from where some later fought on as part of the Free French Forces.

From Great Britain, which now stood alone against the might of Germany and Italy – the latter having declared war on the Allies on 10 June – the voice of the new British Prime Minister, Winston Churchill, resounded throughout the free world: 'The battle which General Weygand has called the Battle of France

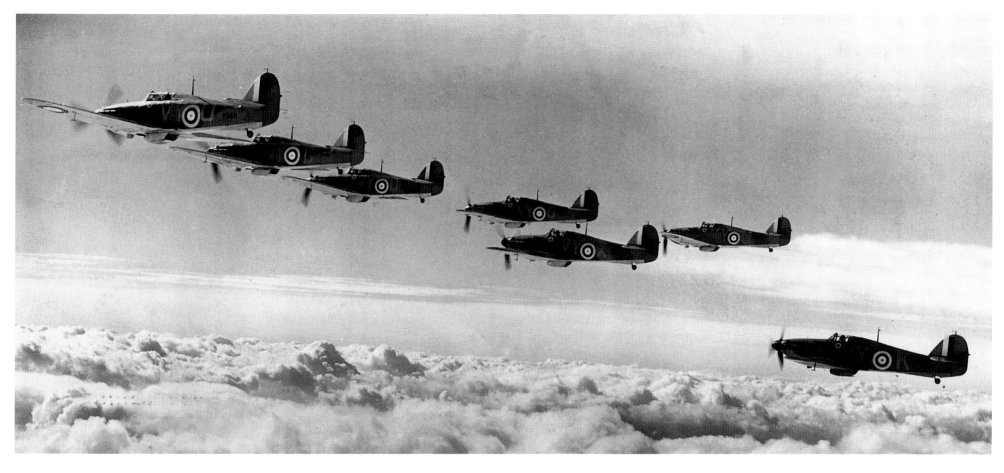

is over. I expect that the Battle of Britain is about to begin ...' For the first time in history, the fate of a nation would soon be decided by young men locked in deadly combat high above the earth, their sacrifice marked by twisting vapour trails etched on a summer sky.

Dowding System

These men would have a priceless asset called the Dowding System. In 1936, the

Air Defence of Great Britain Command had been broken up and replaced by a set of new commands. One of them was Fighter Command, the headquarters of which opened on 14 July that year at Bentley Priory in Middlesex. Its main subordinate formation was No. 11 (Fighter) Group (HQ Uxbridge); its task was the defence of south and southeast England. The other main subordinate formation was No. 12 (Fighter) Group

(HQ Watnall, Nottinghamshire), which was established in April 1937 and was responsible for the defence of the Midlands. Two other groups, No. 10 (covering Wales and the West Country) and No. 13 (covering the north of England and Scotland) were established later.

The man chosen as the head of Fighter Command was Air Marshal Sir Hugh Caswall Tremenheere Dowding, CB, CMG. Under his direction, with

Hurricane Mk Is of No. 242 Squadron pictured during the Battle of Britain. No. 242 was commanded by the famous 'legless ace' Douglas Bader, who went on to command the Tangmere Wing.

Europe accelerating towards war, the most sophisticated air defence system in the world rapidly evolved. At its heart was the apparatus that would become known to the world as radar.

Radar, an acronym of ra(dio) d(irection) a(nd) r(anging) – known by

171

the deliberately misleading title of 'radio direction finding' (RDF) in its early days – had its origin, in so far as it was applied to Britain's defences, in a committee set up in 1934 to examine whether radio waves might be applied in some way to thwart enemy bombers. The committee, called the Committee for the Scientific Survey of Air Defence, and chaired by Henry Tizard, Rector of the Imperial College of Science and Technology, who had been a pilot in the 1914–18 war, enlisted the services of Robert Watson-Watt, a brilliant 42-year-old scientist who swiftly dismissed any fantasy about radio waves being developed into some sort of death ray, one of the many options considered by the committee. He did, however, produce a paper showing the feasibility of using radio waves not to destroy aircraft, but to detect them.

Less than nine months after the Tizard Committee's first meeting, after Watson-Watt's theory had been scientifically proven, the Air Council was recommending the construction of a chain of RDF stations to cover the coast from Southampton to Newcastle. By the summer of 1939, 20 Chain Home (CH) stations had been completed, capable of detecting aircraft at up to 160km (100 miles); they were supplemented by another series, Chain Home Low (CHL), designed to detect aircraft flying below 915m (3000ft). RAF aircraft were fitted with a small transmitter, IFF (Identification Friend or Foe), which enabled controllers to distinguish them from the enemy.

Early Warning

Under Dowding's direction, all the various elements were brought together: the radar stations to provide early warning of attack; the Observer Corps, to track the movements of enemy aircraft once they had crossed the coast; the identical operations rooms at Fighter Command HQ, in the Group HQs and in the Sector stations from which the vital information was relayed to the squadrons; the flexible system whereby, in the vulnerable area of southern England, fighters could be passed from Sector to Sector, from Group to Group by operations room staffs elaborately linked by telephone and teleprinter lines,

Ground crew working on a Heinkel He 111. This bomber was the mainstay of both the day and night offensive against the British Isles, and its armour and armament were progressively upgraded as the battle went on.

The Flying Pencil
Dornier Do 17Z

The Dornier Do 17Z was also used by the Finnish Air Force. This aircraft carries the post-war blue-and-white roundels; the earlier insignia was a blue swastika on a while background.

Although able to outrun most fighters during the Polish campaign, by the time of the Battle of Britain the DO 17Z was challenged by faster fighters.

The narrow cylindrical fuselage quickly earned the Do 17 the name Fliegender Bleistift (Flying Pencil).

installed by the Herculean efforts of the Post Office; the squadrons of eight–gun fighters; and the supply system that kept them flying.

History has defined the Battle of Britain as lasting for a period of 17 weeks, beginning on 10 July 1940, when the Luftwaffe began to attack British convoys in the Channel. In fact, the action started earlier. From 5 June, while the Battle of France was still being fought, the Luftwaffe sent small numbers of bombers to attack 'fringe' targets on the east and southeast coasts of England. These attacks caused little significant damage, and their main purpose was to provide the Luftwaffe's bomber units with experience of Britain's air defences.

On 30 June, Reichsmarschall Hermann Göring, the Luftwaffe Commander in Chief, issued a general directive setting out the aim of the planned air assault on Britain. The Luftwaffe's main target was

to be the Royal Air Force, with particular reference to its fighter airfields and aircraft factories. As long as RAF Fighter Command remained unbroken, the Luftwaffe's first priority must be to attack it at every opportunity, in the air and on the ground, until it was destroyed. Only then would the Luftwaffe be free to turn its attention to other targets, such as the Royal Navy's dockyards and operational harbours, as a preliminary to invasion of Britain.

Early in July, Göring ordered his air commanders to begin attacks on British convoys in the Channel, the twofold object being to inflict serious losses on British shipping and bring Fighter Command to combat. But Air Vice Marshal Keith Park, a New Zealander and a very shrewd leader, who commanded Fighter Command's No. 11 Group in southeast England, refused to be drawn into the trap and committed only a

portion of his precious Hurricane and Spitfire squadrons to battle. The convoy attacks continued during July and the first week of August, and there were several big air battles, mostly in the Dover area. During this phase, the RAF lost 124 aircraft against a Luftwaffe loss of 274.

All-Out Onslaught
At the end of July, Adolf Hitler personally ordered Göring to place his squadrons in a state of immediate readiness for an all-out onslaught on the RAF's fighter airfields, as well as the British aircraft and aero-engine factories. The code name for the offensive was Adler Angriff – Eagle Attack. To put the plan into operation, Göring had three air fleets (Luftflotten) – two in France and the Low Countries, and one in Denmark and Norway – and a total of 3500 bombers and fighters, of which about 2250 were serviceable.

Dornier Do 17Z

Type: (DO 17Z-2) four/five seat medium bomber

Powerplant: two 746kW (1000hp) BMW Bramo 323P Fafnir nine-cylinder single-row radial engines

Maximum speed: 410km/h (255mph)

Ferry range: 1500km (932 miles)

Service ceiling: 8200m (26,905ft)

Weights: empty 5200kg (11,464lb); maximum take-off weight 8590kg (18,937lb)

Armament: one or two trainable 7.92mm machine guns in windscreen, nose, dorsal and ventral positios, plus internal bomb load of 1000kg (2205lb)

Dimensions:
length	15.8m (51ft 9.67in)
span	18.00m (59ft 0.5in)
height	4.6m (15ft 1in)
wing areaa	55m² (590sq ft)

Above: Messerschmitt Bf 110s of Erprobungsgruppe 210. This unit was originally formed to evaluate the unsuccessful Me 210, but operated the Bf 110 during the Battle of Britain.

Left: The Junkers 88 was one of the Luftwaffe's most valuable assets, with 15,000 aircraft being produced in the course of the war.

On the other side of the Channel, the Commander in Chief Fighter Command, Air Chief Marshal Sir Hugh Dowding, had 704 serviceable fighters, including 620 Hurricanes and Spitfires. Iin the beginning, there were about 1000 pilots to fly the RAF's fighters, but the number was to rise to more than 3000 before the battle was over. Eighty per cent were British-born; the rest came from every corner of the dominions, from Poland and Czechoslovakia, from Belgium and France, and from the United States, which was not yet at war. Some were already veterans of the fighting in Europe, before Dunkirk. Most were young men in their late teens or early twenties, barely out of school. All were to experience fear and terrible stress; 520 would lose their lives; others would be maimed, often dreadfully burned as their petrol tanks exploded around them. And in that hectic high summer of 1940, over the harvest fields of England, they would change the course of history.

When the German Luftwaffe was formed after Hitler's rise to power in the early 1930s, its leaders never seriously envisaged that it would have to take part in a long-range strategic bombing offensive. Consequently, its bombers were designed to give tactical support to the army. The concept was proven in Spain, where the new aircraft were tested operationally in the civil war, and worked well in the battles of Poland, Norway and France against limited fighter opposition.

Under the determined attacks of RAF fighters in the Battle of Britain, it was a different story. The Junkers Ju 87 Stuka, which had blasted a path across Poland and western Europe ahead of the Panzer divisions, was massacred by the Spitfires and Hurricanes, and withdrawn from the battle after only a few operations. The twin-engined bombers – Dornier Do 17s, Heinkel He 111s and Junkers Ju 88s – had a limited range and bomb load; they were also lightly armoured and fitted with inadequate defensive armament, which cost them dearly at the hands of Fighter Command. When more armour plate and extra machine guns were fitted, the extra weight reduced their range and bomb load even more.

Of the two German fighter types used in the battle, the Messerschmitt Bf 109 was an excellent fighting machine.

The twin-engined Messerschmitt Bf 110, on the other hand, was not a success story. The Bf110 carried a pilot and rear gunner and was armed with five machine guns and two cannon, but it could be outmanoeuvred by both the Spitfire and the Hurricane. Losses during the battle were heavy, although the Bf 110 did enjoy success as a night fighter over Germany later in the war.

The mainstay of RAF Fighter Command throughout the battle was the Hawker Hurricane. Although somewhat eclipsed by the more glamorous Spitfire, in fact it accounted for 80 per cent of

Below: pilots of No.601 (County of London) squadron scramble for their waiting Hurricanes during the Battle of Britain. In reality, this shot was posed for the camera, but the danger faced hourly by these pilots was all too real.

the enemy aircraft destroyed in the battle. When the conflict began in earnest in July, Hurricanes equipped 29 squadrons of Fighter Command. Another 19 were equipped with the Spitfire. The Spitfire was faster than the Hurricane and more manoeuvrable, but the Hurricane was more robust. Both

fighters were fitted with Rolls-Royce Merlin engines and carried an armament of eight 0.303in Colt-Browning machine guns, which were 'harmonized' so that the bullets converged on a spot 229m (750ft) in front of the aircraft. A two-second burst of gunfire would deliver a cluster of bullets weighing 4.5kg (10lb)

to the target, which was often enough to knock a fatal hole in it.

The critical phase of the battle occurred between 25 August and 6 September 1940. In that fortnight, Fighter Command lost 231 pilots – 103 killed and 128 badly wounded. Savage attacks on airfields and aircraft factories

Above: Trails of condensation in the sky over southern England in 1940 show the extent of the frenzied dogfights between the attacking Luftwaffe and British Hurricanes and Spitfire fighters.

continued. The situation was desperate; inexperienced pilots were being thrown into battle, many to be killed on their first sortie without even seeing the

Although a failure as a day fighter, the Boulton Paul Defiant was successful in the night-fighting role, the favourite technique being to manoeuvre under an enemy bear.

enemy who shot them down. It was then that the Germans made their biggest strategic blunder of the Battle of Britain. On 7 September, Göring ordered the Luftwaffe to switch its effort to an all-out attack on London in an attempt to bring Fighter Command to battle over a single target. The massive airfield attacks ceased, and Fighter Command had the respite it so badly needed.

The daylight battle between 10 July and 31 October 1940 cost Fighter Command 905 aircraft, but the Luftwaffe lost 1529. From now on, the Germans came increasingly under cover of darkness; the period known as the 'Blitz', which would last until the spring of 1941, had begun.

The night Blitz on Britain accelerated the development of dedicated night fighters, equipped with airborne interception (AI) radar. In the summer of 1940 the mainstay of the RAF's hastily organized night-fighter squadrons was the Bristol Blenheim 1F, which was totally unsuited to night operations and which, for the most part, was slower than the bombers it was supposed to catch. Then, in August 1940, the RAF's night-fighter force received unexpected reinforcements in the shape of two squadrons armed with the Boulton-Paul Defiant – unexpected because the debut of the Defiant as a night fighter came about more or less by accident, as a result of the severe mauling the two squadrons had received earlier during daylight operations.

The Defiant was the RAF's third fighter monoplane, and was very different in concept from its contemporaries, the Hurricane and Spitfire. It was designed to Air Ministry Specification F.9/35, calling for a two-seat fighter in which the entire armament was concentrated in a power-operated centrally mounted turret permitting a 360-degree field of fire in the hemisphere above the aircraft. The prototype Defiant flew on 11 August 1937, and some 400 had been ordered by the outbreak of World War II, although a protracted trials programme meant that only three had been delivered. As a day fighter, the Defiant was a disaster, suffering heavy losses in combat, but it went on to enjoy considerable success in the night-fighter/intruder role.

Success at Night
The twin-engined Bristol Beaufighter was an even better proposition. Fast and heavily armed with four 20mm cannon

The Bristol Beaufighter was not an attractive aircraft, but it was immensely strong and surprisingly manoevrable. With the right armament it proved to be a powerful foe when ranged against shipping or – in night attacks – the Luftwaffe.

The Torpedo Biplane
Fairey Swordfish Mk II

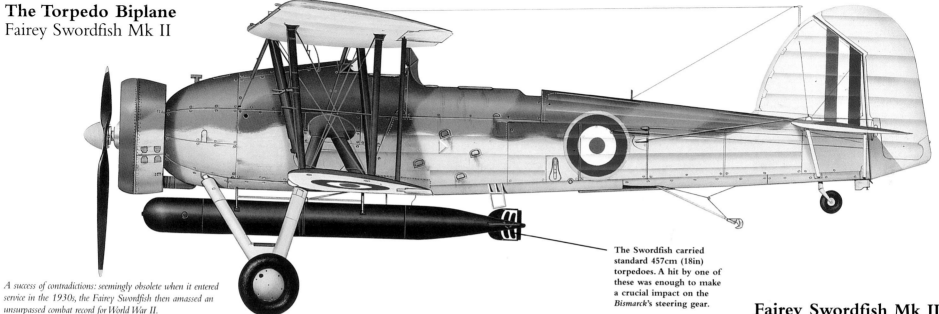

A success of contradictions: seemingly obsolete when it entered service in the 1930s, the Fairey Swordfish then amassed an unsurpassed combat record for World War II.

The Swordfish carried standard 457cm (18in) torpedoes. A hit by one of these was enough to make a crucial impact on the *Bismarck*'s steering gear.

and six machine guns, it got over some initial teething troubles and soon began to register success at night, destroying its first enemy bomber on the night of 25 October 1940. Its score continued to mount steadily from January 1941, with the introduction of Ground Controlled Interception (GCI) stations along the south coast of England. From these stations, the controllers were able to bring the fighters within a mile or so of their target, at which point airborne radar took over to complete the interception. Fourteen Beaufighter

Left: The Gloster Gladiator was quite successful in the early phase of the desert war, when its main opponent was the Italian Fiat CR.42, also a biplane. Gladiators also fought in Greece.

squadrons were assigned to the night defence of Great Britain in 1941–42.

Operation Sea Lion, the planned invasion of Britain, had been postponed indefinitely. Hitler's eyes were now turned east, towards the Soviet Union. First, however, the focus of the air war switched to the Mediterranean theatre, where the strategic island of Malta had been under air attack since Italy's entry into the war in June 1940. Initially, the island was defended by a mere six Gloster Sea Gladiator biplanes, soon reduced to three biplanes that would be immortalized as 'Faith, Hope and Charity', names bestowed on them by the popular press. By the end of the year, the Gladiators had been replaced by

Hawker Hurricanes. Malta had now developed into a vital offensive base, with island-based RAF and Fleet Air Arm aircraft attacking targets in Sicily, Italy and North Africa. Then, in December, came a new development: the Luftwaffe now entered the battle, with the Stukas, Junkers 88s and Messerschmitts of Fliegerkorps X occupying Sicilian airfields in strength.

On 11 January 1941, the Luftwaffe and the Regia Aeronautica began a massive air onslaught against Malta. It continued almost without pause through the first three months of the year and, although the fury of the attacks abated somewhat after March 1941, they did not cease entirely.

Fairey Swordfish Mk II

Type: three-seat carrierborne and land-based torpedo bomber, level bomber and reconnaissance aeroplane

Powerplant: one 578kW (775hp) Bristol Pegasus IIIM3 or 559kW (750hp) Pegasus XXX nine-cylinder single-row radial engine

Maximum speed: 224km/h (139mph); climb to 1525m (5000ft) in 10 minutes 30 seconds

Ferry range: 1657km (1030 miles)

Service ceiling: 3780m (12,400ft)

Weights: empty 2132kg (4700lb); maximum take-off 4196kg (9250lb)

Armament: one 0.303in fixed forward-firing machine gun in the starboard side of the forward fuselage, and one 0.303in trainable rearward-firing machine in the rear cockpit, plus an external torpedo, bomb and rocket load of 726kg (1600lb)

Dimensions: span   13.87m (45ft 6in)
               length (tail up)   111.07m (36ft 4in)
               height (tail up)   4.11m (13ft 6in)
               wing area   50.4m² (542sq ft)

Significant Air Action

Undoubtedly the most significant air action during this phase of the Mediterranean war occurred on 11 November 1940, when 21 Fairey Swordfish strike aircraft from the carrier HMS *Illustrious* attacked heavy units of the Italian fleet at Taranto naval base.

The Fiat CR.42 was the equivalent of the Gloster Gladiator, against which it fought in North African skies. Nimble and relatively fast, it could also hold itself against more modern monoplane fighters.

The battleship *Conte di Cavour* was so badly damaged that she took no further part in hostilities. Her sister ship, the *Caio Duilio*, had to be beached and was out of action for six months, while the *Littorio* was disabled for four months.

At one stroke, the Italian battle fleet had been reduced from six to three capital ships at a crucial point in the Mediterranean war, and for the loss of only two Swordfish. It was the first real demonstration of the aircraft carrier as a means of

exercising flexible, mobile sea power, rather than as a mere adjunct to the fleet, and it was to have a profound effect on the conduct of future air operations. The vital role of naval air power was again demonstrated in May 1941, when Swordfish aircraft torpedoed and crippled the battleship *Bismarck*, allowing surface forces to close in for the kill.

While the RAF battled in the skies of Malta, the air war raged no less

Right: The Fiat G.50 Falco was the Fiat CR.42's monoplane fighter successor. It was never a particular success, and was not a match for the Hawker Hurricane, which it encountered in the Western Desert campaign of World War II.

furiously in other sectors of the Mediterranean theatre, where Gloster Gladiators were pitted against the Fiat CR.42 biplane fighter and Fiat G.50 monoplane. Late in 1940, some of the Gladiator

squadrons were sent to Greece, which had been invaded by the Italians, but their early successes were short-lived, for in April 1941 the Germans entered the battle for Greece. The RAF squadrons were now equipped with Hurricanes, but, by 19 April, heavy attacks on the Greek airfields had reduced the strength of the RAF fighter squadrons to just 22 serviceable aircraft. A few days later, all but seven of these were destroyed in strafing attacks. With this blow, Allied air resistance over Greece virtually ceased to exist.

On 1 May 1941, the last of the Commonwealth forces were evacuated from the Greek mainland, and 30,000 Allied troops prepared the island of Crete to withstand a German invasion. The German attack on Crete began on 20 May with very heavy bombing, followed by a massive airborne assault using both paratroops

and glider troops, and it was not long before the defenders were hard pressed. The Royal Navy, operating off the island without air cover, suffered dreadfully from dive-bomber attacks; three cruisers and six destroyers were sunk, and two battleships, an aircraft carrier, six cruisers and seven destroyers suffered more or less severe damage.

Last Major Operation

By the end of May, the battle for Crete was over, with about half the island's defenders killed or captured. But the German airborne forces had also taken tremendous punishment; Crete was their last major operation of the war.

In March 1941, with the Allies still committed in Greece, the German Afrika Korps arrived in Libya under the command of General Erwin Rommel, and the British forces were soon in retreat along the road they had taken

Curtiss P-40E Kittyhawk IIAs of No. 260 Squadron. This unit, part of the Desert Air Force, fought in North Africa, then in Italy. Kittyhawks were replaced by P-51 Mustangs in 1944.

in their victorious desert offensive against the Italians a few months earlier. New Allied squadrons were being formed to challenge the Luftwaffe's air superiority, and in the spring of 1941 the RAF in the Western Desert was joined by Commonwealth units from Australia and South Africa. The build-up of the Desert Air Force continued throughout the summer months, and, by November 1941, there were 40 squadrons in the Middle East, equipped primarily with Hurricane fighter-bombers and American Curtiss P-40 Kittyhawks. The reasoning behind the German assault on Greece

(and on Yugoslavia, which was attacked simultaneously) soon became clear. With their southern flank now secured, the Germans launched their planned assault on the Soviet Union, Operation Barbarossa, on 22 June 1941. The invasion caught the Soviet High Command completely unawares, and it was not until mid-morning that the Soviet Air Force began operations. These were almost totally lacking in coordination, and communications with ground forces were virtually nonexistent. Priority on this and subsequent days was given to attacks on German armoured and mechanized columns, a task in which the Russian bombers suffered appalling losses. On the Western Front alone (there were five Soviet

fronts in all, Northwestern, Western, Southwestern, Southern and Northern) the Russians were to lose 528 aircraft on the ground and 210 in the air on 22 June.

Above: The LaGG-3 bore a strong resemblance to France's Dewoitine D.520, seen here. The two may have met in combat, as the D.520 was used by some of Germany's allies.

Below: Initially, the LaGG-3 was known under the earlier Russian aircraft designation system as the I-22, in which form it made its first flight on 30 March 1939.

The Soviet Air Force, although it fought desperately, was deficient in equipment and was tactically no match for the experienced Luftwaffe units. For months following the German invasion, it was powerless to prevent one catastrophe after another overwhelming the Soviet armies. It lacked modern aircraft and sufficient trained pilots, and its leadership was too poor, some of the best senior officers having been eliminated in Stalin's pre-war purges.

Soviet Fighters

It was not until 1939–40 that the prototypes of three Soviet fighters that could really be classed as modern made their appearance. The first was the LaGG-1/LaGG-3, which took its name from the initials of the three engineers who conceived it: Lavochkin, Gorbunov and Gudkov. It was a remarkable little aircraft, built entirely of wood and bearing a strong resemblance to France's Dewoitine D.520. The LaGG-1 flew for the first time in March 1940 and was superseded by an improved variant, the LaGG-3, after 100 examples had been built. These still equipped two air regiments at the time of the German invasion of June 1941; however, it was the LaGG-3 that was to hold the line during the first critical months of the German onslaught.

Genesis of a Classic Fighter
MiG-3

Although the forward fuselage was made of steel tubing with an alloy stressed skin, the rear fuselage consisted of four pine longerons with a 0.5mm (⅕₀in) plywood and calico skin.

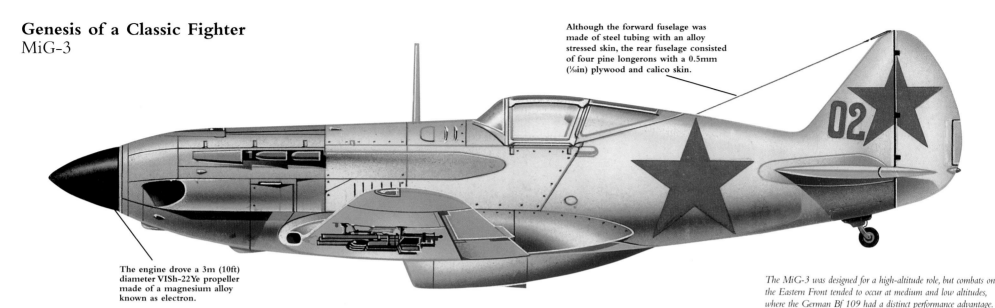

The engine drove a 3m (10ft) diameter VISh-22Ye propeller made of a magnesium alloy known as electron.

The MiG-3 was designed for a high-altitude role, but combats on the Eastern Front tended to occur at medium and low altitudes, where the German Bf 109 had a distinct performance advantage.

The Mikoyan and Gurevich partnership began in 1940 with the design of the I-61 (MiG-1), which flew for the first time 1 March of that year. An open cockpit fighter, it was not a very successful design.

The second was the MiG-1, developed to meet a Soviet Air Force requirement issued in 1938 for a high-altitude fighter. Although it was unstable and difficult to fly, it was rushed into production because of its high performance. The prototype first flew in April 1940, having been built in a record time of only four months. The aircraft was of composite construction; the forward fuselage up to the rear of the cockpit consisted of a steel frame with fabric covering, while the rear section was all wood. The wing centre section was of duralumin, the outer panels wooden. The MiG-1 was redesignated MiG-3 after the 100th machine had been produced, the main improvements being a fully enclosed cockpit and the addition of an auxiliary fuel tank. The resulting increased combat radius meant that MiG-3s were used extensively for fighter reconnaissance.

The third new fighter type was the Yak-1 Krasavyets (Beauty), which made its first public appearance during an air display on 7 November 1940. It was Aleksandr S. Yakovlev's first fighter design and earned him the Order of Lenin, the gift of a Zis car and a prize of 100,000 roubles. Of mixed construction (fabric and plywood covered), the Yak-1 was simple to build and service, and a delight

MiG-3

Type: single-seat fighter

Powerplant: one 1007kW (1350hp) Mikulin AM-35A V-12 piston engine

Maximum speed: 640km/h (397mph) at 7800m (25,600ft)

Range: 1195km (743 miles)

Service ceiling: 12,000m (39,400ft)

Weights: empty 2595kg (5709lb.); maximum take-off 3350kg (7370lb)

Armament: one 12.7mm (.50cal.) Beresin and two 7.62mm (.30cal.) ShKAS machine guns, plus up to 200kg (440lb) of bombs or six RS-82 rocket projectiles on underwing racks

Dimensions:
span	10.20m	(33ft 9in)
length	8.25m	(20ft 9in)
height	3.50m	(11ft 6in)
wing area	17.44m²	(188sq ft)

First of the New Yak Fighters
Yakovlev Yak-1

A slogan painted on the fuselage was a common feature of Soviet fighters. This one reads: 'To the pilot of the Stalingrad front B.N. Yeremin, from the farmers of Stakhanov collective farm.'

The Yakovlev Yak-1, known as 'Krasavyets' (Beauty) was the best of Russia's early monoplane fighters, and was developed into the excellent Yak-3.

Yak-1

Type: single-seat fighter and fighter-bomber

Powerplant: one 782kW (1050hp) Klimov M-105 V-12 liquid-cooled engine

Maximum speed: 530km/h (329mph)

Initial climb rate: 7 minutes to 5000m (16,400ft)

Turning time: 360 degrees in 17.6 seconds

Range: 700km (435 miles)

Service ceiling: 9000m (29,500ft)

Weights: empty 2550kg (5610lb); loaded 3130kg (6886lb)

Armament: one 20mm ShVAK cannon; one or two ShKAS 12.7mm (.50cal.) machine guns; wing racks could carry six RS-82 rockets

Dimensions   span   10.00m (32ft 10in)
                   length   8.48m (27ft 9in)
                   wing area   17.15m² (185sq ft)

to fly. Production was accelerated following the German invasion of Russia in June 1941, and in the second half of the year 1019 Yak-1s were turned out.

Low-Level Attacks

The Russians had only a very small strategic bombing force, equipped with twin-engined Ilyushin Il-4s and Petlyakov Pe-8s, and its medium bomber force was still largely equipped with obsolescent SB-2s. However, a fine medium bomber, the Petlyakov Pe-2, was just entering service. By June 1941, when the Germans invaded the Soviet Union, the total number of Pe-2s delivered had risen to 462, but comparatively few of these saw action during the early days because of a shortage of trained crews. It was not until late August that the Pe-2 was committed to the battle in any numbers,

making low-level attacks on German armoured columns. In these early actions the Pe-2's high speed and defensive armament proved their worth.

By December 1941, German efforts to capture Moscow and Leningrad had failed in the face of growing Soviet resistance; both sides were in the grip of the Russian winter and had fought themselves to a standstill. Half a world away, events were unfolding that would ultimately have a decisive effect on the course of the war. On 7 December 1941 came the first of a series of shattering blows which, in the weeks to come, would alter the whole basis of Allied strategy: the Japanese attack

Right: Built in only small numbers, the Petlyakov Pe-8 was evolved to meet a 1934 Soviet Air Force specification for a four-engine long-range heavy bomber. Its first major operation of the war was an attack on Berlin in 1941.

The Ilyushin Il-4 (DB-3F), the most widely used Soviet bomber of the war years, undertook many of the Soviet Air Force's long-range missions in the early months of the war in the east.

on Pearl Harbor, devastating the US Pacific Fleet and paving the way for further conquests. By the end of December, the Japanese had invaded Thailand, Burma and Malaya, had captured Wake Island and Hong Kong, and had carried out a major landing on Luzon, in the Philippines. Early in 1942 Singapore fell, and the British Army in Burma, under constant Japanese pressure, had embarked

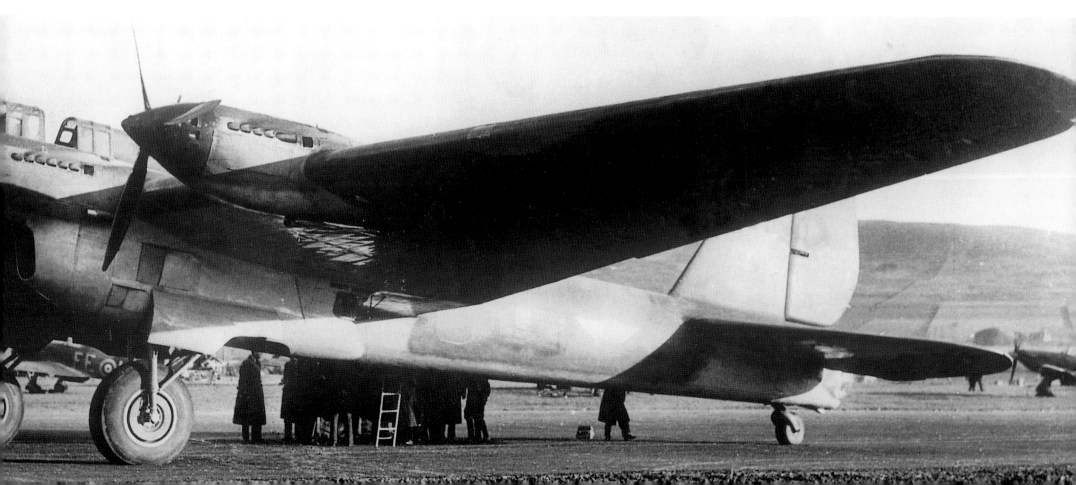

From Pearl Harbor to Kamikaze
Mitsubishi A6M Zero

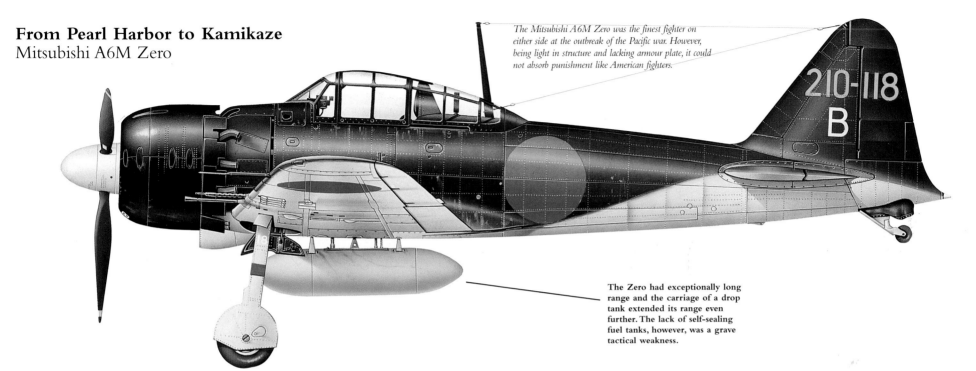

The Mitsubishi A6M Zero was the finest fighter on either side at the outbreak of the Pacific war. However, being light in structure and lacking armour plate, it could not absorb punishment like American fighters.

The Zero had exceptionally long range and the carriage of a drop tank extended its range even further. The lack of self-sealing fuel tanks, however, was a grave tactical weakness.

on the longest fighting retreat in its history. It would end at the frontier of India, where the Allied forces dug in to wait for the day when they were strong enough to go over to the offensive.

The early Japanese conquests were a triumph of air power, and particularly naval air power. The attack on Pearl Harbor was inspired by the British raid on Taranto in November 1940, and it was naval aviation that would be the

The Petlyakov Pe-2, seen here under construction in a Soviet factory where creature comforts were very much a secondary consideration, was an excellent light bomber. A night-fighter version, the Pe-3, was also produced.

dominant factor in the great Pacific battles that were to come. The one significant failure of the Japanese strike on Pearl Harbor was that it had not destroyed the US Pacific Fleet's three aircraft carriers; these now formed the nucleus of the US Navy's first carrier task force, forerunner of a mighty weapon that would ultimately carry the war back across the Pacific to the Japanese home islands.

An Unpleasant Surprise
The quality of Japanese aircraft came as an unpleasant surprise to the Allies, and it was personified in one type, the Mitsubishi A6M Reisen (Zero fighter).

One of the finest aircraft of all time, the Mitsubishi A6M Zero first flew on 1 April 1939, and soon showed itself to be clearly superior to any fighter the Allies could put into the air in the early stages of the Pacific war. Armed with two 20mm cannon and two 7.7mm machine guns, it was highly manoeuvrable and structurally very strong, despite being lightweight. Instead of being built in several separate units, it was constructed in two pieces. The engine, cockpit and forward fuselage combined with the wings to form one rigid unit, the second unit comprising the rear fuselage and the tail. The two units were joined together

Mitsubishi A6M Zero

Type: single-seat carrier based fighter-bomber

Powerplant: one 843kW (1130hp) Nakajima NK1F Sakae 21 radial engine

Maximum speed: 565km/h (350mph)

Ferry range: 1800km (1200 miles) with drop tank

Service ceiling: 11,740m (38,500ft)

Weights: empty 1876kg (4000lb); loaded 2733kg (6025lb)

Armament: two 7.7mm (.303cal.) machine guns with 600 rounds above the engine and two 20mm Type 99 cannon with 100 rounds each in the wings, plus two 60kg (130lb) bombs under wings

Dimensions:		
span	11.00m (36ft 1in)
length	9.12m (29ft 11in)
height	3.60m (11ft 6in)
wing area	21.30m² (230sq ft)

by a ring of 80 bolts. Its main drawback was that it had no armour plating for the pilot and no self-sealing fuel tanks, which meant that it could not absorb as much battle damage as Allied fighters.

The Zero retained its overall ascendancy during the first year of the

The tubby little Grumman F4F Wildcat held the line for the Allies in the Pacific air war until more advanced fighters could be deployed. It particularly distinguished itself in the battles of Midway and Guadalcanal.

Pacific conflict, even though the Japanese suffered some serious reverses during this period. The first of these was the Battle of the Coral Sea in May 1942, when – in the first naval engagement in history fought without opposing ships making contact – American carrier forces prevented the Japanese from carrying out their intended landing at Port Moresby, New Guinea, even though American losses were higher than those of their adversary. Then, in June, came the Battle

of Midway, when US carrier aircraft broke up a strong enemy invasion force, sinking four fleet carriers and destroying 258 aircraft. This battle, in which the Americans lost 132 aircraft and the carrier *Yorktown*, marked a definite turning point in the Pacific war. Not only did it bring an end to Japan's offensive, but it also resulted in the loss of a major part of the enemy's carrier attack force and many of the Imperial Japanese Navy's most experienced pilots.

Fighting Chance

The standard American carrier-based fighter during the first months of the Pacific war was the Grumman F4F Wildcat, a type that was inferior to the Zero on almost every count. Although robust and capable of withstanding a tremendous amount of battle damage, it needed a highly experienced pilot at the controls to give the Wildcat a fighting chance of survival in combat with Japanese fighters. Nevertheless, it was the

The Short Stirling was the first of the RAF's four-engine heavy bombers. Its operational ceiling was poor, and it was progressively relagated to transport duties, which it performed admirably.

The Great All-Rounder
Handley Page Halifax

All Halifax bombers carried a four-gun tail turret to counter German night fighters, which generally attacked from astern.

The Handley Page Halifax, seen here wearing the code letters of No. 76 Squadron, was the second of the RAF's four-engine heavy bombers. Always overshadowed by the later Lancaster, it nevertheless gave excellent service.

Handley Page Halifax

Type: seven-seat long-range heavy bomber; also troop transport and long-range anti-submarine aircraft

Powerplant: four 1214kW (1613hp) Bristol Hercules XVI 14-cylinder radial piston engines

Maximum speed: 500km/h (281mph)

Ferry range: 2000km (1240 miles) with maximum bomb load

Service ceiling: 7315m (24,000ft)

Weights: empty 17,345kg (38,159lb); loaded 29,484kg (64,865lb)

Armament: nine 7.7mm (.303cal.) machine guns in nose and quad dorsal and tail turrets, plus up to 5897kg (13,200lb) of bombs

Dimensions:	span	31.75m (104ft)
	length	21.82m (72ft)
	height	6.32m (21ft)
	wing area	118.45m² (1275sq ft)

Wildcat that held the line in the Pacific during the most desperate days of combat in that theatre of war.

The Japanese attack on Pearl Harbor and its aftermath meant that the British Empire no longer stood alone in its fight against Nazi Germany and its Axis partner, Italy. During the grim days of 1940 and 1941, with one European territory after another falling to Hitler's victorious Wehrmacht (armed forces), Britain had only one means of bringing the war home to the people of Germany: the growing power of RAF Bomber Command. Compared with the mighty Anglo-American strategic bombing offensive that was to unfold later in the war, these early efforts were pinpricks; the crews of the Wellingtons, Whitleys and Hampdens

that were the mainstay of Bomber Command up to 1942 had to battle their way across darkened Europe with little in the way of navigational aids, and only a small percentage of the bombs dropped actually fell in the target areas.

In 1941, however, the squadrons of Bomber Command were re-equipping with two new types of four-engine bomber. The first was the Short Stirling, which entered service in August 1940; it suffered from a relatively low operational ceiling, the result of having its wingspan reduced so that it would fit into existing hangars. The second type, the Handley Page Halifax, also delivered in late 1940, suffered from no such restrictions and went on to become one of the RAF's most successful bombers.

The same could not be said of the Avro Manchester, which was powered by two Rolls-Royce Vulture engines. The airframe was a good design, but the engines were unreliable and prone to overheating, with a consequent risk of fire. The bomber was withdrawn from service in 1942, and the design was modified to take four Rolls-Royce Merlin engines. In this guise, it became the superlative Avro Lancaster, one of the most famous bombers of all time.

Another Merlin-powered aircraft that made its operational debut in 1942 was

An Avro Manchester of the RAF's No. 207 Squadron. Although the Manchester possessed a sound airframe design, its Rolls-Royce Vulture engines proved disastrous and were prone to catching fire unexpectedly.

The Dambusters' Bombers
Avro Lancaster

The key to the Lancaster's success was the capacious bomb bay, which could hold up to seven tons of bombs and, with modification, could house the massive 10-ton 'Grand Slam'.

The twin-tailed layout gave the Lancaster great stability. The extra control surfaces could withstand massive damage and still leave the bomber flyable enough to make it home.

Avro Lancaster B.Mk I

Type: seven-seat heavy bomber

Powerplant: four 1223kW (1750hp) Merlin 24 inverted inline piston engines

Maximum speed: 462km/h (286mph) at 3500m (11,480ft)

Ferry range: 2700km (1674 miles) with 6350kg (13,970lb) bomb load

Service ceiling: 7467m (24,492ft)

Weights: empty 16,783kg (36,923lb); loaded 30,845kg (67,859lb)

Armament: early production model, nine 7.7mm (.303cal.) Browning machine guns plus up to 6350kg (14,000lb) of bombs

Dimensions:
span	31.09m	(102ft)
length	21.18m	(69ft)
height	6.25m	(20ft)
wing area	120.49m²	(1296sq ft)

the all-wood de Havilland Mosquito, without doubt one of the most versatile and successful aircraft of World War II. Official interest in the Mosquito was slow to awaken, but, in March 1940, the Air Ministry issued Specification B.1/40, covering the building of three prototypes (one fighter, one light bomber and one photo-reconnaissance) and an initial production batch of 50 aircraft. The first prototype flew on 25 November 1940.

First Operational Sortie
The PR Mosquito was the first into service, being issued to No. 1 Photographic Reconnaissance Unit at RAF Benson, Oxfordshire, in September 1941. The first operational sortie was flown on 20 September. The first Mosquito B.IV

bombers went to No. 105 Squadron at Marham, Norfolk, in May 1942, and made their first operational sortie on the 31st. A Mosquito night fighter was also produced, and this aircraft gradually took over the night defence of Great Britain from the Beaufighter.

In May and June 1942, the RAF launched thousand-bomber raids against Cologne, Essen and Bremen, causing substantial damage, and the ability of Bomber Command to hit its targets in massive strength began to give rise to serious concern in Luftwaffe circles that the German air defences were badly deficient. German fears increased in the summer of 1942, when the first bomber squadrons of the US Eighth Air Force became operational on British bases. They

were equipped with the Boeing B-17 Flying Fortress, and during the remainder of the year they carried out many daylight attacks with strong fighter escort against targets in France and the Low Countries.

These raids were now opposed by two principal German fighter types, the Messerschmitt Bf 109F and the Focke-Wulf Fw 190, both formidable opponents. Nevertheless, the preliminary attacks on 'fringe' targets in Europe were encouraging enough to persuade the Americans that even without fighter escort, daylight raids on targets in

De Havilland Mosquito B.IV light bombers of No. 139 Squadron. The Mosquito was the most versatile RAF aircraft of World War II, operating in every role from reconnaissance to anti-shipping.

Left: Boeing B-17 Flying Fortresses of the 532nd Squadron, 381st Bomb Group, US Eighth Army Air Force. This group was based at Ridgewell, Essex, in England, from June 1943 to June 1945.

Below: The Focke-Wulf Fw 190 was a formidable fighter and gave the Allies serious problems in 1942. Seen here is a captured example on an evaluation flight in the United States.

Germany itself were feasible – despite the warnings of the RAF, who had bitter experience of the cost of unescorted daylight missions over enemy territory.

While the RAF and USAAF set about planning their respective bombing offensives, the tide of war was changing rapidly in North Africa. In August and September 1942, with the British Army committed to a defensive role while it marshalled its forces to launch a major counteroffensive against the Afrika Korps, practically the whole burden of offensive operations against the enemy devolved on the Desert Air Force, which now had American units under its operational control. With the American contribution – soon to become the Ninth US Army Air Force – the total number of squadrons available to the Allied air forces in the Middle East in October 1942 rose to 96.

On 23 October, the British Eighth Army's counteroffensive began at El Alamein, preceded by a heavy bombardment of enemy airfields. The entire strength of the Desert Air Force's tactical fighter-bomber squadrons was turned on the reeling enemy, who finally broke on 4 November. The coastal roads leading to the west were jammed with enemy convoys, which were harried by the fighter-bombers during the pursuit into Cyrenaica.

Massive Landing

On 8 November, the Allies launched Operation Torch, a massive landing on the coasts of French Morocco and Algeria by seaborne British and US forces. The British landings were supported by the Fleet carriers *Formidable*, *Victorious*, *Furious* and *Argus*, and the escort carriers *Biter*, *Dasher* and *Avenger*, while the American landings were covered by the *Ranger*, *Sangamon*, *Suwannee* and *Santee*. It was a formidable demonstration of naval air power, the naval aircraft providing air cover over the beaches

A Short Sunderland flying boat seen at its moorings at Castle Archdale, Fermanagh, Northern Ireland. From this base, the Sunderlands ranged far out into the Atlantic in pursuit of the German U-boats.

until the capture of airfields enabled fighters to be flown in from Gibraltar.

Caught between the two Allied pincers, the Germans sought to establish new defences in Tunisia and seized a number of ports, through which they attempted to pour in supplies. In April 1943, the Eighth Army linked up with the US II Corps and the final advance through Tunisia began, with the fighter-bomber units in the forefront of the battle all the way. On 13 May 1943, the Axis forces in Tunisia

surrendered, their supply lines shattered by Malta-based aircraft and submarines and by the Desert Air Force, which destroyed huge numbers of German transport aircraft.

Two months later, in an operation that involved the large-scale use of airborne forces, the Allies invaded Sicily, which was to provide them with a springboard for the invasion of Italy a few weeks later. In September, the Italian government concluded an armistice with the Allies, but there was to be no easy victory in Italy. The Germans, and the Italians who remained loyal to them, resisted fiercely as the Allies fought their way doggedly up the

peninsula; however, the capture of key Italian airfields meant that Allied bombers could now reach targets in the German Reich from this area, too.

The Allied landings in North Africa, which had involved the passage of convoys directly from the United States, would not have been possible without Allied control of the Atlantic. In this respect, aviation had played an increasingly vital role. By the end of 1940, the war at sea had cost 1281 British, Allied and neutral ships, of which 585 were sunk by U-boats. German submarine losses during this period amounted to

32 craft, none of which had fallen victim to aircraft alone. Technical improvements were beginning to have an effect in the fight against the submarine, however, and at the beginning of 1941 about a sixth of RAF Coastal Command's maritime patrol aircraft were equipped with ASV (air-to-surface vessel) radar, although this was still in a primitive stage of development and as yet was effective only against U-boats that were fully surfaced and within about 5km (3 miles) of the search aircraft.

A Lockheed A-28 Hudson in the insignia of the US Army Air Corps. The Hudson, which was purchased by the RAF before the outbreak of war, proved to be a useful anti-submarine weapon.

America's Long-Range Bomber
Consolidated B-24 Liberator

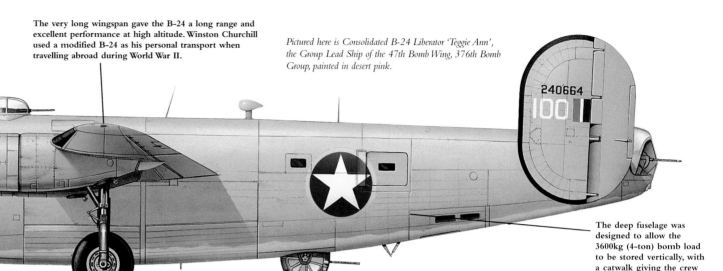

The very long wingspan gave the B-24 a long range and excellent performance at high altitude. Winston Churchill used a modified B-24 as his personal transport when travelling abroad during World War II.

Pictured here is Consolidated B-24 Liberator 'Teggie Ann', the Group Lead Ship of the 47th Bomb Wing, 376th Bomb Group, painted in desert pink.

The deep fuselage was designed to allow the 3600kg (4-ton) bomb load to be stored vertically, with a catwalk giving the crew access to the rear fuselage.

B-24 Liberator

Type: heavy bomber with crew of 10

Powerplant: four 895kW (1200hp) Pratt & Whitney R-1830-43 Twin Wasp radial piston engines

Maximum speed: 488km/h (300mph)

Ferry range: 2896km (2850 miles)

Service ceiling: 9900m (32,500ft)

Weights: empty 15,413kg (34,000lb); maximum 27,216kg (60,000lb)

Armament: one 12.7mm (.50cal) nose gun, two more in dorsal turret, tail turret, retractable ball turret and waist positions, plus maximum internal bombload of 3629kg (8800lb)

Dimensions:
span	33.52m	(110ft)
length	20.22m	(66ft 4in)
height	5.46m	(17ft 11in)
wing area	97.36m²	(1048sq ft)

In these early days, the RAF relied on two main types of maritime patrol aircraft. The first was the Short Sunderland, which had entered service in 1938. One of the principal exponents of the Sunderland as an anti-submarine weapon was No. 10 Squadron RAAF (Royal Australian Air Force), which was based in Britain and first experimented with a group of four 0.303in machine guns mounted on either side of the aircraft's bow, bringing the total armament to 10 guns. The revised forward-firing armament meant that the Sunderland could lay down effective fire on a surfaced U-boat as the aircraft made its run-in, and, with 10 guns, the flying boat presented a dangerous target to enemy fighters, which learned to be wary of it at an early stage of the war.

The Germans nicknamed the Sunderland *Stachelschwein* (Porcupine).

Military Lockheed 14
The other type of maritime patrol aircraft, the Lockheed Hudson, was a military version of the Lockheed Model 14 twin-engined commercial airliner, one of the success stories of the late 1930s. It was developed at short notice in 1938 to meet a British requirement for a maritime reconnaissance aircraft to replace the Avro Anson in the squadrons of RAF Coastal Command. The RAF placed an initial order for 200 aircraft, the first of which were delivered to No. 224 Squadron at Leuchars, Scotland, in May 1939. Lockheed supplied 350 Hudson Is and 20 Hudson IIs (the same as the Mk I except for different

propellers), before introducing the improved Mk III.

Neither the Sunderland or the Hudson, however, had sufficient range to close the dangerous mid-Atlantic gap, where the U-boats prowled in search of Allied convoys. Matters took a turn for the better in 1942, with the introduction of escort carriers and their complement of anti-submarine aircraft, but it was not until the deployment of very long-range maritime aircraft in the shape of the Consolidated B-24 Liberator and the PBY Catalina, operating in concert with naval hunter-killer groups, that the tide of the Atlantic war began to turn.

A Consolidated PBY-5A Catalina. With its very long endurance, the Catalina did much to turn the tide of the Battle of the Atlantic. Fifteen squadrons of the RAF were equipped with it.

Wooden Warrior of the Eastern Front
Lavochkin LA-5

The LA-5's basic wing construction was made of birch wood, cross-grained and impregnated with a resin mixture and covered in plywood.

The Lavochkin La-5FN was basically a radial-engined development of the LaGG-3, and it was a fine aircraft in the hands of an experienced fighter pilot. The type was flown by Russia's leading air ace, Ivan Kozhedub.

This was due, in no small measure, to improved anti-submarine weapons. In early encounters between RAF aircraft and enemy submarines, the standard 113kg (250lb) bomb was used to attack U-boats. It was not until 1940 that the depth charge was acknowledged as the really effective anti-submarine weapon. Even then, the early depth bombs, filled with Amatol, were notoriously unreliable and prone to disintegrate on hitting the sea's surface. Modifications in 1941 introduced a new

The two-seater Ilyushin Il-2m3 Shturmovik made a huge contribution to Russian victories on the Eastern Front in the battles of 1943. It was a very effective ground-attack aircraft and well able to defend itself.

explosive called Torpex, which was 30 per cent more effective than Amatol.

New Weapon
In May 1943, British and American patrol aircraft received a new weapon. Known for security reasons as the Mk 24 mine, it was in fact an air-launched torpedo with an acoustic homing head, developed in the United States. The Liberator squadrons equipped with it carried two of these torpedoes as well as their usual load of depth charges. Rocket projectiles were also used in attacks on surfaced U-boats, and aircraft-mounted searchlights were used to illuminate surfaced U-boats in transit at night across

the Bay of Biscay from their French bases.
Late in 1942, while the western Allies strove to defend their vital Atlantic lifelines, the Battle of Stalingrad raged on the Eastern Front. New Soviet aircraft types were making their appearance, and in the ground-attack role the most important was the Ilyushin Il-2 Shturmovik. This aircraft had entered service in 1941, but the early version was a single-seater, and its lack of rear protection had cost it dearly. A modified single-seat Il-2M, with a boosted engine and new armament, began to reach frontline units in the autumn of 1942, and was used in considerable numbers during the battle for Stalingrad that winter.

Lavochkin La-5FN

Type: interceptor fighter

Powerplant: one 1231kW (1650hp) Shvetsov M-82FN (ASh-82FN) radial piston engine

Maximum speed: 650km/h (403mph)

Ferry range: 765km (475 miles)

Service ceiling: 11,000m (36,000ft)

Weights: empty 2605kg (5737lb); loaded 3360kg (7932lb)

Armament: two or three 20mm shVAK or 23mm NS cannon plus provision for 158kg (350lb) of bombs or four 82mm rockets underwing

Dimensions:		
span		9.80m (32ft)
length		8.67m (28ft)
height		2.54m (8ft)
wing area		17.59m² (189sq ft)

Fighter on the Eastern Front
Yakovlev Yak-9

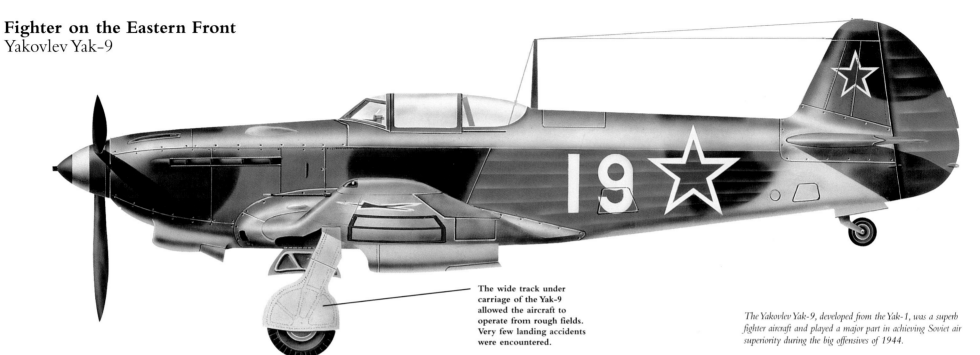

The wide track under
carriage of the Yak-9
allowed the aircraft to
operate from rough fields.
Very few landing accidents
were encountered.

The Yakovlev Yak-9, developed from the Yak-1, was a superb fighter aircraft and played a major part in achieving Soviet air superiority during the big offensives of 1944.

Yak-9D

Type: single-seat long-range fighter/ground-attack aircraft

Powerplant: one 940kW (11,260hp) Klimov VK-105PF-1 liquid-cooled piston engine

Maximum speed: 533km/h (330mph) at sea level; 597km/h (370mph) at 3650m (12,000ft)

Ferry range: 1360km (843 miles)

Service ceiling: 10,000m (33,000ft)

Weights: empty 2420kg (5324lb); maximum take-off 3115kg (6850lb)

Armament: one 20mm shVAK cannon mounted in the spinner; one 12.7mm (.50cal.) machine gun installed in the engine cowling

Dimensions: span   9.74m (31ft 11in)
          length   8.50m (27ft 10in)
          height   2.6m (8ft 6in)
          wing area 17.15m² (185sq ft)

Meanwhile, further modifications were under way. The armoured forward section was extended to accommodate a rear gunner's cockpit. The new two-seater variant, the Il–2m3, entered service in August 1943, and played a prominent and often decisive part on the Eastern Front.

The Russians also, at last, had fighter aircraft that were the equal of their opponents. From the Lavochkin design bureau came the La-5, developed from the earlier LaGG-3 in response to a desperate requirement of the Soviet Air Force, which had suffered appalling casualties at the hands of the Luftwaffe in the second half of 1941, for a modern

fighter that could hold its own with the Messerschmitt 109. Semyon Lavochkin retained the basic LaGG-3 airframe, which was lightweight, of wooden construction and easy to assemble, and married it with a 992kW (1330hp) Shvetsov M-82F radial engine. Other modifications included a cut-down rear fuselage, providing much improved pilot visibility, and a heavier armament. From Yakovlev came the Yak-9, a progressive development of the excellent Yak-1. A superb fighter aircraft, the Yak-9 did much to win air superiority over the eastern battlefront. A further development of the Yak-1 was the Yak-3, which reached the

front line during the early summer months of 1943. In July came the decisive Battle of Kursk, characterized by the massive deployment of armoured formations and large numbers of ground-attack aircraft. It ended in a Russian victory, and launched a Soviet drive across eastern Europe that would end at Berlin.

Spectacular Coup

In the Pacific, too, the war was beginning to turn in the Allies' favour. The principal

The Lockheed P-38 Lightning's principal asset was its long range, enabling it to operate successfully over the vast areas of the Pacific Ocean and to escort bombers deep into Germany.

The Grumman F6F Hellcat incorporated all the design lessons that had been learned the hard way in combat by its predecessor, the F4F Wildcat. It gained air superiority for the Americans from 1943 onwards.

August of that year. The Hellcat was to go on to play a prominent role in all US naval operations.

During 1943, there was a marked and noticeable decline in the level of expertise of Japanese pilots. Loss of the nucleus of the Imperial Japanese Navy's best pilots, many of whom had seen extensive combat in China before the start of the Pacific war, in the great battles of 1942, was at last beginning to have its effect. As new US fighter types arrived in the Pacific, the Japanese began to suffer combat losses that were little short of staggering.

Marianas Turkey Shoot

The most devastating loss suffered in the air by the Japanese during the entire Pacific war occurred during the Battle of the Philippine Sea in June 1944, when carrier-based aircraft provided air cover for the occupation of the Marianas. During the first major fighter sweep over the islands, on 11 June, the carrier aircraft destroyed a third of the defending air force. On 19 June, with the amphibious invasion in full swing, large numbers of Japanese bombers and torpedo-bombers made a

The Mitsubishi G4M, code-named 'Betty' by the Allies, was very vulnerable to attack and burned readily, earning it the nickname of the 'flying lighter'. The green crosses carried by these aircraft indicate that they have surrendered.

Allied fighters in the theatre were still the Grumman F4F Wildcat, the Bell P-39 Airacobra and the Curtiss P-40, but a new long-range fighter, the Lockheed P-38 was becoming available in increasing numbers. On 18 April 1943, P-38 pilots of the US 339th Fighter Squadron pulled off a spectacular coup when they flew to the limit of their combat radius from Guadalcanal and shot down a G4M Betty bomber carrying Admiral Isoroku Yamamoto, Commander in Chief of the Japanese Combined Fleet and architect of the attack on Pearl Harbor. The two top-scoring American pilots of the Pacific

war, Major Richard I. Bong and Major Tommy McGuire, both flew P-38s.

Early in 1943 some US Marine Corps squadrons began to re-equip with a powerful new fighter, the Vought F4U Corsair, which deployed to Guadalcanal in February. One pilot in particular scored spectacular successes while flying this type; he was Lieutenant Robert Hanson of Marine Squadron VMF-215, and he rose to fame in the bitterly contested sky over Rabaul. On 14 January 1944, Hanson fought the first of a series of combats that was to set a record, destroying five out of a formation of 70 Zeros that were

trying to intercept US bombers. His next five sorties over Rabaul netted him 15 more enemy fighters, bringing his score to 20 enemy aircraft destroyed over a period of only 17 days.

The American fighter that really changed the course of the Pacific air war, however, was the Grumman F6F Hellcat. The Hellcat flew for the first time on 26 June 1942, its design having benefited from hard-earned lessons learned by its predecessor, the Wildcat. First deliveries were made on 16 January 1943, and the aircraft saw its first combat over Marcus, one of the Caroline Islands, on 31

Triumph in the Pacific
Vought F4U Corsair

The Corsair's inverted gullwings gave the huge propeller extra ground clearance; they also ensured that the wing met the fuselage at right-angles, causing minimum interference drag.

The cockpit was set right back, making visibility poor and contributing to some of the aircraft's early landing problems.

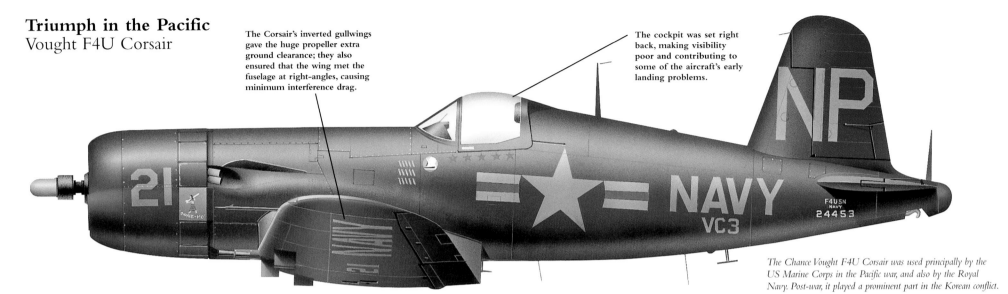

The Chance Vought F4U Corsair was used principally by the US Marine Corps in the Pacific war, and also by the Royal Navy. Post-war, it played a prominent part in the Korean conflict.

F4U-1A Corsair

Type: single-seat carrier-operable fighter-bomber

Powerplant: one 1492kW (2000hp) Pratt & Whitney R-2800-8 Double Wasp 18-cylinder radial piston engine

Maximum speed: 671km/h (417mph) at 6605m (20,000ft)

Ferry range: 1650km (1010 miles)

Service ceiling: 11,247m (37,000ft)

Weights: empty 4074kg (9000lb); loaded 6350kg (14,000lb)

Armament: six 12.7mm (.50cal.) Browning M2 machine guns with 400 rounds (outboard) and 375 rounds (inboard) per gun; up to 1800kg (4000lb) of bombs or rockets

Dimensions:		
span	12.49m	(41ft)
length	10.16m	(33ft 5in)
height	4.90m	(15ft 1in)
wing area	29.17m²	(314sq ft)

series of desperate attempts to hit the task force; they were detected by radar at a range of 240km (150 miles), and the carrier fighters were waiting for them. The great air battle that followed was a one-sided massacre that would go down in history as the 'Marianas Turkey Shoot'. American combat air patrols and anti-aircraft fire destroyed 325 enemy aircraft, including 220 of the 328 launched by Japanese aircraft carriers. American losses were 16 Hellcats in combat, and seven other aircraft shot down by Japanese fighters or ground fire.

In Europe, the strategic air offensive against Germany was now well under way. The first daylight mission undertaken by the Americans against a German target, a raid on Wilhelmshaven by a relatively small number of B-17 Flying Fortresses

in January 1943, was almost unopposed and seemed to bear out the Americans' belief that the heavily armed bombers, flying in tight 'boxes', could bring enough defensive firepower to bear to deter most fighter attacks. Before many weeks had elapsed, however, determined packs of Luftwaffe fighters had shattered this myth once and for all.

The Eighth Air Force's raids continued to grow in size and cost. As the Germans' experience of countering the heavy bombers increased, American losses rose to a serious level in April and May 1943; however, the real test was still to come.

Round-the-Clock Offensive
In June 1943, the RAF and USAAF joined forces in Operation Pointblank, a round-the-clock bombing offensive

against Germany's war industries. In terms of offensive power the Eighth Air Force was well equipped to handle such an operation, its strength having increased to 15 bomber groups. The biggest obstacle to the success of deep-penetration daylight missions was the lack of long-range fighter escorts. The RAF's Spitfires had sufficient range only to escort the bombers halfway across the Netherlands, while the USAAF's P-47 Thunderbolts and P-38 Lightnings could reach Germany's western frontier. In an effort to improve matters, the Americans slung droptanks under the wings and bellies of their P-38s and P-47s, but it was not long before the German fighter leaders developed new combat techniques that went a long way towards eliminating the Americans' advantage.

Biggest, Fastest, Meanest
Republic P-47D Thunderbolt

Known as the 'Jug', the Republic P-47 Thunderbolt fought with distinction in all theatres of war. It was used as an escort fighter, but its true forte lay in ground attack, as it was a very stable weapons platform.

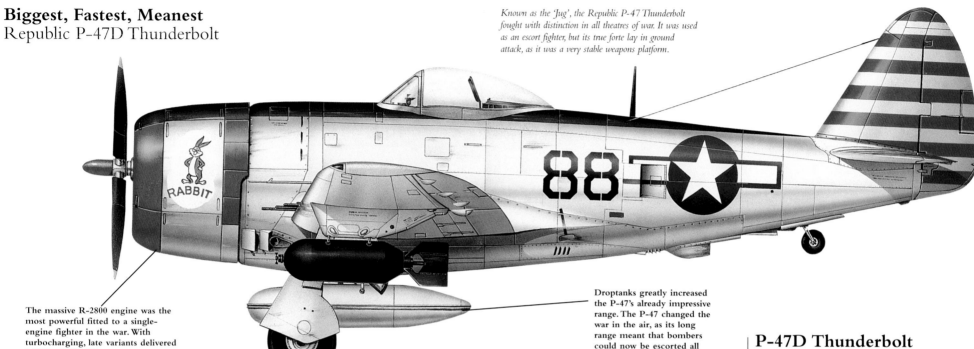

The massive R-2800 engine was the most powerful fitted to a single-engine fighter in the war. With turbocharging, late variants delivered 2,535hp (2090kW).

Droptanks greatly increased the P-47's already impressive range. The P-47 changed the war in the air, as its long range meant that bombers could now be escorted all the way to Berlin and back.

The Focke-Wulfs and Messerschmitts would attack the US fighters as they crossed the Dutch coast, forcing them to jettison their auxiliary tanks in order to increase manoeuvrability.

During the last week of July 1943, the Eighth Air Force carried out five major attacks on enemy targets and lost 88 bombers. Then came August and the first of a series of shattering blows. On 17 August, 376 B-17s were dispatched to attack ball-bearing factories at Schweinfurt and the Messerschmitt assembly plant at Regensburg on the deepest penetration mission mounted so far by the Eighth

Air Force. The Regensburg force was to fly on to North Africa. Both targets were hit, but 60 bombers were shot down and about 100 damaged.

It was five weeks before the Americans recovered sufficiently from this mauling to carry out further long-range missions into Germany. When the attacks did start again, the lessons of August were rammed home even more forcibly. During one week, between 8 and 14 October, the Americans lost 148 bombers and 1500 aircrew. In an attack on Schweinfurt on 14 October, the Luftwaffe's fighters made 500 sorties

and destroyed 60 of the 280 bombers taking part.

Major Battles
Developments in German night-fighting techniques were also beginning to inflict heavy losses on RAF Bomber Command. Three major raids on Berlin in August and September 1943 cost the RAF 123 Lancasters and Halifaxes, with a further 114 damaged. With the introduction of more advanced airborne interception radar and gunnery tactics, such as the installation of upward-firing cannon that could rake a bomber from underneath,

P-47D Thunderbolt

Type: single-seat fighter and fighter-bomber

Powerplant: one 1715kW (2535hp) Pratt & Whitney R-2800-59 Double Wasp 18-cylinder radial engine

Maximum speed: 697km/h (430mph)

Ferry range: 3000km (1860 miles) with droptanks

Service ceiling: 13,000m (42,000ft)

Weights: empty 4853kg (10,660lb); loaded 7938kg (17,500lb); later versions – loaded 9390kg (20,700lb)

Armament: eight 12.7mm (.50cal.) Browning M2 machine guns with 267 to 500 rounds; provision for maximum external load of 1134kg (2500lb), including bombs, napalm or eight rockets

Dimensions:

length	11.02m	(36ft 2in)
span	12.42m	(40ft 9in)
height	4.30m	(14ft 2in)
wing area	27.87m²	(300sq ft)

the German night fighters presented a serious challenge to Bomber Command, and their success rate reached a peak in the spring of 1944. In the course of three major battles over Germany the RAF suffered crippling losses; the worst was on the night of 30 March, when Bomber Command lost 95 heavy bombers in an attack on Nuremberg, with a further 71 damaged.

As the Americans reeled under the

A P-51D Mustang of the 375th Fighter Squadron, 361st Fighter Group, pictured on an escort mission to Germany in late 1944. In England, the 361st Fighter Group was based at Bottisham, Cambridgeshire, and Little Walden, Essex.

losses sustained during the daylight offensive of 1943, it was clear that only a suitable long-range escort fighter could redress the balance in their favour, and by the end of the year they had it. The North American P-51 Mustang was initially produced in response to a 1940 RAF requirement for a fast, heavily armed fighter able to operate effectively at altitudes in excess of 6100m (20,000ft). The Americans built the prototype in 117 days, and the aircraft, designated NA-73X, flew on 26 October 1940. The first of 320 production Mustang Is for the RAF flew on 1 May 1941, powered by an 820kW (1100hp) Allison V-1710-39

engine. RAF test pilots soon found that with this powerplant the aircraft did not perform well at high altitude, but that its low-level performance was excellent. It was therefore decided to use the type as a high-speed ground-attack and tactical reconnaissance fighter, and it was in this role that it entered service with Army Co-operation Command in July 1942.

Luftwaffe Hunted

The USAAF, somewhat belatedly, realized the fighter's potential and evaluated two early production Mustang Is under the designation P-51. The RAF suggested that the P-51 would perform much

better as a high-altitude interceptor if it were re-engined with the Rolls-Royce Merlin, and with a new single-piece cockpit canopy it became the P-51D. The first production P-51Ds began to arrive in England in the late spring of 1944 and quickly became the standard equipment of the USAAF Eighth Fighter Command. There is no doubt at all that the Mustang won the daylight battle over Germany. Operating from bases in England and Italy, it not only provided fighter escort for the bombers engaged in a two-pronged assault on Hitler's

Tank-Buster Supreme
Hawker Typhoon Mk IB

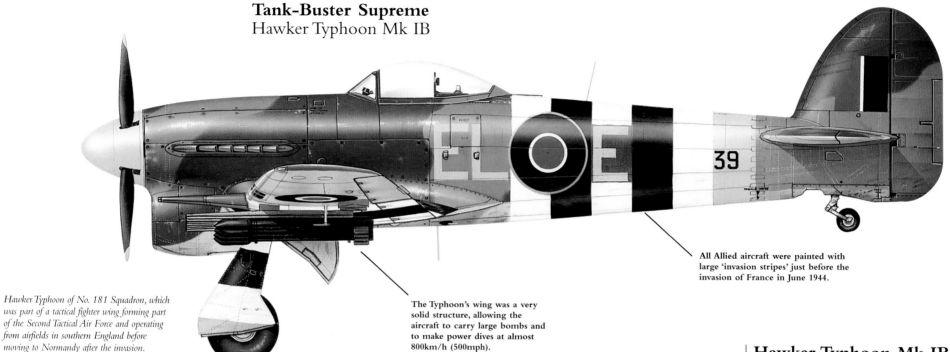

Hawker Typhoon of No. 181 Squadron, which was part of a tactical fighter wing forming part of the Second Tactical Air Force and operating from airfields in southern England before moving to Normandy after the invasion.

All Allied aircraft were painted with large 'invasion stripes' just before the invasion of France in June 1944.

The Typhoon's wing was a very solid structure, allowing the aircraft to carry large bombs and to make power dives at almost 800km/h (500mph).

Reich, but also hunted the Luftwaffe on its own airfields.

On 6 March 1944, Mustangs appeared for the first time over Berlin and took part in one of the most bitterly contested air battles of the war, with 200 German fighters taking on 660 heavy bombers and their escort. When it ended, the Americans had lost 69 bombers and 11 fighters, but the Germans had lost 80 aircraft – almost half the defensive force.

For the next few weeks, the Allied strategic air forces were used in the tactical role, striking at communications, supply depots and gun emplacements

in France in preparation for the coming D-Day landings in Normandy on 6 June 1944. The Allied tactical air forces achieved complete superiority during the Normandy landings, and they never relinquished it during the months that followed – months that witnessed the mounting of the biggest airborne operations of the war, as the Allies attempted to lay an 'airborne carpet' across enemy-held territory to the Rhine bridge at Arnhem in September 1944. It was in the drive across northwest Europe that the Allied fighter-bombers came into their own, the rocket-armed

Hawker Typhoons of the RAF's Second Tactical Air Force and the Republic P-47 Thunderbolts of the US IX Tactical Air Force making the movement of enemy armour by day almost impossible.

On the tactical side, the Luftwaffe was decisively beaten. It made only one serious attempt to deal a crippling blow to the Allied air forces; it happened on 1 January 1945, at the height of the German counteroffensive in the Ardennes – the operation known as the Battle of the Bulge. On New Year's Day, 1000 low-flying German bombers and fighter-bombers struck 27 Allied airfields

Hawker Typhoon Mk IB

Type: single-seat fighter-bomber

Powerplant: one 1626kW (2180hp) Napier Sabre IIA inline piston engine

Maximum speed: 664km/h (413mph) at 6000m (19,685ft)

Ferry range: 975km (606 miles); 1500km (932 miles) with droptanks

Service ceiling: 10,700m (35,100ft)

Weights: empty 3992kg (8800lb); loaded 6010kg (13,250lb)

Armament: four 20mm Hispano cannon each with 140 rounds; two bombs of up to 454kg (1000lb) each

Dimensions:		
span	12.67m	(41ft 7in)
length	9.73m	(31ft 11in)
height	4.52m	(14ft 10in)
wing area	25.90m²	(279sq ft)

in Belgium and the Netherlands, destroying nearly 300 British and US aircraft on the ground in the space of just a few minutes. The attack, which cost the Luftwaffe about 140 aircraft, virtually paralysed the tactical air forces for over a week, but it was not long before the Allied air forces were operating at full strength again. The Luftwaffe had played its last card, and it had lost.

During the following weeks, Mustangs, Thunderbolts, Lightnings, Spitfires and Tempests roved across Germany, ferreting out the dwindling Luftwaffe squadrons and attacking them on their airfields. Fighter-bombers also struck hard at enemy communications in northern Germany in preparation for Operation Varsity, the Allied crossing of the Rhine, which took place on 24 March 1945.

With the Anglo-American forces firmly established across the Rhine and the Russian armies closing in from the east, the collapse of German resistance was rapid. On 30 April 1945, as rocket-firing Hawker Typhoons of the RAF and Thunderbolts of the USAAF harried the last Panzers in the shattered streets of Germany's towns and villages, 50 Focke-Wulf 190s and Messerschmitt 109s attempted to attack the advancing troops of the British Second Army. The Spitfires and Tempests pounced, and, after a fierce

dogfight, the debris of 37 enemy aircraft lay scattered over the countryside.

That same day, Adolf Hitler killed himself beneath the ruins of Berlin; a week later, the war in Europe came to an end.

In the Pacific, the Marianas' capture was of great significance, as the islands provided the USAAF with a platform from which to launch a long-awaited strategic air offensive against the Japanese home islands. At Saipan, Tinian and Guam, work went ahead on the construction of new airfields; by January 1945, these were ready to receive strategic bombers: the mighty Boeing B-29 Superfortresses.

Atomic Bombs

The first units to be equipped with the B-29 were deployed to bases in India and southwest China in the spring of 1944,

the first combat mission being flown on 5 June against Bangkok in Japanese-held Thailand before attacks on the Japanese mainland were initiated 10 days later. The establishment of five operational bases in the Marianas in March 1944 brought the B-29s much closer to Japan, and four bombardment wings were quickly redeployed there from their bases in India and China, being followed a little later by the 58th BW. All of the B-29 wings were now under the control of XXI Bomber Command, with its HQ on Guam. The move was followed by a complete revision of tactics, with B-29s now carrying out large-scale night incendiary area attacks on Japan's principal cities, with devastating results.

By July 1945, huge formations of B-29s, escorted by Mustangs and joined

by fighter-bombers from the carrier task forces that had battled their way across the Pacific, were roaming freely over the skies of Japan. With her aircraft industry in ruins, it was now that Japan keenly felt the effect of the massive losses suffered during the previous months, including the sacrifice of hundreds of aircraft and pilots in kamikaze suicide attacks.

A plan to use almost every remaining aircraft in more suicide missions against the Allied invasion force that was assembling to invade Japan was forestalled in August, with the dropping of atomic bombs on Hiroshima and Nagasaki.

The Boeing B-29 Superfortress had effectively brought Japan to her knees with attacks on the country's industrial cities before the atomic bombs were dropped. Enemy air defences were powerless against it in the end.

Left: During 1944–45 RAF Tempest Mk Vs were successfully engaged in ground attack, train-busting, destroying V-1s and supporting the Allied assault through Belgium and Holland.

Genesis of the Jet

Of all the aviation milestones that were passed during World War II, there was none that would have a greater impact on the future of flight than the deployment of the world's first operational jet aircraft.

The story of the developments that would lead to the biggest leap forward in aviation since the Wright Brothers took to the air in 1903 really begins in 1926, when a young RAF officer cadet named Frank Whittle entered the Royal Air Force College, Cranwell.

A requirement of the Cranwell course was that each student had to produce a thesis for graduation. Whittle's chosen thesis, entitled *Future Developments in Aircraft Design*, was published for circulation within the RAF College in 1928, when Whittle was at the end of his fourth and final term at Cranwell. In it, he described the turbine as a potential prime mover for aero-propulsion and provided the calculations to back his claim. His original idea was to use an internal combustion turbine (ICT) to drive an aircraft's propeller, but about a year later he suddenly realized that the propeller could be dispensed with and that jet propulsion alone might be used as a simple and effective means of driving an aircraft.

Whittle was persuaded to patent his design by a flying instructor friend at Wittering, Pat 'Johnny' Johnson, and, on 16 January 1930, Whittle filed a Provisional Specification for a patent, which was granted in April 1931. Unfortunately, with no public funds forthcoming to develop the idea further, Whittle allowed his patent to lapse in January 1934. Soon afterwards, however, he was approached by a former Cranwell colleague, Rolf Williams, who had retired from the RAF because of poor

Left: The Messerschmitt Me262 was the world's fastest fighter when it entered service, and could have done serious damage to US bomber formations if it had been available in greater numbers.

Right: Air Commodore Sir Frank Whittle patented the design of a jet engine and formed a company called Power Jets to develop it, but constantly came up against government indifference.

health, and another former RAF pilot, J.C.B. Tinling, both of whom offered their support. In 1936, Whittle, Williams and Tinling formed a company, Power Jets Limited, and work was started on an experimental engine at a factory in Rugby, Warwickshire, owned by British Thomson-Houston (BTH), a firm producing steam turbines.

The RAF saw merit in the turbojet idea and agreed to allow Whittle to work on the project for his post-graduate year. Subsequently, he was put on the Special Duties List, and in so doing the RAF ensured continuity of the project, the only stipulation being that Whittle should work no more than six hours per week on it.

Power Jets' formation galvanized the Air Ministry into instructing the Royal Aircraft Establishment (RAE) to restart work on the adoption of the internal combustion turbine for aeronautical application. The RAE complied, but concentrated on developing a device for propulsion via an airscrew. It was not until 1939, following a visit to Power Jets that summer by the Director of Scientific Research at the Air Ministry, Dr D.R. Pye, that the RAE was ordered to convert its energies to turbojet research, and it was only after his visit that an element of secrecy was introduced into the project. It was too late. As early as 1931, the embassies of all European countries, as well as the Soviet Union,

were able to purchase copies of the patent at His Majesty's Stationery Office (HMSO). In the wake of this, the Swedish Milo Company began its own line of turbojet research, while in Germany the concept became available to all the research establishments and to the major aeronautical airframe and engine manufacturing companies.

Whittle Unit

Despite all the problems it faced, both technical and administrative, Power Jets completed the Whittle Unit (WU), as the experimental turbojet engine was known, which had a centrifugal compressor and axial flow turbine. The first test run took place on 12 April 1937, and it was not

without a moment or two of drama. Whittle described the test run as follows:

'The experience was frightening. The starting procedure went as planned. By a system of hand signals from me the engine was accelerated to 2,000rpm by the electric motor. I turned on a pilot fuel jet and ignited it with a hand turned magneto connected to a spark plug with extended electrodes; then I received a "thumbs up" signal from a test fitter looking into the combustion chamber through a small quartz "window." When I started to open the fuel supply valve to the main burner (the fuel was diesel oil), immediately, with a rising scream, the engine began to accelerate out of control. I promptly shut the control valve, but the uncontrolled acceleration continued. Everyone around took to their heels except me. I was paralysed with fright and remained rooted to the spot.'

The reason for the uncontrolled acceleration was that prior bleeding of fuel lines had created a pool of fuel in the combustor. The ignition of this caused the 'runaway.' A drain was quickly fitted to ensure that this could not happen again. Its interest awakened, the Air Ministry signed a contract worth £6000 with Power Jets, with a view to developing a flyable version of the turbojet.

In Germany, unknown to Whittle and his colleagues, turbojet development had

The Heinkel He 178 was the world's first prototype jet-powered aircraft. It was a shoulder-wing monoplane, with the pilot's cockpit set well forward of the wing's leading edge.

First of the Turbojets
Heinkel He 178

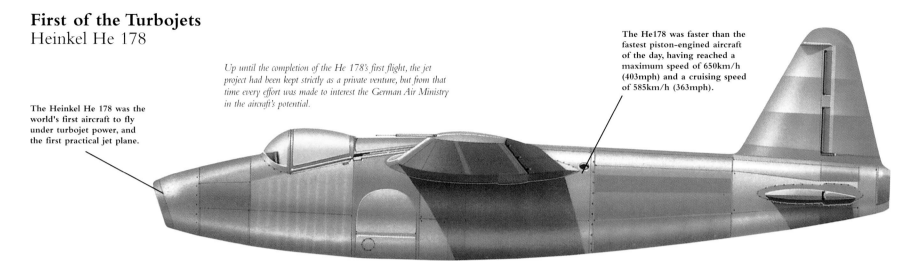

Up until the completion of the He 178's first flight, the jet project had been kept strictly as a private venture, but from that time every effort was made to interest the German Air Ministry in the aircraft's potential.

The He178 was faster than the fastest piston-engined aircraft of the day, having reached a maximum speed of 650km/h (403mph) and a cruising speed of 585km/h (363mph).

The Heinkel He 178 was the world's first aircraft to fly under turbojet power, and the first practical jet plane.

been proceeding under conditions of much greater secrecy than was the case in Britain, where the Air Ministry's lack of interest had ensured that any interested party might have access to Whittle's patent. At the Junkers Flugzeugwerke, Herbert Wagner began developing a turbojet in April 1936. In the same month, at Heinkel AG, Dr Hans Joachim von Ohain, who, like Whittle, had begun development of the turbojet concept in the early 1930s while still at university, began development of his particular internal combustion turbine as a jet propulsion unit. Instead of taking his idea to the German Air Ministry (which, like its British equivalent, would probably have been disinterested), von Ohain approached aircraft manufacturer Ernst Heinkel, who in March 1936 employed both von Ohain and his assistant, Max Hahn.

Von Ohain continued his experiments in a secret shed at Heinkel's Marienehe airfield, and, by September 1937, the first demonstration turbojet, the HeS 1, was being bench-tested (albeit somewhat uncontrollably and only on hydrogen). It produced a thrust of about 250kg (550lb) at 10,000rpm and resembled Frank Whittle's early patents. The HeS 1 bench test was simply a means to prove the concept; the scale model was made with pressed steel.

Heinkel Tests
By March 1938, a much more refined turbojet, the HeS 3, was bench-running at a thrust of about 500kg (1100lb); it was controllable and ran on petrol. The HeS 3, like Whittle's engine, used a centrifugal compressor and inducer. Some of the air from the compressor

passed forwards into a reverse-flow annular combustion chamber, while some went rearwards to mix with the combustion gases before entering the turbine. The radial inflow turbine was of similar configuration to the compressor, and the whole engine had a somewhat large diameter for its size, due to the compressor and combustion chamber arrangement. Maximum rotor speed was 13,000rpm and weight was 360kg (795lb).

While Heinkel set about building an aircraft around the HeS 3, the engine was flight-tested under a Heinkel He 118, which had been an unsuccessful contender in a German Air Ministry requirement for a new dive-bomber (the winner was the Junkers Ju 87). The HeS 3 made many flights under the He 118 before the turbine burned out, by which time a great deal had been

He 178

Type: single-seat experimental monoplane

Powerplant: one 4.4kN (992lb ft) HeS 3 turbojet

Maximum speed: 700km/h (435mph)

Ferry range: 200km (125 miles)

Service ceiling: n/a

Weights: empty 1620kg (3572lb); Max takeoff weight 1998kg (4405lb)

Dimensions:
span	7.20m (23ft 3in)
length	7.48m (24ft 6in)
height	2.10m (6ft 10in)
wing area	9.1m² (98sq ft)

The first prototype of the Gloster-Whittle E.28/39 takes to the air at Farnborough. The aircraft had been fitted with a ventral camera and additional fins on the tailplane.. The E.28/39 was flown by RAF pilots while at Farnborough.

learned and a much-improved engine, the HeS 3b, was ready to be installed in the world's first jet aircraft prototype, the Heinkel He 178. The latter was a simple design, emerging as a shoulder-wing monoplane with the pilot's cockpit situated well forward of the leading edge. On 24 August 1939, with Heinkel test pilot Erich Warsitz at the controls, the He 178 made a short 'hop' along the runway at Marienehe. The first true flight was made three days later, but was marred when the engine flamed out soon after take-off when, according to Ernst Heinkel, a bird was sucked into the intake. Warsitz made a safe landing. A much more plausible explanation was that the flight had to be curtailed because of turbine limitations, as the HeS 3 could be run for only six minutes in flight at high levels of turbine inlet temperature. In November 1939, the aircraft was demonstrated before a group of senior German Air Ministry officials, but the concept was greeted with little enthusiasm. Development of the He 178 was abandoned in favour of the He 280, which had wing-mounted turbojets, and the little aircraft was eventually sent to the Berlin Air Museum, where it was destroyed in 1943 along with the He 176, a rocket-powered research aircraft.

Meanwhile, in Britain, Power Jets

had suffered a serious setback on 6 May 1938, when the WU's turbine failed at 13,000rpm and the engine was wrecked. The WU was rebuilt and modified, the original single combustion chamber being replaced by 10 small ones, but the process of reconstruction took five months and it was not until October 1938 that testing was resumed.

Experimental Aircraft

Whittle had already studied the problem of turning the massive WU into a flyable design and, with an Air Ministry contract secured, work started on the Whittle Type W1A prototype. The W1X ran for the first time on 14 December, 1940. Meanwhile, the Gloster Aircraft Company had been building an experimental aircraft, the E.28/39, and the W1X was installed in it for taxi trials. Fitted with the fully operational W1 engine, the type made its first flight from Cranwell, Lincolnshire, on 15 May 1941, with Gloster's chief test pilot Gerry Sayer at the controls.

The flight lasted 17 minutes and, on this occasion, Sayer kept the speed down, the engine rpm being restricted to about 16,500 to hold back the turbine inlet temperature. This gave a thrust of 390kg (860lb), which was considered adequate for Sayer to ascertain the control qualities of the airframe; the engine had already run for 25 hours on the bench.

Within days, the aircraft was reaching speeds of up to 595km/h (370mph) at 7625m (25,000 feet), with the engine set at 17,000rpm, exceeding the performance of the contemporary Spitfires. Two E.28/39s were built, but the second aircraft was destroyed on 30 July 1943 when its ailerons jammed and it entered an inverted spin. The pilot, Squadron Leader Douglas Davie, baled out at 10,000m (33,000ft), the first pilot to do so from a jet aircraft. The first prototype E.28/39, W4041, is on display in the Science Museum, Kensington, London.

The success of the turbojet was no longer in doubt, and the Air Ministry authorized

development of an improved design, the W2. Like the W1, it featured a unique reverse flow design of the burners, in which the heated air from the flame tubes was piped back towards the front of the engine before entering the turbine area. This allowed the engine to be 'folded', therefore permitting a shorter engine.

In August 1940, well before completion of the experimental E.28/39, the Gloster Aeroplane Company had submitted a preliminary brochure to the Air Ministry, outlining proposals for a turbojet-powered fighter. Realizing that it would take too much time to develop a turbojet of sufficient thrust to power a single-engined fighter, Carter selected a twin-engined configuration, the design having a tricycle landing gear and high-mounted tailplane, with the engines housed in separate mid-mounted nacelles on the low-set wings. In November 1940, the Air Ministry issued Specification F.9/40, written around this

Right: Twenty Meteor F.1s were ordered, and all but five were delivered to the RAF to meet the immediate need for an operational jet fighter. No. 616 Squadron was the world's first operational jet fighter unit.

The Self-Sacrifice Bomb
Fieseler Fi 103 Reichenberg IV

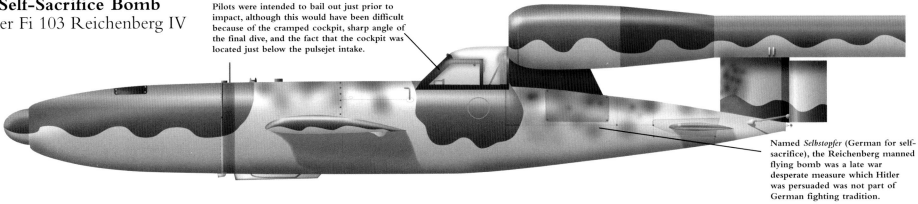

Pilots were intended to bail out just prior to impact, although this would have been difficult because of the cramped cockpit, sharp angle of the final dive, and the fact that the cockpit was located just below the pulsejet intake.

Named *Selbstopfer* (German for self-sacrifice), the Reichenberg manned flying bomb was a late war desperate measure which Hitler was persuaded was not part of German fighting tradition.

Fieseler Fi 103 Reichenberg IV

Type: manned air-to-surface missile

Powerplant: one Argus 014 pulse jet

Maximum speed: 645km/h (400mph)

Service ceiling: 2500m (8200ft)

Range: 330km (205 miles)

Weights: 2250kg (4960lb)

Armament: one 830kg (1830lb) warhead

Dimensions:
span	5.7m (18ft 9in)	
length	7.5m (24ft 7in)	
height	n/a	
wing area	n/a	

proposal, and design arrangements were finalized in the following month. On 7 February 1941, Gloster received an order from the Ministry of Aircraft Production for 12 'Gloster Whittle aeroplanes' to the F.9/40 specification. The planned production target was 80 airframes and 160 engines per month. The first of the 12 flew on 5 March 1943; this aircraft was powered by two 680kg (1500lb) thrust Halford H.1 turbojets, developed by de Havilland, but the first 20 production aircraft were fitted with the 771kg (1700lb) Rolls-Royce Welland, as the W2 engine was now named. Twenty production aircraft were ordered under the designation Meteor F.Mk.1.

Jet Age
It was in June 1944 that the Royal Air Force entered the jet age, and the squadron selected to pioneer its entry into the new era was No. 616, based at Culmhead, near Taunton in Somerset. Following the conversion of a number of the squadron's pilots at Farnborough, No. 616's first Meteors arrived at Culmhead in July 1944, just in time to help counter a serious German threat. It was called the Fieseler Fi 103, better known as the V-1 flying bomb.

The Fieseler Fi 103 was conceived in 1942 as an expendable pilotless aircraft, using as its power source the Argus As 014 impulse duct, or pulsating athodyd, a simple form of jet engine first developed by the fluid dynamicist Paul Schmidt in the 1920s. The first prototypes arrived

Above and right: The V-1 flying bomb evolved into a piloted version, the Reichenberg IV. It was test-flown by the female test pilot Hanna Reitsch, but was never used operationally. It was intended for use against shipping.

Below: The trustworthy Focke-Wulf Fw 200 Condor was used as a 'mother ship' to test missiles such as the V-1 as well as the Henschel Hs 293 anti-ship weapon, which it also carried operationally.

at the Peenemünde research station in December 1942, and to determine the Fi 103's aerodynamic qualities a missile was launched on an unpowered test flight from a Focke-Wulf Fw 200, with the first ramp launch being made on 24 December. Numerous test missiles were fired over the Baltic from the test sites, some even reaching Sweden's southern coast.

The Fi 103 was a simple mid-wing cantilever monoplane, its fuselage being divided into six compartments which contained the compass, warhead, fuel tank, compressed air containers, autopilot and height and range-setting controls, and the servo-mechanisms which controlled the rudder and elevators. The cantilever wing was built around a single tubular spar which passed through the centre of the fuel compartment. The Argus As 014 pulse jet was mounted above the rear portion of the body, supported at its forward end by a crutch and aft by the vertical fin.

A Reichenberg IV, the piloted version of the V-1, slung uder the wing of a He 111 bomber during flight trials. Conventional V-1s were also air-launched by Heinkels after the missiles' launch sites in France were overrun.

The flying-bomb assault on Britain was given the code name Operation Rumpelkammer (lumber room), and

Germany's Wonder Jet
Messerschmitt Me 262

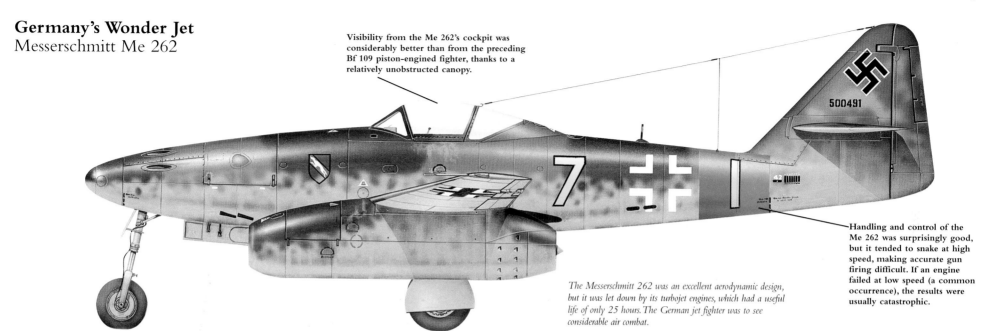

Visibility from the Me 262's cockpit was considerably better than from the preceding Bf 109 piston-engined fighter, thanks to a relatively unobstructed canopy.

Handling and control of the Me 262 was surprisingly good, but it tended to snake at high speed, making accurate gun firing difficult. If an engine failed at low speed (a common occurrence), the results were usually catastrophic.

The Messerschmitt 262 was an excellent aerodynamic design, but it was let down by its turbojet engines, which had a useful life of only 25 hours. The German jet fighter was to see considerable air combat.

such was the success achieved during the initial test phase with the Fi 103 that the date for the start of the operation was set for 15 December 1943. This date proved to be overoptimistic because, by October 1943, only one battery of Flakregiment 155W, the unit trained to operate the Fi 103, had reached the launching sites that were being built in the Pas de Calais, France. Few fully trained personnel were available, and in any case the sites themselves were coming under heavy Allied air attack. By March 1944, of the original 96 launching site, only 14 had escaped damage.

It was not until the night of 12/13 June 1944, that Rumpelkammer began, and from that date until 31 August 1944,

when the majority of the sites had been overrun by British forces, 8564 V-1s were launched against London and 53 against Southampton, the latter being air-launched by Heinkel 111s. The total number of hits recorded on London was 2419. The main problem for the fighter pilots engaged in air defence against the V-1, apart from the fact that the missiles presented very small targets, was their small margin of speed over the flying bombs, coupled with the short time available to make an interception.

Small Fraction
By 31 August 1944, the date when the V-1 sites were finally overrun by Allied ground forces, the squadron's score stood

at 13 destroyed. Although it was only a very small fraction of the total number of missiles destroyed by the air defences, it nevertheless proved the Meteor's capability in action against small high-speed targets.

For the remainder of 1944, No. 616 Squadron settled down to a steady and somewhat dull routine of demonstration flights for the benefit of Allied military dignitaries and air exercises in conjunction with RAF Bomber Command (which was now flying daylight missions in growing numbers) and the US Eighth Air Force. The object of these exercises was primarily to assist the Allied bomber commanders to develop defensive tactics against the German Messerschmitt

Me 262A-2

Type: single-seat air superiority fighter

Powerplant: two 8.82kN (1980lb thrust) Junkers Jumo 004B-1, 2, or 3 axial-flow turbojets

Maximum speed: 870km/h (540mph)

Ferry range: 1050km (650 miles)

Service ceiling: 11,450m (37,500ft)

Weights: empty 3800kg (8738lb); maximum 6400kg (14,100lb)

Armament: four 30mm RheinmetallBorsig MK 108A-3 cannon; upper pair 100 rounds; lower pair 80 rounds; 12 R4M air-to-air rockets; two 226kg (500lb) bombs

Dimensions:	span	12.50m (40ft 11in)
	length	10.58m (34ft 9in)
	height	3.83m (12ft 7in)
	length	21.73m² (234sq ft)

RAF Jet Pioneer
Meteor F3

Among the improvements introduced in the Meteor F.Mk 3 were a sliding cockpit canopy, increased fuel capacity, new Derwent I engines, slotted air brakes and a strengthened airframe.

To correct the directional stability problems exhibited by the F.9/40, an enlarged fin and rudder were fitted, along with flat-sided rudders and an 'acorn' fairing at the intersection of the fin and tailplane.

Gloster Meteor IV
RollsRoyce Derwent Engine

EE455

Above: The Meteor F.3 EE455 was one of two aircraft taken off the production line, brought up to Mk IV standard, less VHF mast and armament, and given a special high-speed finish for an attack on the world air speed record.

Me 262 jet fighters, which were appearing in action against the daylight bomber formations, and against which the piston-engined Allied fighter escorts were virtually powerless.

262 Development

Design work on the Me 262 began in September 1939, a month after the successful flight of the world's first jet aircraft, the Heinkel He 178, but because

The Gloster Meteor F.3, with more powerful jet engines, quickly replaced the Mk I in RAF service. No. 616 Squadron took its F.3s to the Continent early in 1945 and used them for ground attack, but never met the Luftwaffe in combat.

of delays in the development of satisfactory engines, the massive damage caused by Allied air attacks and Hitler's later obsession with using the aircraft as a bomber rather than a fighter, six years elapsed between the 262 taking shape on Messerschmitt's drawing board and its entry into Luftwaffe service. Because of the lack of jet engines, the prototype Me 262V-1 flew on 18 April 1941 under the power of a Jumo 210G piston engine, and it was not until 18 July 1942 that the Me 262V-3 made a flight under turbojet power. In comparison, once the programme of British turbojet engine development had been taken over by Rolls-Royce, progress in Britain had been much faster, and, although British jet engines were less powerful than their German counterparts, they were much more reliable. The Me 262's Jumo engines

Meteor F.Mk 1

Type: single-seat day fighter

Powerplant: two 7.56kN (17000lb thrust) Rolls-Royce W.2B/23C Welland Series 1 turbojets

Maximum speed: 675km/h (419mph) at 3048m (10,000ft)

Service ceiling: 12,192m (40,000ft)

Weights: empty 3737kg (8221lb); loaded 6258kg (13,768lb)

Fuel capacity: 1363 litres (360 gallons)

Armament: four Hispano 20mm cannon in the nose

Dimensions: span 13.10m (42ft 11in)
length 12.50m (41ft)
height 3.90m (12ft 9in)
wing area 34.70m² (373sq ft)

The Night Fighter
de Havilland Vampire FB.Mk 5

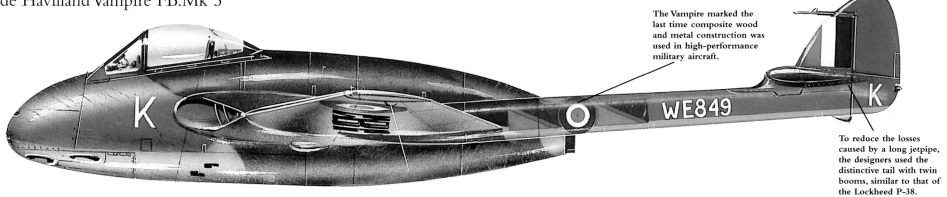

The Vampire marked the last time composite wood and metal construction was used in high-performance military aircraft.

To reduce the losses caused by a long jetpipe, the designers used the distinctive tail with twin booms, similar to that of the Lockheed P-38.

Above: The RAF was remarkably slow to order jet night fighters, and the de Havilland company set about developing the DH113 Vampire NF.Mk 10 as a private venture. The RAF eventually received 95 examples.

were prone to sudden catastrophic failure and had a life of only about 25 hours.

Ground-Attack Role

The second Gloster Meteor variant to enter squadron service, the Meteor F.3, was a much better proposition than the F.1, using the 906kg (2000lb) thrust Rolls-Royce Derwent I engine; however, deliveries to No. 616 Squadron did not begin until December 1944. The Mk 3 version, which eventually equipped 15 squadrons of RAF Fighter Command in the immediate post-war years, and

A de Havilland Vampire F.Mk.6 of the Swiss Air Force pictured against the Alps. The Swiss Air Force was a major customer for the Vampire, and for its successor, the Venom.

which had been operationally tested in a ground-attack role in Belgium with No. 616 Squadron in the closing weeks of the war, was followed into service by the Meteor F.Mk.4. Powered by two Rolls-Royce Derwent 5s, the F.Mk.4 first flew in April 1945 and subsequently, in November, set up a new world air speed record of 975km/h (606mph).

Meanwhile, the second British jet fighter to become operational had made its appearance. Design work on the DH.100 Vampire had begun in May 1942, with the prototype flying for the first time on 20 September 1943, and, in the spring of 1944, it became the first Allied jet aircraft capable of sustained speeds of more than 800km/h (500mph) over a wide altitude range. The first production Vampire flew in April 1945, but it was not until 1946 that the first examples were delivered to operational

squadrons. The Vampire was powered by the 1042kg (2300lb) thrust Halford H.1 engine, now named the Goblin.

America's first jet fighter was the Bell P-59 Airacomet, the prototype of which flew on 1 October 1942 under the power of two General Electric I-A turbojets, derived from the Whittle W.2B engine. A higher powered engine, the 635kg (1400lb) thrust I-16, was installed in the 13 trials aircraft which followed. Two of these were evaluated by the US Navy, and a third was sent to the United Kingdom in exchange for a Gloster Meteor Mk 1. The Airacomet proved to be underpowered and its performance fell far below expectations, and as a result the original order for 100 aircraft was reduced. Twenty P-59As were built with J31-GE-3 engines, and 30 P-59Bs with J31-GE-5s. Although the Airacomet did not serve operationally in World War II,

Vampire FB.Mk 5

Type: single-seat fighter-bomber

Powerplant: one 13.8kN (3100lb) de Havilland Goblin 2 turbojet

Maximum speed: 860km/h (530mph)

Ferry range: 1755km (1090 miles)

Service ceiling: 12,000m (40,000ft)

Weights: empty 3300kg (7270lb); loaded: 5618kg (13,385lb)

Armament: four 20mm Hispano Mk.V cannon

Dimensions:
span	11.6m	(38ft)
length	9.37m	(30ft 9in)
height	1.88m	(6ft 2in)
wing area	24.32m²	(262sq ft)

Left: The United States' first jet fighter was the Bell P-59 Airacomet, the prototype of which flew on 1 October 1942 under the power of two General Electric I-A turbojets, derived from the Whittle W.2B engine.

Right: Pictured here after the end of World War II, the Lockheed P-80 Shooting Star was the United States' first fully operational jet fighter. It later saw service in Korea.

it did provide the Americans with invaluable experience in the operation of jet aircraft, from both the aircrew and engineering points of view.

First US Jet Fighter

The United States' first fully operational jet fighter was the Lockheed P-80 Shooting Star which, like its British counterparts, was of very conventional design and which was to become the workhorse of the American tactical fighter-bomber and fighter-interceptor squadrons for five years after World War II. The prototype XP-80 was designed around a de Havilland H-1 turbojet which was supplied to the United States in July 1943, and the aircraft was completed in just 143 days, making its first flight on 9 January 1944. In April 1945, two YP-80s were sent to England, where they were attached to the Eighth Air Force, and two more went to Italy, but none experienced any operational flying in Europe before the war's end. Early production P-80As entered USAAF service late in 1945 with the 412th Fighter Group, which became the

1st Fighter Group in July 1946 and comprised the 27th, 71st and 94th Fighter Squadrons.

Operational Status

In Germany, production of the Messerschmitt Me 262 had at last accelerated in the closing weeks of 1944, and by the end of the year 730 Me 262s had been completed. A further 564

Early prototypes of the Messerschmitt Me 262 had a tailwheel undercarriage, which made taking off difficult and dangerous. It was soon changed to tricycle landing gear.

were built in the early months of 1945, making a total of 1294 aircraft. The Me 262 initially went into production as a pure fighter, entering service with a trials unit known as Erprobungskommando 262 (EK262) at Lechfeld, near

The World's First Jet Bomber
Arado AR 234

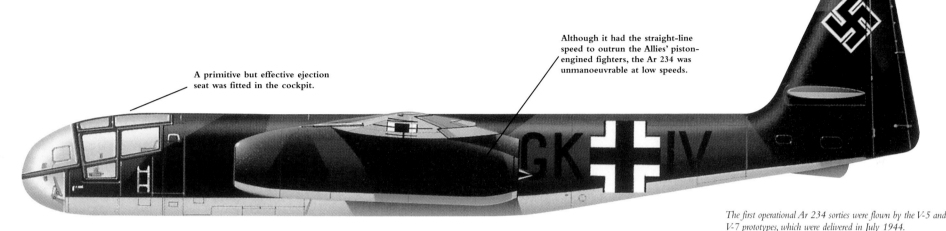

A primitive but effective ejection
seat was fitted in the cockpit.

Although it had the straight-line
speed to outrun the Allies' piston-
engined fighters, the Ar 234 was
unmanoeuvrable at low speeds.

*The first operational Ar 234 sorties were flown by the V-5 and
V-7 prototypes, which were delivered in July 1944.*

Augsburg, in August 1944. It was
originally commanded by Captain
Tierfelder, who was killed when his
aircraft crashed in flames during one of
the unit's first operational missions. His
successor was Major Walter Nowotny,
who, at the age of 23, was one of the
Luftwaffe's top fighter pilots with a
score of 258 kills, 255 of them achieved
on the Eastern Front. By the end of
October, the Kommando Nowotny, as
the unit had come to be known, had
reached full operational status and was
deployed to the airfields of Achmer and
Hesepe near Osnabruck, astride the
main American daylight bomber
approach route. A shortage of
adequately trained pilots and technical
problems meant that the Kommando
Nowotny was usually able to fly only

three or four sorties a day against the
enemy formations, yet in November
1944 the 262s destroyed 22 aircraft. By
the end of the month, however, the unit
had only 13 serviceable aircraft out of
an established total of 30, a rate of
attrition accounted for mainly by
accidents rather than enemy action. The
Me 262 presented a serious threat to
Allied air superiority during the closing
weeks of 1944.

Two versions were now being
developed in parallel: the Me 262A-2a
Sturmvogel (Stormbird) bomber variant
and the Me 262A-1a fighter. In
September 1944, the Sturmvogel was
issued to Kampfgeschwader 51
Edelweiss; other bomber units that
armed with the type at a later date were
KG 6, 27 and 54. Problems encountered

during operational training delayed the
aircraft's combat debut, but, in the
autumn of 1944, the 262s began to
appear in growing numbers, carrying out
low-level attacks on Allied targets, mainly
moving columns. There were also two
reconnaissance versions, the Me 262A-
1a/U3 and Me 262A-5a.

Towards the end of 1944, a new
Me 262 fighter unit, Jagdgeschwader
JG 7 Hindenburg, was formed under the
command of Major Johannes Steinhoff.
Later, authority was also given for the
formation of a second Me 262 jet fighter
unit, known as Jagdverband 44 and
commanded by Lieutenant General
Adolf Galland. It comprised 45 highly
experienced pilots, many of them
Germany's top-scoring aces. Its principal
operating base was München-Riem,

Arado Ar 234B-2

Type: single-seat twin-turbojet tactical
reconnaissance bomber

Powerplant: two 8.8kN (1975lb thrust) Junkers
Jumo 004B-1 Orkan turbojet engines

Maximum speed: 742km/h (460mph) at 6000m
(20,000ft)

Range: 1630km (1010 miles)

Service ceiling: 10,000m (33,000ft)

Weights: empty 5200kg (11,440lb); maximum
take-off 9800kg (21,560lb)

Armament: up to 1995kg (4400lb) of bombs

Dimensions: span   14.44m (46ft)
           length   12.64m (41ft)
           height   4.29m (14ft)
           wing area 27.3m² (294sq ft)

Above: The original trolley-and-skid arrangement of the Ar 234A-1, as the initial production version was designated, was changed to a conventional wheeled undercarriage on the Ar 234B.

Left: The prototype Ar 234V-1, which flew for the first time on 15 June 1943, and the next seven aircraft (Ar 234-2 to V-8) all used a trolley-and-skid landing gear.

where its main targets were the bombers of the Fifteenth Army Air Force, coming up from the south.

Jet Bomber

Two other German jet types became operational before the war's end. The first was the Arado Ar 234 Blitz (Lightning), the world's first operational jet bomber.

Several variants of the Me 262 were proposed, including the radar-equipped Me 262B-1a/U1 two-seat night fighter, which was to see brief operational service from March 1945.

The prototype Ar 234V-1, which flew for the first time on 15 June 1943, and the next seven aircraft (Ar 234V-2 to V-8) all employed a trolley-and-skid landing gear. The second prototype, the Ar 234V-2, was similar in all respects to the first machine, but the Ar 234V-3 was fitted with an ejection seat and rocket-assisted take-off equipment. The trolley-and-skid arrangement was later abandoned and with it the Ar 234A-1,

as the initial production version was to have been designated, the aircraft being fitted with a conventional wheeled undercarriage. In this guise, the aircraft was designated Ar 234B, and 210 were built. Only two versions were used operationally; these were the Ar 234B-1 unarmed reconnaissance variant, and the Ar 234B-2 bomber.

The first operational Ar 234 sorties were actually flown by the V-5 and V-7

Luftwaffe's Last Chance
Heinkel He 162 Salamander

Mounting the BMW 003 engine above the fuselage made the aircraft unstable in pitch, which made it very difficult to fly.

Aerodynamic problems led to the adoption of turned-down wingtips. The wings were mostly of wood, with light alloy flaps.

He 162 Salamander

Type: single-seat jet fighter

Powerplant: one BMW 003E-1 axial-flow turbojet engine rated at 7.80kN (1755lb thrust) for take-off and 9.02kN (2030lb thrust) for maximum bursts of up to 30 seconds

Maximum speed: 890km/h (490mph) at sea level

Range: 620km (384 miles)

Service ceiling: 12,010m (39,400ft)

Weights: empty 1663 kg (3659lb); empty equipped 1758 kg (3868lb); loaded 2805 kg (6171lb)

Armament: two 20mm MG 151 cannon in forward fuselage

Dimensions: span   7.20m (23ft 7in)
         length   9.05m (29ft 8in)
         height   2.60m (8ft 6in)
         wing area   11.20m² (121sq ft)

prototypes, which were delivered to I/Versuchsverband.Ob.d.L (Luftwaffe High Command Trials Unit) at Juvincourt, near Reims, on July 1944. Both aircraft were fitted with Walter rocket-assisted take-off units and made their first reconnaissance sorties on 20 July, photographing harbours on the south coast of England from an altitude of 9000m (29,530ft). Several more sorties were made over the United Kingdom before the unit was transferred to Rheine in September. Other reconnaissance trials units received the Ar 234, and. in January 1945. these were amalgamated into I/F.100 and I/F.123 at Rheine, and I/F.33 at Stavanger, Norway. The jet bombers were very active in the early weeks of 1945, one of their most notable missions being the 10-day series of

attacks on the Ludendorff bridge at Remagen, captured by the Americans in March 1945. Very few Ar 234 sorties were flown after the end of March, although an experimental Ar 234 night-fighter unit, the Kommando Bonow, equipped with two Ar 234s converted to carry upward-firing cannon, continued to operate until the end of the war.

Last-Ditch Air Fighter

The other jet type was the Heinkel He 162. In the winter of 1939–40, Ernst Heinkel abandoned work on the He 178, with its fuselage-mounted turbojet, and concentrated on developing a prototype jet fighter, the twinjet He 280. Problems with the turbojets meant that the inaugural flight on 22 September 1940 was made without these installed, the

The Heinkel He 162 Salamander, also known as the Volksjäger (People's Fighter), was seen by the Germany as the Luftwaffe's last chance in the closing stages of World War II.

aircraft being towed to height by He 111 and released. It was not until April 1941 that the aircraft flew under turbojet power. Nine prototypes were built and flown, some being armed experimentally with cannon, but the aircraft's performance was poor and it did not enter production. The prototypes carried out much trials work, mostly in connection with jet engine development. This culminated, later in the war, in the design of the Heinkel He 162 Salamander. Developed as a last-ditch air fighter in the closing stages of World War II, the Heinkel He 162 progressed from drawing board to first flight, on 6 December 1944, in

Nine prototypes of the Heinkel He 280 jet fighter were built and flown, some being armed experimentally with cannon, but the aircraft's performance was poor and it did not enter production.

only 10 weeks. The type was constructed mainly of wood, due to a shortage of strategic metals. In all, 31 prototypes and 275 production aircraft were built, the first being issued to JG 1 at Leck in Schleswig-Holstein, but this unit did not

become operational before the end of the war. A few contacts were made with Allied aircraft, and one He 162 was possibly shot down by an RAF Tempest on 19 April 1945.

In the Soviet Union, where rocketry had always been a fascination, emphasis was on developing rocket-powered aircraft; turbojet development would be very much a post-war function. The first

Russian attempt to produce a short-range rocket-propelled target defence interceptor was the Berezniak-Isayev BI-1, designed to have a rate of climb of 180m/sec (35,400ft/min). It was to be powered by a Dushkin D-1 rocket motor, which was successfully tested in a glider that had been towed to altitude.

Of mixed construction, the BI-1, a small low-wing monoplane, was built in only

40 days, and was flown as a glider for the first time on 10 September 1941. The first powered test flight was made on 15 May 1942 and was successful, but shortly afterwards the prototype was destroyed when it crashed during a maximum-power run at low level. Despite this setback, seven pre-series aircraft were built, and the programme went ahead. Subsequent flight trials, however, revealed

The BI-1 was the first Russian attempt to produce a short-range rocket-propelled target defence interceptor. It was to be powered by a Dushkin D-1 rocket motor.

unforeseen aerodynamic problems. This, together with the fact that Dushkin's work on a multi-chamber rocket motor encountered innumerable snags, and the powered endurance of eight minutes was considered insufficient for operational purposes, brought an end to the project.

Rocket-powered Flight

The Germans, in contrast, persevered with their efforts to produce an operational rocket-powered fighter, and succeeded, although success came too late to have any impact on the European air war. The aircraft, the Messerschmitt Me 163 Komet, was based on the experimental DFS 194, designed in 1938 by Professor Alexander Lippisch and handed over, together with its design staff, to the Messerschmitt company for further development. The first two Me 163 prototypes were flown in the spring of 1941 as unpowered gliders, the Me 163V-1 being transferred to Peenemünde later in the year to be fitted with its 750kg (1653lb) thrust Walter HWK R.II rocket motor. The fuel used

After landing, the Messerschmitt 163 was loaded on to a special towed trailer for transportation back to its refuelling and rearming point. It was not an easy aircraft to handle on the ground, but its flight characteristics were excellent.

was a highly volatile mixture of T-Stoff (80 per cent hydrogen peroxide and 20 per cent water) and C-Stoff (hydrazine hydrate, methyl alcohol and water). The first rocket-powered flight was made in August 1941, and during subsequent trials the

Me 163 broke all existing world air speed records, reaching speeds of up to 1000km/h (620mph). In May 1944, an operational Komet unit, JG400, began forming at Wittmundhaven and Venlo. Many Me 163s were lost in landing accidents. About 300 Komets were built, but JG400 remained the only operational unit and the rocket fighter recorded only nine kills during its brief career.

The Rotary Wing: Early Developments

World War II saw the fruition of a new concept in aviation: the helicopter. But the idea was by no means new. As long ago as the fourth century BCE, countless children in ancient China were playing with a little toy consisting of a simple round stick with feathers mounted on top, each feather twisted slightly so that it struck the air at an angle when the stick was spun, creating enough lift to enable the device to fly up into the air. In the fifteenth century, Leonardo da Vinci foresaw the development of the rotary-wing principle in remarkable depth, discussing the possibilities of a 'lifting screw' and drawing a detailed sketch. It would be 300 years before another engineer drew up a design for a lifting screw that was sufficiently advanced to enable a working model to be built.

Left: A model of Englishman Sir George Cayley's aerial carriage of 1843, which used four revolving 'vanes' to provide lift in the same manner as a helicopter's rotors. He soon discarded this idea, and went on to pioneering work on fixed-wing aircraft designs.

In the eighteenth and nineteenth centuries, many of aviation's early pioneers, including Sir George Cayley, experimented with the rotary-wing concept, and, in 1842, a British engineer named W.H. Phillips produced a rotary-wing model that flew under the power of a primitive steam engine. The most interesting thing about it was that it used a form of jet propulsion. Steam from a tiny boiler passed through a hollow tube that ran up the rotor shaft and through the two-blade rotor, exhausting into the atmosphere under pressure through small holes at the tip of each blade; the reaction turned the rotor assembly and the model flew, albeit not very successfully. It was the first model aircraft in history to fly under the power of an engine.

The idea of the rotary wing was beginning to catch on. Some scientist-inventors became passionately devoted to it; one of them was the Vicomte Gustave de Ponton d'Amecourt, who formed a small group of enthusiasts dedicated to furthering the development of rotary-wing flying machines. In 1863, he and his colleagues built a small steam-powered model craft fitted with twin rotors mounted on the same shaft. Searching for an appropriate name for his creation, d'Amecourt hit upon the idea of combining the Greek words *helicos* (spiral) and *pteron* (wing). So his model became the *Helicoptère* – and the name now used universally to describe rotorcraft was born.

Viable Proposition

It took the invention of the petrol engine to turn the concept of a full-size rotorcraft into a viable proposition, but it was not until four years after the Wright Brothers made their historic flight at Kitty Hawk that a petrol engine was married to a rotary wing to produce the first helicopter capable of lifting a man clear of the ground. The machine was conceived and built by three Frenchmen, Louis and Jacques Bréguet

The Bréguet-Richet Gyroplane No. 1 had to be steadied by a man standing at the extremities of each of the four arms supporting the rotors when it rose vertically from the ground.

The first aircraft to take off vertically with its pilot and make a free flight entirely without connection to the ground was the 'flying bicycle' designed and built by Paul Cornu in 1907.

and Professor Charles Richet. The engine and pilot's position were located within a rectangular framework of steel tubing, from each corner of which four arms – also of steel tube construction – spread out. Mounted at the end of each arm was a rotor assembly looking something like the wings of a biplane, with four sets of fabric-covered blades mounted in pairs and rotating around a central hub. Altogether, there were 32 lifting surfaces. One pair of rotors revolved clockwise, while the other pair revolved anticlockwise.

With a man named Volumard on board, this contraption made its first short flight on 24 August 1907 at Douai, rising to a height of 61cm (2ft). It was not a free flight; four assistants held on to the rotor arms to prevent the machine from oscillating wildly. Nevertheless, it rose into the air without their assistance and deserves its place in aviation history as the first rotary-wing craft to raise itself off the ground with a pilot aboard.

Another tethered flight was made on 29 September, and this time the Bréguet-Richet Gyroplane No. 1, as the craft was known, rose to a height of 155cm (5ft). It proved, however, to be horribly unstable, and its designers decided to abandon it and build a completely new machine.

The Bréguets and Professor Richet had hoped to be the first to make a free flight with their Gyroplane No. 2; however, this hope was shattered even before the new design was completed. On 13 November 1907, another Frenchman named Paul Cornu beat them to it. Cornu's helicopter design, known as the 'flying bicycle', was powered by a 18kW (24hp) Antoinette engine mounted in an open V-shaped framework, together with the fuel tanks and the pilot's seat. The machine was fitted with tandem rotors, paddle-shaped and fabric-covered; these were mounted on large bicycle-type wheels which were turned horizontally by a belt drive from the engine. A year earlier, Cornu had built and flown a scale model with a 1.5kW (2hp) engine.

The full-size machine made its first flight at Coquainvilliers, near Lisieux, and hovered for 20 seconds at a height of 30 cm (12in).

On subsequent flights, the height was increased to just over 2m (6ft). However, serious snags were encountered – particularly in the transmission system – and Cornu was forced to abandon further development through lack of funds.

Badly Damaged

In the summer of 1908, the Bréguet-Richet Gyroplane No. 2 made its appearance. It bore no resemblance to its predecessor, and was a great deal more advanced. Powered by a 41kW (55hp) Renault engine, it was equipped with two forward-tilting two-blade rotors. On 22 July 1908, it rose to a height of 4.5m (15ft) and flew forwards for 18m (60ft) under some measure of control. Several more successful flights

In 1908, the Bréguet-Richet collaboration produced a No. 2 Gyroplane, powered by a 41kW (55hp) Renault engine and having two forward-tilting two-blade rotors, as well as fixed wings.

were made, but, on 19 September, it made a heavy landing and was badly damaged. In December, after extensive reconstruction, the Gyroplane No. 2 was put on public display in Paris. Another test flight took place in April 1909, but before further experimental work could be undertaken it was destroyed in a storm that struck Bréguet's premises. After its loss, Bréguet concentrated on the development of fixed-wing aircraft; it was 20 years before he once again took a practical interest in helicopters.

Meanwhile, a young aeronautical engineer in tsarist Russia had also turned his thoughts to helicopter design. In 1909, he designed and built a small helicopter fitted with coaxial rotors. The engine turned the rotors all right, but the machine shook and juddered alarmingly during ground tests and never flew. In 1910, the man built a second machine which made one or two short pilotless tethered flights, but was found to have insufficient power to lift anything more than its own weight. After this second failure, the engineer turned his attention to fixed-wing design. Later, after the Russian revolution, he emigrated to the United States, where his name would one day be inscribed on the front page of the helicopter story. He was Igor Sikorsky.

Igor Sikorsky is seen pictured here beside his second unsuccessful helicopter in 1910. It managed to rise a short distance, but was incapable of lifting a pilot. Sikorsky had built his first helicopter the previous year.

Jacob Christian Ellehammer built and flew a helicopter in 1912, and continued testing it until 1916, when it overturned after a take-off and was wrecked when the rotors hit the ground.

The Pescara No. 3 helicopter was Pescara's most successful design; built in 1923, it was capable of making flights of 10 minutes' duration by January 1924. It employed a coaxial rotor system.

The other notable pioneer in the rotary-wing field during the first years of the twentieth century was a Dane, Jacob Christian Ellehammer. In 1911, he built a model helicopter and made several flights with it, and the following year he constructed a full-size machine powered by a 27kW (36hp) engine of his own design. The engine drove both the main rotor system and a tractor propeller. The lifting rotor consisted of two contra-rotating rings mounted on the same axis, the lower ring being fabric-covered to increase lift. After a number of tethered flights indoors, the helicopter made a free vertical take-off in the autumn of 1912. Several more short flights were made until September 1916, when the machine developed a violent oscillation after take-off and disintegrated when its rotor blades hit the ground.

Lacking Stability

In the immediate post-war years, one of the first people to recognize the potential of the rotary engine – which was relatively light and easily cooled – in helicopter design was the Spanish marquess Raul Pateras Pescara. His first helicopter, constructed in Barcelona during 1919–20, was originally powered by a 34kW (45hp) Hispano engine which proved incapable of lifting the craft off the ground.

Early in 1921, Pescara carried out some modifications to his prototype, including replacement of the Hispano engine with a 127kW (170hp) Le

Rhône rotary unit. In this form, the machine made a short vertical flight, but was found to be almost completely lacking in stability. In 1923, Pescara moved to France, where he constructed further helicopters, and in that year his No. 3 design achieved the first helicopter records to be officially recognized. Pescara's first officially logged record was set up on 1 June 1923, when his helicopter made a horizontal flight of 83.2m (273ft) at an average height of 1.83m (6ft); he broke the distance record on 7 June with a flight of 122m (400ft), and went on to crown his success with a flight of 305m (1000ft) on 2 August.

Pescara went on to establish several more helicopter records, but because these attempts were made under the supervision of the Aero Club of France they were not recognized by the Fédération Aéronautique Internationale (FAI), so the honour of being the first to have a record recognised by the FAI, which had just created a Helicopters category, fell to Pescara's leading rival, Etienne Oemichen, an engineer working for the Peugeot Motor Company.

Oemichen's rotorcraft experiments began in the 1920s and he evolved several interesting designs, all powered by rotary engines. His second design

Oemichen's Helicopter No. 2, 1924. This was basically a steel-tube framework of cruciform layout, with two-blade paddle-shaped rotors at the extremities of the four arms.

consisted of a cross-shaped framework of steel tubing. It had a large two-blade lifting rotor at the end of each arm and was equipped with eight propellers, five of them to provide lateral stability, a sixth – mounted on the nose – for steering and the other two for forward propulsion. Powered by a 89kW (120hp) Le Rhône, the machine flew for the first time on 11 November 1922 and showed a high degree of stability and control. Later, the 89kW Le Rhône was

De Bothezat's 'Flying X' helicopter descending for a landing at Cook Field, Dayton, Ohio, on 18 December 1922. The machine performed reasonably well, but it was too complex and the US Army lost interest.

exchanged for a 134kW (180hp) Gnome, and with this powerplant the helicopter went on to make more than a thousand test flights up to the mid-1920s. By the end of 1923, Oemichen's helicopter No. 2 had logged flights of several minutes' duration. On 14 April 1924, he established the first official FAI distance record for helicopters with a flight of 360m (1181ft), and this was followed on 17 April by another record flight of 525m (1722ft).

Cruciform Framework

While Pescara and Oemichen were carrying out their early experiments in Europe, the basis of helicopter development was also being laid in the United States. One of the pioneers in the United States was Dr George de Bothezat, another refugee from the turmoil in Russia, who in 1921 designed and built a helicopter for trials with the US Army Air Corps. The machine had a cruciform framework of metal tubing, a layout that gave it the name 'Flying X', and a 134kW (180hp) Le Rhône rotary drove four big six-blade fan-shaped rotors, mounted at each extremity of the 'X'. With de Bothezat himself at the controls, the helicopter flew for the first time on 18 December 1922, reaching a height of 1.8m (6ft) and drifting downwind for 152m (500ft).

Testing the 'Flying X' continued on and off for the best part of two years, the machine being fitted with a 164kW (220hp) engine at a later stage. In all, more than 100 test flights were made, and the helicopter reached a maximum height of 9m (30ft). The machine performed reasonably well for its day and was test-flown by US Army pilots – but in the end the Army concluded that it was too complex and it was abandoned.

Throughout the 1920s, helicopter design was characterized by totally unnecessary complexity. It was a field of contrasts in which strokes of engineering brilliance such as cyclic pitch (where each blade changes its pitch as it moves round the rotor disc) and collective pitch (where the angle of attack of all the rotor blades is altered simultaneously) control failed to achieve maximum effect because designers persisted in experimenting with inadequate rotor drive systems. It was not until 1930 that designers began to get to grips with the old problems of torque, stability and control, and the development of the helicopter really got under way.

On 26 June 1936, a helicopter took to the air in Germany. Designated Fw 61, its much-publicized performance over the next few months was to eclipse the noteworthy achievements of other helicopter designers the world over. The helicopter was designed by Dr Heinrich Karl Johann Focke, whose name continued to be borne by the famous Focke-Wulf Flugzeugbau even after he left the company. Focke lost no time in forming another company, Focke-Achgelis GmbH, to carry on his work, and, in 1934, a scale model helicopter was built and flown successfully.

Metal Outriggers

For the body of the Fw 61 (the machine, incidentally, retained the 'Fw' designation throughout its career and never carried the 'Fa' which was given to later Focke-Achgelis aircraft), Focke decided to use the fuselage of a Focke-Wulf Fw 44

Stieglitz basic trainer, with the tailplane moved to a new position on top of the fin. The engine, an Sh.14A radial, came from the same source and was mounted in the nose as on the conventional aircraft. The propeller was cut down to the diameter of the engine cylinders to provide a cooling blast of air and gave no assistance to the machine in forward flight, although some of Focke's opponents claimed that it did. The engine drove a pair of three-blade rotors mounted on metal outriggers. By varying the collective pitch of either of these and setting up a lift differential the helicopter pilot had an excellent degree of lateral control.

The first free flight of the Fw 61V-1 (the V standing for *Versuch*,

or experimental) lasted only 28 seconds, but it was not long before the helicopter began to show its true capabilities. After extensive flight testing, it established a series of FAI helicopter records in 1937–38; on one of these attempts, the helicopter was flown by the famous aviatrix Hanna Reitsch, who covered 108.974km (67.713 miles) in a straight line on 25 October 1937. It was Hanna Reitsch who really captured the public's imagination with the Fw 61 when, in February 1938, she demonstrated the helicopter's excellent control by flying it indoors before an audience in Berlin's Deutschlandhalle sports stadium. Two prototypes of the Fw 61 were built and flown, and their successful performance

led to a contract for the development of a large six-passenger transport helicopter, the Fa 266. The outbreak of World War II, however, forced Focke to shelve this project and turn his attention to the design of heavy transport helicopters for service with the German armed forces.

Meanwhile, another type of aircraft had entered the field of rotary-wing design. Called the 'autogiro', it was the brainchild of Juan de la Cierva, who discovered that a rotor, turning freely as it was pulled along through the air, could

The Focke-Achgelis Fw 61's twin rotors were mounted on outriggers on either side of the helicopter's cabin, and were fully articulated three-blade assemblies whose blade angle could be increased or decreased.

be used to produce enough lift to get an aircraft off the ground and sustain it in horizontal flight if forward propulsion were provided by an engine driving a conventional propeller. If the engine failed, the freely-windmilling rotor would go on producing enough lift to lower the aircraft in a descent without the necessity for a nose-down attitude to be adopted; it would even enable a vertical or near-vertical landing to be made.

Traffic Control

After building a number of prototypes, and overcoming the snags that arose during development, Cierva got the formula right. His autogiro designs were immensely popular, and, in the 1930s, some 500 were built throughout the world; by this time, Cierva had formed his own company in Britain, and licences for the manufacture of his autogiros were granted to firms in France, Germany, Japan and the United States. The designs culminated in the C.30A, and the autogiros demonstrated their splendid versatility on many occasions; they were, for example, used extensively by police

Pioneering Transporter
Focke-Achgelis Fa 223 Drache

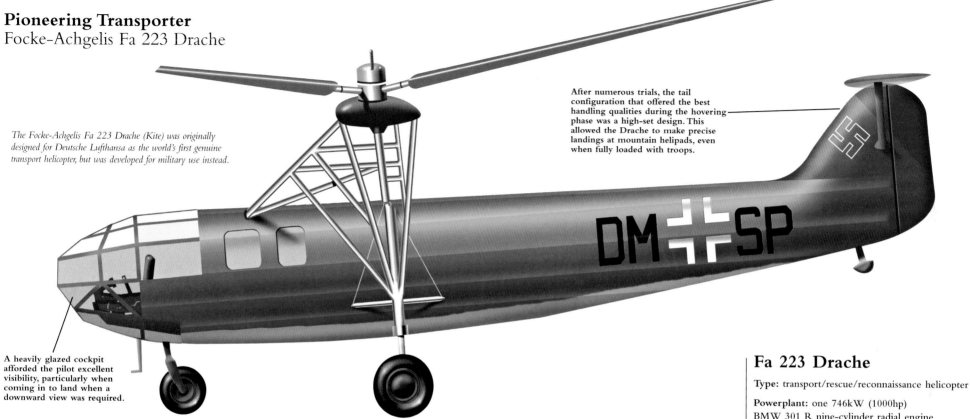

The Focke-Achgelis Fa 223 Drache (Kite) was originally designed for Deutsche Lufthansa as the world's first genuine transport helicopter, but was developed for military use instead.

After numerous trials, the tail configuration that offered the best handling qualities during the hovering phase was a high-set design. This allowed the Drache to make precise landings at mountain helipads, even when fully loaded with troops.

A heavily glazed cockpit afforded the pilot excellent visibility, particularly when coming in to land when a downward view was required.

Left: D-EKRA was the second of two Focke-Achgelis Fa-61 helicopters to be built, and the two machines went on to establish an impressive list of records from 1937 to the beginning of World War II.

for crowd and traffic control duties at major sporting events.

In the late 1930s, the German military establishment was quick to appreciate the potential of both helicopters and autogiros. In 1938, the German navy, while showing an interest in the development of small helicopters for the

fleet spotter role, also issued a requirement for a helicopter which could be used not only for convoy protection but also for mine laying and as a torpedo carrier.

In a bid to meet this requirement, Heinrich Focke considered the possibility of adapting his Fa 266 civil helicopter design for military purposes. The designation was changed to Fa 223, and after about 100 hours of ground testing the first prototype – the Fa 223V-1 Drache (Dragon) made its first flight on 3 August 1940. Like its predecessor,

the much smaller Fa 61, it carried two three-blade rotors mounted on outrigger arms made from steel tubing. The fuselage, too, was of welded steel tube construction, covered with fabric. A crew of two was accommodated in a glazed cockpit, which was completely enclosed, and there was space for four passengers in a freight compartment aft of the flight deck. The engine bay was situated behind the cargo compartment and contained a 731kW (980hp) BMW 323 air-cooled radial which drove the two

Fa 223 Drache

Type: transport/rescue/reconnaissance helicopter

Powerplant: one 746kW (1000hp) BMW 301 R nine-cylinder radial engine

Maximum speed: 175km/h (109mph)

Cruising speed: 120km/h (74mph)

Range: 700km (434 miles) with auxiliary fuel tank

Service ceiling: 2010m (6600ft)

Weights: empty 3175kg (6985lb); maximum take-off 4310kg (9480lb)

Armament: one 7.92mm MG 15 machine gun and two 250kg (550lb) bombs

Dimensions:

span	24.5m (80ft 4in)
length	12.25m (40ft 2in)
height	4.35m (14ft 3in)
rotor disc area	226.19m² (2434sq ft)

rotors by means of shafts via a friction clutch from the engine crankshaft.

Official acceptance trials were carried out early in 1942, and following these the German Air Ministry placed an order for 100 Fa 223s. Allied bombing severely disrupted production of the helicopter, however, and only 19 examples were eventually completed.

The wartime German Navy contract for a shipboard observation helicopter was awarded to another designer, Anton Flettner. In 1937, Flettner had designed a helicopter which incorporated a revolutionary idea: counter-rotating, intermeshing twin rotors. Flettner went ahead with the construction of a prototype, the Fl 265V-1, which was flown for the first time in May 1939.

Successful Trials

The Fl 265V-1 was destroyed when its rotor blades touched one another during a test flight, but the fault that had caused this accident was quickly rectified and the second prototype, the Fl 265V-2, was delivered to the Kriegsmarine (German War Navy) for evaluation, being followed by four pre-production machines. The helicopters underwent successful trials in the Baltic and Mediterranean, flying from platforms erected on various types of naval vessel, and were found to be capable of operating under a wide variety of weather conditions. Several take-offs and landings were made from the decks of U-boats.

These initial operational trials, carried out during the early part of 1940, resulted in Flettner receiving instructions to gear up for full production. By this time, however, work was well advanced on a new Flettner helicopter, the two-seat Fl 282, and since the potential of this aircraft was greater than that of the Fl 265 work on the latter was halted.

Like the Fl 265, the Fl 282 Kolibri (Hummingbird) employed twin intermeshing rotors and was powered by a 112kW (150hp) Sh 14A engine

For early flight trials, which began in 1941, the first three Flettner Fl 282 prototypes were built as single-seaters and had enclosed Plexiglass-panelled cockpits. Subsequent machines, however, were built as open two-seaters.

Hummingbird Goes to War
Flettner FL 282 Kolibri

The Fl 282 underwent exhaustive service trials, and several were used operationally from 1942, usually flying from the gun turrets of convoy escort vessels in the Baltic, Aegean and Mediterranean.

An abnormally large rudder was fitted to the vertical fin. The shape of the rear fuselage was not ideal and caused a great deal of turbulence, which meant that much of the rudder area was ineffective.

An experienced pilot could fly the Kolibri from a ship in almost any weather. Conditions must have been severe, especially during trials in the Baltic, as the forward cockpit was completely open.

mounted in the fuselage aft of the pilot. The Fl 282's cockpit was open, but the fuselage behind it was covered with metal panels. In the summer of 1940, work began at Flettner's Johannisthal factory on 45 Fl 282s to meet a German Air Ministry Order. Flight testing began early in 1941, and in the following year the fifth prototype underwent a series of trials in the Baltic from a platform mounted on a gun turret of the cruiser *Köln*. A few of the 15 pre-production aircraft were completed, and some of these were used operationally aboard

German warships on convoy protection duties in the Mediterranean and Aegean. The helicopters flew in all kinds of weather, including snowstorms, and serviceability remained high throughout; in fact, one Fl 282 in the pre-production batch logged 95 hours' flying time without having to undergo anything more than routine maintenance.

Testing and operational use of the Kolibri proved so satisfactory that, early in 1944, the German Air Ministry placed an order for 1000 production Fl 282s with BMW's factories at Munich and

Eisenach. Everything was ready for production of the helicopter to begin when the plants were wrecked by Allied bombing. Part of Flettner's own works at Johannisthal were also destroyed, and by the end of World War II only 24 Fl 282s had been delivered.

Historic Occasion
On 14 September 1939, a few days after the outbreak of war in Europe, a handful of mechanics in a factory yard at Stratford, Connecticut, in the United States, watched as a little helicopter lifted itself

Flettner Fl 282 Kolibri

Type: single- or two-seater reconnaissance and transport helicopter

Powerplant: one 119kW (160hp) Bramo Sh 14 seven-cylinder radial piston engine

Maximum speed: 150km/h (93mph) at sea level

Vertical climb rate: 91.5m/min (300fpm) at loaded weight

Range: 300km (185 miles) with pilot only

Service ceiling: 3292m (10,800ft)

Weights: empty 760kg (1672lb); maximum take-off 1000kg (2200lb)

Dimensions:

main rotor diameter	11.9m (39ft 3in)
fuselage length	6.56m (21ft 6in)
height	2.20m (7ft 3in)
total rotor disc area	224.69m² (2148sq ft)

off the ground and hovered for a few seconds before settling to earth again. It was an historic occasion, and the prototype they had seen making its first hesitant hop into the air was widely hailed as the first truly practical helicopter in the western hemisphere.

Just how valid this claim was is still a matter of controversy, as when the US machine – the Sikorsky VS-300 – made its first tethered flight other helicopters, such as Germany's Flettner Fl 265, had already flown successfully in the western world. What may be said

with certainty, though, is that the little VS-300, with its single main rotor and a small tail rotor to compensate for torque effect, laid the design foundations for the many helicopters that were subsequently to be produced by the United States' massive industry; in this respect, it was the true father of the many helicopters flying throughout the world today.

The VS-300 was Igor Sikorsky's first helicopter design for 30 years. His first two rotary-wing craft, built when he was a student in tsarist Russia during 1909–10, had both been unsuccessful. After that, he had turned his attention to conventional aircraft, designing the

world's first four-engine machines before World War I's outbreak. Swept into the cauldron of the Russian revolution, Sikorsky had sought refuge in the United States where, as a penniless émigré, he resolutely started his aeronautical career all over again. Gathering together a team of émigré Russians – many of them skilled aeronautical engineers, his colleagues of former days – he founded his own aircraft company which, during the inter-war years,

produced a series of highly successful multi-engine landplanes, amphibians and flying boats. In 1929, the Sikorsky Aviation Corporation became a subsidiary of United Aircraft, developing and building a series of outstanding long-range commercial aircraft at a new factory in Stratford, opposite the Municipal Airport.

The helicopter, however, had always been to the fore in Sikorsky's mind, and as early as 1928 he began a new phase of research into the possibilities of vertical flight, coming up with a number of preliminary designs, which he patented. Finally, in 1938, he received approval from the management of United Aircraft to go ahead with the construction of a helicopter prototype. The result was the VS-300, designed in the spring of 1939 and flown – initially as a tethered test rig,

Left: The Flettner Fl 282 Kolibri (Hummingbird) was a very basic design, as this photograph shows. One thousand were on order, but production was disrupted by the Allied bombing offensive.

Below: In May 1941, Sikorsky's VS-300 helicopter beat the world helicopter endurance record held by the Fw 61 by remaining aloft for more than an hour and a half.

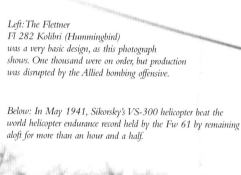

Rotary-winged Warriors
Sikorsky R-4

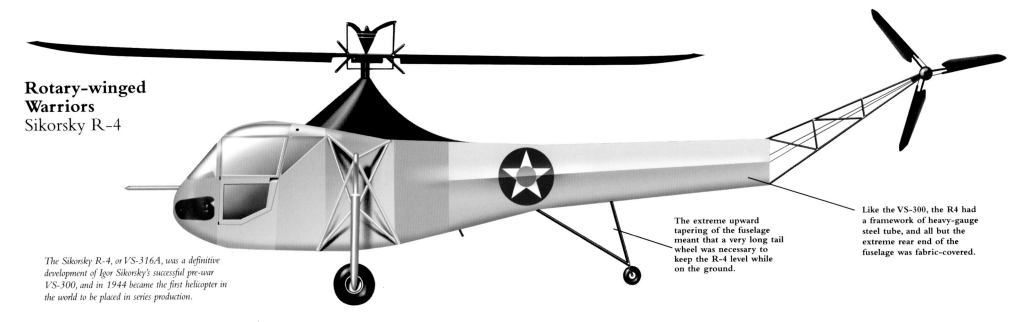

The Sikorsky R-4, or VS-316A, was a definitive development of Igor Sikorsky's successful pre-war VS-300, and in 1944 became the first helicopter in the world to be placed in series production.

The extreme upward tapering of the fuselage meant that a very long tail wheel was necessary to keep the R-4 level while on the ground.

Like the VS-300, the R4 had a framework of heavy-gauge steel tube, and all but the extreme rear end of the fuselage was fabric-covered.

Sikorsky R-4B

Type: experimental training, search and rescue helicopter

Powerplant: one 138kW (185hp) Warner R-550-3 Super Scarab piston engine

Maximum speed: 120km/h (74mph)

Endurance: 2 hours

Initial climb rate: 2440m (8000ft) in 45 minutes

Range: 209km (130 miles)

Service ceiling: 2440m (8000ft)

Weights: empty 913kg (2008lb); loaded 1153kg (2537lb)

Accommodation: two pilots, side by side

Dimensions:

rotor diameter	11.6m (38ft 1in)
length	14.65m (48ft 1in)
height	3.78m (12ft 5in)
wing area	105.3m² (1133sq ft)

with Sikorsky himself at the controls – in the following September. It was powered by a 56kW (75hp) four-cylinder air-cooled engine driving a three-blade main rotor 8.5m (28ft) in diameter and featured a tricycle undercarriage.

Endurance Record

The VS-300 made its first free flight on 13 May 1940, and despite some technical difficulties the VS-300's flight duration of was progressively increased until, on 6 May 1941, it beat the world endurance record for helicopters (then held by the Fw 61) by staying airborne for 1 hour, 32 minutes and 26.1 seconds.

Encouraged by the VS-300's potential, the US Army Air Corps awarded Sikorsky Aircraft a contract for the construction of an experimental development designated XR-4. Following trials, the USAAF (as it now was) ordered three YR-4As in the autumn of 1942, and, in the following year, quantity production began, starting with an order for 27 pre-series YR-4Bs for evaluation by the USAAF, the US Navy, the US Coast Guard and the Royal Air Force.

Four of the USAAF's YR-4Bs were assigned to the First Air Commando Group, operating from advanced bases in India. The first helicopter operation in the China-Burma-India theatre was flown in April 1944, when an L-1 light aircraft was forced down behind enemy lines with engine failure. Apart from the pilot, the aircraft carried three British solders, one with malaria and two with

arm and shoulder bullet wounds. All four survived the forced landing, but they were in an area stiff with Japanese troops and there was no clearing where a rescue aircraft might land.

The pilot of a second light aircraft dropped a message to the stranded men, notifying them of the position of the nearest Japanese troops and advising them to make for a nearby ridge. After several hours of painful progress the small party reached this objective, where they stayed for four days and nights. Food and water was dropped to them by the Air Commando Group's light aircraft, but the condition of the wounded was becoming serious.

Meanwhile, the helicopter detachment at Lalghat had been informed of the situation. On 21 April, a YR–4B piloted by First Lieutenant Carter Harman took off on the long cross-country flight to the front line in Burma. The machine flew in stages through Hailakandi, Khumbirgram, Dimapur and Jorhat, crossing an 1830m (6000ft) mountain range on the way and reaching Jorhat shortly before nightfall. The next day Harman flew on to Ledo and Taro, where an auxiliary fuel tank was fitted for the last and longest leg of the journey, to an airstrip code-named 'Aberdeen.'

The flight to 'Aberdeen' involved another trip across a high mountain range, but the YR–4B arrived safely on the afternoon of 23 April. After refuelling, Harman took off again immediately and flew to another small strip some 32km (20 miles) south of Aberdeen; the four stranded men were hiding near a paddy field 8km (5 miles) away, having descended from their ridge when they learned that help was on the way. A light aircraft circled overhead to make sure the coast was clear, then gave Harman the signal to proceed. The

helicopter made two trips to the paddy field, bringing out one of the soldiers each time. At the small airstrip they were transferred to light aircraft, which flew them to Aberdeen.

No more rescues were made that day; the helicopter became unserviceable due to a badly overheated engine. In the cool of the following morning, however, Harman made two more flights to the paddy field and picked up the remaining men. Later that same day – 24 April – the YR–4B flew back to 'Aberdeen', and during the next 10 days Harman carried

out four more missions, one involving the hazardous rescue of two wounded soldiers from a clearing 915m (3000ft) up on a mountainside. It was a foretaste of what the helicopter would achieve in the years to come.

The helicopter was here to stay, and the next two decades were to witness major strides in its development for both military and commercial use. In both Korea and Malaya, it would become a useful adjunct to military operations; in Vietnam and subsequent conflicts, it would prove indispensable.

This Sikorsky R-4 is pictured taking off from a dusty 10th Air Force base in Burma in January 1945.

Civil Aviation: 1945–1960

Commercial air transport after World War II, particularly in Europe, can best be described as chaotic. For six years, aircraft factories had been mass-producing warplanes, and most transport aircraft used by Britain were supplied by the United States. Even in the USSR, the principal wartime transport was the Lisunov Li-2, a licence-built version of the Douglas DC-3. Only the United States had been in a position to maintain a continuity of transport aircraft production throughout the war, its massive output enabling it to meet its allies' air transport needs as well as its own.

European commercial aircraft operators were forced to rely on stopgap measures to meet their early post-war transport needs. A substantial number of ex-Luftwaffe Junkers Ju 52/3m became spoils of war after VE day, and more than 400 were completed in France and 170 in Spain. In the immediate post-war years, the Ju 52 was used commercially by France, Spain, Norway, Sweden and Denmark, and 10 of them, converted by Short Brothers, were used by British European Airways. The British Overseas Airways Corporation operated the Avro York, derived from the famous Lancaster bomber. The Lancastrian, which did much to put British commercial aviation back on a sound footing, was a more direct transport version of the Lancaster and was operated by several companies, including BOAC, which also used a passenger conversion of the Halifax C.VIII.

Commercial Evolution

The tremendous run-down of the Allied air forces in the months after World War II resulted in many thousands of war-surplus transport aircraft becoming available for sale to airline operators. Foremost among these was the magnificent Douglas C-47, the military transport version of the DC-3 airliner, known to the RAF as the Dakota. These aircraft were snapped up at knock-down prices in their hundreds by embryo airlines and air freight companies around the world, refurbished and pressed into service. Another type was the Curtiss C-46. Although largely eclipsed by the celebrated C-47 Dakota, the Curtiss C-46 Commando was a true workhorse of the USAAF, especially in the Pacific theatre. Originally designed as a civil airliner, the type flew for the first time on 26 March 1940. A preliminary batch of 25 C-46 passenger transports was followed by 1491 C-46A freighters with a single large cargo door, and by 1410 C-46Ds with double doors and a modified nose. The single-door C-46E (17 built) and the double-door C-46F (234 built) were similar except for different powerplants, while 160 aircraft were completed as R5C-1s for the US Marine Corps. Although it had a distinguished career in the Pacific and China-Burma-India theatres, the Commando did not appear in Europe until March 1945, when it took part in the airborne assault on the Rhine. Most examples that passed into civilian use after the war were used in Latin America or in the United States.

The United States had a clear lead when it came to long-haul routes, which were no longer dependent on the flying boats of the pre-war era. Now, airlines

Left: The Douglas DC-3 was used in vast numbers by airlines the world over after World War II, including TWA (pictured). Many surplus C-47s were converted for civilian use.

Below: The Curtiss C-46 Commando was widely used in the Pacific during World War II. Many found their way on to the civil market.

Left: At the end of World War II, the Douglas Aircraft Company found itself seriously behind its main rivals in the long-range air transport market. Its solution was to turn the four-engine C-54 military transport into a successful airliner, the DC-4.

were able to take advantage of the Douglas DC-4 Skymaster.

The evolution of the Douglas DC-4, which was to become one of the most famous civil and military air transports of all time, began in mid-1935 in response to an airline requirement for a medium-range 52-seat airliner. The first DC-4, which featured triple tail fins, flew on 7 June 1938, but was rejected by the airlines, which now felt that a version with smaller capacity would be more viable economically. A modified DC-4 flew on 14 February 1942 and was the subject of 61 firm orders from the main US airlines, but, with the United States at war, all transport aircraft production was devoted to the needs of the US armed forces, and it was not until October 1945 that the DC-4 went into service as a civil airliner. By the time production ceased in August 1947, 1084 C-54 Skymasters and 79 civil DC-4s had been built. Many airlines used the DC-4 in the early post-war years, some buying surplus C-54s for conversion.

The British were less fortunate with their commercial four-engine aircraft designs. The first of these was the Avro Tudor, a commercial derivative of the Lincoln bomber. Two prototypes of the long-range model, the Avro Tudor I, were ordered in September 1944, and

these were followed by a single prototype of the Tudor 2, a high-capacity version with a shorter range. Orders for production aircraft were placed by the three airlines that were planning to operate the new aircraft: BOAC, Qantas and South African Airways. When flight testing of the Tudor I began in June 1945, however, the aircraft showed a disappointing performance, proving difficult to handle. This led to delays while

modifications were carried out, and, to make matters worse for the manufacturer, the customers kept changing their requirements. BOAC cancelled its order, having decided that the Tudor was unsuitable. Twelve Tudors were operated by British South American Airways on its Latin American routes. The Tudor 2 flew in March 1946, but met with as little success; six were built for BOAC as the Tudor 5, but five were soon sold to

The Avro Tudor was an early British attempt to capture a share of both the long-range and short-haul air transport market. The aircraft was not a success, however, and only a few Tudors went into commercial service.

British South American Airways and converted to freighters.

The other new four-engine British airliner of this period was the Handley Page Hermes, which was the civil version of the RAF's Hastings transport.

Globe-Spanning Constellation
Lockheed L-1049G

The Lockheed L-1049G first flew on 12 December 1954, and entered service with Northwest Airlines in the spring of 1955. Many earlier-series Super Constellations were completed as, or converted to, Super-G standard.

The banana-shaped fuselage of the Constellation proved to be a builder's nightmare. The passenger section in later Super Constellations was made cylindrical for ease of manufacture.

The tall, stalky undercarriage, curved fuselage and distinctive triple tail made the Constellation one of the most recognizable aircraft of its time.

L-1049E Super Constellation

Type: long-range civil transport

Powerplant: four 2435kW (3165hp) Wright R-3350-972TC18DA-1 turbo-compound radial piston engines

Maximum speed: 590km/h (370mph) at 5670m (18,000ft)

Range: 7950km (5000 miles)

Service ceiling: 7225m (23,700ft)

Weights: empty 34,665kg (76,500lb); loaded 60,328kg (133,000lb)

Accommodation: flight crew of three; two to four flight attendants; 95 to 109 passengers in various configurations

Dimensions:
span	37.49m	(123ft)
length	34.54m	(113ft 4in)
height	7.54m	(24ft 7in)
wing area	153.29m²	(1650sq ft)

The prototype Hermes I crashed on its maiden flight, on 2 December 1945, but was followed by two more, the last being the prototype of 25 Hermes 4s that were ordered by BOAC.

Last Generation
Neither of these types could compete with the last generation of American piston-engined long-haul airliners which were coming into service. Foremost among them was the Lockheed Constellation. Begun in 1939 as a commercial airliner designed for TWA, the Constellation was taken over as a military project after the United States' entry into World War II, and it first flew on 9 January 1943 with the military designation C-69. Only 20 were delivered before the end of the war, and production for the civil airlines resumed. The first version of the Lockheed

Constellation to be specifically designed for commercial use was the Model 649, which went into service in May 1947, and had improved engines as well as increased load-carrying capacity. This was followed a year later by the Model 749, with increased all-up weight and appropriate modifications to the positioning and capacity of the fuel tanks for overseas operation. This model was joined by a sub-series version, the strengthened Model 749A, which could carry an extra payload of 2200kg (4850lb). These variants of the Constellation won many orders from the large American airlines, Pan American and TWA taking delivery of the biggest numbers, and they were used successfully on both international and internal routes.

Development of the Constellation was ongoing for a decade, culminating in the L-1049G Super Constellation. When it

first took to the air in December 1954, the Lockheed L-1049G Super Constellation was the finest airliner in the world. Structural changes enabled it to carry large wingtip tanks, which combined with its turbo-compound engines to give it the greatest range of any Constellation. One of the main operators of the 99 examples built was TWA, the original pre-war Constellation customer. With these aircraft, the airline pioneered transatlantic and other long-haul services, including its luxury Ambassador class, patronized chiefly by businessmen and using special private suites at the airports. There is no doubt that the L-1049G brought a new degree

Right: When it first took to the air in December 1954, the Lockheed L-1049G Super Constellation was the finest airliner in the world. Structural changes enabled the Super Constellation to carry large wingtip tanks.

of comfort to airline travel, even though its turbo-compound engines generated an excessive amount of noise.

From the Douglas stable came progressive improvements of the DC-4, starting with the DC-6. At the end of World War II, the Douglas Aircraft Company found itself seriously behind its main rivals in the long-range air transport market. Although production of the wartime Douglas DC-4 (C-54) transport had topped the 1000 mark, and the type had proved its reliability by making almost 8000 crossings of the Atlantic and Pacific for the loss of only three aircraft, Boeing's Model 307 Stratoliner and Lockheed's Model 749 Constellation were not only larger in freight capacity, but were also pressurized to carry passengers in comfort. The USAAF therefore financed Douglas in the building of a larger, pressurized version of the DC-4; this was designated XC-112A and the prototype first flew on 15 February 1946. Development as a civil airliner continued under the company designation DC-6.

Different Variants

Many different variants of the DC-6 were produced during the aircraft's long career. The original DC-6A freighter was followed by the DC-6B; first flown on

2 February 1951, the DC-6B was a passenger-only version with windows and a lighter structure, and lacking the cargo door. This was the major production version, and 288 were delivered between 1951 and 1958; several were later fitted with a large underbelly tank to fight forest fires. The DC-6C was completed as a quick-change passenger/freight aircraft with windows; a movable bulkhead could be positioned in any of the four stations for mixed passenger–cargo operations. The DC-6F was a designation applied to DC-6Bs subsequently converted to freighter configuration, often without cabin windows.

The direct successor to the DC-6 was the DC-7, which first flew on 18 May 1953. The DC-7 came about as a result of a requirement issued by American Airlines, which wanted an aircraft that could compete with the Lockheed Super Constellations ordered by its rival, TWA. Wright turbo-compound engines were fitted to 110 DC-7s in the first batch, which retained many features of the DC-6's airframe; these were followed by 112 DC-7Bs (the prototype of which flew in October 1954) for service on transatlantic routes. These two DC-7 variants had a number of faults, not the least of which was excessive engine noise

The end of the commercial flying-boat era was heralded by the cancellation of the Saunders-Roe (Saro) Princess flying-boat programme. Three of these giant aircraft were built, but only one was ever flown.

in the passenger cabin, but these had been eradicated by the time the prototype DC-7C flew in December 1955. This last variant had a restructured wing to allow extra fuel tanks, and a lengthened fuselage.

Other civil aviation projects met with little success. On 2 November 1947, the biggest aircraft ever built, the Hughes H-4 Hercules flying boat, made its first and only flight, becoming airborne for

The gigantic Bristol Brabazon airliner, designed to carry passengers nonstop from London to New York, was overtaken by the march of aviation technology and was left stranded on the shores of the jet age.

about 1.6 km (1 mile) over Los Angeles roadstead at a height of 10m (33ft). Originally designed to ferry large numbers of troops and supplies to various theatres of war, it lost its reason for existence with the end of hostilities and was abandoned by the military, ending its days as a museum piece.

Britain persisted for a time with the development of commercial flying boats, culminating in the giant Saunders–Roe SR.45 Princess. Saunders–Roe had received a specification from BOAC for a flying boat capable of accommodating 200 passengers on intercontinental flights, and in May 1946 an order was placed for three SR.45 prototypes. The construction programme ran into difficulties and fell behind schedule, however, and in 1951 BOAC pulled out of the project, announcing that henceforth it would use only landplanes. A single Princess flew in 1952 and the three aircraft were cocooned at Cowes, on the Isle of Wight, before eventually being scrapped.

White Elephant

The Bristol Brabazon was another white elephant. The biggest and most ambitious project ever undertaken by the British aircraft industry, its design originated in 1943, the idea being to develop an aircraft that would carry 100 passengers nonstop from London to New York. The Brabazon 1 prototype flew for the first time on 4 September 1949, two years behind schedule, and plans were made to produce a Mk 2 version, but the project was abandoned in 1952 and the sole prototype was scrapped.

Meanwhile, a chain of events had taken place that would change the face of civil aviation for ever. It began in 1948, when two Rolls-Royce Nene turbojets were installed in a Vickers

The Vickers Nene Viking was the world's first jet-powered transport aircraft, and proved the concept of the jet airliner by flying from London to Paris in record time, marking the thirty-ninth anniversary of Louis Blériot's cross-Channel flight.

Viking airliner, making it the world's first jet-powered transport aircraft. On 19 July that year, Vickers Chief Test Pilot 'Mutt' Summers flew it from London to Paris in a record time of 34 minutes 7 seconds, at an average speed of 560km/h (348mph), to mark the thirty-ninth anniversary of Louis Blériot's cross-Channel flight.

Just over two years later, on 27 July 1949, de Havilland Chief Test Pilot John Cunningham lifted the prototype of the de Havilland Comet, the world's first jet airliner, off the runway of the company airfield at Hatfield on its maiden flight. Powered by four de Havilland Ghost turbojets mounted in pairs in the wings, the Comet underwent three years of

flight testing before inaugurating the world's first jet passenger service with BOAC in May 1952 with a flight from London to Johannesburg.

The Comet brought unheard-of luxury to its élite clientele. Carrying 36 passengers at 12,190m (40,000ft) in near silence, it was twice as fast as contemporary piston-engined airliners. The aircraft carried 30,000 passengers in its first year of operations, by which time 50 examples had been ordered by BOAC and other airlines.

Then things began to go wrong. On 26 October 1952, BOAC Comet 1 G-ALYZ with 35 passengers on board crashed on take-off at

Rome/Ciampino Airport, fortunately without loss of life; the accident was attributed to the captain having failed to notice that the aircraft had adopted an excessive nose-up attitude during take-off.

Fatal Crash

The first fatal Comet crash occurred on 3 March 1953 and involved Comet 1A CF-CUN, on a delivery flight to Canadian Pacific Airlines via Karachi and Sydney. On take-off from Karachi, the aircraft's wing struck a bridge, and it crashed and caught fire with the loss of all 11 people on board. Pilot error was initially blamed, but flight tests established that lift could be

First Turboprop Airliner
Viscount 708

Air France was a principal customer for the Vickers Viscount, which was one of aviation history's most successful commercial airliners. It was hugely popular and very reliable in service.

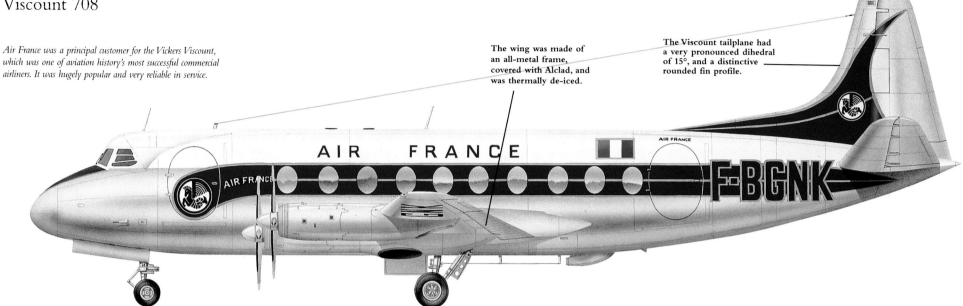

The wing was made of an all-metal frame, covered with Alclad, and was thermally de-iced.

The Viscount tailplane had a very pronounced dihedral of 15°, and a distinctive rounded fin profile.

AIR FRANCE

F-BGNK

AIR FRANCE

Engineers carrying out maintenance work on the de Havilland Ghost engines of a Comet Mk I. The Comet I was somewhat underpowered, which detracted from its take-off performance in 'hot and high' conditions.

lost if the pull-up was made too quickly after take-off. The leading edge of the Comet's wing was redesigned as a result.

There was worse to come. On 2 May 1953, Comet 1 G-ALYV of BOAC disintegrated in a thunderstorm shortly after taking off from Calcutta on a flight from Singapore to London. All 37 passengers and six crew were killed. Two further crashes in January and April 1954, the first involving G-ALYP off the Italian island of Elba and the second

involving G-ALYY off Stromboli, with no survivors and no apparent cause, led to the entire fleet being grounded for investigation. In February 1955, the remnants of the Italian crashes were brought to the surface and shipped back to the United Kingdom for exhaustive testing, while a Comet airframe was tested to destruction. Analysis showed the cause of the crashes to be metal fatigue. After thousands of pressurized climbs and descents, the fuselage metal (which was thinner than standard due to the need to save weight, resulting from the aircraft's underpowered de Havilland Ghost engines) around the Comet's large rectangular windows would begin to

crack and eventually cause explosive decompression of the cabin and catastrophic structural failure.

Later versions of the Comet would fly, and achieve considerable success in airline service, but Britain's lead in the jet transport field had been lost. In another area, however, the British aviation industry remained firmly at the forefront. This was the propeller-turbine, more commonly known as the turboprop. Development of this type of powerplant, which was very efficient at medium altitudes, had been ongoing since 1944, principally by Rolls-Royce. The first flight of a turboprop aircraft in the world was made on 20 September 1945, the

Viscount 810

Type: short-/medium-range transport

Powerplant: four 1566kW (2100hp) Rolls-Royce Dart RDa.7/1 Mk 525 turboprops

Maximum cruising speed: 563km/h (349mph) at 6100m (20,000ft)

Range: 2832km (1755 miles) with no fuel reserve

Service ceiling: 7620 m (25,000 ft.)

Weights: empty 18,854kg (41,479lb); loaded 32,884kg (72,345lb)

Accommodation: two pilots, stewardesses, typically 65 to 74 seats in several configurations; up to 11 tons of cargo in freight configuration

Dimensions:		
span	28.56m (93ft 8in)	
length	26.11m (85ft 8in)	
height	8.15m (26ft 9in)	
wing area	89.46m² (963sq ft)	

Although the SE2010 Armagnac (seen here on the production line) was not a commercial success, it represented an important step forward in French transport aircraft technology.

aircraft being a Gloster Meteor Mk 1 fitted with two Rolls-Royce Trent engines. The Trent was basically a Derwent turbojet fitted with a single-stage reduction gear, a large five-blade propeller and a drive unit.

Rolls-Royce went on to develop the Dart turboprop, and it was this engine that was selected for the Vickers Viscount, the world's first turboprop airliner. The Viscount 630 prototype first flew on 16 July 1948, and on 29 July

1950 British European Airways began a month's trial service on the London–Paris and London–Edinburgh routes using this aircraft. The production 700 Series Viscount began regular services in April 1953, and from then on the Viscount was a major success story, with 445 aircraft being delivered to European and US airlines up to the beginning of 1959.

Substantial Numbers

The commercial advent of the turboprop-powered airliner by no means signalled the early demise of piston-engined types, of which the Vickers Viking was a leading example. Powered by two Bristol Hercules radial engines, the prototype

Viking flew on 22 June 1945 and the type subsequently served in substantial numbers on the domestic and European routes of British European Airways. A thoroughly reliable aircraft, the Viking was also exported, total production being 163 aircraft. In March 1952, the Viking was joined in service by another piston type, the Bristol Centaurus-powered Airspeed Ambassador.

France, anxious to rebuild its aircraft industry, at first relied on aircraft that had been designed before the war, then shelved for obvious reasons. One of the most widely used was the SNCASE SE.161 Languedoc, a four-engine aircraft which had been designed in the

1930s as the Bloch 161 and which was still a viable commercial aircraft. Production totalled 100 aircraft, some for military use, and the type remained in service well into the 1950s.

The SNCASE SE.2010 Armagnac, another French design resurrected after the war, was less successful. Designed as a four-engine transatlantic airliner, the prototype flew on 2 April 1949, but its potential operator, Air France, decided that US equipment would be more appropriate (for one thing, it was cheaper to operate)l only eight Armagnacs were built, finding a role as military transports.

The other four-engine French aircraft of this period was the Bréguet 763 Provence, which had a deep double-deck fuselage and was nicknamed 'Deux Ponts' (Two Bridges) as a consequence. The prototype flew on 15 February 1949, and the first of 12 production aircraft inaugurated a regular Air France

The double-deck Bréguet 763 Provence was used by both Air France and the French air force, both of which used it to transport passengers and freight between France and its colonies.

The Mightiest Turboprop
Tupolev Tu-116

The Tupolev Tu-114 was the largest turboprop-powered aircraft of its time, and used many components of the Tu-95 Bear strategic bomber. It was not an outstanding aircraft, but it was the USSR's prestige airliner in the 1960s.

А Э Р О Ф Л О Т

СССР-Л5442

As a parallel project to support the Tu-114, the Tu-116 was a direct civil variant of the Tu-95. This example was used for crew training for the Tu-114.

All control surfaces were hydraulically operated, a major innovation in this successor to the B-29–derived designs by Tupolev. The tailplane was of the variable incidence type.

service to North Africa in March 1953. The French airline later sold six of the Bréguets to the French air force to supplement the military version, the Bréguet 765 Sahara, and the others were converted to the cargo role.

The Soviet Union, for its part, concentrated on the development of medium-range transports during the early post-war years, as these were best suited to serving Aeroflot's substantial network of internal routes and the links with neighbouring countries, such as Poland, Hungary and Czechoslovakia. The most successful of these aircraft was the Ilyushin Il-12, a twin-engined

Left: A development of the twin-engined Il-12 transport, the Il-14 represented a determined effort to eliminate the snags that had plagued the earlier aircraft. The Il-14 was widely exported.

airliner of all-metal construction with a tricycle undercarriage. It flew for the first time in August 1945 and entered service with Aeroflot in 1947.

Determined Attempt
The Il-12's successor, the Ilyushin Il-14, represented a determined (and successful) attempt to produce a better all-round transport that had none of the snags that had beset the earlier machine. The first variant, the Il-14P, could take off on one engine, even from elevated airfields, and was fitted with updated blind-flying equipment. The aircraft could carry only 18 passengers, however, which was not economically viable, and so it was redesigned as the Il-14M, with a longer fuselage accommodating 24 passengers. The Il-14 was hugely successful, being

widely exported and built under licence in Czechoslovakia and the German Democratic Republic.

To western eyes, there was little remarkable about aircraft such as the Il-14, but western eyes were opened sharply when, on 22 March 1956, a Soviet jet airliner arrived at London Heathrow Airport carrying a Soviet government delegation. The aircraft was a Tupolev Tu-104, a type first flown in June 1955, and, on 15 September 1956, the Soviet Union became the second nation (after the United Kingdom) to inaugurate scheduled passenger services using this turbojet-powered aircraft. The route was Moscow–Irkutsk. The Tu-104 had some advanced features, including slotted trailing-edge flaps, boundary layer fences, and an anti-skid braking system on the

Tu-114 'Cleat'

Type: long-range airliner and transport

Powerplant: four 11,033kW (14,784hp) Kuznetsov NK-12MV turboprop engines

Maximum speed: 880km/h (545mph) at 7100m (23,000ft)

Cruising speed: 770km/h (477mph)

Range: 6200km (3853 miles)

Service ceiling: 12,000m (39,500ft)

Weights: empty 88,200kg (194,000lb); loaded 179,000kg (393,800lb)

Accommodation: flight crew of five (two pilots, engineer, navigator and radio/radar operator); typically eight or nine flight attendants; typically 170 passengers in three cabins holding 42, 48 and 54; maximum seating of up to 220 passengers

Dimensions:
span	51.10m (168ft)	
length	54.10m (177ft)	
height	13.31m (44ft)	
wing area	311.10m² (3349sq ft)	

main undercarriage units. A braking parachute was also fitted. The airliner retained the Tu-16 bomber's wings, tail unit and undercarriage, but the fuselage was new, having a circular section and a pressurized cabin for 50 passengers. Later models could carry 100 passengers. As well as Aeroflot, Tu-104s served with the Czech National Airline, CSA.

Meanwhile, the French aviation industry had produced a major success story. It was the Sud-Aviation SE.210 Caravelle, the first twin-jet to have its engines mounted at the rear. This configuration was to become a classic formula for medium- and short-range commercial transport aircraft. The

Caravelle prototype first flew on 27 May 1955, only two years after the project had been given the go-ahead, and the commercial sales drive received massive support from the French government. The first Caravelle Series I service was opened by Air France on the Paris–Rome–Istanbul route. Other versions were produced into the 1970s, 280 Caravelles of all variants being built.

Latest Knowledge
In the United Kingdom, the Comet was once more in the air, in a much-modified guise. De Havilland had already embarked on a study of a 'stretched' version of the Comet 1 before the latter suffered its

disastrous series of crashes, and this flew on 19 July 1954 as the Comet 3. By the end of 1954, with all the accident findings available, the company incorporated the latest knowledge into a Mk 4 version. The prototype was the Comet 3, G-ANLO, fitted with uprated Rolls-Royce Avon 523 engines and with various modifications. This aircraft began a test flight programme in February 1957, and the first of 19 production Comet 4s for BOAC followed in April 1958. The Comet 4 was well liked by its operators, who were mostly in the Middle East and Latin America.

It was on 4 October 1958 that a BOAC Comet 4 inaugurated the first

Right: In the early 1950s, Boeing took advantage of the expertise it had gained in its B-47 and B-52 jet bomber programmes to design what was to become a world-beating jet airliner, the Boeing 707.

Below: Hawker Siddeley, into which the old de Havilland firm had been absorbed, ended its Comet 4 programme with the Mk 4C, produced by merging the long body with a large pinion-tanked wing. The Comet 4C was the most successful model of all.

fare-paying transatlantic jet service from London to New York. Three weeks later, Pan American Airways inaugurated its own transatlantic jet service with an aircraft which, before long, would take the airlines of the world by storm. That aircraft was the Boeing 707.

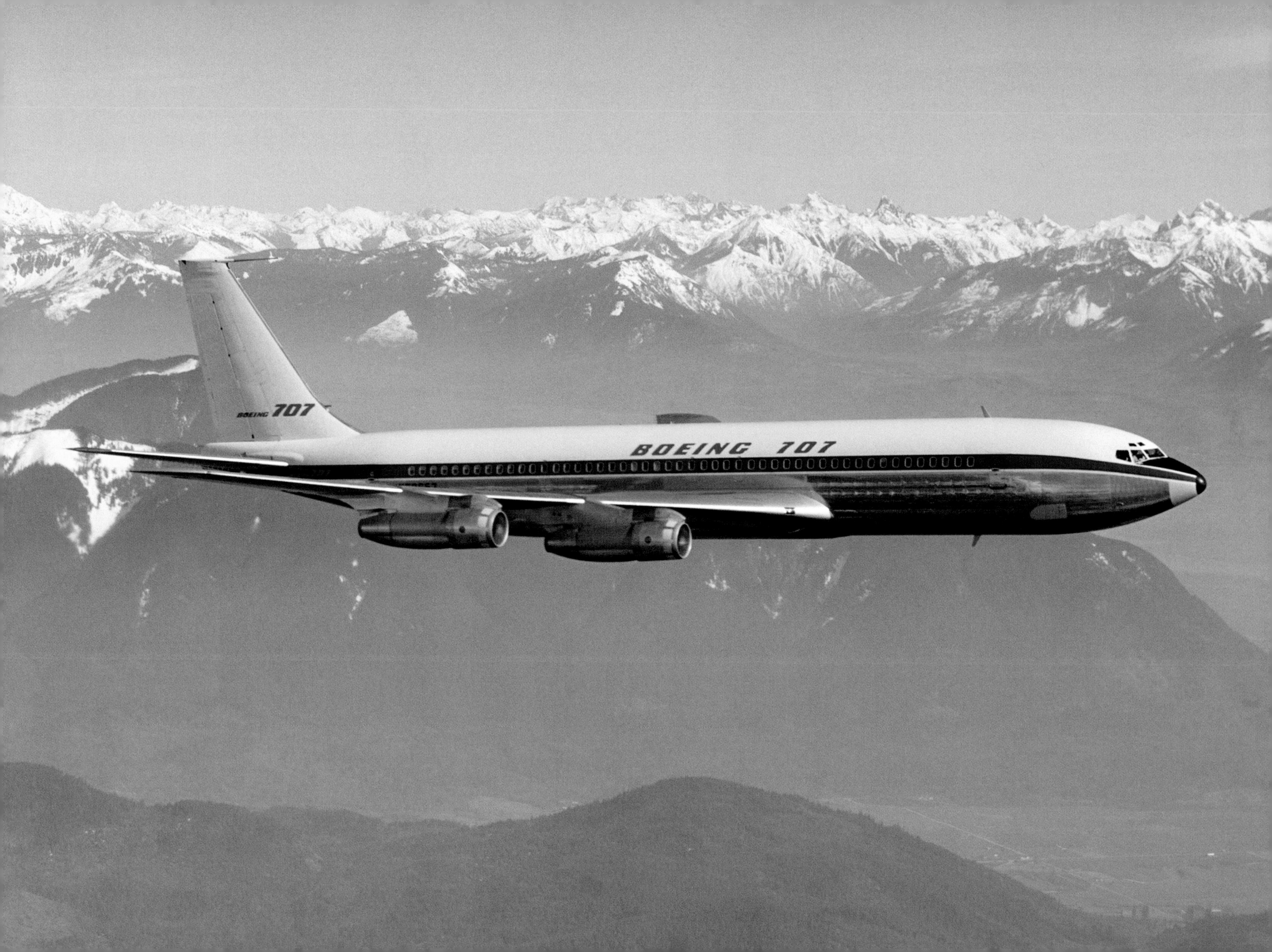
BOEING 707
BOEING 707

The Quest for Speed

The Allied jet fighter designs that had evolved by the end of World War II were strictly conventional. Apart from the fact that it was turbojet-powered, there was nothing at all unconventional about the Gloster Meteor which, apart from one or two idiosyncrasies, had turned out to be a very good fighter. The second British jet fighter, the de Havilland Vampire, was also of conventional design, and was of simple configuration, comprising a nacelle housing the engine and cockpit, a very straightforward wing with slightly tapered leading and trailing edges, twin tail booms and twin fins.

Apart from the Meteor and Vampire, in the immediate post-war period, the squadrons of RAF Fighter Command and 2nd Tactical Air Force in Germany were equipped with piston-engined types such as the Tempest Mk 2, which had a Bristol Centaurus radial engine; the Tempest Mk VI; and the later marks of Spitfire. Perhaps the ultimate in British piston-engined fighter design was the de Havilland Hornet, the fastest twin piston-engined fighter in the world. The Hornet began life as

a private venture in 1942 to meet the need for a long-range escort fighter for service in the Far East, but major orders for the Hornet F.1 were cancelled at the end of the war and only 60 were built, entering RAF service in 1946. These were followed by 132 Hornet F.3s, which served with four first-line RAF air defence squadrons until they were withdrawn in 1951. Many were subsequently sent to the Far East, where they were used in the ground-attack role against communist terrorists in Malaya.

Fighter Assets

As was the case with the RAF, the USAAF's principal fighter assets at the end of World War II comprised the later versions of well-tried piston-engined designs such as the P-51 Mustang and P-47 Thunderbolt. The United States' first fully operational jet fighter was the Lockheed P-80 (later F-80) Shooting Star, which, like its British counterparts, was of very conventional design and was to become the workhorse of American tactical fighter-bomber and fighter-interceptor squadrons for five years after the war. The Republic F-84 Thunderjet, which was to provide many of NATO's air forces with their initial jet experience, began life in the summer of 1944, when Republic Aviation's design team investigated the possibility of adapting the airframe of the P-47 Thunderbolt to take an axial-flow turbojet. This idea proved impractical and, in November 1944, the design of an entirely new airframe was begun around the General Electric J35 engine. The first of three XP-84 prototypes was

Left: TG370 was an early production de Havilland Vampire F.Mk.1. The Vampire was the second jet fighter to enter RAF service, equipping many tactical fighter-bomber squadrons overseas.

Right: A Westland Welkin prototype high-altitude interceptor is pictured here. A twin-engined heavy fighter meant to fight at extremely high altitudes, the Welkin never entered service.

completed in December 1945 and made its first flight on 28 February 1946. Three prototypes were followed by 15 YP-84As for the USAF. The F-84B was the first production model, featuring an ejection seat, six 12.7mm (0.5in) M3 machine guns and underwing rocket rails. Deliveries of the F-84B began in the summer of 1947. The F-84C, of which 191 were built, was externally similar to the F-84B, but incorporated an improved electrical system and an improved bomb release mechanism. The next model to appear, in November 1948, was the F-84D, which had a strengthened wing and a modified fuel system. Production

totalled 151 aircraft. The F-84D was followed, in May 1949, by the F-84E, which, in addition to its six 12.7mm (0.5in) machine guns, could carry two 454kg (1000lb) bombs, two 298mm (11.75in) rockets or thirty-two 127mm (5in) rockets.

During 1952, this model began to give way to the F-84G, which was the first Thunderjet variant to be equipped for flight refuelling from the outset. It was also the first USAF fighter to have a tactical nuclear capability; atomic weapons development had advanced considerably in the United States since 1950, and the device carried by the F-84G (the Mk 7 nuclear store), although still bulky, weighed less than 908kg (2000lb).

Lightest Jet Fighter

Of all the aviation booty that the Russians uncovered during their advance into Germany, the most important haul was a large quantity of BMW 003A and Junkers Jumo 004A turbojets, which were distributed among the various aircraft designers for experimental use, while the engine manufacturers geared up to produce them in series.

One of the designers involved was Aleksandr S. Yakovlev, who set about adapting a standard Yak-3 airframe to accommodate a Jumo 004B. The

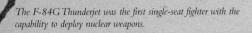

The F-84G Thunderjet was the first single-seat fighter with the capability to deploy nuclear weapons.

At the time of its introduction the Yak-15 was the lightest jet fighter in the world. It featured the wings, tail-wheel undercarriage, rear fuselage and tail unit of the piston-engined Yak-3U.

resulting aircraft, designated Yak-15, flew for the first time on 24 April 1946. At the time of its introduction, the Yak-15 was the lightest jet fighter in the world, the lightweight structure of the Yak-3's airframe compensating for the relatively low power of the RD-10 (Jumo 004B) engine. Although the Yak-3 was an interim aircraft, bridging the gap until the advent of more modern jet fighters, it was important in that it provided the Soviet Air Force with the jet experience it badly needed.

Meanwhile, in February 1945, Artem Mikoyan had also begun work on a jet aircraft, the I-300, built around two BMW 003A engines. The prototype I-300 flew on the same day as the prototype Yak-15, and the production version, designated MiG-9, entered service in small numbers in mid-1947, having been selected in preference to a rival design, the Su-9, offered by Sukhoi.

In the spring of 1947, in a deal seen by many as a misplaced gesture of socialist solidarity, the British Labour Government authorized the delivery of 30 Rolls-Royce Derwent and 25 Nene jet engines to the Soviet Union. The Russians lost no time in applying this technology to their latest fighter designs, which now featured swept wings. Prototype aircraft were produced by both Lavochkin and Mikoyan, and both of these were very similar in appearance. Lavochkin's aircraft, the La-15, went on to be produced in small numbers, but the rival MiG design was destined to become one of the most famous jet fighters of all time. It was the MiG-15. Production

The Barrel-bodied Fighter
Lavochkin La-15

The Lavochkin La-15 was a refined version of the La-168 experimental interceptor and flew for the first time early in 1948. The type was ordered into production, but only a few tactical fighter units were equipped with it.

The La-15 had a barrel-like fuselage, swept wings and stabilizers mounted high on the fin, almost like a T-tail.

Lavochkin La-15

Type: jet fighter

Powerplant: one 15.6kN (3495lbf) thrust Klimov RD-500 engine

Maximum speed: 1026km/h (638mph) or Mach 0.00

Ferry range: 1170km (730 miles)

Service ceiling: 13,000m (42,650ft)

Weights: empty 2575kg (5677lb); loaded 3850kg (8490lb)

Armament: three 23mm Nudelman-Suranov NS-23 cannon

Dimensions:
span	8.83m (29ft)
length	9.56m (31ft 4in)
height	n/a
wing area	16.2 m² (174sq ft)

of the MiG-15 would eventually total some 18,000 aircraft, this figure including a tandem two-seat trainer version, the MiG-15UTI.

Naval Jet Fighter
In 1944, before German advanced aeronautical research data became available, the USAAF issued specifications drawn up around four different fighter requirements, the first of which involved a medium-range day fighter that could also serve in the ground-attack and bomber-escort roles. The first of these requirements awakened the interest of North American Aviation, the design team of which was then working on the NA-134, a projected carrier-borne jet fighter for the US Navy. This, like the XP-59A and XP-80, was of conventional

straight-wing design and was well advanced, so North American offered a land-based version to the USAAF under the company designation NA-140. On 18 May 1945, North American received a contract for building three NA-140 prototypes under the USAAF designation XP-86. At the same time, 100 NA-141s (production developments of the NA-134 naval jet fighter) were ordered for the US Navy as FJ-1s, although this order was subsequently reduced to 30 aircraft. Known as the Fury, the FJ-1 flew for the first time on 27 November 1946 and went on to serve with Navy Fighter Squadron VF-51, and was to remain in service until 1949.

While construction of the XFJ-1 prototypes got under way, design development of the XP-86 and FJ-1

proceeded in parallel. A mock-up of the XP-86 was built and, in June 1945, was approved by the USAAF. It was at this point that material on German research into high-speed flight, in particular swept-wing designs, became available, and the XP-86 was redesigned to carry swept flying surfaces. On 8 August 1947, the first of two flying prototypes was completed, making its first flight under the power of a General Electric J35 turbojet. The second prototype, designated XF-86A, made its first flight on 18 May 1948, fitted with the more powerful General Electric J-47-GE-1

F-86K Sabres of the Royal Norwegian Air Force. The F-86K was a straightforward development of the F-86D, which was originally intended to be a two-man aircraft with a weapons systems operator in the rear seat.

left: Claimed to have been the first turbojet-powered aircraft in the world to exceed Mach 1, the DH.108 was designed for research into swept-wing behaviour. Three aircraft were built, the first flying on 15 May 1946; two were destroyed in accidents.

engine, and deliveries of production F-86As began 10 days later. On 4 March 1949, the North American F-86 was officially named the Sabre.

In Britain, high-speed research had been hampered by the lack of facilities to carry out advanced aerodynamic research,

with most of the equipment captured in Germany, such as a high-speed wind tunnel, having gone to the United States. The British consequently had to start almost from scratch, and de Havilland built an experimental aircraft, the DH.108, which was basically a tailless Vampire with swept wings attached, to investigate the properties of the swept wing. Three aircraft were built, each one with the specific task of testing the swept-wing configuration at various speeds. The third DH.108, VW120,

was the high-speed aircraft of the trio, and, on 9 September 1948, flown by test pilot John Derry, it exceeded Mach 1, the speed of sound, in a steep dive between 12,000 and 10,000m (40,000 and 30,000ft). Despite conflicting claims that arose thereafter, the DH.108 appears to have been the first turbojet-powered aircraft in the world to exceed Mach 1. All three DH.108s were destroyed in fatal crashes, two after disintegrating in midair.

Advanced Project

Although the US Bell X-1 rocket-powered aircraft (see Chapter 13) became the first in the world to exceed the speed of sound in 1947, the British might have beaten them to it some months earlier with a turbojet-powered design, the Miles M.52.

The M.52 was an extremely advanced project on which Miles Aircraft Ltd had been working for three

The first of the so-called X-craft, funded for research purposes by the US Air Force and US Navy under the supervision of NACA (later NASA), the Bell X-1 was the first US aircraft to be rocket-powered.

Left: The Miles E.24/43, or M.52, was an extremely advanced project which had been in development for three years when a high-level decision was taken to suspend further work.

which the pilot sat semi-reclined, could be detached in an emergency by firing small cordite charges; the pilot would then bale out normally when the capsule reached a lower altitude.

The M.52 was fitted with bi-convex section wings, mounted at mid-point on the fuselage. A full-scale wooden mock-up of this unique high-speed wing design was built and tested on a Miles Falcon light aircraft in 1944. As design work progressed, various refinements were incorporated. Split flaps were fitted, together with an all-moving tailplane. The addition of rudimentary afterburners in the form of combustion cans situated at the rear of the engine duct was calculated to produce much greater thrust at supersonic speed. The position of the undercarriage presented some headaches; the very thin wing section meant that the wheels had to be positioned to retract into the fuselage, a narrow-track arrangement which, it was recognized, might cause landing problems.

Detailed design work on the M.52 was 90 per cent complete by the start of 1946, and the jigs were ready for assembly of three planned prototypes. No problems were envisaged in construction, and it was expected that the first M.52 would fly within six to eight months. In February 1946, with no warning, F.G. Miles received word that all work on the M.52

years when a high-level decision was taken to suspend further work after the prototype had been half built. It was a decision which may well rank as one of the major tragedies of British aviation.

The Miles company began work on the M.52 in 1943, at a time when knowledge of high-speed aerodynamics was strictly limited. As the project was masked in secrecy, Miles set up its own foundry for the production of the necessary metal components and also built a high-speed wind tunnel. The design that gradually evolved featured a bullet-like fuselage of circular section, 1.5m (5ft) in diameter, constructed of high-tensile steel with an alloy covering. The powerplant, a Power Jets W.2/700, was centrally mounted and fed by an annular air intake, the cockpit forming a centre cone. The whole cockpit cone, in

First of the 'Century' Fighters
F-100D Super Sabre

The D-model had a taller vertical tail, introduced to improve handling. This incorporated a deeper fairing for the fuel dump pipe (later used to mount the radar warning receiver antenna).

The F-100D's redesigned wings had kinked trailing edges, which incorporated broad slotted landing flaps. These were much appreciated by pilots used to the high-speed landing run of the F-100C.

The North American F-100 Super Sabre was the first American jet aircraft capable of exceeding the speed of sound in level flight. This F-100D is armed with Bullpup air-to-surface missiles.

project was to cease at once. Secrecy surrounded the M.52's cancellation, just as it had surrounded its design, and it was not until September 1946 that the British public was made aware that its aircraft industry had been within sight of flying the world's first supersonic aircraft, only to have the chance snatched away.

Unmanned Models

The stated reason behind the decision to cancel the M.52 was that it had already been decided, early in 1946, to carry out a supersonic research programme with the aid of unmanned models developed by Vickers Ltd. Between May 1947 and October 1948, eight rocket-powered models were launched, only three of which were successful. In each case of failure

(apart from the first attempted launch when the Mosquito launch aircraft lost control in cloud and the model broke away), it was the rocket motor that failed, not the airframe. The irony was that most of the models were based on the M.52's design. What's more, in the light of current knowledge, the full-size M.52 would almost certainly have been a success.

Only a year after cancellation of the M.52 was made public, Major Charles Yeager, USAF, made history's first supersonic flight in the rocket-powered Bell X-1 research aircraft.

Although the first generation of swept-wing jet fighters could exceed supersonic speed in a dive, it took some time before the goal of exceeding Mach 1 in level flight was reached by a

turbojet-powered aircraft. The type that did it was the North American F-100 Super Sabre, which exceeded Mach 1 on its maiden flight on 25 May 1953. The first Soviet turbojet-powered type to achieve this was the MiG-19, designed as a successor to the MiG-17.

Although Britain lacked an operational aircraft that could reach supersonic speed in level flight, it had two research aircraft that could do so with ease. The first was the English Electric P.1, conceived just after World War II, at a time when RAF Fighter Command had one jet fighter, the Gloster Meteor, in operational service and another, the de Havilland Vampire, scheduled for delivery in 1946. Early in that year both Hawker and Supermarine were studying schemes for

F-100D Super Sabre

Type: single-seat fighter-bomber

Powerplant: one 75.4kN (16,958lbf) thrust Pratt & Whitney J57-P-21A afterburning turbojet

Maximum speed: 1436km/h (892mph) at altitude

Initial climb rate: 5045m/min (16,552fpm) (clean)

Range: 2494km (1550 miles) with two drop-tanks

Service ceiling: 14,020m (45,997ft)

Weights: empty 9526kg (21,000lb); maximum take-off 15,800kg (34,833lb)

Armament: four M-39E 20mm cannon plus up to 3402kg (7500lb) of external stores including bombs, napalm tanks, rockets and missiles

Dimensions:		
span	11.82m	(38ft 9in)
length	14.36m	(47ft 1in)
height	4.94m	(16ft 2in)
wing area	35.77m²	(385sq ft)

MiG Goes Supersonic
MiG-19S 'Farmer'

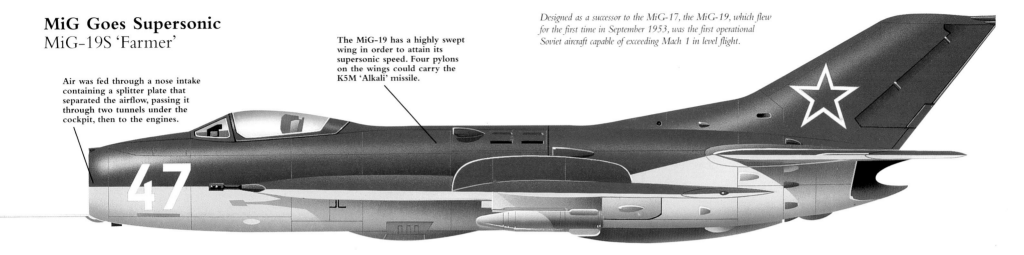

Air was fed through a nose intake containing a splitter plate that separated the airflow, passing it through two tunnels under the cockpit, then to the engines.

The MiG-19 has a highly swept wing in order to attain its supersonic speed. Four pylons on the wings could carry the K5M 'Alkali' missile.

Designed as a successor to the MiG-17, the MiG-19, which flew for the first time in September 1953, was the first operational Soviet aircraft capable of exceeding Mach 1 in level flight.

MiG-19SF 'Farmer-C'

Type: single-seat day fighter–bomber

Powerplant: two 32.66kN (7346lbf) thrust MNPK 'Soyuz' (Tumansky) RD-9BM afterburning turbojets

Maximum speed: 1452km/h (902mph) at high altitude

Ferry range: 2200km (1367 miles)

Service ceiling: 18,500m (60,695ft)

Weights: empty 5760kg (12,700lb); maximum take-off 9100kg (20,062lb)

Armament: two or three 30mm NR-30 cannon each with 73 rounds; provision for two bombs of up to 454kg (1000lb) (usually 227kg/500lb) bombs carried), various single or multi-barrel pod rockets, two 767-litre (203-US gallon) fuel tanks or four missiles

Dimensions:
span	9.20m (30ft 2in)
length	12.60m (41ft 4in)
height	3.88m (12ft 9in)
wing area	25.00m² (269sq ft)

swept-wing jet fighters which would eventually materialize as the Hunter and Swift; experimentation with a truly supersonic design was then focused on the Miles M.52.

When the M.52 project was cancelled, English Electric's talented young design team, under the leadership of its chief engineer, W.E.W. 'Teddy' Petter, began to turn its thoughts to designing an aircraft that would not only be capable of sustained supersonic flight, but also be capable of reaching Mach 2. Preliminary sketches were produced showing a radical design: an aircraft with a wing swept at 60 degrees, powered by two engines mounted one above the other in a slab-sided fuselage with a single-seat cockpit perched on top, advanced avionics, missile armament, powered controls and an all-moving tailplane. Perhaps the most amazing thing about the design was that

the Ministry of Supply, which had begun to have serious doubts about the practicability of sustained supersonic flight while the M.52 project was in being, decided that it merited further investigation, and in 1947 issued an experimental study contract, ER.103.

Research Aircraft

This was followed, two years later, by a contract for two prototypes and an airframe to be used for static testing. To investigate the characteristics of a wing with high sweep angle, a research aircraft, the Short SB.5, was built and flown with varying degrees of sweep, starting with 50 degrees in December 1952 and gradually working up to a full 60 degrees.

The SB.5's test programme proved that the English Electric design team had its figures right, and construction of two experimental prototypes, designated P.1

and P.1A, continued. The first of these was flown at Boscombe Down on 4 August 1954 by English Electric's chief test pilot, Wing Commander R.P. Beaumont. The aircraft was powered by two Bristol Siddeley Sapphire turbojets and reached supersonic speed on its third flight.

Later in 1954, English Electric received a contract for the construction of three P.1Bs, which were effectively to be the prototypes of the operational version. The P.1B, which was the first British aircraft to be designed as an integrated weapons system, was powered by two Rolls-Royce RA24 engines. The first example flew on 4 April 1957 – ironically, the very day that the British government produced a White Paper on Defence

Right: The Short SB.5, flown in 1953, was built to carry out low-speed trials of the wing planform intended for the English Electric Lightning supersonic fighter.

Britain's Front Line
English Electric Lightning F.Mk 1A

An English Electric (BAC) Lightning F.Mk.3 of No. 56 Squadron RAF. The first production Lightning F.Mk.1 flew on 29 October 1959, and fully combat-equipped Lightnings began entering RAF service in July 1960.

Although popular with its pilots, the Lightning was not an easy aircraft to fly. The cockpit was fairly cramped, and instruments and controls were of 1950s vintage.

XMI74

The two Avon engines were mounted one on top of the other, minimizing handling problems if one failed.

Lightning F.Mk 6

Type: single-seat air-defence fighter

Powerplant: two 72.77kN (16,367lb-thrust) Rolls-Royce Avon 302 afterburning turbojets

Maximum speed: 2415km/h (1500mph) at 12,000m (39,370ft), or Mach 2.3

Range: 1200km (746 miles)

Service ceiling: 16,500m (54,134ft)

Weights: empty 12,700kg (28,000lb); loaded 22,500kg (73,820lb)

Armament: two ADEN 30mm cannon with 120 rounds each; two Red Top or Firestreak heat-seeking missiles; 2500kg (5512lb) of under- and over-wing stores (export variants only)

Dimensions: span   10.62m (34ft 10in)
           length   16.84m (55ft 3in)
           height   5.97m (19ft 7in)
           wing area 35.31m² (380sq ft)

forecasting the end of piloted combat aircraft and their replacement by missiles.

The original intention was that operationally, the P.1B – which was given the name Lightning – was to form a mixed interceptor force together with the Saunders-Roe SR.177, a target defence aircraft powered by a jet engine and a rocket motor. Along with other promising military aircraft projects, the SR.177 fell victim to the 1957 policy changes, leaving the Lightning alone to make the jump from subsonic to supersonic flight.

The second British supersonic design, the Fairey FD.2 (Fairey Delta Two) research aircraft, was assured of its place in aviation history when, on 10 March 1956, it became the first aircraft to set a world speed record of more than 1600km/h (1000mph). On that date, test pilot Peter Twiss flew the aircraft to a new record speed of 1821km/h (1132mph).

Like the P.1, the FD.2 also originated in ER.103, and in December 1949 Fairey came up with firm proposals for a highly streamlined delta-wing machine that was in essence a supersonic dart just big enough to house a pilot, engine and fuel. The first of two FD.2 prototypes flew on 6 October 1954. From the start, it showed its enormous potential. The second FD.2 flew on 15 February 1956, and the two aircraft had made well over 100 flights by the time Peter Twiss

captured the speed record, at that time held by a North American F-100C Super Sabre. The achievement astounded the aviation world, and Fairey felt certain that the Delta Two's design had proven itself to the point where proposals could be put forward for a family of supersonic fighters based on it. Fairey proceeded to develop a military variant, but this project was terminated in April 1957. Still, the two FD.2s made an enormous contribution to high-speed flight research, the first

The record-breaking Fairey FD.2 (Fairey Delta 2) research aircraft, later used in the development of the Concorde supersonic airliner. Both aircraft featured a nose section which could 'droop' to improve pilot visibility on landing.

Development of the F-104 was begun in 1951, when the lessons of the Korean air war were starting to bring about profound changes in combat aircraft design. The first Starfighter flew on 7 February 1954.

aircraft later being fitted with a model of the ogival (dual-curve) wing planform that was to be used on the Concorde.

Mach 2

On 12 December 1957, the United States recaptured the world air speed record with a McDonnell F-101A Voodoo. The Voodoo retained the record for only five months before it passed to another American aircraft in May 1958. This time the aircraft involved was one that really lifted turbojet flight into the realms of Mach 2, the Lockheed F-104 Starfighter.

Development of the F-104, the first American jet aircraft capable of sustained flight at Mach 2, was begun in 1951, when the lessons of the Korean air war were starting to bring about profound changes in combat aircraft design. A contract for two XF-104 prototypes was placed in 1953, and the first of these flew on 7 February 1954, only 11 months later. The two XF-104s were followed by 15 YF-104s for USAF evaluation, most of these, like the prototypes, being powered by the Wright J65-W-6 turbojet. The aircraft was ordered into production as the F-104A, deliveries to the USAF Air Defense Command beginning in January 1958. Its lack of all-weather

The World's Most Popular Fighter
MiG-21FL 'Fishbed'

The Mig-21's 'tailed delta' wing design helped to make it one of the nimblest fighters of its era – more than a match for the Phantom, which opposed it in Vietnam.

This MiG-21FL was built in India by Hindustan Aeronautics Ltd and served with No 1 'Tiger' Squadron of the Indian Air Force until 1973. The MiG-21 was widely exported and its handling qualities were well liked.

This version of the 'Fishbed', the MiG-21FL, did not have any internal guns, but carried a 23mm cannon pack under the fuselage.

capability meant that the F-104A saw limited service with Air Defense Command, equipping only two fighter squadrons. F104As were also supplied to Nationalist China and Pakistan, and saw combat during the Indo-Pakistan conflict of 1969. The F104B was a two-seat version, and the F-104C was a tactical fighter-bomber, the first of 77 examples being delivered to the 479th Tactical Fighter Wing (the only unit to use it) in October 1958. Two more two-seat Starfighters, the F-104D and F-104F, were followed by the F-104G, which was numerically the most important variant.

The Starfighter achieved a speed of 2259.7km/h (1404.1mph) and held the record until 31 October 1959, when the speed was raised to 2387.99km/h (1483.83mph) by an aircraft reportedly

designated Ye-66. Its designation was actually Ye-6/3, and it was the prototype of an aircraft that came as a profound shock to western air intelligence experts: the MiG-21.

Target Defence

Like the F-104, the MiG-21, which was codenamed 'Fishbed' by NATO, was a child of the Korean War, where Soviet air combat experience had identified a need for a light single-seat target defence interceptor with high supersonic manoeuvrability. Two prototypes were ordered, both appearing early in 1956; one, which received the code name 'Faceplate', featured sharply swept wings and was not developed further.

The initial production versions (Fishbed-A and Fishbed-B) were built in only limited numbers, being short-range

day fighters with a comparatively light armament of two 30mm NR-30 cannon, but the next variant, the MiG-21F Fishbed-C, carried two K-13 Atoll infrared homing air-to-air missiles, and had an uprated Tumansky R-11 turbojet as well as improved avionics. The MiG-21F was the first major production version; it entered service in 1960 and was progressively modified and updated over the years that followed.

There were more shocks to follow. When the Soviet Union put its latest combat aircraft on display at Tushino in 1961, there were indications that the Russians might not only have caught up with the western world in terms of military aviation technology, but also even have captured the advantage. The two power blocs were now entering the most dangerous phase of the Cold War.

Lightning F.Mk 6

Type: single-seat interceptor and fighter

Powerplant: one 63.65-kN (14,316-lb-thrust) Tumanskii R-13 afterburning turbojet engine

Maximum speed: 2230km/h (1,386mph)

Range: 1480km (917 miles)

Service ceiling: 18,500m (60,696ft)

Weights: empty 5350kg (11,795lb); loaded 9400kg (20,723lb)

Armament: one twin-barrel 23-mm (0.91-in) GSh-23 cannon with 200 rounds; four wing pylons for heat-seeking or radar-guided 'Atoll' air-to-air missiles; up to 2000kg (4,409lb) of bombs or rocket pods

Dimensions:

span	7.15m (23ft 5in)
length	15.76m (51ft 8in)
height	4.50m (14ft 9in)
wing area	23.00m² (248 sq ft)

Cold War I: Birth of the Nuclear Era

The period known as the Cold War began almost as soon as World War II ended and lasted for nearly half a century. When the Cold War began, the United States had the monopoly on nuclear weapons and the means to deliver them, but that was quickly eroded after 1949, when the Soviet Union detonated its first nuclear device.

In 1945, the principal US strategic bomber was the Boeing B-29, which was replaced by a more powerful variant, the B-50, from 1947. Also in that year, the newly formed US Strategic Air Command (SAC) received the first Convair B-36, the first bomber with a truly global strategic capability to serve with any air force. The B-36 flew for the first time on 8 August 1946, powered by six Pratt & Whitney pusher engines developing 2237kW (3000hp) each. The first XB-36 was followed by two more prototypes, the YB-36 and YB-36A, both of which flew in 1947. The B-36 was a massive aircraft, with a wing span of 70m (230ft) and a length of 49m (162ft).

Left: The Convair B-36 gave the US Strategic Air Command the capability to deliver nuclear weapons to targets in the USSR while operating from bases in the continental United States. Its huge size led to the nickname 'Aluminium Overcast'.

Above right: For a brief period, the Boeing B-50 Superfortress was the backbone of the US Strategic Air Command (SAC). A heavy bomber, tasked with the delivery of the first nuclear bombs in the US Cold War arsenal, it was developed from the B-29.

It carried a crew of 16. Maximum speed over the target was 700km/h (435mph); service ceiling was 12,800m (42,000ft) and range 12,875km (8000 miles). The aircraft carried a heavy defensive armament, being equipped with six retractable remotely controlled turrets, each housing twin 20mm cannon, plus two 20mm cannon in the nose and two in the tail. Normal bomb load was a single 4536kg (10,000lb) nuclear store, but the aircraft could lift a maximum conventional bomb load of 38,102kg (84,000lb) over short ranges. The definitive bomber version of the B-36 was the B-36D, which was equipped with four auxiliary turbojet engines pairs mounted in twin pods under the outboard wing sections.

From March 1946, the strategic bomber forces of the US came under the control of a new formation known as Strategic Air Command. At that time the command, still equipped with B-29s, was still a conventional bombing force; only one unit, the

509th Bomb Group – the group responsible for dropping the first atomic bombs on Hiroshima and Nagasaki – had aircraft that were suitably modified to carry these large, bulky, first-generation nuclear weapons.

In July 1946, the 509th Bomb Group took part in Operation Crossroads. Centred on Bikini Atoll, the object of this exercise was to study the effects of two nuclear explosions on a simulated naval force consisting of captured and time-expired warships. On 1 July 1946, *Dave's Dream*, a 509th Bomb Group B-29

The Boeing B-47 Stratojet was fast enough to evade most Soviet fighters when it first entered service, but it did not have an exceptional operational ceiling and was tricky to handle on the ground.

piloted by Major Woodrow P. Swancutt and temporarily based on the island of Kwajalein, dropped a Nagasaki-type plutonium bomb on 73 ships assembled off Bikini. The air-bursting weapon, of about 17 kilotons yield, destroyed five ships and severely damaged nine others.

Nuclear-armed Bomber

The real American goal was to produce a nuclear-armed jet bomber that could strike any target in the Soviet Union from bases in the continental United States, flying high and fast enough to evade any air defence systems that the Soviet Union might put in place in the foreseeable future. In September 1945, the Boeing Aircraft Company commenced

design of a strategic jet bomber project designated Model 450. The aircraft, which was a radical departure from conventional design, featured a thin, flexible wing – based on wartime German research data – with 35 degrees of sweep and carrying six turbojets in underwing pods, the main undercarriage being housed in the fuselage. Basic design studies were completed in June 1946, and the first of two XB-47 Stratojet prototypes flew on 17 December 1947, powered by six Allison J35 turbojets. Later, the J35s were replaced by General Electric J47-GE-3 turbojets, the XB-47 flying with these in October 1949.

Meanwhile, Boeing had received a contract for ten B-47A

Stratojets in November 1948, and the first of this pre-production batch flew on 25 June 1950. The B-47A was used for trials and evaluation and, to some extent, for crew conversion. The first production model was the B-47B, which was powered by J47-GE-23 engines and featured a number of structural modifications, including a strengthened wing. It carried underwing fuel tanks, and was fitted with 18 solid-fuel rockets to give an emergency take-off thrust of up to 89kN (20,000lb). These were not used during normal operational training, but would have been necessary in a real combat situation to get the B-47, carrying a full fuel load and a 4536kg (10,000lb) bomb load, off the ground, as the aircraft

The most numerous version of the Stratojet was the B-47E, which first flew on 30 January 1953. At the peak of its deployment in the mid-1950s the Stratojet equipped 27 Strategic Air Command medium bombardment wings.

needed a very long take-off run and was tricky to handle during the take-off phase.

The B-47's undercarriage consisted of two pairs of main wheels mounted in tandem under the fuselage and outrigger wheels under each wing. The main gear folded up into the fuselage, while the outriggers retracted into the inboard engine nacelles. The arrangement was light and space-saving, but gave the B-47 a tendency to roll on take-off, so that in a strong crosswind the pilot had to hold the control column right over to one side. Steering on the ground was accomplished by the nosewheel, which was adjusted to prevent the aircraft swinging more than six degrees either way. However, the aircraft's optimum attitude for take-off was the one it assumed as it sat on the ground, and at about 140 knots (260km/h; 161mph), depending on its weight, the Stratojet literally flew itself off the runway with no need for backward pressure on the control column. Once off the ground, with flaps up and the aircraft automatically trimmed, the technique was to hold it down until safe flying speed had been reached, then climb at a shallow angle until 310 knots (574km/h; 357mph) showed on the airspeed indicator, after which the rate of

The Veteran Bomber
English Electric Canberra B.Mk.52

The enormous slab-like wing was the key to the Canberra's enormous range and load-carrying capabilities.

The Avon engines were mounted at the front of the nacelles, with a long jetpipe trailing back to the exhaust nozzle.

A Canberra B.Mk.52 of the Ethiopian Air Force. Ethiopia ordered four ex-RAF Canberras in 1968, and used them in its various anti-guerrilla campaigns in the 1970s.

climb was increased to 1200 or 1500m (4000 or 5000ft) per minute, depending on the aircraft's configuration.

At its operating altitude of around 12,000m (40,000ft) the B-47 handled lightly and could easily be trimmed to fly hands off. The quietness of the cockpit, the lack of vibration, and the smoothness of the flight were noticeable, the only exception being when turbulence was encountered at high altitude in jet streams. Then, looking out of the cockpit, the crew could see the B-47's long, flexible wings bending up and down, a rather unnerving phenomenon when experienced for the first time.

Left: Canberra PR.3 prototype VX181 pictured over the Needles during a test flight from Boscombe Down in the United Kingdom. The PR.3 gave the RAF a photo-reconnaissance capability that was second to none.

Landing Technique

The B-47 had a spectacular landing technique that began with a long, straight-in approach from high altitude when the pilot lowered his undercarriage to act as an air brake; with landing gear down the Stratojet was capable of descending 6100m (20,000ft) in four minutes. Flaps were not lowered until final approach, which started several miles from the end of the runway and demanded great concentration. The bomber must not be allowed to stall, yet its speed had to be kept as low as was safely possible to prevent it from running off the far end of the runway. Each additional knot above the crucial landing speed added another 150m (500ft) to the landing run, so the pilot had to fly to an accuracy of within two knots of the landing speed, which was usually about

130 knots (240km/h; 150mph) for a light B-47 at the end of a sortie.

Ideally, the Stratojet pilot aimed to touch down on both tandem mainwheel units together because if one or the other made contact with the runway first the aircraft bounced back into the air. With the wheels firmly down, the pilot used his ailerons to keep the wings level, much as a glider pilot does after touchdown; as the ailerons were moved, the flaps automatically adjusted their position to counteract roll. Rudder had to be used very cautiously and sparingly or the aircraft might turn over. To slow the fast-rolling B-47, a brake parachute was deployed immediately on touchdown, and the pilot applied heavy braking. The aircraft was also fitted with an anti-skid device, which automatically released the brakes, then reapplied them to give fresh

English Electric Canberra B.Mk.6

Type: light bomber

Powerplant: two 33.36kN (7503lbf) Rolls-Royce Avon Mk 109 turbojet engines

Maximum speed: 871 km/h (541mph) at 12,190m (39,993ft)

Ferry range: 5842km (3630 miles)

Service ceiling: 14,630m (48,000ft)

Weights: empty 10,099kg (22,264lb); normal take-off 19,597kg (43,204lb); maximum take-off 24,041kg (78,875lb)

Armament: up to nine internal 454kg (1000lb) bombs or other ordnance loads; two wing-mounted 454kg (1000lb) bombs, gun pods, AS.30 or Martel missiles, or rocket launchers

Dimensions:
span	19.51m (64ft)
length	19.96m (65ft 6in)
height	4.75m (15ft 7in)
wing area	89.19m² (960sq ft)

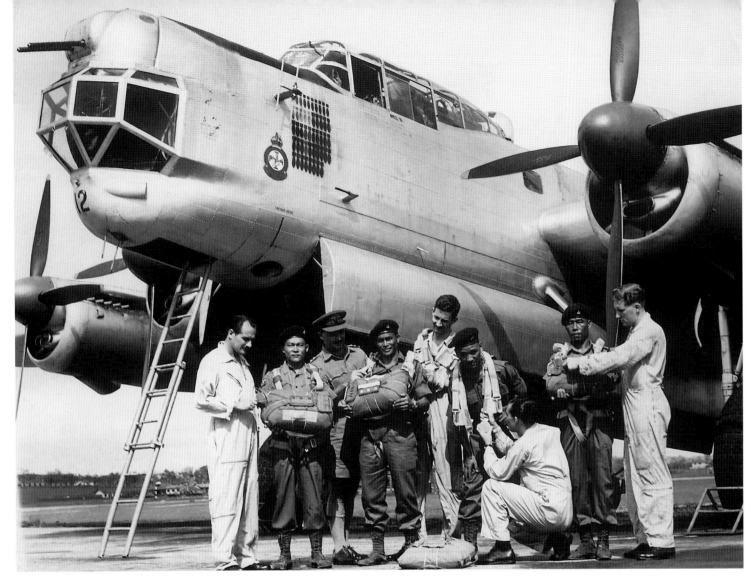

In 1948, the Cold War spread to Malaya. Pictured here is an Avro Lincoln B.30 of No 1 Squadron, RAAF, deployed to Butterworth for operations against communist terrorists.

'bite'. On average, the B-47's landing roll used up 2100m (7000ft) of runway.

The first B-47 was delivered to the 306th Bomb Wing at McDill AFB, Florida, on 23 October 1951, and 11 more were delivered by the end of the year, replacing the wing's B-50s. The 306th Bomb Wing was given the task of evaluating the B-47 under operational conditions and formulating appropriate tactics. This culminated in an exhaustive exercise known as Sky Try, during which all operational procedures were tested. These included the carriage and release of dummy bomb shapes, having the exact configuration of the Mk 7 atomic bomb, which the B-47 was initially to carry. This weapon, with a yield of 30–40 kilotons (kT), weighed 770 kg (1700lb) and was almost 5m (15ft 6in) long, with a diameter of 76cm (30in). Its casing was streamlined, with three stabilizing fins. The Mk 7 was the result of a crash programme, initiated by President Truman in 1948 at the time of the Berlin crisis, and designed to give the United States a substantial stockpile of atomic weapons. The programme was continued under President Eisenhower's administration, and in 1952 Mk 7 bombs were being produced at the rate of one a day. By early 1953, the stockpile stood at about 1500. Later in the 1950s, SAC's B-47 fleet standardized on the Mk 28 thermonuclear weapon, up to four of which could be carried by the Stratojet. This weapon could be assembled in five different configurations, with yields controllable between 1.1 and 20 megatons (mT). Depending on the chosen yield, its length varied between 2.74 and 4.27m (9 and 14ft). Its diameter was 50cm (20in), and weight varied with the selected yield. It could be dropped in free fall, or retarded with a parachute.

Variants of the B-47 included the RB-47E, RB-47H and RB-47K reconnaissance aircraft. About 1800 B-47s of all variants were built between 1946 and 1957. Boeing also developed a flight refuelling tanker version of its C-97 transport to support the B-47 force, with 20 tankers assigned to every SAC bomber wing.

Prior to 1954, SAC's concept of war operations was based on the deployment of its bombers to forward bases outside the continental United States, for

The first prototype of the Vickers Type 660 Valiant, WB210, powered by four Rolls-Royce Avon RA.3 engines, made its first flight on 18 May 1951. Note the original slot intakes.

example in the United Kingdom. The combination of B-47 and KC-97 now made it feasible for SAC's bomber wings to strike directly at targets inside the Soviet Union from the United States, afterwards recovering to bases in Europe or North Africa. The B-47 force reached its peak in 1956, by which time 1260 aircraft, mostly B-47Es, were in service.

Britain, meanwhile, was an early participant in the jet bomber field with the English Electric Canberra.

Success Story
Originally designed for the radar bombing role as a replacement for the de Havilland Mosquito, the Canberra was the greatest success story of Britain's post-war aviation industry and was only retired from first-line service in 2006, more than 50 years after the prototype was rolled out. Four prototypes of the Canberra B.Mk.1 were produced, and the first of these flew on 13 May 1949, powered by Rolls-Royce Avon turbojets.

Problems with the radar bomb-aiming equipment, however, led to the redesign of the nose with a visual bomb-aiming position, and with this modification the fifth aircraft became the Canberra B.2. A photo-reconnaissance version, the Canberra PR.3, was basically a B.2 with a battery of seven cameras.

While awaiting the deployment of the Canberra, the RAF relied on the Avro Lincoln, a development of the Lancaster,

Above: The first bomber in the world to employ the delta wing planform, the Avro Type 698 Vulcan prototype (VX770) first flew on 30 August 1952, following extensive testing of its then radical configuration in the Avro 707 series of research deltas.

Right: The Handley Page Victor demonstrates its awesome conventional bombing capability by releasing a load of 35 454kg (1000lb) bombs. The Victor was the fastest of the V-bombers.

and on a batch of B-29s supplied by the United States.

It was not until the beginning of 1947 that the decision to produce atomic bombs was made by the British government. In the meantime, however, the Air Staff, under the direction of Marshal of the RAF Lord Tedder, had drafted a requirement for a British nuclear bomb and the specification of an aircraft that would be capable of delivering it, an advanced jet bomber capable of carrying a 10,000lb 'special' weapon at 500 knots (926km/h; 575mph) over a combat radius of 1500 nautical miles (2780km), with a ceiling of 15,200m (50,000ft) over the target.

Five aircraft companies submitted designs to meet the specification; the two eventually selected by the Ministry of Supply were those tendered by A.V. Roe and Co. Ltd, and Handley Page, respective manufacturers of the wartime Lancaster and Halifax bombers. A third design, the Type 660, submitted by Vickers, was less advanced in concept than the other two and was initially rejected. Later, when it was realized that the lower performance of the Vickers design was greatly outweighed by its ability to be developed more quickly than the others, it was decided to proceed with it as an 'interim' aircraft, a kind of insurance against the failure of the more radical bombers. It was a fortunate decision, and one which was to have far-reaching consequences. In March 1948, when a new specification

The Victor B.1 and its load of conventional 454kg (1000lb) bombs. Unlike the Vulcan, the Victor never dropped bombs in combat, but did see action in its flight refuelling tanker role during the Gulf War of 1991.

(B9/48) was written around the Vickers Type 660, not even its designers could have envisaged the role that this aircraft would play over the years to come. This was the aircraft that would form the backbone of the RAF's nuclear strike force during the dangerous years of the 1950s, and would pioneer the operational techniques of what would become the V-Force. In service, it would chalk up an impressive series of 'firsts', and would become the only British aircraft ever to release nuclear weapons. The name chosen for it was Valiant.

The Vickers Type 660's high-mounted wing had a mean sweep of 20 degrees, the angle being increased towards the wing root – at the thickest part – to improve lift/drag ratio. In this section, the engines were buried. The structure of the wing, and indeed of the whole aircraft, was entirely conventional. In fact, the only major innovation lay in the electrical systems, with which the bomber was crammed.

The prototype 660, WB210, was powered by four Rolls-Royce Avon RA3 turbojets of 28.9kN (6500lbf) thrust. After a period of systems testing and pre-flight trials, WB210 made its first flight on 18 May 1951, with Vickers's chief test pilot J. 'Mutt' Summers as captain and G.R. 'Jock' Bryce as co-pilot.

The Tupolev Tu-4 was a Russian copy of the Boeing B-29, several USAAF examples of which made emergency landings on Soviet territory towards the end of World War II. Soviet scientists successfully reverse-engineered the aircraft.

The name Valiant was officially adopted for the Vickers design in June 1951, and in 1952 it was decided that the Avro and Handley Page aircraft should have names beginning with 'V' as well.

Overshadowed

The Valiant tended to be overshadowed by the RAF's later V-bombers, the Vulcan and Victor. The first bomber in the world

to employ the delta wing planform, the Avro Type 698 Vulcan prototype (VX770), flew for the first time on 30 August 1952, following extensive testing of its then radical configuration in the Avro 707 series of research deltas. The first prototype was fitted with four Rolls-Royce Avon turbojets and was later re-engined with Bristol Siddeley and finally Rolls-Royce Conways, but the second prototype (VX777) employed Bristol Siddeley Olympus 100s. This aircraft, which flew on 3 September 1953, featured a slightly lengthened fuselage and was later fitted with wings

having redesigned leading edges with compound sweepback, flying in this configuration on 5 October 1955. It was later used to test the larger wing designed for the Vulcan B.Mk.2, being finally retired in 1960.

The first production Vulcan B.Mk.1 was delivered to No. 230 Operational Conversion Unit in July 1956, and No. 83 Squadron became the first unit to equip with the new bomber in July 1957. The second squadron to receive the aircraft, in October that year, was No. 101, followed in May 1958 by No. 617, the famous 'Dam Busters'. Production of the

greatly improved Vulcan B.Mk.2 was well under way by this time. On 30 August 1958, the first production Vulcan B.2 flew, powered by Olympus 200 engines. The second production aircraft featured a bulged tail cone housing electronic countermeasures equipment, and this became standard on subsequent aircraft.

The third design, the HP.80 Victor, was the last in a long line of Handley Page bombers. The Victor's design owed much to research into the crescent wing carried out by the German Arado and Blohm & Voss firms in World War II. The prototype HP80 Victor, WB771, was flown from Boscombe Down on 24 December 1952 by Handley Page's Chief Test Pilot, Squadron Leader H.G. Hazelden, with E.N.K. Bennett as his flight observer. The maiden flight was effortless, and it was during the landing that the Victor displayed one of its finest handling characteristics; if set up properly on final approach, it would practically land itself. When most aircraft entered the ground cushion in the round-out stage just prior to touchdown, the ground effect tended to destroy the downwash from the tailplane, causing a nose-down moment and making it necessary for the pilot to hold off with backward pressure on the control column; the Victor's high-set tailplane eliminated this effect almost entirely. Also, the aircraft's crescent wing

The Tu-85, which began flight testing in 1951, was Russia's first real attempt to produce an intercontinental bomber. It had a very good performance, but was not ordered into production. It was known as 'Barge' to NATO.

configuration reduced downwash at the root and upwash at the tips, a characteristic of normal swept wings. This produced a nose-up pitch that contributed to a correct landing attitude. The Victor prototype was destroyed when the tailplane broke away during a low-level run. The second prototype flew on 11 September 1954, followed by the first production Victor B.Mk.1 on 1 February 1956.

The first Victor squadron, No. 10, became operational in April 1958, and three more, Nos. 15, 55 and 57, had formed by 1960. The B.Mk.1A was an updated variant with more advanced equipment, including ECM in the tail, and the B.Mk.2 was a more powerful version with a larger span.

Nuclear Weapons Trials

It was the Valiants of No. 49 Squadron, however, that conducted Britain's air-dropped nuclear weapons trials, the first live drop of a British atomic bomb

(Blue Danube) having been made on 11 October 1956 during a series of trials codenamed 'Buffalo' at Maralinga, South Australia. The Blue Danube detonated at between 150 and 180m (500 and 600ft). The fissile material had been loaded into the nuclear capsule in flight and the weapon had a modified fusing system. Fears that the fusing system might fail, resulting in a 40kT ground burst and unwanted contamination, meant that a low-yield (3kT) version was used, rather than a standard production bomb. Nevertheless, this was the climax of the development effort, bringing together the bomb and the V-bomber in an operational configuration.

On 15 May 1957, Valiant XD818 of No. 49 Squadron, captained by Wing Commander K.G. Hubbard, successfully dropped the first nuclear weapon in the Operation Grapple series of trials over Malden Island in the southwest Pacific. The bomb, which consisted of a Blue

Danube ballistic case, was armed with a 'Short Granite' physics package that detonated at an altitude of about 2440m (8000ft), producing a yield of 100-150kT. It was later publicized as a 'megaton-range device', which it was not. It was a so-called 'fall-back' fission device, a lightweight fission bomb producing a considerably higher yield than the first-generation atomic bombs.

The Grapple trials continued on and off for the next 18 months, the first phase being completed in June 1957. It was clear that all had not gone well with the tests, and that further experimentation was necessary to provide a greater

Left: Although never an outstanding success in the long-range strategic bombing role, the Myasishchev Mya-4 was nevertheless the Soviet Union's first operational four-engined jet bomber, and was roughly comparable with early versions of the Boeing B-52.

understanding of the triggering mechanisms that were needed to produce high-yield thermonuclear explosions. To this end, a series of tests called 'Antler' was set up at the Maralinga range in Australia, taking place in September to November 1957.

Testing at the Pacific Range, based on Christmas Island, resumed on 8 November 1957, when Valiant XD825 flown by Squadron Leader B.T. Millett dropped a fission device. The explosion produced a high yield, possibly as high as 300kT, according to some estimates, and was probably the first really successful test to have taken place at the Pacific Range.

Medium Bomber Force

The Valiant, Vulcan and Victor, armed with nuclear weapons of British and American origin, were to form the RAF's Medium Bomber Force in the late 1950s and early 1960s, but in the meantime it was the US Strategic Air Command that continued to provide an effective deterrent against the growing strategic might of the Soviet Union.

In the closing months of World War II, three B-29s fell into Soviet hands when their crews were forced to land inside the Soviet Union after attacking Japanese targets in Manchuria. After a good deal of reverse engineering, the Tupolev

Design Bureau produced a copy, named the Tu-4. A prototype Tu-4 flew in 1946, but the Russians encountered numerous engineering problems in copying the complex American type. The first production aircraft were not issued to the Soviet long-range bomber force until early in 1948, and was not until the middle of 1949 that the type was declared fully operational.

With the B-29/Tu-4, the Russians now had the means to deliver a nuclear weapon. By the time the Tu-4 entered production, Soviet nuclear research was

well advanced. The first Soviet atomic device (not yet a bomb) was detonated at the Semipalatinsk test site in Kazakhstan on 29 August 1949. The test, which was a tower shot, used plutonium as the fissionable material and produced a yield of 10–20kT. A second device was exploded on 24 September 1951 and produced a yield of at least 25kT; another, detonated on 18 October 1951, was a composite design using uranium and plutonium as fissionable materials. This shot produced a yield of 50kT and was probably the prototype of an operational bomb.

Deployed in the mid-1950s, Tupolev's Tu-16 was the most effective of Russia's trio of new strategic bombers, and was destined to become the most important bomber type on the inventories of the Soviet Air Force and Naval Air Arm.

Meanwhile, the Tupolev design team had been turning its attention to improving the basic Tu-4 design, the principal object being to increase the bomber's range. Retaining the basic structure of the Tu-4, Tupolev's engineers set about streamlining the fuselage, increasing its length by several feet and redesigning the nose section, replacing

Given the NATO reporting name 'Bear', the Tupolev Tu-95 flew for the first time on 12 November 1952. The type entered service with the Soviet Strategic Air Forces in 1957, early examples having played a prominent part in Soviet nuclear weapons trials.

the Tu-4's rather bulbous cockpit with a more aerodynamically refined stepped-up configuration. The area of the tail fin was also increased and the fin made more angular in design. To reduce drag, the nacelles of the Ash-73TK engines (copies of the B-29's Wright R-3350s) were redesigned. The outer wing sections were also redesigned and the span increased slightly, allowing for an increase in fuel tankage of 15 per cent.

The redesigned aircraft, designated Tu-80, flew early in 1949. Two prototypes were built, and the operational version, while carrying a payload similar to that of the Tu-4, was to have had a defensive armament of ten 23mm cannon or ten 12.7mm machine guns in remotely controlled barbettes. By this time, however, the Soviet Air Force had begun to think in terms of an aircraft that would compare with the Convair B-36, which was beginning to enter service with Strategic Air Command, and the Tu-80 was not ordered into production.

In mid-1949, Tupolev embarked on the design of the biggest aircraft so far constructed in the Soviet Union, and the last Russian bomber type to be powered by piston engines. At this time, several engine design bureaux in the Soviet Union were working on powerful jet and turboprop engines that would power

the next generation of Soviet combat aircraft, but it would be some time before these became operational. In the meantime – with relations between east and west deteriorating rapidly, particularly as a result of the Russian blockade of Berlin – the race to achieve parity with the United States assumed a high degree of urgency.

This was especially true in the strategic bombing field; it was of little use if the Russians broke the American nuclear weapons monopoly by building up their own stockpile of atomic bombs, only to lack the means of delivering them to their targets. The B-36 had given Strategic Air Command the capability to deliver nuclear bombs deep into the heart of the Soviet Union, but in 1949 the Russians had no comparable bomber. The Tu-4 had the capacity to lift Russia's early, cumbersome nuclear weapons, but over only limited ranges; it could theoretically strike at targets in North America across the Arctic regions, but the mission would be strictly one-way.

Intercontinental Bomber
The new specification called for an intercontinental bomber capable of carrying a 5200kg (11,500lb) bomb load over a combat radius of 7040km (4375 miles), then returning to base without refuelling. Tupolev's answer was to produce a scaled-up version of the Tu-80 powered by new 2983kW (4000hp) piston engines. In this way, Tupolev succeeded not only in retaining the

Bombing in the Beagle
Ilyushin Il-28 'Beagle'

To save weight, the gunner's cockpit was constructed entirely of magnesium, with armoured ammunition boxes and feeds. The structure (minus NR-23 guns) weighed only 375kg (827lb). The gunner was cut off from the other crewmembers.

The fuselage construction was conventional, except that the airframe was built in separate halves, complete with equipment, then joined later to save time. The sections were bolted together, which was heavy, but quick and cheap.

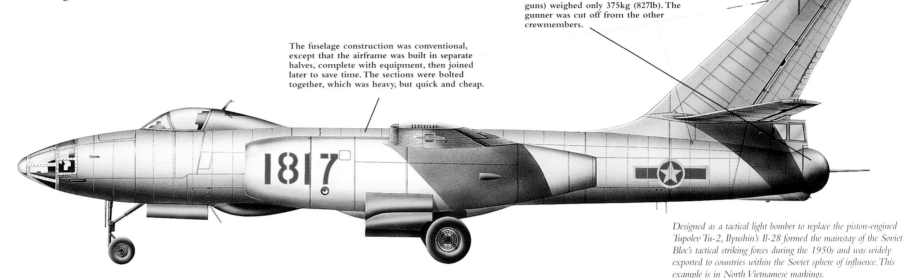

Designed as a tactical light bomber to replace the piston-engined Tupolev Tu-2, Ilyushin's Il-28 formed the mainstay of the Soviet Bloc's tactical striking forces during the 1950s and was widely exported to countries within the Soviet sphere of influence. This example is in North Vietnamese markings.

Ilyushin Il-28 'Beagle'

Type: three-seat twin-jet light bomber, torpedo bomber and reconnaissance aircraft

Powerplant: two 26.87kN (6403lbf) Klimov VK-1 (Rolls-Royce Nene) turbojets

Maximum speed: 900km/h (559mph) at 4500m (14,764ft)

Initial climb rate: 770m/min (2526fpm) to 5000m (16,404ft)

Combat radius: 1135km (705 miles)

Service ceiling: 12,300m (40,354ft)

Weights: empty 12,890kg (28,418lb); maximum take-off 23,200kg (51,147lb)

Armament: two 23mm cannon in nose (fixed) and two in tail turret; 3000kg (6614lb) of bombs

Dimensions:
span	21.45m	(70ft 4in)
length	17.65m	(57ft 11in)
height	6.70m	(22ft)
wing area	60.8m²	(654sq ft)

proven aerodynamic and technical qualities of the Tu-80 and its predecessor, the Tu-4, but also in saving time. Only two years elapsed between the start of the intercontinental bomber programme and the first flight of a prototype. By way of comparison, it took the Americans five years to produce the B-36, although the latter was somewhat more revolutionary in concept.

The new bomber, designated Tu-85, began flight-testing at the beginning of 1951. The structure was light, employing a number of special alloys (although for some reason magnesium, which was used in the structure of the B-36, was not incorporated), and the long, slender, semi-monocoque fuselage was split into four compartments, three of which were pressurized and housed the 16-man crew. Defensive armament was the same as the Tu-4's, comprising four remotely controlled turrets each with a pair of 23mm cannon. The roomy weapons bay could accommodate up to 20,000kg (44,000lb) of bombs. With a 5000kg (11,000lb) bomb load, the Tu-85 had a range of 12,070km (7500 miles) at 547km/h (340mph) and 10,000m (33,000ft); normal range was 8900km (5530 miles). Maximum speed over the target was 653km/h (406mph).

Several Tu-85 prototypes were built and test flown in 1951–52, but the aircraft was not ordered into production. Times were changing fast. In February 1951, before the Tu-85 began its flight test programme, the US Air Force had decided to order the Boeing B-52 Stratofortress, which was capable of attacking targets in the Soviet Union from bases in the continental United States, and it was clear that the day of the piston-engine bomber was over. The Russians therefore decided to abandon further development of the Tu-85 in favour of turbojet-powered strategic bombers, although they fostered the

Right: During the dangerous years of the 1960s, the mighty Boeing B-52 was the symbol of the United States' awesome striking power. Few could have imagined that the B-52 would still be in first-line service half a century later, and due to serve for another 30 years.

The Ultimate Nuclear Bomber

B-52F Stratofortress

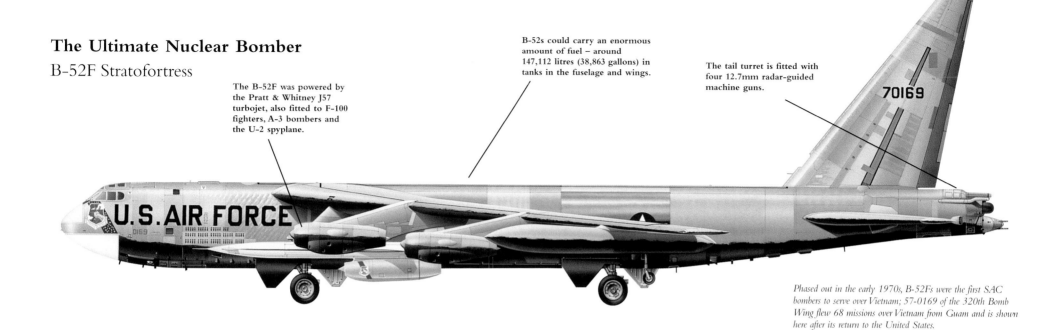

The B-52F was powered by the Pratt & Whitney J57 turbojet, also fitted to F-100 fighters, A-3 bombers and the U-2 spyplane.

B-52s could carry an enormous amount of fuel – around 147,112 litres (38,863 gallons) in tanks in the fuselage and wings.

The tail turret is fitted with four 12.7mm radar-guided machine guns.

Phased out in the early 1970s, B-52Fs were the first SAC bombers to serve over Vietnam; 57-0169 of the 320th Bomb Wing flew 68 missions over Vietnam from Guam and is shown here after its return to the United States.

impression that it was in service by showing the prototypes, escorted by jet fighters, at Aviation Day flypasts.

The production of a strategic jet bomber was entrusted to Tupolev and also to the Myasishchev design bureau; the latter's efforts were to culminate in the four-engine Mya-4, which first appeared at Tushino in 1954 and received the NATO reporting name 'Bison'. Although never an outstanding success in the long-range strategic bombing role

Left: B-52s climbing hard from their home base following the call to 'scramble'. The trick was to get away from the airfield as fast as possible before an enemy nuclear strike came in. The thick black exhaust smoke is actually water vapour; water is injected into the exhaust to give added boost at take-off.

for which it was intended, the Bison was nevertheless the Soviet Union's first operational four-engine jet bomber. Its main role in later years was maritime and electronic reconnaissance, and some were converted as flight refuelling tankers.

Tupolev's strategic jet bomber design was much more successful. Deployed in the mid-1950s, the Tu-16 flew for the first time in 1952 under the manufacturer's designation Tu-88, and was destined to become the most important bomber type on the inventories of the Soviet Air Force and Naval Air Arm. The first production version was the Badger-A, which had a fuselage, structure, systems and defensive armament based on those of the Tu-4, combined with a new swept

wing, retractable landing gear of tricycle configuration, and new indigenous AM-3 turbojets designed and developed by the Mikulin Bureau. Production of the Tu-16, which was allocated the NATO reporting name 'Badger', began in 1953. The aircraft began to enter service with the Soviet Air Force's Long-Range Aviation in 1955. Later production aircraft were powered by the uprated Mikulin AM-3M, providing improvements in both maximum range and speed. The Badger-A was also supplied to Iraq (9) and Egypt (30).

The principal subvariant of the Badger-A was the Tu-16A, configured to carry the Soviet Union's air-deliverable nuclear weapons. This variant featured

B-52D Stratofortress

Type: heavy bomber

Powerplant: eight 53.82kN (12,105lbf) Pratt & Whitney J57-P-19W turbojet engines

Maximum speed: 893km/h (555mph) at altitude

Combat range: 11,730km (7290 miles)

Service ceiling: 11,600m (38,000ft)

Weights: empty 74,893kg (165,111lb); maximum 204,117kg (450,000lb)

Armament: four 12.7mm machine guns in tail turret and up to 27,215kg (60,000lb) of bombs internally and on external racks

Dimensions:		
span	56.39m	(185ft)
length	47.73m	(156ft 7in)
height	14.73m	(48ft 4in)
wing area	47.73m²	(156ft 7in)

P-51D Mustangs dropping napalm. The World War II-era Mustang was still in the front line at the outbreak of the Korean war in June 1950, and it was some time before it was replaced by jet equipment.

prominently in the Soviet atmospheric nuclear test programme, which took place in the mid-1950s. The Tu-16 went on to have a long and illustrious career, its many roles including electronic intelligence gathering and anti-shipping strike. Some Badgers were converted to flight refuelling tankers. The Tu-16, more than 2000 examples of which are thought to have been produced, was also licence-built in China as the Xian H-6.

Turboprop-powered
Tupolev also adopted the Tu-85's basic fuselage structure in the design of a new turboprop-powered strategic bomber, the Tu-95. To bring the project to fruition as quickly as possible, the Tupolev team married swept flying surfaces to what was basically a Tu-85 fuselage.

Development of the Tu-95 and Mya-4 proceeded in parallel, and it was intended that both types should be ready in time to take part in the Aviation Day flypast at Tushino in May 1954. Some delay was experienced with the Tu-95's engines, however, and in the event only the Mya-4 was test-flown in time.

The other principal piston-engined American type in service at the start of the Korean War was the Vought F4U Corsair, which equipped many US Navy and Marine Corps units.

Left: The Grumman F9F Panther was the workhorse of the US Navy's jet fighter-bomber squadrons throughout the war in Korea. It carried out sustained attacks on enemy communications and was often equipped with unguided rockets.

Below: The MiG-15 formed the backbone of Soviet and Warsaw Pact air forces for most of the 1950s. The Allies in Korea offered a $100,000 reward to any pilot who would defect in a MiG-15.

Despite some early problems, the principal key to the Tu-95's long-term success was its powerplant. A massive engine, the NK-12, was developed by the Nikolai D. Kuznetsov Engine Design Bureau at Kuibyshev. It was designed with a single shaft, the five-stage turbine driving a 14-stage compressor, with variable guide vanes and blow-off valves, and a complex power-dividing gearbox, which coupled the power into tandem co-axial propellers. The huge AV-60 series propellers had two units each with four blades, with a diameter of 5.6m (18ft 4in).

Flight testing of the Tu-95 began in the summer of 1954, and seven pre-series aircraft made an appearance at Tushino on 3 July 1955, the type being allocated the NATO reporting name 'Bear'. By this time, the importance of the Tupolev bomber was growing, as

the performance of the Mya-4 had fallen short of expectations, and as a result production orders were cut back drastically. Even though the Tu-95's engines were still causing problems, it was realized that the Tupolev design would form the mainstay of the Soviet Air Force's strategic air divisions for at least the next decade.

Russia's new strategic bomber assets were divided in the main between three formations, the 30th Air Army (HQ Irkutsk), the 36th Air Army (HQ Moscow), and the 46th Air Army (HQ Smolensk). The 46th Air Army, forming the Western Theatre Strike Force, was numerically the most important, being eventually expanded to a strength of four bomber divisions, each of 12 bomber regiments. The other Soviet air armies of the Cold War era, the 4th at Legnica in Poland and the 24th at Vinnitsa, were essentially tactical formations. The other tactical air army, the 16th, which was also the largest, was based in the German Democratic Republic.

While the build-up of the strategic bomber force was progressing, so was the development of Russia's nuclear weapons. On 12 August 1953, the Russians exploded their first thermonuclear device, which produced a yield of 200-300kT. At about this time,

The First Cold War Superfighter
MiG-15UTI

The MiG-15UTI was the two-seat trainer version of the MiG-15 fighter. This one is seen in the insignia of the Iraqi Air Force, which received substantial quantities of Soviet equipment after 1959.

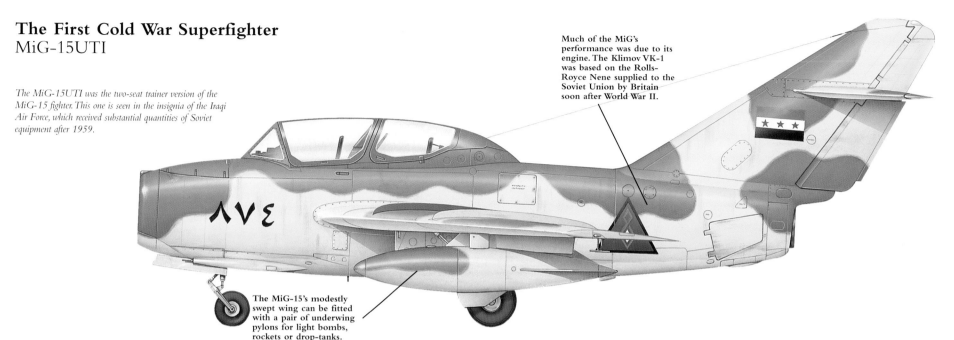

Much of the MiG's performance was due to its engine. The Klimov VK-1 was based on the Rolls-Royce Nene supplied to the Soviet Union by Britain soon after World War II.

The MiG-15's modestly swept wing can be fitted with a pair of underwing pylons for light bombs, rockets or drop-tanks.

the Soviet Air Force received its first issue of atomic bombs, and in September 1954 the Russians conducted their first large-scale exercise involving an atomic bomb detonation. By 1955 small numbers of nuclear weapons were being produced for the army and navy as well as the air force, and in that year a series of tests took place involving the delivery of nuclear weapons by aircraft. These culminated in two significant shots, both occurring in November; the first was a thermonuclear bomb reduced in size to fit the bomb bays of a planned new generation of jet bombers, while the second was the first Soviet high-yield (1.6 megaton) weapon.

Tactical Light Bomber

Backing up the strategic arsenal was a formidable array of tactical aircraft, led by the Ilyushin Il-28, which was roughly in the same class as the Canberra. Designed as a tactical light bomber to replace the piston-engine Tupolev Tu-2, the Il-28 formed the mainstay of the Soviet block's tactical striking forces during the 1950s and was widely exported to countries within the Soviet sphere of influence. The first VK-1-powered Il-28 flew on 20 September 1948, and deliveries to Soviet tactical squadrons began in the following year. Around 10,000 Il-28s were produced, variants including the Soviet Navy's Il-28T

torpedo bomber and the Il-28U two-seat trainer (NATO code name 'Mascot'). Some 500 Il-28s were supplied to China, where the type was also built under licence as the Harbin H-5.

Overshadowing all other bombers of the 1950s, however, was the mighty Boeing B-52, the aircraft that was to remain the backbone of the west's airborne nuclear deterrent forces for three decades. The B-52 was the product of a USAAF requirement, issued in April 1946, for a new jet heavy bomber to replace the Convair B-36 in Strategic Air Command. Two prototypes were ordered in September 1949, the YB-52 flying for the first time on 15 April 1952 powered

MiG-15UTI 'Midget'

Type: two-seat advanced pilot and weapons trainer

Powerplant: one 26.48kN (5956lbf) VK-1 centrifugal-flow turbojet (derived from Rolls-Royce Nene)

Maximum speed: 107km/h (66mph) at sea level

Range: 142km (88 miles)

Service ceiling: 15,600m (51,180ft)

Weights: empty 4000kg (8818lb); loaded 5400kg (11,905lb)

Armament: often not fitted, or one 23mm cannon with 80 rounds or one 12.7mm cannon with 150 rounds, plus option of two 500kg (1100lb) bombs carried underwing as an alternative to drop-tanks

Dimensions:		
span	10.08m	(33ft 1in)
length	10.04m	(33ft)
height	3.74m	(12ft 3in)
wing area	20.60m²	(222sq ft

The Lockheed F-80C Shooting Star performed excellent ground-attack work in the Korean War. It was a very stable gun platform, and was also able to carry a substantial load of bombs and rockets.

by eight Pratt & Whitney J57-P-3 turbojets. On 2 October 1952, the XB-52 also made its first flight, both aircraft having the same power plant. The two B-52 prototypes were followed by three B-52As, the first of which flew on 5 August 1954.

These aircraft featured a number of modifications and were used for extensive trials, which were still in progress when the first production B-52B was accepted by SAC's 93rd Bomb Wing at Castle AFB, California. Fifty examples were produced for SAC (including ten of the 13 B-52As originally ordered, which were converted to B-52B standard), and it was followed on the production line by the B-52C, 35 of which were built.

The focus of B-52 production then shifted to Wichita, Kansas, with the appearance of the B-52D, the first of which flew on 14 May 1956; 170 were eventually built. Following the B-52E (100 built) and the B-52F (89) came the major production variant, the B-52G.

The B-52G was the first aircraft to be armed with a long-range stand-off air-to-surface missile, the North American GAM-77 Hound Dog, a system designed to enhance the bomber's chances of survival. The missile was designed to carry a one-megaton warhead over a range of between 500 and 700 nautical miles (926 and 1297km) depending on the mission profile, and could operate between treetop level and 16,775m (55,000ft) at speeds of up to Mach 2.1. The weapon was fitted with a North American Autonetics Division inertial system, which was linked to the aircraft's navigation systems and continually updated by a Kollsman astro-tracker in the launch pylon.

All B-52Gs and, later, B-52Hs armed with the Hound Dog carried one pylon-mounted round under each wing. The Hound Dogs' turbojets were lit up during take-off, effectively making the B-52 a ten-engined aircraft, and were subsequently shut down, the missile's tanks being topped up from the parent aircraft. After launch, the missile could follow a high or low flight profile, with dog legs and diversions as necessary. Later, antiradar and terrain contour matching (TERCOM) modifications were introduced. At the missile's peak in 1962, there were 592 Hound Dogs on SAC's inventory, and it is a measure of the system's effectiveness that it remained in operational service until 1976.

The Republic RF-84F Thunderflash was the reconnaissance version of the F-84F Thunderstreak, which replaced aircraft such as the F-80 in the USAF's tactical fighter-bomber squadrons.

Robust, Resilient Hunters
Hawker Hunter F.Mk 5

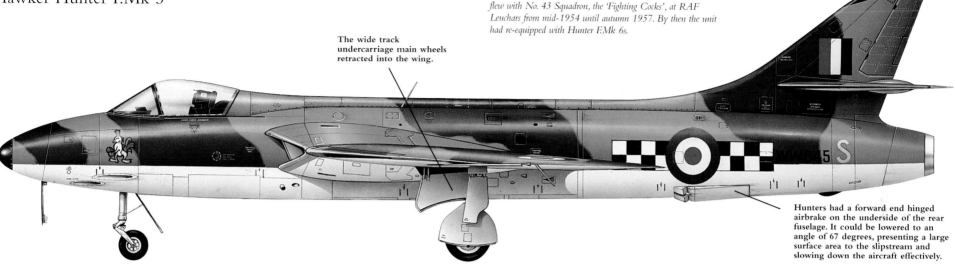

WW645 was the last Hunter Mark 1 built for the RAF. It flew with No. 43 Squadron, the 'Fighting Cocks', at RAF Leuchars from mid-1954 until autumn 1957. By then the unit had re-equipped with Hunter F.Mk 6s.

The wide track undercarriage main wheels retracted into the wing.

Hunters had a forward end hinged airbrake on the underside of the rear fuselage. It could be lowered to an angle of 67 degrees, presenting a large surface area to the slipstream and slowing down the aircraft effectively.

B-52G production totalled 193 examples, 173 of these being converted in the 1980s to carry 12 Boeing AGM-86B Air Launched Cruise Missiles. The last version was the B-52H, which had been intended to carry the cancelled Skybolt air-launched IRBM, but was modified to carry four Hound Dogs instead. The B-52 was also armed with the Short-Range Attack Missile (SRAM), the first being delivered to the 42nd Bomb Wing at Loring AFB, Maine, on 4 March 1972. The B-52 was capable of

Left: The Gloster Meteor F.Mk 8 was the RAF's main single-seat fighter during the early 1950s, and was exported to several nations including Israel (pictured), Denmark and Australia. F.Mk 8 Meteors saw considerable service during the Korean War.

carrying 20 SRAMs, 12 in three-round underwing clusters and eight in the aft bomb bay, together with up to four Mk 28 thermonuclear weapons.

By the end of the 1950s, the power blocks of east and west had come into open confrontation on several occasions. In June 1948, the Russians cut off land access to Berlin. British and US transport aircraft began flying supplies into the city, marking the start of the Berlin Airlift, a massive operation that lasted a year. In June 1949, the airlift began to run down with the lifting of the Soviet blockade; it continued to operate at a reduced rate until October. Between June 1948 and September 1949, 2,325,809 tons of supplies were flown into Berlin, more than half the tonnage consisting of coal.

Carrier-borne Support

The global threat presented by Soviet-backed communism escalated into armed conflict in 1950, when North Korean forces launched a massive invasion of South Korea. The mainstay of the North Korean Air Force during the early stages of the communist offensive was the Yak-9 fighter, the type that had helped to carry the Soviet Air Force to victory five years earlier. Other types in service with the Soviet-trained air arm were the Yak-3, the Lavochkin La-7 and the Ilyushin Il-10 Sturmovik. Opposing them were North American F-51 Mustangs and F-82 Twin Mustangs, together with smaller numbers of F-80 Shooting Stars. The US Navy provided carrier-borne support in the form of F4U Corsairs and F9F Panthers.

Hawker Hunter F.Mk 5

Type: single-seat interceptor fighter

Powerplant: one 35.59kN (8005lbf) Armstrong Siddeley Sapphire 101 turbojet

Maximum speed: 978km/h (608mph) at 11,000m (36,089ft)

Initial climb rate: 8 minutes 12 seconds to 13,720m (45,000ft)

Range: 689km (428 miles)

Service ceiling: 15,240m (50,000ft)

Weights: empty 5689kg (12,542lb); loaded 'clean' 7756kg (17,100lb); maximum take-off weight 10,886kg (24,000lb)

Armament: four 30mm ADEN cannon

Dimensions:		
span	10.29m	(33ft 9in)
length	13.98m	(45ft 10in)
height	4.01m	(13ft 2in)
wing area	33.42m²	(360sq ft)

The T.7 was the two-seat trainer version of the Hawker Hunter. Other Hunter two-seater variants were the Mks 8, 12, T52, T62, T66, T67 and T69.

At a later date, the Royal Navy also provided a strike component with its Hawker Sea Furies and Fairey Fireflies.

The Americans, operating with the sanction of the United Nations, quickly established air superiority, and by the end of August the North Korean Air Force had been practically wiped out. Then, in October, Chinese Communist forces intervened on a massive scale, and United Nations aircrews began to encounter large numbers of Russian-build MiG-15 jet fighters. The only US fighter that could match the MiG-15 in performance was the North American F-86A Sabre, and by the middle of December 1950 the first Sabre unit – the 4th Fighter Interceptor Wing (FIW) – had been rushed into action in Korea.

During preliminary skirmishes with the MiGs, it was found that the Sabre's biggest disadvantage was its limited radius of action. Whereas the MiGs operated within sight of their airfields, the Sabres had to make the long trip north to the Yalu River from their bases at Kimpo or Taegu, which reduced the

Right: Later versions of the Gloster Javelin all-weather fighter were fitted with a lance-type flight refuelling probe to extend their combat radius. The reheat nozzles for the Sapphire Sa.7R engines are clearly seen in this photograph.

The Original French Jet Fighter
Dassault Ouragan

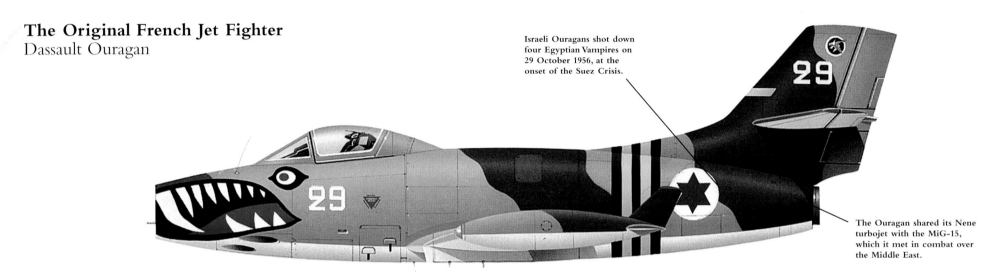

Israeli Ouragans shot down four Egyptian Vampires on 29 October 1956, at the onset of the Suez Crisis.

The Ouragan shared its Nene turbojet with the MiG-15, which it met in combat over the Middle East.

A shark-toothed Dassault Ouragan in the black-and-yellow identification markings worn by Israeli Air Force ground-attack aircraft during the Sinai campaign of 1956.

Dassault Ouragan

Type: single-seat fighter/ground-attack aircraft

Powerplant: one 2300kg (5070lb) Hispano-Suiza Nene 104B turbojet

Maximum speed: 940km/h (584mph)

Ferry range: 1000km (620miles)

Service ceiling: 15,000m (49,210ft)

Weights: empty 4150kg (9150lb); loaded 7600kg (17,416lb)

Armament: four 20mm Hispano 404 cannon; underwing hardpoints for two 454kg (1000lb) bombs, or 16 105mm rockets, or eight rockets and two 458-litre (101-gallon) napalm tanks

Dimensions:
span	13.2m	(43ft 2in)
length	10.74m	(35ft 3in)
height	4.15m	(13ft 7in)
wing area	23.8m²	(256sq ft)

time they could spend in the combat area to a matter of minutes.

To extend their patrol time, the Sabres were forced to fly at relatively low airspeeds to conserve fuel, which placed them at a disadvantage. The MiG pilots were quick to exploit this weakness, attacking from above at near-sonic speed and making their escape before the Sabre pilots could increase their own speed in time to react. To counter this inherent advantage, the Sabre pilots adopted new tactics which involved sending four flights of F-86s into the combat area at five-minute intervals and high speed; from then on, although the MiGs almost always enjoyed the initial advantage in combat, the Sabres began to establish definite air supremacy.

Superiority Challenge

By June 1951, some 300 MiG-15s were deployed on the cluster of airfields north of the Yalu, a formidable force against which the Americans had only 44 Sabres in Korea. It was a considerable source of annoyance and frustration to the United Nations' pilots that they were not allowed to cross the river to strike at the enemy on his bases. Nevertheless, despite the fact that they were often outnumbered by two to one in air combat, the Sabres managed to hold their own, although the MiGs challenged their overall superiority several times. It was touch and go in September and October 1951, when the MiGs succeeded for the first time in seriously interfering with American bombing raids on North Korean targets,

and the situation eased only in January 1952, with the arrival in Korea of a second Sabre wing, the 51st Fighter Interceptor Wing.

Not until much later – nearly four decades later, in fact – did it become generally known that the MiG pilots in combat over Korea were almost entirely Russian. The first Soviet fighter units to deploy to Manchuria in the second half of 1950 were the 151st Guards Fighter Division (28th and 139th Guards Fighter regiments) and the 28th Fighter Division (67th and 139th Fighter regiments). At

Right: The Dassault Mystère IV was unquestionably one of the finest combat aircraft of its era. Israel acquired the first of 60 in April 1956, the type replacing the Gloster Meteor F.8 in Israeli Air Force service.

Left: The carrier-borne Hawker Sea Hawk saw much service during the Suez Crisis, caused by Egypt's nationalization of the Suez Canal.

the end of November 1950, the 64th Fighter Corps was created by amalgamating the 151st Guards Fighter Division and the 28th and 50th Fighter divisions, but in December the 28th Fighter Division was transferred to central China, where it began training pilots on the MiG-15. Soon afterwards, the 151st Guards Fighter Division was assigned a similar task, so that at the end of the year the only MiG-15 unit taking an active part in the air war over Korea was the 50th Fighter Division, comprising the 29th Guards Fighter Regiment and the 177th Fighter Regiment.

The 50th Division was the first formation in China to use the uprated version of the MiG-15, the MiG-15B.

At the beginning of 1951, the 50th Guards Fighter Division was recalled to the Soviet Union. Its place in the front line was taken by the 151st Guards Fighter Division, which took over the 50th's MiG-15Bs and relinquished its own earlier-model MiGs to the 3rd Fighter Division of the Chinese People's Air Force. The 151st rotated its regiments to the combat area, sending the 28th Fighter Regiment forward to Antung on 8 February 1951 and two squadrons of the 72nd Regiment in March. In April 1951, the 1151st Division deployed to Anshan, where the rest of 64th Air Corps was located, and was replaced in the Antung area by

the 324th Fighter Division. The unit was very well trained and highly motivated, which was hardly surprising in view of the fact that it was commanded by Brigadier General Ivan Kozhedub, the top-scoring Soviet and Allied fighter pilot of World War II. The division was armed with 62 MiG-15Bs, and soon began to make its presence felt. Other Soviet air divisions deployed to Manchuria were the 303rd and 324th.

Ground-Attack Role

The United Nations retained its air superiority throughout 1952, the F-80 gradually being replaced in the ground-attack role by the F-84 Thunderjet. As a Korean

armistice became a possibility in the early summer of 1953, the last great jet-versus-jet battles of the conflict took place, with the communists briefly taking the offensive again. By the time the last shots of the Korean war were fired, United Nations airmen claimed to have destroyed 900 enemy aircraft in three years of fighting, a total that included 792 MiG-15s claimed by the Sabre pilots for the loss of 78 of their own number.

De Havilland Sea Venoms and their crews on board a Royal Navy aircraft carrier. The Sea Venom played a prominent part in the Fleet Air Arm's attacks on Egyptian airfields during the 1956 Suez crisis.

Left: The rocket-armed Republic F-84F Thunderstreak proved to be an extremely potent tactical fighter in the 1950s and 1960s. The aircraft was to remain in service with Greece and Turkey until the early 1980s.

Later, this claim was reduced to 379 MiG-15s, the Sabre losses being increased to 106. Russian records admit the loss of 335 MiG-15s, which rises to 550 if Chinese and North Korean MiGs are included. The Russians and their allies, however, claim to have destroyed 181 F-86 Sabres out of a total of 271 UN aircraft, which included 27 Thunderjets and 30 Shooting Stars.

The MiG-15 revealed the inadequacy

of Britain's principal air defence fighter, the Gloster Meteor F.8, which was used by No. 77 Squadron RAAF in the fighter escort and, later, the ground-attack roles. Two new swept-wing fighter types, the Hawker Hunter and Supermarine Swift, were to replace the Meteor in the air defence role; their prototypes flew on 20 July and 1 August 1951, respectively, and both types were ordered into 'super-priority' production for RAF Fighter Command. The Swift, however, was found to be unsuitable for its primary role of high-level interception, being prone to tightening in turns and suffering frequent high-altitude flame-outs as

a result of shock waves entering the air intakes when the cannon were fired. It was later adapted to the low-level fighter/ reconnaissance role and, as the Swift FR.5, equipped two squadrons in Germany.

The Hunter F.Mk.1, which entered service early in 1954, also suffered from engine surge problems during high-altitude gun firing trials, resulting in some modifications to its Rolls-Royce Avon turbojet, and this – together with increased fuel capacity and provision for underwing tanks – led to the Hunter F4, which gradually replaced the Canadair-built F-86E Sabre (which had been supplied to the RAF as an interim fighter) in the German-based squadrons of the 2nd

Tactical Air Force. The Hunter Mks 2 and 5 were variants powered by Armstrong Siddeley Sapphire engines. In 1953, Hawker equipped the Hunter with the large 4535kg (10,000lb) thrust Avon 203 engine. This variant, designated Hunter F.MK.6, flew for the first time in January 1954. Deliveries began in 1956, and the F6 subsequently equipped 15 squadrons of RAF Fighter Command. The Hunter FGA.9 was a development of the F6 optimized for ground attack.

The Lockheed F-94 Starfire all-weather fighter was developed from the T-33A trainer, with two production T-33 airframes being converted as YF-94s.

A Northrop F-89D Scorpion firing a salvo of folding-fin aircraft rockets (FFAR) from its wingtip pods. The F-89D was followed into production by the F-89H, which could carry Falcon missiles as well as the MB-1 Genie nuclear AAM.

Last Day Fighter

The Hunter was the last of the RAF's pure day fighters. In the late 1950s, it shared the UK air defence task with the Gloster Javelin, developed as a replacement for the night-fighter versions of the Meteor, Vampire and Venom aircraft that had equipped the RAF's night-fighter squadrons during the first part of the decade. Construction of the Javelin prototype, the Gloster GA5 – the world's first twin-jet delta and an extremely radical design for its day – began in April 1949, and the aircraft flew for the first time on 26 November 1951, powered by two Armstrong Siddeley Sapphires. As the Javelin FAW1, the new fighter was ordered into 'super-priority' production for the RAF. Several variants of the type were produced, culminating in the FAW.9.

In the early 1950s, France made great strides in the deployment of jet combat aircraft of its own design, the first being the Dassault Ouragan. Begun as a private venture in 1947, the prototype Ouragan first flew on 28 February 1949. A straightforward no-frills fighter, the Ouragan (Hurricane) was powered by a Rolls-Royce Nene 102 turbojet, built under licence by Hispano-Suiza, and became the first jet fighter of French design to be ordered in quantity, some 350 production aircraft being delivered to the French Air Force from 1952. The Ouragan was exported to India, where it was known as the Toofani (Whirlwind), and to Israel, which received 75 examples.

Right: An unusual view of the Avro Canada CF-100 all-weather fighter. The CF-100, the largest fighter in the world at its conception, was designed as a long-range night and all-weather interceptor to counter a Soviet air attack across the Arctic.

The Dassault MD 452 Mystère IIC, first flown on 23 February 1951, was in turn a straightforward swept-wing development of the Ouragan. The French Air Force took delivery of 150 aircraft, and Israel had plans to purchase some in 1954-55, but in view of the type's poor accident record – several of the earlier machines having been lost through structural failure – it was decided

The Avro Canada CF-105 Arrow was one of the most advanced interceptors in the world, but escalating development costs and an offer by the US government to equip three RCAF air defence squadrons with the F-101B Voodoo brought about its demise.

to buy the far more promising Mystère IV instead. The latter was unquestionably one of the finest combat aircraft of its era.

The prototype Mystère IVA flew for the first time on 28 September 1952, and early trials proved so promising that the French Government placed an order for 325 production aircraft six months later in April 1953. The fighter was also delivered to India, and Israel acquired the first of 60 in April 1956, the type replacing the Gloster Meteor F.8 in Israeli Air Force service.

Another important French type of this period was the Sud-Ouest SO.4050

Vautour. Designed from the outset to carry out three tasks - all-weather interception, close support and high-altitude bombing - the Sud-Ouest SO.4050 Vautour (Vulture) flew for the first time on 16 October 1952. Two production versions were ordered, the Vautour IIB light bomber and the IIN all-weather interceptor. The final version of the Vautour was the IIBR, a bomber-reconnaissance variant. The close-support version of the Vautour, the IIA, was not used by the French Air Force; however, 20 examples were supplied to Israel, together with four IINs.

Right: The first Convair F-102A Delta Dagger was handed over to US Air Defense Command in June 1955, but it was another year before the type was issued to squadrons. In total, 875 were delivered.

Ill-fated Venture

Israel's Ouragans and Mystères saw combat in October 1956, when Israeli forces invaded the Sinai Peninsula in collusion with Anglo-French forces that were seizing key points in the Suez Canal Zone, an ill-fated venture mounted as a consequence of the Egyptian President

In the early 1960s the F-106A was the most important type on the inventory of US Air Defense Command, with which it served exclusively. The type also equipped several units of the Air National Guard. This example belongs to the New Jersey ANG.

Nasser's nationalizing of the Suez Canal Company some months earlier. Attacks on Egyptian airfields were made by Vickers Valiant and English Electric Canberra bombers operating from Malt and Cyprus, by carrier-borne Hawker Sea Hawk, de Havilland Sea Venom and Westland Wyvern fighter-bombers, by RAF Venoms based on Cyprus, and by French F4U Corsairs and F-84F Thunderstreaks, the latter based in Cyprus and Israel. The swept-wing F-84F replaced the Thunderjet in several NATO air forces, giving many European pilots their first experience of modern, swept-wing jet aircraft. During the Suez operation, the Israel-based F-84Fs carried out an attack on Luxor airfield, destroying most of the Egyptian Air Force's Il-28 jet bombers.

By the mid-1950s, with the Soviet Union's jet bomber force growing, the US Air Force had a clear requirement for a long-range all-weather fighter capable of intercepting nuclear-armed bombers before they could reach the coastline of the North American continent. As a stopgap measure, an all-weather version of the Sabre, the F-86D, was produced; it had a complex fire control system and a ventral rocket pack. From Lockheed came the F-94 Starfire, which entered service in 1950 and saw action in Korea,

while Northrop produced the F-89 Scorpion, which could carry the Genie nuclear-tipped air-to-air missile.

It was the Canadian aircraft industry, however, that fielded one of the most important aircraft of this type. The Avro Canada CF-100, the largest fighter in the world at the time of its conception, was designed as a long-range night and all-weather interceptor to counter a Soviet air attack across the Arctic. The prototype CF-100 Mk 1 flew on 19 January 1950, an order for 124 production CF-100 Mk 3s being followed by further orders for 510 Mk 4As and 4Bs; the latter had Orenda 11 engines. Nine RCAF squadrons operated the type, providing round-the-clock air defence coverage. CF-100 squadrons served in Germany as part of Canada's NATO commitment, and 53 examples of the last production version, the Mk 5, were delivered to the Belgian Air Force.

All-Weather Interceptor

The CF-105 was to have been replaced by the Avro Canada CF-105 delta-wing all-weather interceptor, which flew for the first time on 25 March 1958, powered by two Pratt & Whitney J75 turbojets that gave it a speed of over Mach 2.0. Four more aircraft were built, designated CF-105 Mk 1; four more – designated Mk 2, with Orenda PS-13 engines – were almost complete when the project was abruptly cancelled in February 1959. The CF-105 was one of the most advanced interceptors in the world, but escalating development costs

Left: An F-106A Delta Dart passes over the Mojave Desert. The aircraft, the second-to-last F-106 in active service, had been used as a chase aircraft in the B-1B supersonic bomber programme.

and an offer by the US government to equip three RCAF air defence squadrons with the F-101B Voodoo brought about its demise. All that remained was the knowledge that, during its brief career, it had made a significant contribution to the advance of aviation technology.

The two-seat F-101B, the all-weather variant of the McDonnell Voodoo, equipped 16 squadrons of the US Air Defense Command and served alongside the supersonic Convair F-102A Delta Dagger, which entered service only after a protracted and troubled development career and which was supplanted by the Convair F-106 Delta Dart. The first production F-106 was delivered in June 1959, and production ended in 1962 after 257 examples had been built, equipping 13 fighter interceptor squadrons. In the early 1960s the F-106A was the most important type on the inventory of Air Defense Command.

Convair was also responsible for developing the world's first operational supersonic bomber, the B-58 Hustler, which first flew on 11 November 1956. The B-58 was a bold departure from conventional design, having a delta wing with conical-cambered leading edge, an area-ruled fuselage and four turbojets in pods under the wing. The crew occupied tandem cockpits, and the B-58 was the first aircraft in the world in which the

crew had individual escape capsules for use at supersonic speeds. Weapons and extra fuel were carried in a large, jettisonable underfuselage pod. It was anticipated that the type would replace the B-47, but it was technically too complex and had an appalling accident rate. In the end, only the 43rd and 305th Bomb Wings were equipped with it.

Potent Combat Aircraft
The year 1958 saw the first flight of one of the most potent and versatile combat aircraft in the history of aviation, the McDonnell F-4 Phantom II, which

stemmed from a 1954 requirement for an advanced naval fighter. The XF4H-1 prototype first flew on 27 May 1958. Twenty-three development aircraft were procured, followed by 45 production machines for the US Navy. These were originally designated F4H-1F, but this was later changed to F-4A. The F-4B was a slightly improved version with J79-GE-8 engines, and between them the F-4A and F-4B captured many world records over a four-year period. Carrier trials were carried out in 1960; in December that year, the first Phantoms were delivered to training squadron VF-121.

The first supersonic bomber to enter service with the USAF, the Convair B-58 prototype flew in November 1956. It was anticipated that it would replace the B-47, but in the end only the 43rd and 305th Bomb Wings were equipped with it.

The first fully operational Phantom squadron, VF-114, commissioned with F-4Bs in October 1961, and in June 1962 the first USMC deliveries were made to VMF(AW)-314. Total F-4B production was 649 aircraft.

Twenty-nine F-4Bs were loaned to the USAF for evaluation in 1962 and proved superior to any Air Force fighter-bomber. A production order was quickly

Left: An F-4E Phantom releasing a salvo of cluster bombs. One of the most potent and versatile combat aircraft ever built, the McDonnell (later McDonnell Douglas) F-4 Phantom II stemmed from a 1954 project for an advanced naval fighter.

placed for a USAF variant; this was originally designated F-110A, but later changed to F-4C. Deliveries to the USAF began in 1963. The RF-4B and RF-4C were unarmed reconnaissance variants for the USMC and USAF, while the F-4D was basically an F-4C with improved systems and redesigned radome. The major production version was the

F-4E, 913 of which were delivered to the USAF between October 1967 and December 1976. F-4E export orders totalled 558. The RF-4E was the tactical reconnaissance version. The F-4F (175 built) was a version for the Luftwaffe, intended primarily for the air superiority role, but retaining multi-role capability, while the F-4G Wild Weasel was the F4E modified for the suppression of enemy defence systems. The F-4B's successor in USN/USMC service was the F-4J, which possessed greater ground-attack capability; the first of 522 production

aircraft was delivered in June 1976. The Phantom served with most of the United States' NATO partners, including Britain, which was the first overseas customer, and with other friendly air forces, including Japan's.

The F-4 entered US Navy service in time to be involved in the US blockade of Cuba, imposed in October 1962 when it was found that the Russians had infiltrated intermediate-range ballistic missiles into the island. The missiles and their associated equipment were revealed by photographs brought back by a

reconnaissance aircraft that was already the subject of much controversy: the Lockheed U-2. First flown in 1955, the U-2 had made reconnaissance sorties over the Soviet Union from 1956 until 1 May 1960, when one flown by a Central Intelligence Agency pilot, Francis G. Powers, was shot down near Sverdlovsk by a Soviet SA-2 missile battery.

Lockheed's 'Black Lady', the U-2 high-altitude reconnaissance aircraft. U-2 overflights of the USSR and Warsaw Pact territories began in 1956 and continued until 1 May 1960, when a U-2 was shot down near Sverdlovsk.

The Later Cold War

During 1958, with the process well under way of building up Strategic Air Command's ground alert force to the point where one-third of its bombers would be combat-ready at all times, Strategic Air Command was taking other action to ensure that a high proportion of its bomber force would survive a surprise attack and be in a position to launch a massive retaliatory strike. The main problem that had to be overcome was one of overcrowding. The tremendous expansion that had taken place during the 1950s meant that some bases were supporting as many as 90 B-47 bombers and 40 KC-97 tankers. The first B-52 wings were also very large, consisting of 45 bombers and 15 or 20 KC-135 tankers, all located on one base.

The obvious answer was dispersal and, as a first step, several KC-97 squadrons were separated from their parent B-47 wings and relocated on northern bases, which in fact were strategically better placed to support the B-47s' Arctic operations. The B-47 dispersal programme itself was a long-term one, and was to be achieved mainly through the phasing out of B-47 wings in the late 1950s and early 1960s. The B-52 force, on the other hand, was still growing, and in this case the dispersal programme called for the larger B-52 wings to be broken up into three equally sized units of 15 aircraft each. Two of these units, which were redesignated Strategic Wings and given full supporting services, included an attached KC-135 squadron, were relocated to other bases.

The RAF's V-Force, which unlike Strategic Air Command never maintained an airborne alert force, relied entirely on dispersal as an insurance against surprise attack, the V-bombers

Republic F-105 Thunderchiefs from Hill AFB, Utah, pictured in formation with US Navy A-4 Skyhawks. In October 1962, both types stood ready to carry out strikes on Soviet military sites in Cuba.

being dispersed in clutches of four to any of 36 airfields in the United Kingdom and overseas. The V-Force's viability as an effective strategic deterrent was constantly put to the test by war-situation exercises of varying intensity; for example, those named 'Kinsman' meant dispersal, while 'Micky Finn' meant dispersal without notice, at any time of the day or night.

In February 1962, the state of readiness of the V-Force was further improved with the inauguration of the Bomber Command Quick Reaction Alert (QRA) plan, which initially involved one aircraft from each V-Force squadron being maintained in an armed condition, on specially designed operational readiness platforms (ORPs), prepared to scramble at a moment's notice. The ORPs were angled into the main runway so that the bombers could become airborne very quickly. As expertise grew, a section of four Vulcans could be off the runway within 90 seconds of the order to scramble being received.

East–West Confrontation

Crisis followed crisis during this dangerous period of east–west confrontation. The most serious erupted in the autumn of 1962. At 1900 on 22 October, President John F. Kennedy, in a televised speech lasting 17 minutes, announced to an unsuspecting American public the discovery of Russian intermediate-range ballistic missiles in Cuba and the immediate imposition of a naval blockade around the island. Within two days, ships of the blockading force were in position at sea, including the attack carriers *Enterprise* and *Independence*, and the anti-submarine carriers *Essex* and *Randolph*, while shore-based maritime aircraft maintained constant patrols.

The Cuban Missile Crisis of October 1962 brought Strategic Air Command up to full alert. Battle staffs were placed on 24-hour alert duty, leaves were cancelled and personnel were recalled. B-47s were dispersed to their pre-selected civil and military airfields, additional bombers and tankers were placed on ground alert, and the B-52 airborne alert training programme was quickly expanded into an actual airborne alert involving 24-hour sorties by fully armed aircraft and the immediate replacement of each B-52 that landed. The Intercontinental Ballistic and Cruise Missiles (ICBM) forces, which then numbered about 200 missiles, were also brought into alert configuration.

Had war come, the spearhead of an attack on Soviet facilities in Cuba would have been the Republic F-195 Thunderchiefs of Tactical Air Command's 4th Tactical

Left: First seen publicly in 1961, the turboprop-powered Beriev Be-12 amphibian aircraft was the type selected to replace the Be-6 as the Soviet Navy's principal maritime patrol flying boat. The prototype first flew in 1960.

Fighter Wing, which deployed to McCoy AFB in Florida on 21 October. The 4th Tactical Fighter Wing began a one-hour alert status at 0400 the next day, and this was reduced to 15 minutes in the afternoon. However, the F-105s were held back while international negotiations proceeded, and when they flew it was in the air defence role, patrolling the southern Florida peninsula on the lookout for Il-28 jet bombers. Meanwhile, Cuba was kept under constant surveillance by McDonnell RF-101 Voodoo and Lockheed U-2 reconnaissance aircraft.

In Europe, which would certainly have been the first to feel an armed Soviet backlash against any armed American action in Cuba, the nuclear alert force comprised USAF F-100 Super Sabre tactical fighter-bombers deployed on British bases, backed up by Thor IRBMs deployed with the RAF in the United Kingdom, and RAF Valiant bombers armed with Mk 28 nuclear weapons of American origin.

Right: The first land-based aircraft designed specifically for the long-range maritime reconnaissance role, the Lockheed Neptune was destined to be one of the longest-serving military aircraft ever built. Seen in this photograph are P2V-7s of the Japanese Maritime Self-Defence Force.

Left: A development of the Lockheed Electra airliner, the P-3 (formerly P3V-1) Orion has seen service with 17 different air arms, including that of Japan, pictured. It is slated for replacement by around 2013, by which time it will have been in service for more than 50 years.

Covert Alert

The commanding general of the United States Air Forces Europe, General Truman H. Landon, and his subordinate commanders were briefed on the Cuban situation by General Lauris Norstad, the Supreme Commander, Allied Powers Europe (SACEUR), at a hastily convened conference called at Orly airfield, Paris, at 1500 GMT on 22 October. Immediately afterwards, a procedure called 'Covert Alert' was initiated at RAF Wethersfield and RAF Lakenheath, Suffolk, where the nuclear-capable F-100s of the 20th and 48th Tactical Fighter Wings were based. This involved key personnel being contacted by radio telephone and ordered to report to their duty stations; it also involved the arming of some, but not all, aircraft in the Theatre Tactical Nuclear Force. As the crisis deepened, the tactical squadrons stepped up their state of alert. At the more critical points of the crisis, pilots adopted a cockpit alert posture, ground power units were engaged, all covers were removed from weapons and engines readied for an immediate start.

On 25 October 1962, RAF Bomber Command was informed that SAC had raised its alert status to DEFCON 2 – the second highest short of all-out war – in connection with the Cuban crisis. At this time, the Bomber Command was carrying out a routine manoeuvre called Exercise Mick, which involved practising alert and arming procedures without dispersing the aircraft. A no-notice exercise, it required all bomber airfields to generate – in other words, prepare for war operations – all available aircraft, bringing together the three elements of

The first of 77 production Avro Shackleton MR.1s entered service with No. 120 Squadron at Kinloss, Scotland, in April 1951. The Shackleton MR.2 had a ventral radome, while the MR.3 had a redesigned wing and a tricycle undercarriage.

each weapons system: aircraft, weapons and aircrew. On 26 October, the exercise was extended and the readiness state of the V-Force was increased to Alert Condition 3 of the Bomber Command Alert and Readiness Procedures; all civilians employed on the bomber airfields were sent home and armed patrols doubled on the airfield perimeters. HQ Bomber Command ordered stations to double the number of aircraft on Quick Reaction Alert, so that most stations had six fully armed bombers at 15 minutes' readiness. The exception was RAF Waddington, where nine fully armed Vulcans were brought to 15 minutes' readiness.

The first major break in the crisis came on 28 October, when the Soviet administration agreed to move its IRBMs from Cuba, subject to verification by the United Nations. During the next few days, SAC aircraft maintained close aerial surveillance while the missiles were dismantled, loaded on to ships and sent back through the quarantine. The quarantine was maintained until 20 November, when the Russians agreed to move their Il-28 light bombers from the island. SAC then began running down its high-alert state. The B-47s returned to their home bases, the ground alert force dropped back to its normal 50 per cent standard, and the B-52 wings resumed their routine airborne alert training.

By the time of the Cuban crisis, it had become apparent that the Russians had made big strides in their military aviation technology. The annual air display at

Developed from the de Havilland Comet 4C airliner, the Nimrod, which first flew on 23 May 1967, was intended to replace the Shackleton as the RAF's standard long-range maritime patrol aircraft.

Tushino, near Moscow, in May 1961 had produced revelations that had startled western observers, not the least of them being that the Russians appeared to be producing supersonic bombers. One type first seen publicly at Tushino that year was the Tupolev Tu-22, code-named 'Blinder' by NATO, designed as a supersonic successor to the Tu-16 Badger. The Tu-22s seen at Tushino were pre-series trials aircraft, and first deliveries of the type to the Dalnaya Aviatsiya (Soviet Strategic Air Force) were not made until the following year. The first operational version, code-named 'Blinder-A', was produced in limited numbers only. The second variant, the Tu-22K Blinder-B, was equipped with a flight refuelling probe; 12 aircraft were later supplied to Iraq and 24 to Libya.

Another type that took part in the Soviet Aviation Day flypast, escorted by MiG-21s and appearing to be a four-engine supersonic bomber, turned out to be only a prototype. It was the Myasishchev M-50, an extremely advanced turbojet-powered bomber with supersonic flight capability. The M-50 was first flown in November 1959, and several prototypes were built, but the project was abandoned in favour of ICBM development.

Also seen at Tushino in 1961 was a turboprop-powered amphibian, the Beriev Be-12, which was allocated the NATO reporting name 'Mail' and which was a very capable anti-submarine aircraft. In the early 1960s, with both east and west deploying, or about to deploy, nuclear submarines, the importance of the anti-submarine warfare (ASW) aircraft increased immeasurably.

American ASW Types

At this time, two principal American types were in use, the first being the Lockheed P2V Neptune. The first land-based aircraft that had been designed specifically for the long-range maritime reconnaissance role, the Lockheed Neptune, was destined to be one of the longest-serving military aircraft ever built. The first of two XP2V-1 prototypes flew on 17 May 1945, with orders already having been placed for 15 pre-production and 151 production P2V-1s. Deliveries to the US Navy began in March 1947, by which time another variant, the P2V-2, had also flown. The next variant of the Neptune was the P2V-3, and another engine change produced the P2V-4, which carried underwing fuel tanks. The P2V-6 (P2F) Neptune had a mine-laying capability in addition to its ASW role; 83 were delivered to the US Navy and

The prototype Saab A-32 Lansen (Lance) flew for the first time on 3 November 1952, powered by a Rolls-Royce Avon RA7R turbojet. Three more prototypes were built, and one of these exceeded Mach One in a shallow dive on 25 October 1953.

12 to France's Aéronavale. The last production version was the P2V-7. The other main US anti-submarine aircraft was the Lockheed P-3 Orion. A development of the Lockheed Electra

After a short career as a fighter the J.21 was converted to the attack role as the A-21R. The type was the only aircraft ever to see first-line service with both piston and jet power.

airliner, the P-3 (formerly P3V-1) Orion was Lockheed's winning submission in a 1958 US Navy contest for a new off-the-shelf ASW aircraft which could be brought into service very rapidly by modifying an existing type. The first of two YP3V-1 prototypes flew on 19 August 1958, and deliveries of production P-3As began in August 1962. The definitive P-3C

variant appeared in 1969. The Orion also served with the RAAF and was built under licence by several other nations.

The Royal Air Force used the Avro Shackleton, a derivative of the Lincoln bomber. The first of 77 production Shackleton MR.1s entered service with No. 120 Squadron at Kinloss, Scotland, in April 1951. The Shackleton MR.2 had

a ventral radome, while the MR.3 had a redesigned wing, wingtip tanks and a tricycle undercarriage. The MR.3 was later fitted with Armstrong Siddeley Viper turbojets in the outboard engine nacelles, and these aircraft were designated MR.3 Phase 3.

From October 1969, the Shackleton was replaced by the Hawker Siddeley Nimrod, derived from the Comet 4C airliner. The prototype

Sweden's Double-Delta Dragon
Saab J-35 Draken

The cockpit is narrow, cramped, and uses very old control technology. Yet the J-35 remains popular with pilots, possibly because it is a challenge to fly.

The Saab J-35 Draken represented a quantum leap over anything that had gone before and was, at the time of its service debut, a component of the finest fully integrated air defence system in western Europe.

Saab J-35J Draken

Type: single-seat interceptor

Powerplant: one 78.46kN (17,647lbf) Volvo Flygmotor RM6C turbojet (Rolls-Royce RB.146 Avon 300 fitted with Volvo-designed afterburner)

Maximum speed: 2125km/h (1320mph) at 11,000m (36,089ft) or Mach 2

Combat radius: 720km (447 miles)

Service ceiling: 20,000m (65,617ft)

Weights: empty 8250kg (18,188lb); loaded 12,270kg (27,051lb)

Armament: one 30mm ADEN M/55 cannon with 90 rounds, two Rb 27 radar missiles and four Rb 28 Falcon or Rb 24 Sidewinder infrared missiles, or 2900kg (6393lb) of ordnance

Dimensions: span   9.40m (30ft 10in)
           length   15.35m (50ft 4in)
           height   3.89m (12ft 9in)
           wing area   49.20m² (530sq ft)

Nimrod flew for the first time on 23 May 1967, and deliveries of production Nimrod MR.Mk.1 aircraft began in October 1969. The first 38 Nimrods were delivered between 1969 and 1972, equipping five squadrons and No. 236 OCU; another eight were delivered in 1975, while three, designated Nimrod R.1, were converted to the electronic intelligence role. From 1979, the Nimrod fleet was significantly upgraded to MR.2 standard, with improved avionics and weapon systems. Flight refuelling equipment was added at the time of the 1982 Falklands War. All Nimrods were scheduled to be rebuilt between 2003 and 2008, retaining only the fuselage shell of existing aircraft. The new aircraft, which is designated

Nimrod MRA.4, features new wings and undercarriage, and BMW/Rolls Royce fuel-efficient engines.

Swedish Engineering
Sandwiched between NATO and the Warsaw Pact was Sweden, which in the 1950s and 1960s produced some of the world's finest aircraft in defence of its neutrality. Sweden's entry into the jet age began with the Saab J-21R; this was a jet-powered version of the piston-engined twin-boom J-21A. The J-21R flew on 10 March 1947 but, because of many modifications that had to be made to the airframe, production deliveries did not take place until 1949, and an order for 120 aircraft was cut back to 60. After a short career as a fighter, the

J.21 was converted to the attack role as the A-21R. The type was the only aircraft ever to see first-line service with both piston and jet power. The J-21R was followed into service by the Saab J-29, the first swept-wing fighter of western European design to enter service following World War II. The first of three prototypes flew on 1 September 1948 and the first production model, the J-29A, entered service in 1951. Other variants of this aircraft's basic design were the J-29B, which featured increased fuel tankage;

Right: One of the most potent combat aircraft of the 1970s, the Saab 37 Viggen (Thunderbolt) was designed to carry out the four roles of attack, interception, reconnaissance and training. The first of seven prototypes took its maiden flight on 8 February 1967.

France's Export Success
Dassault Mirage III

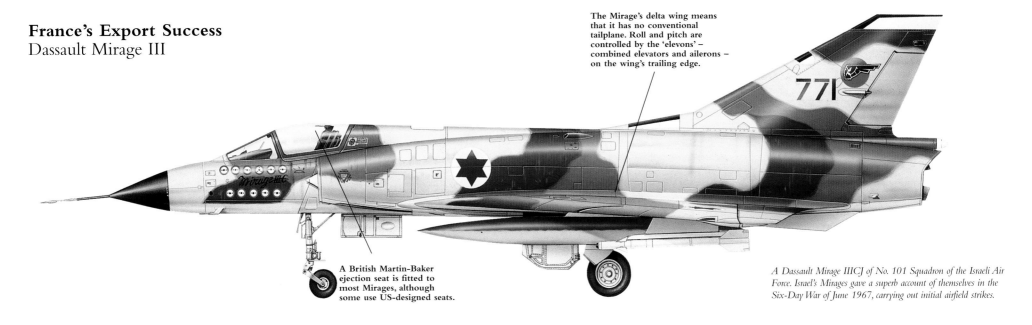

The Mirage's delta wing means that it has no conventional tailplane. Roll and pitch are controlled by the 'elevons' – combined elevators and ailerons – on the wing's trailing edge.

A British Martin-Baker ejection seat is fitted to most Mirages, although some use US-designed seats.

A Dassault Mirage IIICJ of No. 101 Squadron of the Israeli Air Force. Israel's Mirages gave a superb account of themselves in the Six-Day War of June 1967, carrying out initial airfield strikes.

Mirage IIIE

Type: single-seat fighter

Powerplant: one SNECMA 41.97kN (9440lbf) Atar 9C-3 (60.80kN/13,674lbf with afterburning) and provision for one jettisonable 14.71kN (3308lbf) SEPR 844 rocket booster

Maximum speed: 2350km/h (1460mph) or Mach 2.1

Range: 2400km (1491 miles)

Service ceiling: 14,440m (47,375ft)

Weights: empty 7050kg (15,543lb); loaded 13,700kg (30,203lb)

Armament: 30mm DEFA 552 cannon with 125 rounds; Nord 5103, MATRA R.511, MATRA T.53 or Hughes AIM-26 Falcon missiles

Dimensions:	span	8.22m (27ft)
	length	15.03m (49ft 4in)
	height	4.50m (14ft 9in)
	wing area	35.00m² (377sq ft)

the A-29 ground-attack version, which was identical to the J-29 except for underwing ordnance racks; and the S-29C reconnaissance version.

Attack Aircraft
In the autumn of 1946, Saab had also begun design studies of a new turbojet-powered attack aircraft for the Swedish Air Force, and two years later the Swedish Air Board authorized the construction of a prototype under the designation P1150. This aircraft, now known as the A-32 Lansen (Lance), flew for the first time on 3 November 1952, powered by a Rolls-Royce Avon RA7R turbojet. Three more prototypes were built, and one of these exceeded Mach 1

in a shallow dive on 25 October 1953. The A-32A attack variant was followed by the J-32B all-weather fighter, which first flew in January 1957.

Meanwhile, design work had been proceeding on the next-generation Swedish combat aircraft, the Saab J-35 Draken, which represented a quantum leap over anything that had gone before. Designed from the outset to intercept transonic bombers at all altitudes and in all weathers, the Draken was, at the time of its service debut, a component of the finest fully integrated air defence system in western Europe. The first of three prototypes of this unique 'double delta' fighter first flew on 25 October 1955; the initial production version, the J-35A,

entered service early in 1960. The major production version of the Draken was the J-35F, which was virtually designed around the Hughes HM-55 Falcon radar-guided air-to-air missile and was fitted with an improved S7B collision-course fire control system, a high-capacity datalink system integrating the aircraft with the STRIL 60 air defence environment, an infrared sensor under the nose and PS-01A search and ranging radar. The J-35C was a two-seat operational trainer, while the last new-build variant, the J-35J, was a development of the J-35D with more capable radar, collision-course fire control and a Hughes infrared sensor to enable carriage of the Hughes Falcon

Multi-faceted Fresco
MiG-17F 'Fresco-C'

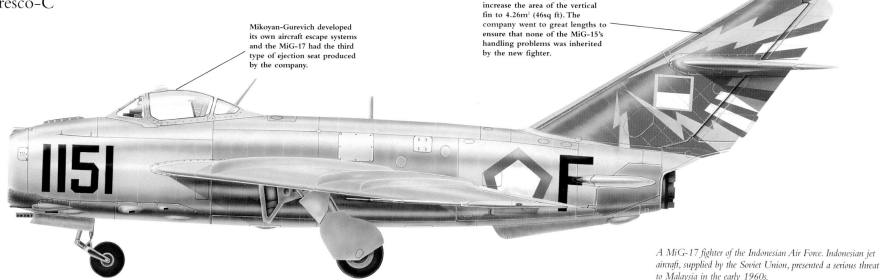

Mikoyan-Gurevich developed its own aircraft escape systems and the MiG-17 had the third type of ejection seat produced by the company.

MiG found it necessary to increase the area of the vertical fin to 4.26m² (46sq ft). The company went to great lengths to ensure that none of the MiG-15's handling problems was inherited by the new fighter.

A MiG-17 fighter of the Indonesian Air Force. Indonesian jet aircraft, supplied by the Soviet Union, presented a serious threat to Malaysia in the early 1960s.

air-to-air missile. The Saab RF-35 was a reconnaissance version, which continued to serve with Eskadrille 729 of the Royal Danish Air Force until the unit was disbanded as an economy measure and its task was taken over by the F-16s of Esk 726 in January 1994. Total production of the Draken was around 600 aircraft, equipping 17 RSAF squadrons; the type was exported to Finland as well as Denmark. The Draken was the first fully supersonic aircraft in western Europe to be deployed operationally.

Saab's next design, the Viggen, was arguably the most advanced combat aircraft produced in Europe during the 1970s, possessing a far more advanced radar, greater speed range and a more comprehensive avionics fit than its contemporaries. Certainly one of the most potent combat aircraft of its time, the Viggen (Thunderbolt) was designed to carry out the four roles of attack, interception, reconnaissance and training. Like the earlier J-35 Draken, it was fully integrated into the STRIL 60 air defence control system. Powered by a Swedish version of the Pratt & Whitney JT8D turbofan engine, with a powerful Swedish-developed afterburner, the aircraft had excellent acceleration and climb performance. Part of the requirement was that it should be capable of operating from sections of Swedish motorways. The first of seven prototypes flew for the first time on 8 February

1967, followed by the first production AJ-37 single-seat all-weather attack variant in February 1971. Deliveries of the first of 110 AJ-37s to the Royal Swedish Air Force began in June that year. The JA-37 interceptor version of the Viggen, 149 of which were built, replaced the J35F Draken; the SF-37 (26 delivered) was a single-seat armed photo reconnaissance variant; and the SH-37 (26 delivered) was an all-weather maritime reconnaissance version, replacing the S-32C Lansen. The SK-37 (18 delivered) was a tandem two-seat trainer, retaining a secondary attack role.

France continued to produce superlative combat aircraft, Dassault's Mystère series of fighters giving way to

MiG-17F 'Fresco-C'

Type: single-seat fighter

Powerplant: one 33.2kN (7467lbf) Klimov VK-1F afterburning turbojet

Maximum speed: 1100km/h (684mph) at 3000m (9843ft)

Initial climb rate: 3900m/min (12,795fpm)

Combat radius: 700km (435 miles) on a hi-lo-hi mission with two 250kg (550lb) bombs

Service ceiling: 16,600m (54,462ft)

Weights: empty 3930 kg (8664lb); maximum take-off 6069kg (13,380lb)

Armament: two 23mm NR-23 and one 37mm N-37D cannon, plus 500kg (1100lb) of bombs

Dimensions:		
span	9.63m	(31ft 7in)
length	11.26m	(36ft 11in)
height	3.80m	(12ft 6in)
wing area	22.60m²	(243sq ft)

the Mirage III. Developed from the Mirage I of 1954, the Mirage III made its first flight on 17 November 1956, and the aircraft exceeded Mach 1.5 in level flight on 30 January 1957.

Auxiliary Rocket

The French government instructed Dassault to proceed with a multi-mission version, the Mirage IIIA, the prototype of which (Mirage IIIA-01) flew on 12 May 1958, and, in a test flight on 24 October 1958, this aircraft exceeded Mach 2 in level flight at 12,500m (41,000ft). The Mirage IIIC, which flew on 9 October 1960, was the first production version and was identical to the IIIA, with an Atar 09 B3 turbojet and a SEPR 841 or 844 auxiliary rocket motor. 100 Mirage IIICs were ordered by the Armée de l'Air. The aircraft was widely exported, those supplied to Israel later playing a significant part in subsequent Arab–Israeli wars, notably the Six-Day War of June 1967.

Without doubt, the most significant development in military aviation in the 1960s, a decade that saw the United States embroiled in a protracted conflict in Vietnam, was the development of the short take-off vertical-landing (STOVL) aircraft, epitomized by the Hawker Siddeley Harrier. The most revolutionary combat aircraft to emerge during the post-war years, the Harrier STOVL tactical fighter-bomber began its career as a private venture in 1957 following discussions between Hawker Aircraft Ltd

British Jaguars were fitted with two weapon guidance systems: a Laser Ranging and Marked Target Seeker (LRMTS) and a Navigation and Weapon Aiming Subsystem (NAVWASS).

and Bristol Aero-Engines Ltd, designers of the BS53 Pegasus turbofan engine. Development of this powerplant, which featured two pairs of connected rotating nozzles, one pair to provide jet lift, was partly financed with US funds. In 1959–60, the Ministry of Aviation ordered two prototypes and four development aircraft under the designation P.1127. The first prototype made its first tethered hovering flight on 21 October 1960 and began conventional flight trials on 13 March 1961.

In 1962, Britain, the United States and West Germany announced a joint order for nine Kestrels, as the aircraft was now known, for evaluation by a tripartite handling squadron at RAF West Raynham in 1965. Six of these aircraft were subsequently shipped to the United States for further trials. In its single-seat close support and tactical reconnaissance version, the aircraft was ordered into production for the RAF as the Harrier GR.Mk.1, the first of an initial order of 77 machines flying on 28 December 1967. On 1 April 1969, the Harrier entered service with the Harrier OCU at RAF Wittering, and the type subsequently equipped No. 1 Squadron at Wittering and Nos. 3, 4 and 20 Squadrons in Germany. The version chosen for service with the US Marine Corps, and produced by McDonnell Douglas, was designated AV-8A.

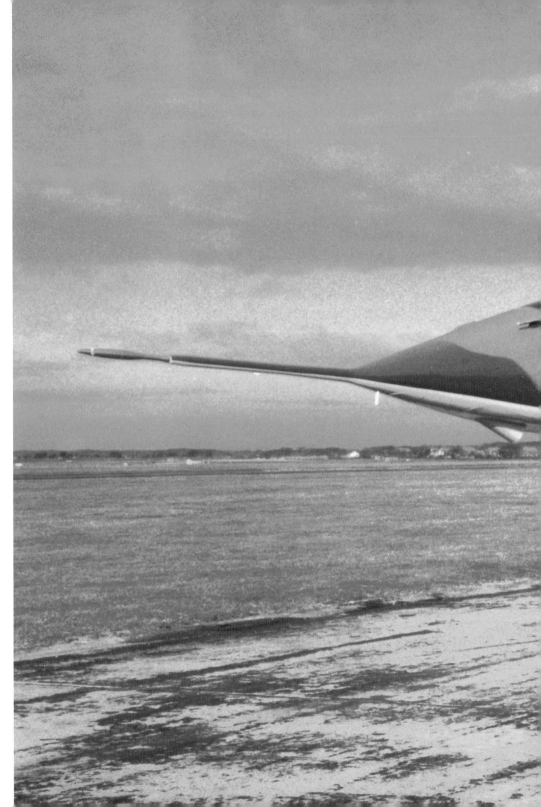

Serving alongside the Harrier in the short-range strike/attack role was an aircraft symbolic of what might be achieved in international cooperation. Developed jointly by the British Aircraft Corporation and Breguet (later Dassault–Breguet) under the banner of SEPECAT (Societé Européenne de Production de l'Avion Ecole de Combat et Appui Tactique), the Jaguar emerged from protracted development as a much more powerful and effective aircraft than was

originally envisaged. The first French version to fly, in September 1968, was the two-seat E model; 40 examples of this aircraft were ordered by the French air force. The E model was followed in March 1969 by the single-seat Jaguar A tactical support aircraft. Service deliveries of the E began in May 1972, the first of 160 Jaguar As following in 1973. The British versions, known as the Jaguar S (strike) and Jaguar B (trainer), flew on October 12 1969 and 30 August 1971,

respectively, being delivered to the RAF as the Jaguar GR.Mk.1. In the European context at least, cooperation was to be the keyword from now on.

Confirmed Victories

On 5 August 1964, in response to earlier attacks on US warships by North Vietnamese torpedo boats in the Gulf of Tonkin, US naval strike aircraft attacked four torpedo boat bases and oil storage facilities. It was the beginning of the

The MiG-21 is a top-notch dogfighter, prized by pilots for its agility and speed. It might not have the range of other fighters of its generation, but it is deserves its reputation as the most successful fighter jet ever built.

United States' air war over North Vietnam, and the F-4 Phantom was in it from the start, flying combat air patrols to fend off the MiG-17 fighters which the North Vietnamese were known to have deployed, and which soon showed themselves to be formidable opponents.

Flight refuelling was a vital adjunct to American air operations in the Vietnam War, enabling aircraft such as this Republic F-105 Thunderchief to return safely to base after a mission.

The first confirmed American victories came on 17 June 1965, when two Phantoms of VF-21, USS *Midway*, destroyed two MiG-17s with their long-range Sparrow air-to-air missiles. The USAF's first victories of the Vietnam War were to come a few weeks later, when two MiG-17s were destroyed over North Vietnam by two F-4C Phantoms of the 45th Tactical Fighter Squadron, recently arrived in the theatre.

By September 1966, the North Vietnamese Air Force had received some numbers of the MiG-21, armed with Atoll infrared air-to-air missiles and operating from five bases in the Hanoi area. The tactics employed by the MiG pilots involved flying low, then zooming up to attack the heavily laden fighter-bombers, mainly F-105 Thunderchiefs, forcing them to jettison their bomb loads as a matter of survival. To counter this, Phantoms armed with Sidewinder air-to-air missiles flew at lower altitudes than the F-105s, enabling the crew to sight the MiGs at an early stage in their interception attempt, then use the Phantom's superior speed and acceleration to engage the enemy.

The Republic F-105D Thunderchief, along with the Phantom, was the principal US fighter-bomber used in Vietnam, especially in attacks on targets in the north. The F-105D, which first

flew on 9 June 1959 and entered service with Tactical Air Command the following year, embodied what was at the time the most advanced automatic navigation system in the world. Production of the F-105D totalled 610 aircraft. Although the type was initially unpopular, mainly because of early snags with its avionics systems, it proved its worth over Vietnam, where it flew more than 70 per cent of USAF strike missions with an abort rate of less than 1 per cent. For the largest and heaviest single-seat fighter-bomber in the world, it also showed an astonishing ability to absorb tremendous battle damage and still get back to base; however, 397 F-105s were lost on operations in Vietnam. A two-seat version, the F-105F, of which 143 were built, had full operational capability and was assigned in small numbers to each F-105D squadron. In Vietnam, F-105Fs frequently led strikes, providing accurate navigation to the target. F-105Fs were the first Thunderchiefs to assume the 'Wild Weasel' defence suppression role. F-105Fs fitted with improved defence suppression equipment were designated F-105G.

Left: An A-4 Skyhawk of Fighter Squadron Composite 13 (VFC-13), Fighting Saints, Naval Air Station (NAS) Fallon, Nevada. The Skyhawk is carrying an Air Combat Manoeuvring Instrumentation (ACMI) pod.

A Sikorsky HH-3E Jolly Green Giant rescue helicopter. During the Vietnam War, the crews of these large helicopters took enormous risks to penetrate into enemy territory and bring downed aircrews to safety.

The US Navy's workhorse in the Vietnam War was the Douglas A-4 Skyhawk shipboard attack aircraft, which had been in service since 1956. The Skyhawk bore the brunt of the Navy offensive against the North from the Gulf of Tonkin reprisal raids of 1964 until 1968. Although replaced on the large fleet carriers by the Vought A-7 Corsair II, Skyhawks continued to serve on the smaller carriers until the US withdrawal. As a result of their long and active combat career, more Skyhawks were lost during the Vietnam War than any other type of naval aircraft.

It was in Vietnam that the helicopter came into its own. The conflict saw the development of the helicopter gunship

and the battlefield reconnaissance helicopter, and also honed search-and-rescue techniques to a fine art. Some of the most dangerous missions carried out by the USAF in Vietnam were flown by the crews of the big Sikorsky HH-3E rescue helicopters, nicknamed 'Jolly Green Giants'. These helicopters went to the aid of pilots shot down during the 'Out-Country War', the bombing of North Vietnam.

Vietnam Reconnaissance

The air reconnaissance task over Vietnam was performed by a variety of aircraft, beginning with the Lockheed U-2. One of the principal types used

in this role was the North American RA-5C Vigilante, which started life as a heavy naval attack bomber. First flown in 1958, the Vigilante's career as an attack bomber was relatively short-lived, the majority of A-5A and A-5B airframes being converted to RA-5C reconnaissance configuration. First service deliveries of the RA-5C were made in January 1964. Of the ten RA-5C squadrons activated, eight were to see service in Vietnam. The RA-5C proved so successful in action over Vietnam that the production line was reopened in

1969 and an additional 48 aircraft built. Eighteen aircraft were lost on operations.

In the spring of 1968, because of the growing vulnerability of the U-2 in a surface-to-air missile environment, it was decided to deploy four Lockheed SR-71s to Kadena Air Base, Okinawa, for operations over Southeast Asia. This remarkable aircraft, whose performance included a maximum speed of 3220km/h (2000mph) at 24,385m (80,000ft) and a range of 4800km

Right: The aircraft that became known as the SR-71 was actually designated RS (Reconnaissance System) 71, but it was erroneously referred to as the SR-71 by US President Lyndon B. Johnson when the secret programme was first unveiled.

(2983 miles) could literally outrun the enemy's SA-2 Guideline surface-to-air missiles. The first SR-71 mission over Vietnam was flown in April 1968; up to three missions per week were flown thereafter.

The North American A-5 Vigilante was a huge aircraft, ill-suited to its naval role, and soon found a second life as a reconnaissance platform.

The Boeing-Vertol CH-47 Chinook was a vital component of US airlift operations in Vietnam and also in later conflicts such as the two Gulf wars. The Chinook is exceptionally reliable under the most adverse conditions.

Backbone of the World's Air Forces
Lockheed C-130 Hercules

A high-set taill allows for a rear ramp which can be lowered in flight to make drops in combat zones.

The spacious, high-set cockpit offered superb visibility and was a huge improvement over the flight decks of previous transports. In addition, it was quiet and vibration-free.

The Allison T56 engines are fitted with four-bladed propellers.

Without doubt the most versatile tactical transport aircraft ever built, the Lockheed C-130 Hercules flew for the first time on 23 August 1954, and many different variants were produced over the next half-century. The RAF is the second-largest Hercules user, operating 80 aircraft.

The American commitment in Vietnam could not have been sustained without the biggest airlift operation in history. In the field, apart from the widespread use of transport helicopters such as the Boeing-Vertol CH-47 Chinook, the main effort was supported by the Lockheed C-130 Hercules. Without doubt the most versatile tactical transport aircraft ever built, the C-130 Hercules flew for the first time on 23 August 1954, and many different variants were produced over the next half century. The initial production versions were the C-130A and C130-B, of which 461 were built, and these were followed by the major production variant, the C-130E, 510 of which were produced. Other versions include the AC-130E gunship, the WC-130E weather reconnaissance aircraft, the KC-130F assault transport for the USMC and the HC-130H for aerospace rescue and recovery.

Airlift

Long-range airlift operations were undertaken by the Boeing C-135, the military transport version of the Boeing 707 airliner, and the Lockheed C-141 StarLifter. First flown on 17 December 1963, the StarLifter heavy-lift strategic transport was designed to provide the USAF Military Air Transport Service with a high-speed global airlift and strategic deployment capability. Deliveries to the USAF began in April 1965. The

aircraft ultimately equipped 13 squadrons of Military Airlift Command, with 277 being built in total.

As the Vietnam War progressed, it revealed the increasing inability of combat aircraft to survive in an environment dominated by surface-to-air missiles. During a week-long bombing campaign against North Vietnam in December 1972, for example, 15 B-52 bombers were shot down by SA-2s, despite the use of electronic countermeasures.

Six-Day War

On 5 June 1967, while the United States remained embroiled in Vietnam, Israeli combat aircraft carried out heavy dawn attacks on Egyptian airfields in Sinai and

C-130A Hercules

Type: four-engined military transport aircraft

Powerplant: four 2796kW (3749hp) Allison T56-A9 turboprop engines

Maximum speed: 616km/h (383mph)

Cruising speed: 528km/h (328mph)

Initial climb rate: 783m/min (2569fpm)

Range: 4110km (2554 miles)

Service ceiling: 12,590m (41,306ft)

Weights: empty 26,911kg (59,329lb); loaded 48,988kg (108,000lb)

Dimensions:
span	40.41m	(132ft 7in)
length	29.79m	(97ft 9in)
height	11.66m	(38ft 3in)
wing area	162.12m²	(1745sq ft)

the Suez Canal Zone in what was the
first of a series of pre-emptive strikes
designed to neutralize the power of
Egypt and its allies. Airfields in Jordan,
Syria and Iraq were also attacked. By the
end of the day, the Israeli Air Force had
flown about 1000 sorties for the loss of
20 aircraft, all but one to ground fire.
Arab losses totalled 308 aircraft, of which
240 were Egyptian; 30 were destroyed in
air combat. In these first strikes of what
was to become known as the Six-Day
War, the Mirage III reigned supreme, its
prowess lending more impetus to an
already healthy export drive by its
manufacturer, Dassault.

Ground operations in Sinai, on the
Golan Heights and the West Bank of the
Jordan were supported by Fouga
Magister light attack aircraft, Dassault
Ouragans, Mystère IVAs and Super
Mystère B.2s. By the time a UN
ceasefire was imposed on 10 June, the
Arab air forces had lost 353 aircraft,
about 43 per cent of their effective
strength, and the Israeli Air Force
31 aircraft, just over 10 per cent of its
effective strength. The Israelis, therefore,
had achieved overwhelming air
superiority in the most efficient way, by
destroying a high proportion of the
enemy's air forces on the ground.

The Germans had attempted to achieve
a similar result towards the end of World
War II, when they launched Operation
Bodenplatte (Baseplate), a major attack
on Allied airfields in northwest Europe,
on 1 January 1945, in support of their

The major production Hercules was the C-130E, 510 of which were produced. Other versions include the AC-130E gunship, the WC-130E for weather reconnaissance, the KC-130F for assault transport, and the HC-130H for aerospace rescue and recovery.

flagging offensive in the Ardennes. Like
the Israelis, the Germans had achieved
complete surprise and had destroyed
some 300 Allied aircraft on the ground;
however, by contrast, they had lost
around one-third of the attacking force,
mostly destroyed by friendly fire because
of faulty communications.

The Israeli attack, very carefully
planned and brilliantly executed, left
nothing to chance, and so succeeded. A
primary threat to the attacking aircraft –
the SA-2 Guideline surface-to-air
missile, which had recently been deployed
in Egypt – was quickly eliminated, the
Israelis having assimilated the American
experience of this weapon in Vietnam.

Yom Kippur

In the wake of the Six-Day War, the
Israeli Air Force received two new types
of combat aircraft, the Phantom and the
A-4 Skyhawk attack aircraft, both of
which had performed very successfully
in Vietnam. The IAF's Phantoms first
went into action in 1969, in a series of
air strikes against Egyptian artillery
positions on the west bank of the Suez
Canal. The strike squadrons then set about
the systematic destruction of Egyptian
missile and radar sites in the Canal Zone,
concentrating on installations spread
along an 18-mile-wide defence perimeter

In addition to its original role of flight refuelling tanker, the KC-135 has been adapted to perform other vital tasks. This example is a specially equipped test aircraft, designed to evaluate the communications performance of satellites.

between the Suez Canal and Cairo, and on strategic roads in the same area. The Russians augmented the Egyptian air defences, supplying several more squadrons of MiG-21s, and air combat between the opposing sides intensified.

On 30 July 1970, a section of four Phantoms was attacked by 16 MiG-21s over the Gulf of Suez, but the Egyptian (or Soviet) pilots failed to see the Mirage top cover, and in the battle that followed the Mirages and Phantoms shot down five MiGs for no loss. In another action, on 23 September 1973, Mirages and Phantoms engaged Syrian MiG-21s and shot down 13 for the loss of one Mirage.

For the Israelis, however, the sternest test was still to come. On 6 October 1973, the Jewish Day of Atonement (Yom Kippur), Egypt launched a surprise attack with some 70,000 troops, supported by 400 tanks, against Israeli positions across the Suez Canal. At the same time, Syrian forces attacked the Golan Heights. In support of the Egyptian attack, an estimated 250 MiG-21s and Sukhoi Su-7 fighter-bombers struck at Israel air bases, radar and missile sites in

the Sinai. The Israelis counterattacked strongly, using all available air power, but the IAF now had to contend with a formidable arsenal of air defence weaponry. As well as fixed SA-2 and SA-3 missile sites, mobile SA-6 surface-to-air missile systems and ZSU-23/24 tracked anti-

Right: Deliveries to the C-141 to the USAF began in April 1965 and the aircraft ultimately equipped 13 squadrons of Military Airlift Command with 277 aircraft.

Warsaw Pact's Fighter
Sukhoi Su-7B 'Fitter-A'

The cockpit had poor
visibility and no instrument
landing system.

The thin- highly-swept wing
made for dangerously fast
take-off and landing speeds.

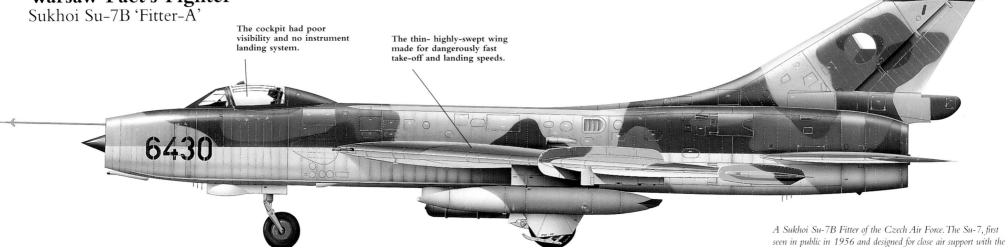

6430

*A Sukhoi Su-7B Fitter of the Czech Air Force. The Su-7, first
seen in public in 1956 and designed for close air support with the
Soviet Frontal Aviation, remained the Warsaw Pact's standard
tactical fighter-bomber throughout the 1960s.*

Sukhoi Su-7B 'Fitter-A'

Type: ground attack fighter

Powerplant: one 66.6kN (14,980lbf) dry
thrust Lyulka AL-7F turbojet; 94.1kN (22,150lbf)
with afterburner

Maximum speed: 1700km/h (1056mph) at
11,000m (36,000ft)

Combat radius: 320km (199 miles)

Service ceiling: 15,150m (49,700ft)

Weights: empty 8620kg (19,000lb); loaded
13,500kg (29,750lb)

Armament: two 30mm NR-30 cannon with
70 rpg; four external pylons for two 750kg
(1650lb) and two 500kg (1100lb) bombs, but with
two tanks on fuselage pylons

Dimensions:
span	8.93m	(29ft 3½in)
length	17.37m	(57ft)
height	4.7m	(15ft 5in)
wing area	34m²	(366sq ft)

aircraft artillery systems, each with four
radar-controlled 23mm guns, were
brought into play. The IAF's Phantoms
were used mainly in the defence
suppression role and suffered heavy
losses, mainly because the relatively flat
terrain offered no cover for aircraft
carrying out low-level attacks.

New Tactics
Israeli pilots adopted new tactics which
involved diving their aircraft steeply on
the surface-to-air missile sites, which
kept their aircraft outside the low-angle
missile launch trajectory; unfortunately
this brought them within range of the
anti-aircraft artilly, which in fact
accounted for the majority of the Israeli
losses, which were high. In the first week
of the conflict the IAF lost more than

80 aircraft, mostly victims of suface-to-
air missiles and anti-aircraft artillery, and
38 more were lost in the second week.

Having outfought the Syrians, the
Israelis turned the full weight of their
counteroffensive against the Egyptians,
pushing forces across the Suez Canal and
encircling the Egyptian Tenth Army
before a ceasefire was arranged by the
UN on 24 October. In all, the Israeli Air
Force lost 118 aircraft, the Egyptians 113
and the Syrians 149. The Iraqi Air Force,
assisting the Syrians, lost 21. For once,
Arabs and Israelis had fought each other
to a standstill.

Air Superiority Fighter
During the air war over Vietnam, the
Americans had quickly learned one
important lesson: that speed and

sophistication were no substitutes for
manoeuvrability, and an all-missile
armament was no substitute for guns.
Aircraft such as the F-4 Phantom,
designed for combat at supersonic speeds
and for multiple roles, found themselves
fighting nimble MiG-17s and MiG-21s
in turning combats at relatively low
speeds, and they had to be retrofitted
with 20mm cannon for this close-in
work. What was required was a dedicated
air superiority fighter, a highly
manoeuvrable aircraft capable not only
of engaging an opponent in close combat
and winning, but also of engaging him
with missiles at beyond visual range.

The need for such an aircraft only
intensified when it was discovered that
the Russians were developing a radical
new interceptor, the MiG-25. The

prototype MiG-25 was flown as early as 1964, and the aircraft was apparently designed to counter the projected North American B-70 supersonic bomber, with its Mach 3.0 speed and ceiling of 21,350m (70,000ft). The cancellation of the B-70, however, left the Foxbat in

Between them, the twin Tumanskii R-15 engines of the MiG-25 generate a remarkable 219kN (49,409lbf) of thrust in full afterburner.

search of a role. It entered service as an interceptor in 1970 with the designation MiG-25P (Foxbat-A).

The United States Air Force and various aircraft companies in the United States began discussions on the feasibility of just such an aircraft and its associated systems to replace the F-4 Phantom in 1965, and four years later it was announced that McDonnell Douglas had been selected as prime airframe

contractor for the new aircraft, then designated FX. As the F-15A Eagle, it flew for the first time on 27 July 1972, and first deliveries of operational aircraft were made to the USAF in 1975.

The secret of the F-15's success lay in the design of its wing. The F-15C – the main interceptor version – had a wing loading of only 24kg (54lb) per square foot and this, together with its two Pratt & Whitney F-100 advanced technology

turbofans, gave it an extraordinary turning ability and the combat thrust-to-weight ratio (1.3:1) necessary to retain the initiative in a fight. The high thrust-to-weight ratio permitted a scramble time of only six seconds, using 183m (600ft) of runway, and a maximum speed of more than Mach 2.5 gave the pilot the margin he needed if he had to break off an engagement. Primary armament of the F-15 was the AIM-7F Sparrow

The McDonnell Douglas F-15 Eagle was designed for the air superiority role. It flew for the first time on 27 July 1972, and first deliveries of operational aircraft were made to the USAF in 1975. These examples are from Kadena Air Base in Japan.

A Boeing (formerly McDonnell-Douglas) F-15A Eagle launching an AIM-7 Sparrow air-to-air missile. The F-15 is one of the world's fastest and most deadly warplanes, and in its F-15E guise it is also a formidable tactical bomber.

radar-guided air-to-air missile, with a range of up to 56km (35 miles). The Eagle carried four of these, backed up by four AIM-9L Sidewinders for shorter range interceptions and a General

Electric 20mm M61 rotating-barrel cannon for close-in combat. This armament, together with the Hughes pulse-Doppler radar that could be used in a variety of modes, made the F-15 a very viable fighter aircraft.

Lightweight Fighter
Another US combat aircraft that was to perform with distinction in the Gulf War

was the Lockheed Martin F-16 Fighting Falcon. The F-16, designed and built by General Dynamics, had its origin in a USAF requirement of 1972 for a lightweight fighter and first flew in February 1974. The F-16 Fighting Falcon, now produced by Lockheed Martin, went on to become the world's most prolific combat aircraft and was constantly upgraded to extend its life

well into the twenty-first century.

The US Navy's air superiority fighter was the Grumman F-14 Tomcat, a formidable interceptor designed from the outset to establish complete air superiority in the vicinity of a carrier task force and also, as a secondary role, to attack tactical objectives. Selected in January 1969 as the winner of a US Navy contest for a carrier-borne fighter

(VFX) to replace the Phantom, the prototype F-14A flew for the first time on 21 December 1970 and was followed by 11 development aircraft. The variable-geometry fighter completed carrier trials in the summer of 1972, and deliveries to the US Navy began in October that year, the Tomcat forming the interceptor element of a carrier air wing. The Tomcat's two Pratt & Whitney TF30-P414 turbofans gave it a maximum low-level speed of Mach 1.2 and a high-level speed of Mach 2.34.

Two highly agile Soviet fighters, the MiG-29 Fulcrum and Sukhoi Su-27 Flanker, were designed in response to the F-15 and Grumman F-14 Tomcat. Both Russian aircraft shared a similar configuration, combining a wing swept at 40 degrees with highly swept wing root extensions, underslung engines with wedge intakes, and

twin fins. The Fulcrum-A became operational in 1985. The Sukhoi Su-27, like the F-15, is a dual-role aircraft; in addition to its primary air superiority task it was designed to escort Su-24 Fencer strike aircraft on deep-penetration missions. The prototype flew for the first time in May 1977, the type being allocated the code name 'Flanker' by NATO. Although full-scale production of the Su-27P Flanker-B air defence fighter began in 1980, the aircraft did not become fully operational until 1984.

The variable-geometry concept, built into the design of many combat aircraft in the 1970s, was by no means new. It was applied to at least one German jet fighter project, the Messerschmitt P.1101, in World War II, tested on the experimental Bell X-5 aircraft post-war and built into the design of was a carrier-borne jet fighter, the Grumman XF10F-1 Jaguar. Two prototypes of this aircraft were built, but only one flew, in 1953.

Battlefield Support Variant

The MiG-23, which flew in prototype form in 1967 and entered service with the Frontal Aviation's attack units of the 16th Air Army in East Germany in 1973, was a variable-geometry fighter-bomber with wings sweeping from 23 to 71 degrees, and was the Soviet Air Force's first true multi-role combat aircraft. The MiG-23M Flogger-B was the first series production version, and it equipped all the major Warsaw Pact air forces. The MiG-27, which began to enter service in the late 1970s, was a dedicated battlefield support variant which was known to NATO as Flogger-D.

Variable geometry was also applied to one American design, first used in the Vietnam War, which went on to become one of the most important weapons in NATO's arsenal. This was the General Dynamics F-111A, interdictor/strike aircraft, which flew for the first time on 21 December 1964, the initial variant being followed into service by the F-111E, which featured modified air intakes to improve performance above Mach 2.2.

The Sukhoi Su-27 was hailed as an aerodynamic miracle when it was first revealed to western observers. The aircraft's incredible agility, which allows spectacular manoeuvres such the 'Cobra', would make it a dangerous opponent in any dogfight.

The F-111F was a fighter-bomber variant combining the best features of the F-111E and the FB-111A (the strategic bomber version) and fitted with

Left: The MiG-23 was a variable-geometry fighter-bomber with wings sweeping from 23 to 71 degrees, and was the Soviet Air Force's first true multi-role combat aircraft.

The 48th TFW, based at Lakenheath in the United Kingdom, was armed with the F-111F, a fighter-bomber variant combining the best of the F-111E and the FB-111A (the strategic bomber version) and fitted with more powerful TF30-F-100 engines.

the more powerful TF30-F-100 engines. The F-111C (24 of which were built) was a strike version for the RAAF.

In 1965, the Soviet government instructed the Sukhoi design bureau to begin design studies of a new variable-geometry strike aircraft in the same class

as the General Dynamics F-111. One specified criteria was that the new aircraft be able to fly at very low level in order to penetrate increasingly effective air defence systems. The resulting aircraft, named the Su-24, made its first flight in 1970, and deliveries of the first production version, the Fencer-A, began in 1974. Several variants of the Fencer were produced, culminating in the Su-24M Fencer-D, which entered service in 1986.

Another variable-geometry type, the Tornado, was the result of a 1960s requirement for a strike and reconnaissance aircraft capable of carrying a heavy and varied weapons load and of penetrating foreseeable Warsaw Pact defensive systems by day and night, at low level and in all weathers. To develop and build the aircraft, a consortium of companies was formed under the name of Panavia; it

consisted principally of the British Aircraft Corporation (later British Aerospace), Messerschmitt-Bölkow-Blohm (MBB) and Aeritalia, together with many subcontractors. Another consortium, Turbo-Union, was formed

The EF-111A Raven was an electronic warfare variant of the F-111, which could unleash a potent array of electronic countermeasures to protect an attacking force from enemy radar and fighters.

by Rolls-Royce, MTU of Germany and Fiat to build the Tornado's Rolls-Royce RB-199 turbofan engines.

The first of nine Tornado IDS (Interdictor/Strike) prototypes flew in Germany on 14 August 1974. The RAF took delivery of 229 GR.1 strike aircraft, the Luftwaffe 212, the German Naval Air Arm 112, and the Italian Air Force 100. RAF and Italian Tornados saw action in the 1991 Gulf War.

The Tornado GR.1A is a variant with a centreline reconnaissance pod, with deliveries of this aircraft beginning in 199. The GR.4, armed with Sea eagle anti-shipping missiles, is an anti-shipping version, while the GR.4A is the tactical reconnaissance equivalent.

Effective Interceptor

In 1971, the UK Ministry of Defence issued Air Staff Target 395, which called for a minimum-change, minimum-cost but effective interceptor to replace the British Aerospace Lightning and the F.4 Phantom in the air defence of the United Kingdom. This resulted in the Tornado ADV (Air Defence Variant), which served with the RAF, Italy and Saudi Arabia.

Right: Several variants of the Su-24 Fencer were produced, culminating in the Su-24M Fencer-D, which entered service in 1986. This variant has in-flight refuelling equipment, upgraded nav/attack systems, and laser/TV designators.

With the threat of a massive Warsaw Pact armoured attack across the north German plain a constant threat during the Cold War, the means to counter it assumed high priority and culminated in the development of a dedicated anti-tank aircraft, the Fairchild Republic A-10 Thunderbolt II, designed to operate from short unprepared strips less than 457m (1500ft) long. Deliveries began in March 1977 to the 354th Tactical Fighter Wing at Myrtle Beach, South Carolina; in all, the USAF took delivery of 727 aircraft for service with its tactical fighter wings, the emphasis being on European operations. The operational tactics developed for the aircraft involved two A-10s giving one another mutual support, covering a swathe of ground three to five kilometres (two to three miles) wide, so that an attack could be quickly mounted by the second aircraft once the first pilot had made his firing pass on the target. The 30mm ammunition drum carried enough rounds to make 10–15 firing passes.

In general, operations by the A-10s envisaged cooperation with US Army helicopters; the latter would hit the mobile surface-to-air missiles and anti-aicraft artillery systems accompanying a Soviet armoured thrust, and, with the enemy's defences at least temporarily stunned or degraded, the A-10s would then be free to concentrate their fire on the tanks. Twelve years later, these tactics were used to deadly effect in the 1991 Gulf War.

Russia's equivalent of the A-10 was the Sukhoi Su-25 Frogfoot. Deployment of the single-seat close-support Su-25K began in 1978, and the aircraft saw considerable operational service during the former Soviet Union's involvement in Afghanistan. As a result of lessons learned during the Afghan conflict, an upgraded version known as the Su-25T was produced, with improved defensive systems to counter weapons such as the Stinger. The improvements included the insertion of steel plates, several millimetres thick, between the engine bays and below the fuel cell. After this modification, no further Su-25s were lost to shoulder-launched missiles. In total, 22 Su-25s and eight pilots were lost in the nine years of the Afghan conflict.

Supersonic Bomber

The 1970s saw the resurrection of the supersonic bomber concept in the Rockwell B-1. Designed to replace the B-52 and FB-111 in the low-level penetration role, the B-1 prototype flew on 23 December 1974. The operational designation of the supersonic bomber, 100 of which were to be built for SAC, was B-1B, the prototypes being known as B-1As. The first B-1B flew in October 1984 and was well ahead of schedule, despite the crash several weeks earlier of

The first of nine Tornado IDS (Interdictor/Strike) prototypes flew in Germany on 14 August 1974, aircrews of the participating nations having been trained at RAF Cottesmore in the United Kingdom, which received the first Tornado GR.1s in July 1980.

The Fairchild A-10 was designed to operate on only one engine and with large portions of the aerodynamic surfaces damaged. Its tough construction proved vital in the 1991 Gulf War.

Fairchild A-10 Thunderbolt II

Tank-busting Warthog

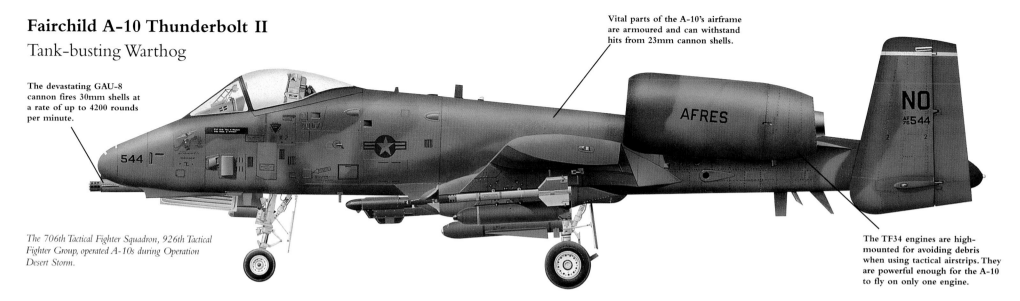

Vital parts of the A-10's airframe are armoured and can withstand hits from 23mm cannon shells.

The devastating GAU-8 cannon fires 30mm shells at a rate of up to 4200 rounds per minute.

The 706th Tactical Fighter Squadron, 926th Tactical Fighter Group, operated A-10s during Operation Desert Storm.

The TF34 engines are high-mounted for avoiding debris when using tactical airstrips. They are powerful enough for the A-10 to fly on only one engine.

one of the two B-1A prototypes taking part in the test programme. The first operational B-1B (83-0065) was delivered to the 96th Bomb Wing at Dyess AFB, Texas, on 7 July 1985.

From the Soviet Union came one of the later Cold War era's most important combat aircraft, the Tupolev Tu-22M. Allocated the NATO reporting name Backfire, the Tupolev Tu-22M first flew in 1971, reached initial operational capability (IOC) in 1973 and, during the following years, replaced the Tu-16 Badger in Soviet service. The mission of the new bomber, peripheral attack or intercontinental attack, became one of the most fiercely contested intelligence debates of the Cold War. It was a long time before the true nature of its threat – anti-shipping attack – became known.

During the Cold War, the Tu-22M was operated by the VVS (Voenno-Vozdushnye Sily; Soviet Air Force), in a strategic bombing role, and by the AVMF (Aviatsiya Voenno-Morskogo Flota; Soviet Naval Aviation) in a long-range role. The United States was highly concerned about the threat that this new bomber posed. In fact, it was unable to complete a round trip to the United States and back, and by 1982 fewer than 200 had been built. The US Navy and USAF cited the bomber as a serious threat, however, and the result was a budget infusion for the US air defence effort. The Tu-22M saw its first combat use in Afghanistan from 1987 to 1989, where it was used in a tactical support role, dropping large amounts of conventional ordnance in support of

ground operations. In fact, it operated in much the same way as the USAF's B-52s had done in Vietnam and, as was the case in that conflict, the usefulness of such saturation attacks was very limited. The CIS also used the Backfire in combat against forces in carrying out strikes near Grozny against Chechyan forces.

At the time of the collapse of the Soviet Union some 370 Tu-22Ms remained in CIS service, but this number was drastically reduced over the following decade by financial constraints. The complex nature of the Tu-22M led to serious servicing problems, with the result that production was halted in 1993. Although the Soviet Union did not export the Tu-22M, the break-up of the Soviet Union did leave some aircraft in the possession of former Soviet republics.

Fairchild A-10

Type: single-seat anti-tank aircraft

Powerplant: two 40.31kN (9066lbf) General Electric TF34-GE-100 non-afterburning turbofans

Maximum speed: 682km/h (424mph)

Ferry range: 4000km (2485 miles)

Service ceiling: 10,575m (34,695ft)

Weights: 10,977kg (24,200lb); loaded 21,500kg (47,400lb)

Armament: one General Electric GAU-8/A 30mm cannon with 1350 rounds plus up to 7258kg (16,000lb) of mixed ordnance including laser-guided bombs, cluster bombs and AGM-65 Maverick missiles on 11 weapons pylons

Dimensions: span   17.53m (57ft 6in)
          length   16.25m (53ft 4in)
          height   4.47m (14ft 8in)
          wing area   47.01m² (506sq ft)

The Tu-22M Backfire was followed by the Tu-160 supersonic bomber which, like the Backfire, had a variable-geometry wing. The Tu-160, code-named 'Blackjack' by NATO, first flew on 19 December 1981, but one of the two prototypes was lost in an accident. Comparable to but much larger than the Rockwell B-1B, the type entered series production in 1984, and the first operational examples were deployed in May 1987.

The 1980s, the end of which witnessed the collapse of the Soviet regime and with it the end of the Cold War, saw a series of limited conflicts in which the technology of the previous decade was put to use. The first was the Falklands War of 1982, in which Britain's Harriers and Sea Harriers were tested in combat against Argentina. In the same year, Israel's F-15s and Syrian MiG-23s fought one another over the Lebanon.

Sea Harrier

The Sea Harrier, in particular, proved a remarkable asset in the Falklands conflict. Developed from the basic Harrier

Right: Most B-1B missions are flown at high subsonic speeds; the aircraft is fitted with fixed-geometry engine inlets which feed the engines through curved ducts incorporating stream-wise baffles, blocking radar reflections from the fan.

Below: A Russian requirement for an attack aircraft in the A-10 Thunderbolt II class materialized in the Sukhoi Su-25 Frogfoot, which was selected in preference to a rival design, the Ilyushin Il-102.

Su-25

A good deal of so-called 'stealth' technology has been built into the B-1B, greatly enhancing its prospects of penetrating the most advanced enemy defences. With flight refuelling, it can carry very heavy weapons loads over long distances.

airframe, the Sea Harrier FRS.1 was ordered to equip the Royal Navy's three Invincible class aircraft carriers. The nose was lengthened to accommodate the Blue Fox A I radar, and the cockpit was raised to permit the installation of a more substantial avionics suite and to provide the pilot with a better all-round view. An initial production batch of 24 aircraft, plus three development aircraft, was ordered to expedite testing and clearance, and while the first Sea Harrier neared completion in the summer of 1978, the testing of its entire range of operational equipment was under way in two specially modified Hawker Hunter T.8 aircraft.

The first Sea Harrier FRS.1 took off for its maiden flight from Dunsfold on 20 August 1978; this aircraft, XZ450, was not in fact a prototype, but the first aircraft of a production order that had now risen from 24 to 31 examples. On 13 November, it became the first Sea Harrier to land on an aircraft carrier, HMS *Hermes*. In addition to the production batch, three development Sea Harriers had been ordered in 1975. The first of these, XZ438, flew on 30 December 1978 and was retained by the manufacturers for performance and handling trials. The second, XZ439, flew on 30 March 1979 and went to the

Aeroplane and Armament Experimental Establishment (A&AEE) at Boscombe Down for stores clearance trials, while the third, XZ440, flew on 6 June 1979 and was employed in handling and performance trials at B.Ae Dunsfold, Boscombe Down, and with the RAE and Rolls-Royce (Bristol).

The second production Sea Harrier, XZ451, flew on 25 May 1979 and became the first example to be taken on charge by the Royal Navy, being accepted on 18 June 1979 for service with the Intensive Flying Trials Unit. No. 800A Naval Air Squadron was commissioned at Royal Naval Air Station, Yeovilton, Somerset, on 26 June 1979 as the Sea Harrier Intensive Flying Trials Unit (IFTU), and on 31 March 1980 this unit was disbanded and re-formed as No. 899 Headquarters and training squadron. A second Sea Harrier squadron, No. 800, was commissioned on 23 April 1980, and was followed by No. 801 Squadron on 26 February 1981. The planned peacetime establishment of each squadron was five Sea Harriers; No. 800 was to embark on HMS *Hermes*, while No. 801 was to go to HMS *Invincible*.

Meanwhile, an additional batch of 10 Sea Harriers had been ordered from British Aerospace; the first of these flew on 15 September 1981 and was delivered to No. 899 Squadron. Armed with Sidewinder air-to-air missiles, the Sea Harrier FRS.1 distinguished itself in the 1982 Falklands War, its pilots destroying 23 Argentine aircraft. At the campaign's

height, on 21 May 1982, Sea Harriers were being launched on combat air patrols at the rate of one pair every 20 minutes. The Sea Harrier force was later upgraded to FA.2 standard, the forward fuselage being redesigned to accommodate the Ferranti Blue Vixen pulse-Doppler radar. The avionics suite was wholly upgraded and the aircraft armed with the AIM-120 AMRAAM medium-range air-to-air missile, enabling it to engage multiple targets beyond visual range.

The Falklands conflict also saw the first and only combat operation of the aircraft that had been mainly responsible for maintaining Britain's nuclear deterrent for so long, the Avro Vulcan. Having relinquished the QRA (Quick Reaction Alert) role to the Polaris-armed nuclear submarines of the Royal Navy in 1968, the RAF's Vulcan force was assigned to NATO and CENTO in the free-fall bombing role. No. 27 Squadron's B.2s also operated in the maritime radar

reconnaissance role for a time, their aircraft being redesignated Vulcan B.2 (MRR). In May 1982, Vulcans operating from Ascension Island in the Atlantic carried out attacks on the Falkland Islands in support of British operations to recapture these from Argentina. These operations, code-named 'Black Buck', involved both conventional bombing sorties and anti-radar missions by individual aircraft, each mission being supported by no fewer than 11 sorties by

The Tupolev Tu-22M was a very viable and advanced variable-geometry bomber which was designed specifically to attack NATO naval task forces far out to sea with stand-off missiles.

Victor K.2 tankers. For the anti-radar missions the Vulcan received the AGM-45A Shrike missile, which had a high-explosive fragmentation warhead and could be launched from a distance of 12km (7.5 miles). The Shrikes were delivered to the United Kingdom slung under the wings of USAF Phantoms, flying in from Germany – another fine example of the cooperation that existed between the USAF and the RAF throughout the Cold War era and, indeed, has continued since then. Total Vulcan production was 136 aircraft, including the two prototypes and 89 B.2s. The last operational Vulcans were six aircraft of No. 50 Squadron, converted to the flight refuelling role.

Harrier II

Although it was the British who were responsible for the early development of this remarkable aircraft, it was the US Marine Corps that identified the need to upgrade its original version, the AV-8A. The Harrier used 1950s technology in airframe design and construction, and in systems, and by the 1970s, despite

systems updates, this was restricting the further development of the aircraft's potential. In developing the USMC's new Harrier variant, the basic design concept was retained, but new technologies and avionics were fully exploited. One of the major improvements was a new wing, with a carbonfibre composite structure, a super-critical aerofoil and a greater area and span. The wing has large slotted flaps linked with nozzle deflection at short take-off unstick to improve control precision and increase lift. Leading-edge root extensions (LERX) are fitted to enhance the aircraft's air combat agility by improving the turn rate, while longitudinal fences (LIDs, or lift improvement devices) are incorporated beneath the fuselage and on the gun pods to capture

The Tupolev Tu-160 Blackjack was an ambitious Soviet attempt to produce a long-range variable-geometry supersonic bomber similar to America's Rockwell B-1, but larger. Escalating costs caused serious production cutbacks.

Left: The Royal Navy's Sea Harrier leaped to prominence during the Falklands War of 1982, when it flew effective combat air patrols. Pictured here is the last variant, the Sea Harrier FRS.2.

ground-reflected jets in vertical take-off and landing, give a much bigger ground cushion and reduce hot gas recirculation.

A prototype YAV-8B Harrier II first flew in November 1978, followed by the first development aircraft in November 1981, and production deliveries to the USMC began in 1983. The first production AV-8B was handed over to Training Squadron VMAT-203 at Cherry Point, North Carolina, on 16 January 1984, the aircraft

making its acceptance check flight four days later. VMAT-203 began training pilots exclusively for the AV-8B in the spring of 1985, and 170 had completed their conversion course by the end of 1986. Operational Harrier pilots were assigned to Marine Air Group (MAG) 32, the first tactical squadron (VMA 331) reaching initial operational capability (IOC) with the first batch of 12 aircraft early in 1985. The squadron's strength had risen to

15 in the autumn of 1986 and had reached the full complement of 20 by March 1987. The second AV-8B tactical squadron, VMA-231, achieved IOC in July 1986 with 15 aircraft, and a third squadron, VMA-457, also achieved IOC at the end of 1986. The fourth squadron to equip was the first of the West Coast units, VMA-513, which had stood down as the last of the Marine Corps AV-8A squadrons in August 1986.

Delivery of the RAF's equivalent, the Harrier GR5, began in 1987; production GR5s were later converted to GR7 standard. This version, generally similar to the

USMC's night-attack AV-8B, has FLIR, a digital moving map display, night-vision goggles for the pilot and a modified head-up display. The Spanish navy also operated the AV-8B, delivered from October 1987. The survivors of an earlier batch of AV-8As were sold to Thailand in 1996.

The hectic developments of the Cold War brought a whole new range of words and expressions into the language of aviation technology. In the 1980s, one rather intriguing word stood out above the rest. It was 'stealth'.

The US Marine Corps took the basic Harrier design and developed it into the AV-B Harrier II, with greatly increased striking power. The original AV-8A is seen here undergoing deck landing trials.

X-Craft: The Road to the Space Shuttle

Soon after the end of World War II, the USAAF, the National Advisory Committee for Aeronautics (NACA) and the Bell Aircraft Company began joint design studies with the object of producing a research aircraft to probe into the realms of high-speed flight beyond Mach 1. In layman's terms, Mach 1, as the speed of sound designated under the scale devised by the Austrian Professor Ernst Mach in 1887, is equivalent to a speed of 1224.68km/h (760.98mph) at sea level at a temperature of 15°C (59°F), falling to a constant 1061.81km/h (659.78mph) above 11,000m (36,098ft).

The resulting research aircraft was the Bell XS-1, the designation soon being changed simply to X-1. Sleek and bullet-shaped, the X-1 sported ultra-thin unswept wings and conventional tail surfaces. It was powered by a Reaction Motors bi-fuel rocket motor capable of developing a maximum static thrust of 2721kg (6000lb) for two and a half minutes.

Supersonic Flight

The X-1 made its first flight in the autumn of 1946, being carried to altitude recessed into the bomb bay of a modified B-29 bomber, then released to glide to earth. The first flight under its own power was made over the Muroc Flight Test Base (later renamed Edwards AFB) on 9 December that year, the pilot being Chalmers Goodlin. By the summer of 1947, the X-1 had made several flights, the speed being pushed up steadily to beyond the 965km/h (600mph) mark, and much information had been assembled on the aircraft's handling characteristics.

On 14 October 1947, the X-1 became the first aircraft in the world to achieve supersonic flight, being launched from a B-29 Superfortress at 9000m (29,500ft).

Left: The first of three X-1 prototypes became the first aircraft in the world to achieve supersonic flight on 14 August 1947. The X-1 was designed to mimic the streamlined shape of a rifle bullet.

Right: Fuelling the Bell X-1, as with all rocket-propelled aircraft, was always a dangerous operation, as the rocket fuels used were highly volatile and a mistake could lead to disaster.

Twice the Speed of Sound
Bell X-1A

Although the X-1 series of the aircraft were later painted white, the middle of the fuselage was always left unpainted because the extreme cold of the liquid oxygen tanks adversely affected the paint.

Like the X-1, the X-1A had a four-chamber XLR11 rocket engine fuelled by liquid oxygen.

US AIR FORCE
81384

BELL Aircraft

The X-1A's career began with Chuck Yeager's first Mach 2 flight, but ended unceremoniously when it was jettisoned to destruction after an explosion.

Bell X-1A

Type: high-altitude high-speed research aircraft

Powerplant: one 26.7kN (6000lbf) (at sea level) four-chamber Reaction Motors XLR11-RM-5 rocket engine

Maximum speed: 2655.4km/h (1646.35mph) or Mach 2.44

Endurance: about 4 minutes 40 seconds

Service ceiling: over 27,432m (90,000ft)

Weights: empty 3296kg (7251lb); loaded 7478kg (16,452lb)

Armament: always unarmed

Dimensions:		
span	8.53m	(28ft)
length	10.90m	(35ft 8in)
height	3.30m	(10ft 10in)
wing area	39.6m²	(426sq ft)

Piloted by Major Charles E. Yeager, who had joined the test programme a few months earlier and now had eight flights in the X-1 behind him, the aircraft reached a speed of Mach 1.015 in level flight.

'Chuck' Yeager went on to make 53 more flights in the X-1, most of them at supersonic speed. On 5 January 1949, he took the aircraft off the ground for the first time under its own power and climbed to 7015m (23,000ft) in 1 minute 40 seconds, exceeding the speed of sound in the climb. On 8 August 1949, Major Frank Everest flew the X-1 to a record altitude of 21,925m (71,881ft). Another three improved aircraft were built (the X-1A, X-1B and X-1D), and in the first of these Yeager reached a

speed of Mach 2.435 on 12 December 1953. On 4 June 1954, another pilot, Arthur Murray, reached 27,435m (more than 90,000ft). The last of the series was the X-1E, converted from the second X-1 to test a new high-speed wing. In all, the X-1 series aircraft made 231 flights.

In 1950, the X-1s were joined at Muroc by the Douglas Skyrocket. First flown in February 1948, this sleek swept-wing aircraft was originally powered by both turbojet and rocket motors, enabling a normal take-off to be made from the ground. Later, the turbojet was deleted and the Skyrocket, now powered solely by a rocket engine, was carried to altitude under a B-29 in the same way as the X-1. On 21 November 1953, the

Skyrocket became the first piloted aircraft to exceed Mach 2, reaching Mach 2.01 at 19,825m (65,000ft).

Although marred by a number of accidents and technical setbacks, the NACA piloted rocket research aircraft programme did not result in loss of life until 1954, and the aircraft involved was another Bell design, the X-2. Unlike the X-1, the X-2 had swept wing and tail surfaces and was designed to reach speeds in the order of 3218km/h (2000mph).

Right: The swept-wing Douglas Skyrocket was first flown in February 1948, originally powered by a Westinghouse J34 turbojet and an XLR-8 rocket motor. The aircraft later became the first piloted aircraft to exceed Mach 2 when it reached Mach 2.01 at 19,825m (65,000ft), in November 1953.

Bell Goes Even Faster
Bell X-2

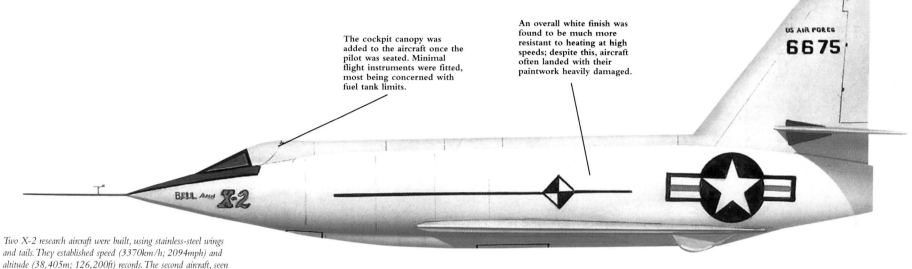

The cockpit canopy was added to the aircraft once the pilot was seated. Minimal flight instruments were fitted, most being concerned with fuel tank limits.

An overall white finish was found to be much more resistant to heating at high speeds; despite this, aircraft often landed with their paintwork heavily damaged.

US AIR FORCE 6675

Two X-2 research aircraft were built, using stainless-steel wings and tails. They established speed (3370km/h; 2094mph) and altitude (38,405m; 126,200ft) records. The second aircraft, seen here, was destroyed in a fatal crash.

To counter the high temperatures that would be met at such speeds, stainless steel featured predominantly in the aircraft's construction. The X-2 was powered by a Curtiss XLR-25 rocket motor.

Fatal Crash

Two X-2s were built. Disaster overcame the first in May 1954, when an explosion ripped through it as its liquid oxygen tank was being topped up in the belly of the B-50 mother ship. The X-2 pilot and one B-50 crew member were killed, but quick action in jettisoning the rocket

Left: The remains of the first Bell X-2 after it was recovered from the desert following a mid-air explosion that caused it to be jettisoned by the B-50 'mother' aircraft in May 1954.

aircraft by the B-50 pilot prevented further casualties. The second X-2 made its first powered flight on 18 November 1955, piloted by Lieutenant-Colonel Frank Everest, but this aircraft was also destroyed in a fatal crash on 27 November 1956 after a flight in which the pilot, Captain Milburn Apt, recorded a speed of Mach 3.2 and was officially recorded as having flown faster than any other human being.

Following preliminary design studies made by NACA, together with a design competition that involved most of the US aviation industry, North American Aviation was awarded, in December 1955, a contract for three prototypes of a manned research aircraft which was to

have a design speed of at least Mach 7 and be capable of reaching an altitude of at least 80,000m (264,000ft), or 80km (50 miles) above the earth. In other words, the aircraft was designed to fill the gap between embryo rocket-powered research types and the space vehicles that would eventually place an American in orbit. The powerplant was to be a Thiokol XLR-99-RM-1 rocket motor developing a thrust of 26,000kg (57,600lb), although initial flight tests with the first two X-15As were made with two Reaction Motors LR-11-RM-5s, each of 3624kg (8000lb) thrust, the larger engine not being ready. The high friction that would be encountered at hypersonic speeds meant that the X-15's basic structural materials

Bell X-2

Type: supersonic research aircraft

Powerplant: one 66.7kN (15,000lbf) Curtiss-Wright XLR25-CW-1 rocket engine

Maximum speed: 3058km/h (1896mph)

Endurance: 10 minutes 55 seconds of powered flight

Fuel capacity: 2960 litres (782 gallons) of liquid oxygen; 3376 litres (892 gallons) of ethyl alcohol and water

Accommodation: one pilot

Service ceiling: 38405m (126,000ft)

Weights: empty 5314kg (11,690lb); maximum take-off 11,299kg (24,858lb)

Dimensions:		
	span	9.75m (32ft)
	length	13.41m (44ft)
	height	4.11m (13ft 6in)
	wing area	24.19m² (260sq ft)

Faster than a Bullet
North American X-15

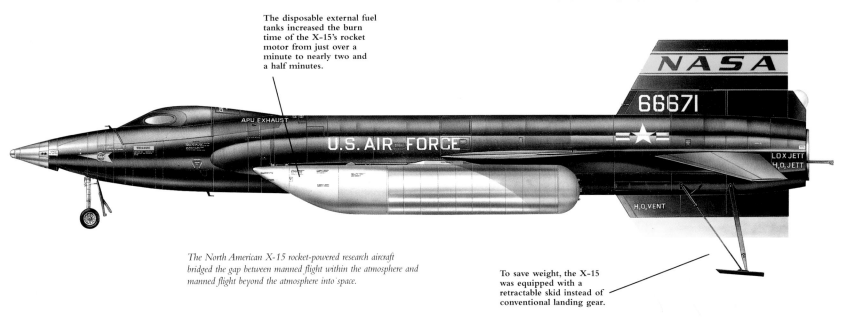

The disposable external fuel tanks increased the burn time of the X-15's rocket motor from just over a minute to nearly two and a half minutes.

APU EXHAUST

RESCUE

NASA

66671

U.S. AIR FORCE

LOX JETT
H.O. JETT

H.O. VENT

The North American X-15 rocket-powered research aircraft bridged the gap between manned flight within the atmosphere and manned flight beyond the atmosphere into space.

To save weight, the X-15 was equipped with a retractable skid instead of conventional landing gear.

North American X-15A-2

Type: single-seat hyper-velocity rocket-powered research aircraft

Powerplant: one Thiokol (Reaction Motors) XLR99-RM-2 single-chamber throttleable liquid-propellant rocket engine, with a thrust rating of 26,000kg (57,200lb) at 14,000m (46,000ft) altitude and 32,000kg (70,400lb) at 30,000m (98,400ft)

Max speed: 7297km/h (4534mph)

Maximum altitude: 107,960m (354,000ft)

Time to height: 140 seconds from launch at 15,000m (49,212ft) to 100,000m (320,000ft)

Range: 450km (280 miles) on a typical test flight

Weights: loaded 25,460kg (56,000lb)

Dimensions:		
span	6.81m	(22ft 4in)
length	15.47m	(50ft 9in)
height	3.96m	(12ft 11in)
wing area	18.58m²	(200sq ft)

were titanium and stainless steel, the entire airframe being covered with an 'armoured skin' of nickel alloy steel which was designed to withstand temperatures of up to 550°C (1022°F).

Supersonic Climb

The first X-15A flew for the first time on 10 March 1959, carried under the starboard wing of a B-52 'mother' aircraft; it was not released on that occasion. The first free flight, without power, was made on 8 June, with test pilot Scott Crossfield at the controls. On 17 September, with Crossfield once again in the pilot's seat, the X-15A was launched

on its first powered flight, dropping from a height of 11,590m (38,000 feet). The rockets cut in 1525m (5000ft) lower down, and Crossfield took the aircraft in a shallow climb to Mach 2.3. The fuel was exhausted four minutes after launch, and Crossfield came round in a turn to make a dead-stick landing on Lake Muroc, touching down at 240km/h (150mph). When ground crew inspected the X-15A, they found that alcohol from a broken fuel pump had flowed into the aft engine bay and an undetected fire had broken out, burning through a large area of aluminium tubing, fuel lines and valves. Repairs were carried out in

23 days and the aircraft was soon ready for its second powered flight.

A number of snags, mostly associated with the fuel system, were encountered, and these had to be solved before the second flight could be made. Eventually, however, on 17 October 1959, Crossfield and the X-15 were launched from the B-52 at 12,505m (41,000ft) over the desert. With all eight rocket tubes firing, the X-15 quickly accelerated. The pilot

Right: Three X-15s were built, the aircraft being air-launched at altitude from a B-29. The second X-15A was rebuilt after a landing accident to become the X-15A-2, and it was the fastest aircraft ever flown.

took it in a supersonic climb to 16,775m (55,000ft), where he levelled out and made some high-speed manoeuvres before climbing again to 20,435m (67,000ft), the maximum altitude for this flight. After the rockets burned out, Crossfield took the X-15 in a supersonic glide at Mach 1.5, levelling out at 15,250m (50,000ft).

Five days later, Crossfield was airborne in the X-15 again, with plans to push the speed up to Mach 2.6 at an altitude of 25,925m (85,000ft). The flight had to be abandoned, however, when the pilot detected a malfunction in his oxygen system, and bad weather delayed further testing until 5 November. This time, the weather was perfect, and the pre-flight checks indicated no snags at all. The X-15 was dropped, the rockets ignited and the

aircraft began to accelerate. Then, from his position a quarter of a mile behind the X-15, test pilot Major Bob White, flying an F-104 chase plane, saw a red glare blossom out near the X-15's rocket exhaust and knew that Crossfield had a fire to cope with. As soon as he heard White's warning, Crossfield shut down the X-15's rocket motor, jettisoned his fuel load and, following a terrifying fast glide, made an emergency landing on Rosamund Dry Lake. Crossfield escaped without injury, but the X-15's back was broken and its rocket motor burnt out.

After a two-month delay, the research programme resumed with the X-15A-1, now fitted with the XLR-99-RM-1 rocket motor; it flew for the first time under power on 23 January 1960. Crossfield's damaged aircraft was repaired and returned to service as the X-15A-2. A

third aircraft, the X-15A-3, had been made ready for flight in the summer of 1960, but was seriously damaged by a propellant explosion in the ground on 8 June. It was several months before it was airworthy again. This was not the end of the disasters. On 9 November 1962, the X-15A-2 landed without flaps, collapsed its undercarriage and ended on its back, fortunately without serious injury to the pilot.

Record Flights
By this time, the X-15s had made a number of notable record flights. On 27 June 1962, Joe Walker, Chief Test Pilot with the National Aeronautics and Space Administration (NASA), reached a speed of Mach 6.06 in the X-15A-1 after the engine burned

Right: The Northrop HL-10 was one of six lifting-body vehicles tested at NASA's Dryden Flight Research Center, Edwards AFB, from 1966 to 1975 as part of the programme to develop a space shuttle.

for 89 seconds instead of the normal 84 seconds. On 17 July 1962, Major Bob White climbed to an altitude of 95.89km (59.6 miles) to capture the absolute world altitude record. It also qualified White for US Astronaut Wings, which are awarded to those who have travelled more than 80km (50 miles) above the earth.

Following its accident in November 1962, the X-15A-2 was almost

Towards the end of its operational life the X-15A-2 received a coat of ablative material, enabling it to withstand the higher temperatures that were generated at speeds of up to Mach 8.0.

The Martin X-24 series of lifting bodies was designed to investigate flight characteristics within the atmosphere from high altitude supersonic speeds to landing, and to prove the feasibility of using lifting bodies for return from space.

spin during its descent and disintegrated. Further, by the late 1960s, the X-15 was coming to the end of its useful life. On 3 October 1967, Major William J. Knight, USAF, reached the highest speed ever attained by the aircraft, Mach 6.72.

The X-15 made its last flight on 24 October 1968, and soon afterwards the programme was suspended. The eyes of Americans were now on the *Apollo* lunar landing programme, and the first manned moon landing in 1969 largely eclipsed the efforts of the X-15 team. Yet the contribution made by the X-15 to the United States' space programme was incalculable, particularly in the development of reusable space vehicles.

An important step towards achieving this goal was taken with the design of a series of experimental lifting-body research vehicles, starting with two wingless aircraft built by Northrop. The vehicles, designated M2-F2 and HL-10, were very similar. The M2-F2 had a basic delta planform and its fuselage was D-shaped in cross-section, the flat side of the D forming the top. In the case of the HL-10, the flat surface was on the underside. The 'lifting bodies' were taken to altitude by NASA's specially modified B-52, then dropped, making controlled gliding descents to earth. The M2-F2 was delivered to NASA on 15 June 1965; it

completely rebuilt, with a lengthened fuselage and large external fuel tanks. Its entire airframe was coated with ablative material, enabling it to withstand higher temperatures of 1400°C (2552°F) at speeds of up to Mach 8. This aircraft flew

in its new form on 28 June 1964, when Major Robert Rushworth achieved a speed of 4769km/h (2964mph) at 25,315m (83,000ft). On 18 November 1966, the X-15A-2 reached a speed of 6838km/h (4250mph) in level flight at

30,500m (100,000ft), piloted by Major Pete Knight of the USAF.

The X-15 programme suffered its only fatality on 15 November 1957, when test pilot Michael J. Adams was killed after the X-15A-3 went into a

made its first unpowered flight on 12 July 1966 and began tests under power at the end of the year. On 10 May 1967, the M2-F2 suffered a spectacular crash on landing (made famous in the opening sequences of the 1970s TV series *The Six Million Dollar Man*) and was completely rebuilt, completing its test programme in December 1972.

Maximum Altitude

The HL-10 was delivered to NASA on 19 January 1966. It made its first unpowered flight on 22 December, and went on to complete a programme of 37 flights by the end of 1971, 25 under its own power. The HL-10 was flown to a maximum altitude of 27,500m (90,200ft) and reached a speed of Mach 1.861.

The Martin Marietta Corporation was also involved in lifting-body research, producing four small-scale unmanned vehicles known as SV-5D PRIME (Precision Recovery Including Manoeuvring Entry); their USAF designation was X-23A. Then, in 1966, the USAF ordered a manned vehicle, the SV-5P (X-24A) to investigate the low-speed flight regime. The X-24A was delivered on 11 July 1967. The flight test profile involved the vehicle being carried to 13,715m (45,000ft) by the B-52 and released, using its rocket motor to reach Mach 2 and an altitude of 30,480m (100,000ft), after which it would make a powerless glide descent and landing, the flight lasting 15 minutes from launch. The vehicle had a very high landing speed,

with a design maximum of more than 560km/h (350mph). The X-24A made its first powered flight on 19 March 1970; it was rebuilt in 1972 and flew again in August 1973 as the X-24B, making its final flight on 23 September 1975.

Meanwhile, the Space Shuttle programme, which had been initiated in July 1972, had been taking shape. Rockwell International was awarded the contract for two Orbiters, later increased to five; the first of these was rolled out in September 1976. The first unmanned flight was made in February 1977, the Orbiter being mounted on top of a specially modified Boeing 747. The first release and gliding flight was made on 18 June 1977. The first fully functional shuttle, officially known as the Space Transportation System (STS), was made by the Orbiter *Columbia* on 12 April 1981.

On 28 January, 1986, the Orbiter *Challenger* was destroyed when it disintegrated during ascent, with the loss of all seven astronauts on board. *Endeavour* was built to replace *Challenger* (using spare parts originally intended for the other Orbiters) and delivered in May 1991; it was first launched a year later. Seventeen years after *Challenger*, *Columbia* was also lost, together with all seven crew members, during re-entry on 1 February 2003, and was not replaced.

The experience gained with the lifting bodies and earlier X-craft culminated in one of the greatest technological achievements of all time, the Space Transportation System, or Space Shuttle.

Commercial Aviation: 1950 to the Present Day

In the early 1950s, Boeing took advantage of the expertise that it had gained during its B-47 and B-52 jet bomber programmes to design what was to become a world-beating jet airliner, the Boeing 707. The prototype was built in great secrecy, and it flew for the first time on 13 July 1954. The principal series models of the Boeing 707 were the 707-120, which first flew in December 1957, and the 707-320, which first flew in January 1959.

The potential of the Boeing 707, and indeed all other jet airliners, improved immeasurably with the introduction of the turbofan engine. The first turbofan engine in the world was the Rolls-Royce Conway. Developed from the axial-flow turbojet, the turbofan features an enlarged first-stage compressor which acts as a ducted fan, blowing air past the core of the engine to produce additional thrust. The engine was first air-tested in 1955 under an Avro Ashton test-bed, mounted in an underfuselage pod approximating to the contours of the nacelle that was to be fitted

under the wing of the Boeing 707, the Conway-powered version of which was to be purchased by the British Overseas Airways Corporation.

The Boeing 707's direct rival was the Douglas DC-8, the second commercial jet aircraft produced by the United States. Originally known as the Douglas Model 1881, and conceived as a four-jet domestic airliner, the Douglas DC-8 was announced in June 1955, made its first flight on 30 May 1958 and entered airline service about a year after the Boeing 707.

Less Expensive Option

By the time the prototype DC-8 flew, the order book stood at more than 130 aircraft; the first customer was Pan American, which ordered 25 aircraft in October 1955. Ironically, these were to operate alongside the Boeing 707 on the airline's routes to Europe during the 1960s. On 21 August 1961, a modified DC-8-40 became the first jet airliner to exceed Mach 1, reaching 1073km/h (667mph) in a shallow dive. The DC-8 was slightly less expensive than the Boeing 707, and a little slower, although the speed difference was barely

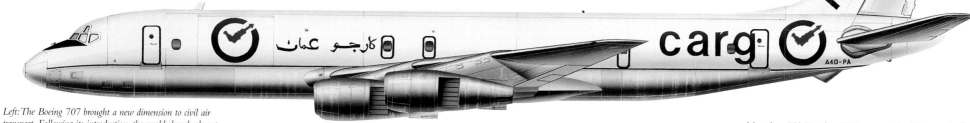

Left: The Boeing 707 brought a new dimension to civil air transport. Following its introduction, the world shrank almost overnight. This is one of BOAC's early examples.

More than 550 Douglas DC-8s were produced between 1959 and 1972. Pictured here is a DC-8F cargo version.

Britain's Last Big Jet Airliner
Vickers VC.10

The VC-10 Model 1151, 17 of which were operated by BOAC, was the basic passenger transport. Five more aircraft, designated Model 1154, were purchased by East African Airways, the only other airline to order the type.

The spoilers on the top of the wings were used as airbrakes.

G-ASGM

The cantilever all-metal tail had the tailplane set at the top of the fin, ahead of a large bullet-shaped fairing at the junction. The fin also had an integral fuel tank.

BOAC

Super VC.10

Type: four-engined long-range passenger/cargo jet airliner

Powerplant: four 100.08kN (23,030lbf) Rolls-Royce Conway RCo.43 turbofans

Maximum speed: 935km/h (580mph)

Initial climb rate: 700m/min (2300fpm)

Cruise height: 11,600m (38,000ft)

Range: 7560km (4698 miles) with maximum payload

Weights: empty 66,660kg (146,960lb); basic operating weight 70,479kg (155,054lb)

Maximum payload: 27,043kg (59,495lb)

Dimensions: span 44.55m (146ft)
     length 52.32m (172ft)
     height 12.04m (39ft)
     wing area 272.4m² (2931sq ft)

noticeable, even on long trips. After an early flurry of accidents, mostly linked to the vastly greater complexity and performance of the jets, they proved to be safe and reliable aircraft. The 707, overall, was more efficient in service.

In April 1965, Douglas announced three new variants of the DC-8. The first was the DC-8 Super 61, a high-capacity transcontinental aircraft with the same wing and engines as the DC-8-50; the second was the Super 62, which was only slightly longer than the standard aircraft, but which was stretched just enough to match the seating capacity of the Boeing 707-320 and which had a completely redesigned engine installation; and the third was the Super 63, which combined the DC-8-61 fuselage with the Super 62 wing and uprated engines. The first Super 61 flew in March 1966,

and all three passenger versions were in service by mid-1967.

Britain, having lost the commercial jet airliner leadership with the misfortunes of the de Havilland Comet, tried to re-enter the field with the Vickers (British Aircraft Corporation) VC-10, a truly beautiful design powered by four tail-mounted Rolls-Royce Conway turbofans. Designed to operate on both long-distance routes with a high subsonic speed and hot-and-high operations out of African airports, the VC-10 first flew in 1962. A further developed version, the Super VC-10, was designed to carry larger payloads than the standard VC-10 at the cost of a relatively small increase in take-off distance, the fuselage being lengthened by 4.27m (14ft). The VC-10 was not a commercial success, being operated only by BOAC and East

African Airways, and only 54 VC-10s and Super VC-10s were built. Some of the latter were converted as flight refuelling tankers for the RAF.

Prestige Airliner

In 1957, a few days before the fortieth anniversary of the Russian Revolution, the largest Soviet turboprop aircraft of the time and the largest commercial aircraft in the world made its first flight. It was the Tupolev Tu-114 Rossiya, Andrei Tupolev's response to a requirement for an aircraft capable of literally circumnavigating the globe. Based on the Tu-95 Bear Strategic bomber, using the same wing mounted

Right: The Ilyushin Il-62, initially flown in January 1963, was the first commercial long-range four-jet aircraft produced in the Soviet Union. The Il-62M was a more powerful version.

American Turboprop
Lockheed 188 Electra

First flown on 6 December 1957, the Lockheed Electra short-/ medium-range airliner was an immediate success, the company having 144 orders on its books by the time the prototype made its maiden flight.

The Electra was the first turboprop airliner designed and built in the United States.

This aircraft was built in 1961 for Western Airlines and converted into a freighter in 1969.

The Allison 501 engine also powered the L-100 Hercules and the Convair 580 airliner.

FRED. OLSEN

LN-FOG

low on the fuselage so that the passenger cabin was unobstructed by the wing main spar structure, it broke new ground in the history of air transportation. One of its most successful routes was the joint Aeroflot/Japan Air Lines service between Moscow and Tokyo, which was operated with mixed Russian/Japanese crews. The performance of the airliner, given the NATO reporting name 'Cleat', was not outstanding, but its load carrying and speed made it the Soviet Union's prestige airliner throughout the 1960s.

The other Soviet long-haul airliner of the 1960s was the Ilyushin Il-62. The

Il-62, which was given the NATO reporting name 'Classic', flew for the first time in January 1963 and was the first long-range four-jet commercial aircraft produced in the USSR. After a series of proving flights by one of the prototypes and three pre-production aircraft, the Il-62 began scheduled services with Aeroflot on the Moscow–Khabarovsk and Moscow–Novosibirsk routes. From September 1967, the type began to replace the Tu-114 on the Moscow–Montreal route, and this service was extended to New York in July 1968. The Il-62M was a version with more powerful engines and extended range.

In December 1960, Boeing announced its intention to produce a short- to medium-range jet transport, designated Model 727. The aircraft made its first

flight in February 1963, and the type entered scheduled service with Eastern Airlines in February 1964. By April 1967, the Boeing 727 was the most widely used commercial jet airliner in the world.

The British equivalent of the Boeing 727 was the Hawker Siddeley Trident, although it never enjoyed anything like the success of the American airliner. The Trident originated in a requirement issued by British European Airways in 1957, calling for a new short-range commercial jet with an in-service date of 1964. The prototype flew on 9 January 1962, and BEA began regular services with its first batch of 24 aircraft on 1 April 1964. In June 1965, a BEA Trident I made the first automatic landing during a scheduled passenger service. In all, 117 Tridents were produced in five versions.

Left: In many ways the Russian equivalent of the Boeing 727, the Tupolev Tu-154 is widely used on domestic routes in Russia and other states of the former Soviet Union. It is also used by the air forces of at least ten countries worldwide.

Lockheed 188A Electra

Type: turboprop airliner

Powerplant: Four 2800kW (3750hp) Allison 501 turboprop engines

Cruising speed: 600km/h (373mph)

Range: 4458km (2770 miles)

Service ceiling: 8565m (28,400ft)

Weights: loaded 51,257kg (113,000lb)

Accommodation: flight crew of three, plus 66–98 passengers

Dimensions: span   30m (99ft)
            length   32.15m (105ft 4in)
            height   10.25m (33ft 7in)

The massive Antonov An-125 is offered for cargo duty anywhere in the world, to any customer. Here, a US Navy Deep Submergence Rescue Vehicle (DSRV) is being swallowed into the maw of one such giant.

Russia's medium-range tri-jet airliner was the Tupolev Tu-154, which flew for the first time in October 1968 and went on to become one of the world's leading medium-haul airliners. This aircraft found itself in widespread service with Aeroflot on both domestic and international services, and also with the airlines of nations allied to the former Soviet Union. The Tu-154 entered regular service on Aeroflot's internal routes in November 1971.

In the wake of the Vickers Viscount, a new generation of turboprop-powered airliners entered service in the late 1950s and early 1960s. From Britain came the Bristol Britannia, which stemmed from a BOAC requirement for a Medium Range Empire (MRE) transport aircraft, originally intended to be powered by four Centaurus piston engines. In 1950, BOAC expressed a preference for the Bristol Proteus turboprop, and it was with this

powerplant that the Britannia made its first flight on 16 August 1952. The type entered service on BOAC's London–Johannesburg service on 1 February 1957. Although a fine aircraft, the Britannia entered the world airliner market too late, as potential operators now had their eyes fixed on all-jet equipment. Nevertheless, the Britannia gave excellent service with a number of airlines, and also equipped two squadrons of RAF Transport Command.

The first turboprop airliner designed and built in the United States was the Lockheed L-188A Electra. First flown in December 1957, the type began scheduled services with Eastern Airlines and American Airlines in 1959 and commercial success seemed assured, but two subsequent fatal accident revealed

Two Boeing 747s were extensively modified so that they were capable of carrying the Space Shuttle 'piggyback' fashion. Seen here is the Space Shuttle Atlantis.

The Douglas Aircraft Company developed two versions of the DC-9 specifically for Scandinavian Airlines System. These were the DC-9-40 and the DC-9-20, a 'hot-and-high' version.

structural weaknesses in the aircraft's wing, and production of the Electra was halted while major modifications were made. A speed restriction was placed on the aircraft and no further orders were forthcoming; however, the military variant, the P-3 Orion, went on to be an outstanding success.

From the Soviet Union came a succession of turboprop designs, starting with the Ilyushin Il-18, which first flew

in July 1957 and entered service with Aeroflot in April 1959. Unsophisticated and crude by western standards, the Il-18, branded 'Coot' under the NATO reporting system, became a mainstay of Soviet civil aviation scene and did much to expand Aeroflot's routes in the 1960s.

The Antonov An-10 Ukraina heavy transport, which went into military service in 1959, was another four-engined Russian turboprop. The An-10A was the passenger version and the An-12, known to NATO as 'Cub', was a cargo variant. It went on to become one of the period's most successful transport aircraft

and was roughly the equivalent of the Lockheed Hercules. Antonov was also responsible for a hugely successful series of twin-engined transports, beginning with the An-24 of 1959, and for the remarkably versatile An-2 utility biplane.

Heaviest Aircraft

At the Paris Air Show in June 1965, Oleg K. Antonov revealed his latest creation, and it stunned the aviation world. The huge An-22 heavy transport was in service with both Aeroflot and the Soviet Air Force, which used it to transport large cargoes such as missiles

on tracked launchers and dismantled aircraft. When the An-22 made its debut, it was the heaviest aircraft ever built. Fifty examples were completed up to 1974, when production ended.

Antonov had more surprises in store a few years later, the first being the Antonov An-124 Ruslan. One of the largest aircraft ever built, the mighty An-124 transport, designed for very heavy lift, proved a winning design from the outset. Dubbed

Sales of the Boeing 737 were steady but unspectacular until 1978, when the market suddenly erupted. Many US regional airlines began buying the 737 to hasten their expansion.

'Condor' under the NATO reporting system, it was more popularly and correctly known by its Russian name, Ruslan, which first appeared on the second prototype. (Ruslan is a giant folk hero of Russian literature and music.) The first prototype An-124 opened the flight test programme on 26 December 1982; the aircraft was making proving flights on Aeroflot routes by the end of 1985. At least 23 An-124s were in service by 1991, and the Antonov bureau had formed a special company to sell cargo space all over the world.

The concept of a transport aircraft to carry orbital space vehicles between locations on the ground was pioneered by NASA's Boeing 747/Space Shuttle combination, but the idea reached a new peak of development in the former Soviet Union. Trials with a much-modified Myasishchev Mya-4 Bison bomber (named VM-t *Atlant*) proved that the 'piggyback' method of transporting heavy and outsize loads was feasible by carrying components of the *Energiya* booster that would be used to launch the Russian space shuttle, *Buran* (Snowstorm), and the massive Antonov An-225 *Mriya* (Dream) appeared in 1988. The An-225 was developed specifically with the Russian space programme in mind and was the first aircraft in the world to be flown at a gross weight of 453,000kg (1,000,000lb).

The early 1960s produced a British success story in the short-haul jet market, in the shape of the British Aircraft

Few aerodynamic engineering achievements ever matched that of the Anglo-French Concorde, designed to fly at an economical cruising speed of just over Mach 2.

The Tupolev Tu-144 was the world's first supersonic transport to fly, on 31 December 1968, beating the Anglo-French Concorde into the air by two months. Unlike Concorde, it was not a success.

Corporation (BAC) One-Eleven, which first flew in August 1963. Several versions were produced to suit the requirements of various airline customers. Total One-Eleven production was 244, the airliner also being built under licence in Romania.

American Equivalent

The One-Eleven's American equivalent was the Douglas DC-9, which was a familiar sight on the short- and medium-haul routes of many airlines around the world for many years. The prototype flew in February 1965, and it, too, was produced in several versions. When Douglas was taken over by McDonnell in 1967, the DC-9 became the McDonnell Douglas MD-80. With total sales of more than 2400 units, the DC-9 became one of the most successful airliner families in aviation history.

The Russian airliner that fell into this class was the Tupolev Tu-134, known to NATO as 'Crusty'. A progressive development of the Tu-104 and its successor, the Tu-124, it was originally designated Tu-124A, but incorporated so many changes that an entirely new bureau number was allocated. Work on the Tu-134 project began in June 1962, and the prototype flew in December 1963, with the type entering service with Aeroflot on internal routes in 1966. It began international services in September 1967 on the Moscow–Stockholm route. The original 64-seat Tu-134 was followed in 1958 by a stretched version, the 80-seat Tu-134A.

Four Boeing 747-200s were bought by the US Air Force to serve as National Emergency Airborne Command Posts, fitted with an extensive communications suite and in-flight refuelling capability.

The most phenomenal short-haul success story of this period, however, was the Boeing 737. Development of this famous airliner began in 1964, with the prototype flying in April 1967. Sales of the type were steady but unspectacular until 1978, when the market erupted. No fewer than 145 sales were recorded in that year, for a number of reasons. Boeing took two large 'one-off' orders from British Airways and Lufthansa, and the US government abolished the rules that had prevented small but efficient regional airlines from competing on many routes. The regional airlines purchased Boeing 737s to hasten their expansion, and Boeing produced several variants to meet the surge in demand.

As intended, the advanced Model 737 was attractive to 'Third World' operators, and the airliner became a familiar sight in the Middle and Far East, Africa and Latin America. In Europe, the holiday charter business had matured to the point where airlines could afford brand-new aircraft; the advanced Model 737, with 130 seats and plenty of range, proved ideal. In 1980, the 737 overtook the Boeing 727 as the world's bestselling airliner.

Stunning Achievement

In commercial aviation, the most stunning achievement of the 1960s was the development of the supersonic

transport, epitomized by the Anglo-French Concorde. A fine example of international cooperation, development and production of the west's first (and to date only) supersonic airliner was a joint undertaking by Britain and France, formal agreements being signed in November 1962. Intended to cruise at Mach 2.05, Concorde employed an ogival (dual-curve) wing planform, the

Left: The second wide-bodied high-density aircraft to enter airline service (the first being the Boeing 747), the McDonnell Douglas DC-10 flew for the first time on 29 August 1970, and production aircraft entered service on 5 August the following year.

characteristics of which were exhaustively tested on the BAC-221, a research aircraft rebuilt from the record-breaking Fairey Delta 2. Another research aircraft, the Handley Page HP.115, was built to test low-speed handling characteristics of the wing. Concorde was provided with four Rolls-Roycel/SNECMA Olympus 593 engines. Aérospatiale was responsible for the first prototype, F-WTSS, which flew for the first time at Toulouse on 2 March 1969, and the British Aircraft Corporation for the second, G-BSST, which made its first flight at Filton, Bristol, on 9 April 1969.

The first prototype, Concorde 001, exceeded Mach 1.0 in October 1969 and Mach 2.0 in November 1970. By this time, 16 airlines had taken out options on the purchase of 74 aircraft, but in the event Concorde was used only by British Airways and Air France. These two airlines inaugurated Concorde passenger services in January 1976, BA between London and Bahrain, and Air France between Paris and Rio de Janeiro, followed by services to Caracas, Washington and New York.

The elegantly simple lines of Concorde tended to disguise the

extreme complexity of the aircraft's engineering and aerodynamic systems. For example, the ogival wing had cambered leading edges that created powerful vortices on which the aircraft 'rode' at cruising speed, while the four

Developed from the earlier Il-86, the Il-96 turned out to be virtually a new design, with only sections of the fuselage and the landing gear barely unaltered.

The market requirements that had led to the development of the McDonnell Douglas DC-10 in 1966 also resulted in the Lockheed TriStar high-density jet airliner programme. The project, designated L-1101, was launched in March 1968.

underslung engines were fed with carefully controlled air, involving a complex series of intake ramps. Concorde's long nose and high angle of attack meant that the crew had no forward vision at low speed, so the nose 'drooped' for take-off and landing. Concorde's excellent safety record was blemished on 25 July 2000, when an Air France machine crashed

near Charles de Gaulle Airport, Paris, killing all on board. The accident was caused by debris on the runway rupturing one of the aircraft's fuel tanks as it took off. All Concordes were withdrawn from service in 2003.

Design Changes

Concorde was not the first supersonic transport (SST) to fly. It was beaten into the air by the Tupolev Tu-144, which made its first flight on 31 December 1968. The development of the Tu-144 was protracted, spanning a period of

nearly 10 years, during which it underwent major design changes, including a new wing, relocated engine nacelles, a new undercarriage and retractable canard foreplanes (small, wing-like projections forward of the main lifting surface) to improve low-speed handling. The Tu-144 exceeded Mach 1 on 5 June 1969 and Mach 2 just over a month later. The second production aircraft was involved in a fatal accident at the Paris Air Show on 3 June 1973, breaking up in midair after executing a violent manoeuvre. No report on the crash was ever released by

the Russians. The Tu-144 was initially used to carry mail and cargo between Moscow and Alma Ata, and began carrying passengers on that route in November 1977; the aircraft was abruptly withdrawn from service in June 1978.

The Americans also made a bid for a share of the SST market, with the Boeing 2707. Unlike Concorde and the Tu-144,

The Airbus A310 has achieved excellent sales, largely on account of its excellent economy and range performance. It is a very safe aircraft, with numerous high-lift devices providing good safety factors close to the ground.

this was to be constructed largely of titanium, making it capable of Mach 3, and was to have a variable-geometry wing. A full-scale mock-up was built in 1966, but the VG concept was abandoned in 1968 as being too complex, and a smaller fixed-wing version was planned, with test flights scheduled for 1970 and commercial service in 1974. Two prototypes were begun, but the US SST project was cancelled in 1971 on the grounds of escalating fuel costs and environmental concerns.

Exciting and imagination-catching though the supersonic transport concept might have been, it was a far different aircraft that brought about the true revolution in air transport in the 1970s. The age of the wide-bodied jet transport came into being on 9 February 1969, with the first flight of the Boeing 747 'Jumbo Jet', developed initially to rival and surpass the 'stretched' version of the Douglas DC-8. Numerous variants of the 747 were subsequently produced, the first production model, the 747-100, going into service with Pan American on the London–New York route on 22 January 1970. Originally planned as a double-decker, the 747 eventually became essentially a single-deck design, seating 385 people in the basic passenger model, including 16 in an upper-deck lounge.

In October 1970, Boeing flew the first Model 747-200, with a greater fuel capacity and increased gross weight. The basic passenger version was the Model 747-200B, while the Model 747-200F

was a dedicated cargo version with no windows and a hinged nose for straight-in loading of pallets and containers. Variants include the 747SP, a special-performance long-range version with a shortened fuselage and an enlarged tail fin. Among other notable flights, a Pan American 747SP flew around the world in 1 day, 22 hours and 50 minutes at an average speed of 809km/h (503mph); another traversed the globe by crossing both poles.

Intercontinental Routes

The second wide-bodied high-density aircraft to enter airline service was the McDonnell Douglas DC-10, which flew for the first time on 29 August 1970, and production aircraft entered service on 5 August the following year with American Airlines on the Los Angeles–Chicago route. An extended-range variant, the DC-10-30, flew on 21 June 1972; intended for intercontinental routes, this had more powerful engines, a third main undercarriage unit and increased wingspan. It was followed by several other variants, including the more powerful Series 40. Later, the aircraft was redesignated MD-11; subsequent versions had a stretched fuselage in order to provide greater accommodation for both passengers and luggage, while the wings were lengthened and incorporated winglets. The MD-11's overall design was more advanced than the DC-10's, resulting in greater efficiency, while the earlier analogue cockpit display was replayed by multifunction CRT displays.

The same market requirements that had led to the development of the McDonnell Douglas DC-10 resulted in the Lockheed TriStar high-density jet airliner programme. The project, which was designated L-1101, was launched in March 1968, by which time 144 orders and options were in place, and the first aircraft flew on 16 November 1970. The initial version available was the Lockheed L-1011-1, which entered regular airline service with Eastern Air Lines on 26 April 1972. By late 1973, some 56 were in service, with orders and options for a further 199. It was not enough as, by this time, the DC-10 was making inroads into the intercontinental market, so Lockheed set about increasing the TriStar's range and payload, starting with the L-1011-100 series. Powered by three Rolls-Royce RB.211 turbofans, this became the most adaptable of the TriStar series, but it failed to match the DC-10 Series 30's range and payload capability. In an attempt to bring about a radical improvement of the TriStar's range capability, Lockheed introduced the L-1011-500, this aircraft receiving FAA certification in December 1979.

Improved Version

The Soviet Union emerged on to the wide-body stage in December 1976, with the first flight of the Ilyushin Il-86. Aeroflot began services with the type in October 1977, but these were mostly restricted to destinations within the USSR because of the airliner's poor

range. This resulted in the development of an improved version, the Il-96, which was virtually a new design. Almost the only components left unaltered, or only slightly modified, were major sections of the fuselage (though this was made much shorter) and the four units of the landing gear. The first prototype of the Il-96 flew on 28 September 1988, and the type made its international debut at the Paris Air Show in the following June. Aeroflot placed orders for about 100 aircraft for service on its long-range high-density routes both at home and overseas, but only about 16 were in service in September 2006. Further developments of the type are the Il-96M with 350 seats for medium-range sectors and the Il-90 twin-engine version.

During the 1980s, the Boeing family continued its expansion with the introduction of the twinjet Model 757, which began to replace the 727 in airline service. Next came the Model 767, which was similar to the 757, but with a wider body. Then, neatly filling the gap between the 767 and the 747, came the Boeing 777, an all-new wide-body design that built on Boeing's tried and tested concepts for twin turbofan airliners and also offered a choice of engine to suit the requirements of potential customers. Its structure made extensive use of advanced materials, and the latest avionics included a 'fly-by-wire' control system.

By now, however, Boeing's apparent monopoly of the civil airliner market had

The largest airliner in the world, the Airbus A380 was scheduled to enter airline service in 2007, but suffered serious delays during its development phase because of differing customer requirements.

come under serious and sustained attack by the European consortium Airbus Industries, which by 1981 had captured more than 55 per cent of the world market for twin-aisle transport aircraft. In 1972, the company flew the Airbus A300, the first wide-body twin-engine commercial aircraft to enter service. Initial sales were poor, but then Airbus launched the A300B4, designed for medium-haul routes. Four aircraft were

taken by Eastern Air Lines on a six-month lease, beginning in late 1977. The airline was so impressed by the aircraft that it bought the original four, along with 25 more. It was the beginning of the Airbus success story; by 1978, Airbus had secured orders from other American airlines, and had come second only to Boeing in wide-body sales. Within three years, it had pushed Boeing into second place.

Modified Wings
The A310 was a shorter version of the A300 with modified wings, and tended to be overshadowed by the A320, the

model that heralded the age of the truly high-technology airliner. In 1981, the A320 guaranteed Airbus's position as a leading participant in the world airliner market. The A320 had secured 400 orders before it even flew. The A318, A319 and A321 are short-haul derivatives, while the twin-jet A330 and four-jet A340 are long-range models.

On 27 April 2005, Airbus flew the prototype of its latest product, the A380, which is the largest airliner in the world, with seating for 555 passengers in standard three-class configuration or up to 853 passengers in full economy-class

configuration. The A380 was scheduled to enter airline service in 2007.

Boeing decided not to develop a direct competitor to the Airbus A380, but instead proposed a fast subsonic replacement for the 767, called the Sonic Cruiser. Unconventional in design, Boeing's proposal produced no serious interest in airline circles and the project was subsequently abandoned in 2001, although some of the technology involved is being used in Boeing's latest venture, the fuel-efficient 7E7 Dreamliner, a conventional design incorporating all the latest technology.

The Boeing (McDonnell Douglas) AH-64 Apache is a potent combat helicopter and first demonstrated its awesome firepower in the 1991 Gulf War, when it knocked out Iraqi radar stations with rockets and cannon.

Wings of Tomorrow: Military Aviation in Tomorrow's World

The Lockheed F-117A played a prominent part in the Gulf wars of 1991 and 2003, making first strikes on high-priority targets; it was also used in the Balkans and Afghanistan.

On the night of 16/17 January 1991, eight McDonnell Douglas AH-64A helicopters began the air assault phase of Operation Desert Storm with an attack on two radar stations on the approaches to Baghdad, using Hellfire ASMs, 70mm rockets and 30mm gunfire. The mission was completely successful and both stations were destroyed. Initial attacks on Baghdad were made by Tomahawk cruise missiles launched by US warships in the Gulf and by Lockheed F-117As, directed at command and control centres, ministries, barracks and individual targets such as the Presidential Palace.

Throughout the approach to Baghdad and the subsequent attack, the F-117A strike aircraft remained undetected, for this was 'stealth' technology in action. The amazing F-117A Stealth aircraft began life in 1973 as a project called 'Have Blue', launched to study the feasibility of producing a combat aircraft with little or no radar and infrared signature. Two Experimental Stealth Tactical (XST) Have Blue research aircraft were built and flown in 1977 at Groom Lake, Nevada (Area 51). One was destroyed in an accident, but the other went on to complete the test programme successfully in 1979. The Have Blue prototypes validated the faceting concept of the stealth aircraft, and the basic aircraft shape.

The evaluation of the two Have Blue aircraft led to an order for 65 production F-117As. The type made its first flight in June 1981 and entered service in October 1983. The F-117A is a single-seat subsonic aircraft powered by two non-afterburning GE F404 turbofans with shielded slot exhausts designed to dissipate heat emissions (aided also by heat-shielding tiles), thus minimizing the infrared signature. The use of faceting (angled flat surfaces) scatters incoming radar energy, while radar-absorbent materials and transparencies treated with conductive coating reduce the F-117A's radar signature still further. The aircraft has highly swept wing leading edges, a W-shaped trailing edge and a V-shaped tail unit. Armament is carried on swing-down trapezes in two internal bays. The F-117A has quadruple redundant fly-by-wire controls, steerable turrets for forward-looking infrared (FLIR) and laser designator, head-up and head-down displays, laser communications and nav/attack system integrated with a digital avionics suite.

F-117As of the USAF 37th Tactical Fighter Wing played a prominent part in the 1991 Gulf War, making first strikes on high-priority targets; since then they have been used in both the Balkans and Afghanistan, and in the second invasion of Iraq in 2003. The last of 59 F-117As was delivered in July 1990.

The Sinister Boomerang
Northrop B-2A Spirit

Development of the Northrop B-2 was begun in 1978. The prototype flew on 17 July 1989 and the first production B-2 was delivered to the 393rd Bomb Squadron of the 509th Bomb Wing at Whiteman AFB, Missouri, on 17 December 1993.

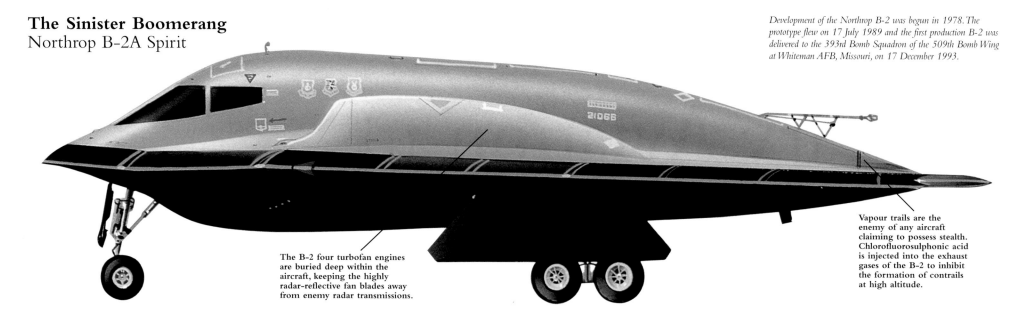

The B-2 four turbofan engines are buried deep within the aircraft, keeping the highly radar-reflective fan blades away from enemy radar transmissions.

Vapour trails are the enemy of any aircraft claiming to possess stealth. Chlorofluorosulphonic acid is injected into the exhaust gases of the B-2 to inhibit the formation of contrails at high altitude.

B-2A Spirit

Type: two-seat long-range strategic bomber

Powerplant: four 84.52kN (19,017lbf) General Electric F118-GE-100 turbofan engines

Maximum speed: about 960km/h (597mph) above 12,200m (40,000ft)

Range: 12,225km (7,596 miles)

Service ceiling: over 16,920m (53,440ft)

Weights: empty 79,380kg (175,995lb); loaded 181,437kg (400,000lb)

Armament: eight B61 or B83 nuclear bombs or 16 stand-off nuclear missiles on rotary launcher in bomb-bay or 80 Mk 82 227kg (500lb) bombs or up to 22,600 kg (50,000 lb) of other weapons

Dimensions: span   52.43m (172ft)
          length   21.03m (69ft)
          height   5.18m (17ft)
          wing area   196m² (2110sq ft)

The second US stealth design, the Northrop Grumman B-2 bomber, is even more awesome. Development of the B-2 was begun in 1978, and the USAF originally wanted 133 examples, but by 1991 successive budget cuts had reduced this to 21 aircraft. The prototype flew on 17 July 1989 and the first production B-2 was delivered to the 393rd Bomb Squadron of the 509th Bomb Wing at Whiteman AFB, Missouri, on 17 December 1993.

Flying Wing

In designing the Advanced Technology Bomber (ATB), as the B-2 project was originally known, the Northrop company, with its experience in the design of 'flying wing' aircraft going back to World War II,

decided on an all-wing configuration from the outset. The argument is that a flying wing will carry the same payload as a conventional aircraft while weighing less and using less fuel. The weight and drag of the tail surfaces are absent, as is the weight of the structure that supports them. The wing structure itself is far more efficient because the weight of the aircraft is spread across the wing rather than concentrated in the centre. The all-wing approach was also selected because it promised to result in an exceptionally clean configuration for minimizing radar cross-section, including the elimination of vertical tail surfaces, with added benefits such as span-loading structural efficiency and high lift/drag ratio for efficient cruising. Outboard wing panels were

added for longitudinal balance, to increase lift/drag ratio and to provide sufficient span for pitch, roll and yaw control. Leading-edge sweep was selected for balance and transonic aerodynamics, while the overall planform was designed to have neutral longitudinal (pitch) static stability. The aircraft's short length meant that it had to produce stabilizing pitchdown moments beyond the stall for positive recovery. The original ATB design had elevons on the outboard wing panels only, but as the design progressed additional elevons were added inboard, giving the B-2 its distinctive 'double-W' trailing edge.

Right: The B-2's wing leading edge is so designed that air is channelled into the engine intakes from all directions, allowing the engines to operate at high power and zero airspeed.

Today's Stealth Fighter
Lockheed F-22 Raptor

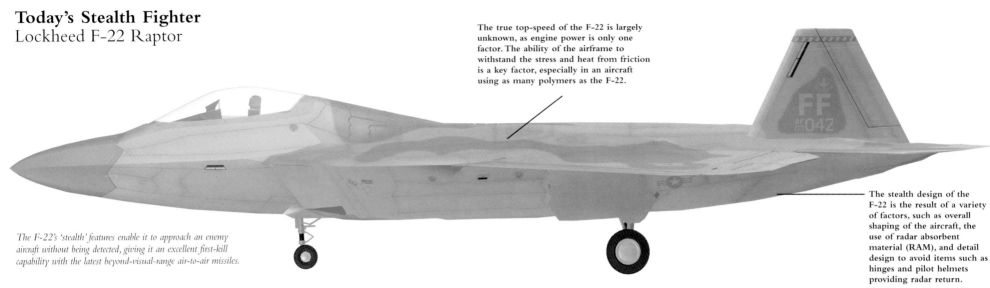

The true top-speed of the F-22 is largely unknown, as engine power is only one factor. The ability of the airframe to withstand the stress and heat from friction is a key factor, especially in an aircraft using as many polymers as the F-22.

The F-22's 'stealth' features enable it to approach an enemy aircraft without being detected, giving it an excellent first-kill capability with the latest beyond-visual-range air-to-air missiles.

The stealth design of the F-22 is the result of a variety of factors, such as overall shaping of the aircraft, the use of radar absorbent material (RAM), and detail design to avoid items such as hinges and pilot helmets providing radar return.

The B-2 lifts off at 140 knots (260km/h), the speed independent of take-off weight. Normal operating speed is in the high subsonic range; maximum altitude is around 15,200m (50,000ft). The aircraft is highly manoeuvrable, with fighter-like handling characteristics.

Winning Combination

A good deal of stealth technology is incorporated in the design of what is without doubt the most exciting combat aircraft of the early twenty-first century, the Lockheed Martin F-22 Raptor. The USAF identified a requirement for 750 examples of an Advanced Tactical Fighter

Left: The F-22 Raptor is designed to be deployed rapidly to any part of the world, forming a rapid reaction force in combination with combat aircraft such as the B-1 Lancer, B-2 Spirit and F-15E Strike Eagle.

(ATF) to replace the F-15 Eagle in the late 1970s. Two companies, Lockheed and Northrop, were selected to build demonstrator prototypes of their respective proposals. Each produced two prototypes, the Lockheed YF-22 and Northrop YF-23, and all four aircraft flew in 1990. Two different powerplants, the Pratt & Whitney YF119 and the General Electric YF120, were evaluated, and in April 1991 it was announced that the F-22 and F119 were the winning combination. The first definitive F-22 prototype was rolled out at the Lockheed Martin plant at Marietta, Georgia, on 9 April 1997. There were numerous problems with this aircraft, including software troubles and fuel leaks, and the first flight was delayed to 7 September 1997. The second prototype first flew on 29 June 1998. By late 2001, there were eight F-22s flying.

The F-22 combines many stealth features. Its air-to-air weapons, for example, are stored internally; three internal bays house advanced short-range, medium-range and beyond-visual-range air-to-air missiles. After an assessment of the aircraft's combat role in 1993, a ground-attack capability was added, and the internal weapons bay can also accommodate 454kg (1000lb) GBU-32 precision guided missiles. The F-22 is designed for a high sortie rate, with a turnaround time of less than 20 minutes. Its avionics are highly integrated to provide rapid reaction in air combat, much of its survivability depending on the pilot's ability to locate a target very early and hit it with its first shot. The F-22 was designed to meet a specific threat, which at that time was presented by large numbers of highly agile Soviet combat

Lockheed F-22 Raptor

Type: single-seat supersonic air superiority fighter

Powerplant: two 15,87kN (35,000lbf) Pratt & Whitney F119-P-100 turbofans

Maximum speed: 2575km/h (1600mph), or Mach 2.42

Combat radius: 1285km (800 miles)

Service ceiling: 19,812m (65,000ft)

Weights: empty 14,061kg (31,000lb); maximum take-off 27,216kg (60,000lb)

Armament: production aircraft have common armament plus next generation air-to-air missiles in the internal weapons bay

Dimensions:		
span	13.1m (43ft)
length	19.55m (64ft 2in)
height	5.39m (17ft 8in)
wing area	77.1m² (830sq ft)

aircraft, its task being to engage them in their own airspace with beyond-visual-range weaponry. It is a key component in the Global Strike Task Force, formed in 2001 to counter any threat worldwide.

The F-22 programme was beset by delays, but far fewer than those afflicting Europe's fighter hope for the twenty-first century, the Eurofighter Typhoon. An outline staff target for a common European fighter aircraft was issued in December 1983 by the air chiefs of staff of France, Germany, Italy, Spain and the United Kingdom; the initial feasibility study was completed in July 1984, but France withdrew from the project a year later. A definitive European Staff Requirement (Development) giving operational requirements in greater detail was issued in September 1987, and the main engine and weapon system development contracts were signed in November 1988. To prove the necessary technology for Eurofighter, a contract was awarded in May 1983 to British Aerospace for the development of an agile demonstrator aircraft – not a prototype – under the Experimental Aircraft Programme, or EAP. The demonstrator flew for the first time on 8 August 1986.

Swedish Superfighter
Saab JAS 39 Gripen

The fuselage is approximately 30 per cent composite materials. The structure proved to be far stronger than designers had predicted when it was tested. The Gripen's airframe can withstand 9g.

The Saab JAS-39 Gripen lightweight multi-role fighter was conceived in the 1970s as a replacement for the attack, reconnaissance and interceptor versions of the Viggen.

Power is provided by a single Volvo RM12 turbofan, which is a licence-built General Electric F404. This is the same engine that powers the Boeing F/A-18 Hornet.

SAAB JAS 39 Gripen

Type: single-seat high-performance fighter

Powerplant: one 54.0kN (12,150lbf) Volvo Flygmotor RM12 turbofan (General Electric F404-GE-400); 80.49kN (18,110lbf) with afterburning

Maximum speed: 2126km/h (1321mph) at 11,000m (36,000ft)

Service ceiling: over 14,000m (46,000ft)

Weights: empty 6622kg (14,600lb); loaded 8300kg (18,298lb)

Armament: one 27mm Mauser BK27 cannon; two wingtip Rb 74 (AIM-9L Sidewinder) or other air-to-air missiles; underwing air-to-ground or Saab Rb 15F anti-shipping missiles

Dimensions:
span	8.00m	(26ft 3in)
length	14.10m	(46ft 3in)
height	4.70m	(15ft 5in)
wing area (est.)	80m²	(267sq ft)

The end of the Cold War led, in 1992, to a reappraisal of the whole programme, with Germany in particular demanding substantial cost reductions. Several low-cost configurations were examined, but only two turned out to be cheaper than the original European Fighter Aircraft; both were inferior to the MiG-29 and Su-27. Finally, in December 1992, the project was relaunched as Eurofighter 2000, the planned in-service entry having now been delayed by three years.

The first two Eurofighter prototypes flew in 1994, followed by several more. The original customer requirement was 250 each for the United Kingdom and Germany, 165 for Italy and 100 for Spain. The latter country announced a firm requirement for 87 in January 1994, while Germany and Italy revised their respective needs to 180 and 121, the German order to include at least 40 examples of the fighter-bomber version. The United Kingdom's order was 232, with options on a further 65. Deliveries to the air forces of all four countries were scheduled to begin in 2001; not for the first time, the schedule slipped. The RAF received its first aircraft on 30 June 2003. Eurofighter has broken into the export market, with an Austrian order for 35 aircraft.

France, originally a member of the European consortium that was set up to develop Eurofighter, decided to withdraw at an early stage and develop its own agile combat aircraft for the twenty-first century. France had plenty of experience to build on; its Mirage 2000 multi-role combat aircraft, successor to the Mirage III, had been a huge success.

French Squall

The French agile combat aircraft emerged as the Dassault Rafale (Squall). On the basis of an airframe with overall dimensions little greater than those of the Mirage 2000, Dassault set out to produce a multi-role aircraft capable of destroying anything from supersonic aircraft to helicopters in the air-to-air role, and able to deliver at least 3500kg (7715lb) of bombs or modern weapons on targets up to 650km (400 miles) from its base. The ability to carry at least six air-to-air missiles, and to fire them in rapid succession, was considered essential, together with the ability to launch

While the F-14 replaced the Phantom in the naval air superiority role, the aircraft that replaced it in the tactical role (with both the US Navy and USMC) was the McDonnell Douglas F-18 Hornet, first flown on 18 November 1978.

electro-optically guided and advanced 'fire and forget' stand-off air-to-surface weapons. High manoeuvrability, high angle of attack flying capability under combat conditions, and optimum low-speed performance for short take-off and landing were basic design aims. This led to a choice of a compound-sweep delta wing, a large active canard foreplane mounted higher than the mainplane, twin engines, air intakes of new design in a semi-ventral position, and a single fin.

Three Versions

As with Eurofighter, a technology demonstrator was built; known as Rafale-A, this flew for the first time on 4 July 1986. Powered by two SNECMA M88-2 augmented turbofans, each rated at 7450kg (16,424lb) thrust with reheat, Rafale is produced in three versions, the Rafale-C single-seat multi-role aircraft for the French Air Force, the two-seat Rafale-B and the navalized Rafale-M. In the strike role, Rafale can carry one Aérospatiale ASMP stand-off nuclear bomb; in the interception role, armament is up to eight AAMs with either IR or active homing; and in the air-to-ground role, a typical load is 16 227kg (500lb) bombs, two AAMs and two external fuel tanks. The aircraft is compatible with the full NATO arsenal of air-to-air and air-to-ground weaponry. Built-in armament comprises one 30mm cannon in the side of the starboard engine duct.

Competing with Eurofighter and Rafale in the lucrative export market is

The F-35 Joint Strike Fighter is intended for service with the US Navy, US Marine Corps and the Royal Air Force. It traces its ancestry back to the vertical take-off Harrier.

Sweden's JAS-39 Gripen. The Saab JAS-39 Gripen (Griffon) lightweight multi-role fighter was conceived in the 1970s as a replacement for the attack, reconnaissance and interceptor versions of the Viggen. The prototype rolled out on 26 April 1987 first flew on 9 December 1988. The loss of this aircraft in a landing accident on 2 February 1989 led to a revision of its advanced fly-by-wire control system. Orders for the Gripen totalled 140 aircraft, all for the Royal Swedish Air Force. The type entered service in 1995.

The 1991 Gulf War, in which air power was used on a massive scale, and subsequent operations conducted by the United Nations and NATO in Iraq, Afghanistan, the Balkans and elsewhere saw the use of all the conventional weapons developed during the later years of the Cold War, from cluster bombs to cruise missiles. These conflicts also confirmed that the aircraft carrier, with its mixture of attack aircraft, remained the most effective means of projecting military force across the globe. One of the most effective aircraft of this type remains the McDonnell Douglas F/A-18 Hornet, which first saw action in a reprisal attack on Libya in April 1986. First flown on 18 November 1978, the prototype Hornet was followed by 11 development aircraft. The first production versions were the fighter/attack F-18A and the two-seat F-18B operational trainer; subsequent variants are the F-18C and F-18D, which have provision for AIM-120 AAMs and Maverick infrared missiles, as well as an airborne self-protection jamming system. The aircraft also serves with the Canadian Armed Forces as the CF-188. Other customers include Australia, Finland, Kuwait, Spain and Switzerland.

Joint Strike Fighter

The Hornet operates in conjunction with the US Marine Corps' Av-8B Harrier II, and both aircraft will eventually be replaced by the F-35 Joint Strike Fighter, an Anglo-American venture which will be deployed in three variants. The F-35A conventional take-off and landing aircraft will replace the USAF's F-16 Fighting Falcons and A-10 Thunderbolt IIs, beginning in 2011; the F-35B is a short take-off and vertical landing variant intended to replace the USMC AV-8B Harrier IIs and F/A-18 Hornets, and also the RAF/Royal Navy's Harrier GR.7/9s, beginning in 2012; the F-35C carrier-borne variant will replace part of the US navy's Hornet fleet from 2012.

Effective though they are in a modern combat environment, the fact remains that the latest combat aircraft, such as the F-35, are prohibitively expensive, and, although pilots remain essential, increasing reliance will be placed in the future on unmanned combat aerial vehicles. These are already with us in prototype form, and will be the warriors of tomorrow's air wars.

Index

Page numbers in *italics* refer to illustrations

Picture Credits